GERALD R. FORD

GERALD R. FORD

An Honorable Life

JAMES CANNON

Afterword by Scott Cannon

THE UNIVERSITY OF MICHIGAN PRESS

Ann Arbor

Published in the United States of America by
The University of Michigan Press
Manufactured in the United States of America
⊗ Printed on acid-free paper

2016   2015   2014   2013   4   3   2   1

A CIP catalog record for this book is available from the British Library.

Library of Congress Cataloging-in-Publication Data

Cannon, James M., 1918–2011.
    Gerald R. Ford : an honorable life / James Cannon ; afterword by
Scott Cannon.
      pages   cm
    Includes index.
    ISBN 978-0-472-11604-1 (cloth : alk. paper) — ISBN 978-0-472-
02946-4 (e-book)
    1. Ford, Gerald R., 1913–2006.   2. Presidents—United States—
Biography.   3. United States—Politics and government—1974–1977.
I. Title.
E866.C35   2013
973.925092—dc23 [B]   2013006632

Although James Cannon had planned to provide source notes and
bibliography for this book as he had in previous books, he did not
complete that portion of the manuscript before his death.

FOR

James Monroe Cannon IV
Scott Dawson Cannon

Gerald Ford was our only President to be a normal human being.

—HENRY KISSINGER

Contents

PART 3

PART I

A Crisis of the Regime

The day: Thursday, August 8, 1974. The hour: 11:10 a.m. With one fateful question dominating his thoughts, Gerald Ford waited in the sunny and deceptively calm reception room next to the Office of the President of the United States. The question: would Richard Nixon resign, or would he fight on and put himself, and all three branches of the Federal government, and the American people through the agony of a President's impeachment, trial, conviction, and dismissal from that high and once-honored office?

Vice President Ford was there to hear the answer. Minutes earlier, Chief of Staff Alexander Haig had telephoned: "The President wants to see you now." In that instant, Ford knew the months of crisis and anticipation had reached a turning point. Deep in his soul, Ford knew that this encounter, whatever the outcome, would live in history. Responding to the call, he left the Vice President's suite in the Old Executive Office Building and walked quickly across West Executive Avenue, wondering along the way, "Will he go, or will he continue to fight?"

Up the stairs of the West Wing, Ford paused at Haig's imposing corner office for last-minute guidance. Haig, haggard and grave, walked with Ford to the door of the reception room. "The President wants to see you alone, Mr. Vice President."

Poised, intent, Ford sat by himself on a small couch, "waiting to hear, waiting to get the word," he said later. "I knew the odds, that Nixon would resign and I would take over. But I had been cautioned, repeatedly, by Haig that Nixon kept changing his mind, and I should believe no decision had been made until I heard it from Nixon himself. So it all depended on what Nixon would finally decide to do. I expected, I strongly expected that he would leave, yet I couldn't be positive. I was certain of one thing: If it happened, I was confident that I could handle the job. So I just sat there and waited."

As Ford waited, so also did all America await a resolution of this "crisis of the regime." For more than two years, the infamy of Watergate had paralyzed President Nixon, occupied both the U.S. Senate and the U.S. House of Representatives, dominated the national press, and implanted in the public mind doubt and distrust of Richard Nixon, and everything he and his White House had done and stood for.

Watergate: code word for the most improbable White House scandal in history. It was not a case of Presidential appointees taking bribes, as with Grant and Harding; it was instead an intentional criminal act by a President in the Oval Office. By deliberately breaking laws he had taken an oath to uphold, Nixon provoked the most serious Constitutional crisis since the Civil War.

The scandal began in the summer of 1972 when managers for Nixon's reelection campaign concocted, inexplicably, a plan to burglarize Democratic headquarters in the Watergate office building in downtown Washington. Five CIA-trained operatives hired by the Nixon campaign broke into the Democratic Chairman's office, and were rifling his files when police caught them in the act. All five were jailed and indicted.

President Nixon, also inexplicably, did not distance himself from the break-in by campaign hirelings. He could have dismissed his political managers responsible for the crime and that might have ended the incident. Instead, Nixon tried to cover up the crime by telling his Chief of Staff, Bob Haldeman, and White House Counsel, John Dean, to bribe the burglars to keep silent; but, the men caught in the break-in talked. Bit by bit they gave evidence marking a trail that led to Nixon's campaign staff, then to hush money in a White House safe, on to Nixon's most trusted aides, and, in time, to Nixon himself.

A fool's errand, followed by Nixon's monstrous misjudgment, turned into catastrophe. The President's close friend and most able mentor, former Attorney General John Mitchell, and four senior White House aides were indicted, forced to resign, and faced trial for perjury—or worse. For his part in the attempt to cover up the Watergate crime, President Nixon faced impeachment in the House, conviction in the Senate, and prosecution in the courts.

As Ford sat in suspense, waiting to see the President that August morning, there was no question in his mind about what Nixon should do. White House tape recordings, made public by court order just four days earlier, revealed astonishing evidence: President Nixon, in his own voice, conspiring to obstruct justice. Consequently, it was certain that Nixon would be impeached, convicted, and removed from office. No President—indeed, no man—had ever faced such a formidable array of legal power: the Senate Watergate Committee, the House Judiciary Committee, a Special Prosecutor, a tenacious Federal Judge, and the Supreme Court of the United States.

Grim though his legal predicament was, Nixon's standing with the American people was even worse. He had lied to them—not once, but repeatedly; not inadvertently, but intentionally. He had defiled the Presidency. He was a crook. Angry crowds gathered in historic Lafayette Park across from the White House shouting: "Jail to the Chief! Jail to the Chief!"

By any measure, Richard Nixon had lost the legitimacy of authority essential to any President. As a consequence, he could no longer govern. Ford knew that, as did Congress, the Federal bureaucracy, the press, and all the other diverse powers in Washington. But Ford did not know whether Nixon was yet ready to accept the reality that as President, he was finished.

Such a sad time, Ford thought as he sat waiting—such a tragedy for his good friend and political ally for a quarter century. Now that friend was ruined—ruined in his time, and in the verdict of history. Nixon's accomplishments as President would be diminished, perhaps forgotten.

At that moment, Ford's reflections were interrupted. The door into the Oval Office was opening. "Mr. President," a Nixon aide announced with terse formality, "the Vice President is here to see you."

Nixon stood as Ford entered and reached forward to shake hands. Strain and despair evident on his face, he gestured for his Vice President to sit in the chair at his right. Nixon then turned to White House photographer Oliver Atkins, standing near the wall in the Oval Office.

"Ollie," Nixon said, "take this photograph for history."

As soon as the photographer left the room, Nixon turned and looked Ford in the eye. In a voice calm and matter of fact, he spoke slowly and deliberately. "I have made the decision to resign. It is in the best interest of the country. I won't go into the arguments, pro and con. I have made my decision."

The answer at last: Nixon will go. It is over. At that moment, Ford felt a sense of liberation, of deliverance; but he did his best to contain his emotions and mask his relief that the government and the people could soon move past Watergate to a better time.

Still looking Ford in the eye, Nixon said: "Jerry, you will become President. I know you'll do a good job. You have the background, the training. You are capable. You have the experience of political management, all the other things that go with the job. So I feel certain the country will be in good hands."

Speaking from the heart, Ford said: "Mr. President, you know I am saddened by this. You know I would have wanted it to be otherwise. I was hoping you could continue. Under the circumstances I think your decision is the right one, but I'm sorry about it."

Ford had more to say. He wanted Nixon to know that he had no hesitation about becoming President himself. "I am ready to do the job," he said in a firm voice, "and I think I am fully qualified to do it."

"I know you are too," Nixon said.

The moment always remained vivid in Ford's mind. "Dick's face was solemn, taut, drawn, obviously under great strain. His shoulders sagged. But he was such a proud person that he would not collapse, or even show distress. I could see it was very, very hard for him to say he had decided to resign; but once he did, it was like a burden had been lifted from him."

After their solemn exchange, Nixon's manner and comportment quickly changed. Rolling back in his chair, propping his feet on his desk, and in a voice sure and confident, Nixon began a tutorial to his successor on the state of the world. Continent by continent, country by country, he identified critical problems, evaluated leaders, and calculated U.S. interests. He talked about the necessity for nuclear-arms limitation, and the obligation to continue supporting South Vietnam, characterized Leonid Brezhnev ("tough but flexible") and Mao Zedong ("pragmatic, patient"), identified the strengths and weaknesses of NATO, and discussed the prospects for peace in the Middle East. "He showed his mastery at surveying the world on a global basis," Ford said. "I listened. I learned."

"Keep Kissinger," Nixon said. "Henry is not the easiest person to work with, but he is an outstanding foreign policy strategist and conceptualizer."

Turning to domestic affairs, Nixon spoke bluntly and in detail about the state of the economy—increasing inflation, rising unemployment rates, the possibilities of a recession—and urged Ford to work closely with Federal Reserve Chairman Arthur Burns.

"Who will be your Vice President?" Nixon asked. Ford had made no decision; had not yet even given it a thought. "You will want someone who will add stature to your Administration, someone who will generate international as well as national confidence," Nixon said. Governor Nelson Rockefeller of New York, he suggested, would be a wise choice. Nixon also urged Ford to keep Haig as Chief of Staff, for the transition, if not longer; he would be "an invaluable source of advice and experience."

After an hour of passing along lessons from his years in office, Nixon turned to the practical business of executing an orderly transition. He would address the nation that evening and announce his intention to resign as President. On the next morning, his last in office, he would say farewell to his Cabinet and White House staff in the East Room. From there, he and his family would go to the Diplomatic Reception Room. He asked that Ford and his wife Betty meet him and Pat Nixon there, and walk with them to the presidential helicopter. After this last ride to Andrews Air Force Base, he would depart for California aboard Air Force One.

President Nixon's letter of resignation would be delivered to Secretary of State Kissinger shortly before noon. At that hour, Nixon expected to be high in the air over Missouri or Kansas; at that moment, he would no longer be President.

Where, he asked, would Ford take the oath of office? He had not decided, Ford replied. Nixon suggested that Ford hold a small ceremony in the Oval Office, "as Truman did."

With that, Nixon rose and put his arm around Ford as they walked out the east door that leads to the Rose Garden. For a moment, the two stood in silence on the covered porch outside the Oval Office. Their eyes met. They shook hands. "No historic words were spoken," Ford said. "There was just the recognition on the part of both of us that the time had come. His choice had been made, and my fate decided."

Their meeting had taken seventy minutes.

From the President's porch, Ford walked quickly across the South Lawn—not looking right or left, nor at the Secret Service agent holding open the door to the Vice Presidential limousine. "I wanted to get out of this terribly dramatic circumstance and in the car," Ford said. "I really just wanted to be alone."

CHAPTER 2

Resolve

On the two-minute ride out the southwest gate and onto West Executive Avenue, Ford regained full control over his emotions. His earlier anxiety about what Nixon *might* do quickly turned into resolution about what he, the new President-to-be, *must* do.

Time was precious. This was Thursday: he had less than twenty-four hours before his swearing-in. He must get to work.

Ford's first concern, as it is with every new President, was national security. Striding to his desk in the Vice President's office, he telephoned Secretary of State Kissinger. The exchange reflects Ford's modesty and Kissinger's diplomacy.

"I have just finished talking with the President, and he gave me his decision," Ford said. "I want you to stay, Henry. I need you. The country needs you. I'll do everything I can to work with you."

"Mr. Vice President," Kissinger replied, "it is my job to get along with you and not yours to get along with me."

"I would hope we could get together sometime this afternoon at your convenience," Ford said.

"Would 3:00 p.m. suit you, Mr. Vice President?"

"Fine, Henry. I would appreciate it very much."

"I have prepared some tentative suggestions for your consideration," Kissinger said. "Might I bring these along?"

"Bring anything along that you want, Henry. I will be delighted to see you."

Continuity at the Department of State affirmed, Ford brought in his two most trusted aides—Robert Hartmann and John Marsh—for the next decision: Where should he be sworn in? "They're talking about the Oval Office," Ford said.

"The hell with what *they* want," said Hartmann, Ford's plain-speaking counselor and principal speechwriter. "It's what do *you* want. *You* are going to be President."

Ford's first choice was to take the oath of office at the U.S. Capitol. Not only was it the traditional site of Presidential inaugurals; the Capitol was home to Ford. There, in the House of Representatives, he had served the Fifth District of Michigan for twenty-five years; there, his peers had chosen him to be Vice President, and confirmed him by a landslide vote. But, after discussion, all three agreed that this unprecedented inaugural should take place in the White House.

"The Chief Justice!" Ford said. "He *must* administer the oath of office." No lesser personage, the three agreed, would bring the legitimacy and appropriate dignity to this unprecedented occasion. In minutes, the White House switchboard operators found Chief Justice Warren Burger, traveling in the Netherlands.

"Mr. Chief Justice, I guess you've heard the news," Ford said. "I hate to interrupt your trip, but I would like it very much if you could be here for the swearing-in."

"Oh, I *want* to be there," Burger said. "I've *got* to be there."

Marsh, Ford's national security adviser and former colleague in the House, quickly arranged for an Air Force plane to pick up the Chief Justice in Europe, and fly him to Washington.

Since the East Room—the largest in the White House—could hold no more than 275 guests, Marsh recommended an order of priority for the invitations: the Ford family, the Cabinet and senior White House staff, the bipartisan leaders of Congress, the chairmen and ranking members of House and Senate committees, the diplomatic corps, Ford's fellow Representatives in the Class of 1948, and the entire Michigan delegation. All would have to be invited by telephone.

To begin the invitations, Ford telephoned two of his closest Congressional friends: Hugh Scott, Republican leader of the Senate, and Democrat Tip O'Neill, Majority Leader of the House and Ford's favorite golfing partner. "Are wives invited, Jerry?" O'Neill asked.

"They are now," Ford said cheerfully.

O'Neill read a statement he planned to make: Democrats would cooperate with Ford, but he must listen to and work closely with Congress.

"That's fine," Ford said, "and Tip, I will rely on you for advice and assistance."

Ever the partisan, O'Neill said: "Christ, Jerry, isn't this a wonderful country? Here we can talk like this and you and I can be friends, and eighteen months from now I'll be going around the country kicking your ass in."

As both laughed, Ford said: "That's a hell of a way to speak to the next President of the United States."

Ford asked Hartmann to bring in his inaugural speech; he wanted to go over it again. It was an excellent draft, for Hartmann could put into words what Ford was thinking but could not readily articulate. Ford particularly liked the opening: "Not an inaugural address, not a fireside chat, not a campaign speech, just a little straight talk among friends . . ."

Reading on, Ford paused as he neared the concluding paragraphs. "Bob, just one thing troubles me and that's this line, 'Our long national nightmare is over.' Isn't that a little hard on Dick? Could we soften that?"

"No, no, no!" Hartmann said. "That's what you have to proclaim to the whole country, to the whole world. That's what everybody needs to hear, wants to hear, has got to hear you say. You have to turn the country around. That sentence will be the headline in every paper, the lead in every story. Junk all the rest of the speech if you want to, but not that."

Ford had never seen Hartmann so adamant, or so vehement. He did not always agree with Hartmann, but he always listened to him. During their eight years of working together, Ford had come to trust Hartmann's political wisdom as much as his insight into the inscrutable ways of the press. Turning back to the draft, Ford read the last part of the speech again. "Okay, Bob, I guess you're right. I hadn't thought about it that way."

What had weighed too heavily on Ford's mind was compassion for Richard and Pat Nixon, and their two daughters. Ford knew Nixon; knew his pride and yearning for a place in history along with his enervating insecurities and gnawing fear of being thought a loser. For Nixon to be forced out of the Presidency was, in Ford's judgment, capital punishment—not so much political execution as a life sentence to ignominy. Ford could not help feeling some sympathy for his disgraced friend; Hartmann had the better grasp of the public mind and what should be said.

Turning back to Hartmann, Ford said: "Thank you, Bob. You did a wonderful job." He folded the speech and put it in his pocket. He planned to rehearse it with Betty that evening.

As soon as Kissinger arrived, Ford brought in Marsh and moved right to the point: "Henry, I am going to announce this evening, even before I take the oath of office, that you will continue as Secretary of State and National Security Adviser." Briefly, they spoke of their long friendship and beneficial exchanges. In the 1950s, then Harvard Professor Kissinger had invited Ford, then serving on the House Appropriations Subcommittee on Defense, to speak at Harvard seminars on defense priorities; Ford, in turn, had invited Professor Kissinger to discuss national-security issues with fellow House members.

Turning to the transition, they addressed an immediate danger: an adversary somewhere in the world might seize on the fall of the U.S. President as an opportunity to send troops across a border, or, in some other way, instigate a crisis threatening U.S. national interests. Kissinger suggested, and Ford agreed, that the new President would send a message to all governments warning that any such adventure would be met by force. The cables would also make the point that while the President had changed, U.S. foreign policy would not. To make sure that all governments understood, Ford agreed to meet with all ambassadors accredited to Washington on the day of his swearing-in.

For an hour, Kissinger analyzed the most troubling situations in the world, concluding with one promising opportunity: Nixon had initiated a meeting with Brezhnev on strategic arms limitations later in the year, and Brezhnev had agreed. Would the Vice President want to proceed with plans for that meeting? "Yes, of course," Ford replied. "Anything that would bring the arms race under control would be a plus for the entire world."

Kissinger, no stranger to discourse with world leaders, was not only impressed by the calm and order in the Vice President's office on that busy and historic afternoon, but he was also reassured by his exchange with Ford. The President-to-be had spoken plainly, read position papers with care, asked the right questions, and made his decisions without hesitation. Of that comprehensive session Kissinger wrote later: "Ford's inner peace was precisely what the nation needed."

While Ford had been meeting with Nixon, Haig—at the direction of a desperate President Nixon—had met secretly with Watergate Special Prosecutor Leon Jaworski. Haig had asked for the meeting to consider two issues critical to Nixon—issues that would, as it turned out, bedevil, taint, and diminish Ford's Presidency. First on Haig's agenda: what would happen to the Nixon tapes and papers? Second, would Nixon be prosecuted?

Previously, Jaworski had initiated meetings with Haig to request Nixon tapes or documents, and they had done so openly in the Map Room at the White House. Invariably, Nixon had rejected these requests. Though adversaries, Haig and Jaworski had come to respect and trust each other. This time, Haig asked for the meeting. To avoid the cordons of reporters staked out at every White House gate, Haig proposed that they travel in unmarked cars and meet at noon at his house on Edmunds Street, in northwest Washington.

After Mrs. Haig served tea, Jaworski opened with a firm statement: "I think we should have a clear understanding, Al, that we are not going to reach any kind of agreements about the President at this meeting."

"I know that," Haig said. He had asked for the meeting, he said, to inform the Special Prosecutor that the President was going to resign the next day. Jaworski already knew that; the news had been leaked to his press assistants. Haig made his next point: "He's going to be taking his tapes and papers with him. He's going to San Clemente tomorrow and the papers and tapes will be shipped out later." Haig said he would personally guarantee that Jaworski would have access to the tapes as needed.

That was imperative, Jaworski responded. He emphasized that he and his fellow prosecutors must have access to Nixon tapes and any relevant documents needed for the trials of Mitchell, Haldeman, Ehrlichman, and the other Watergate defendants. Or, he emphasized, he would take Nixon to court.

For more than an hour the two talked. At one point, Haig raised the subject of pardons. He said that both Haldeman and Ehrlichman had asked Nixon to pardon them, but Nixon turned them down. He also observed that Nixon was deteriorating physically; not only that, Haig said, but the President's judgment was becoming more and more erratic.

Haig, in asking for the meeting, was well aware that Jaworski had previously intervened in Nixon's behalf at a critical point in the Watergate prosecutions. In a May 5, 1974, meeting Jaworski informed Haig that he had blocked the Watergate grand jury from indicting Nixon by refusing to sign any such indictment. In that meeting, Jaworski told Haig: "I have no interest whatsoever in trying the President of the

United States in open court." Was that still true? Jaworski did not say.

Nevertheless, Jaworski did ask Haig: "Are Nixon's supporters in Congress going to pass a resolution that would, in effect, tell me not to move against him?"

"Oh, yes," Haig said. "I think it will be passed in a day or two. With no difficulty."

Jaworski was relieved; he would welcome such an action by Congress. For weeks, he had been searching for a convincing legal basis to avoid bringing Nixon to trial. Convicting a President, he told one staff member, "would be regicide."

After the Haig meeting, Jaworksi secluded himself in the Jefferson Hotel. He invited three of his senior prosecutors to his hotel room and told them Haig had made no request for a deal to encourage Nixon's resignation, and that there had been none. His visitors were openly skeptical; they did not believe that it would take almost two hours for Haig simply to inform Jaworski of Nixon's decision. Perhaps, they surmised, in their long session Haig had hoped for a sign, perhaps a silent nod of sympathy, indicating that Jaworski still did not intend to prosecute Nixon.

Haig returned to the White House and gave Nixon an encouraging report on his talk with Jaworski. "From their conversation," Nixon wrote, Haig "got the impression that that I had nothing further to fear from the Special Prosecutor."

Ford was told nothing of Haig's machinations in behalf of Nixon that day—not then, nor later. It was Ford's nature to look ahead, to pack this momentous day with activity as he had all his professional life, insisting on a full schedule and sticking to it, always on time, never wasting a minute. This day, the eve of his taking over as President, was no exception. Task by task, he worked at his desk through the late afternoon. He cancelled a political appearance in California; Republican National Chairman George Bush and Governor Ronald Reagan would substitute. He appointed a transition team—former House colleagues Bob Griffin, John Byrnes, Mel Laird, and Bill Scranton; veteran Presidential adviser Bryce Harlow; fellow golfer and U.S. Steel lobbyist Bill Whyte; Philip Buchen, Ford's fraternity brother at the University of Michigan and first law partner; and William Seidman. Buchen had been serving as part-time counsel to the Vice President. Seidman, a highly successful Grand Rapids businessman, a brainy and versatile executive, had been brought in three months earlier to organize Ford's Vice Presidential office.

Ford directed Buchen and Seidman to assemble the transition team and draft a plan. First priority: no Chief of Staff. Ford was convinced that Nixon had delegated far too much authority to his staff, especially to the arrogant Haldeman. To organize and bring about a swift and orderly Presidential transition, Ford knew just the man to do it. "Send for Rummy," he told Buchen.

Donald Rumsfeld, then U.S. Ambassador to NATO, had planned, organized, and managed both of Ford's campaigns for House leadership. First elected in 1962 to represent Illinois's affluent 13th Congressional District, Rumsfeld—then 30 years old—worked closely with Ford for six years to increase the party's numbers and advance the party's interests in the House. Their mentoring was mutual: the younger man learning congenial leadership from the older; the older learning planning and organizing from the younger.

Rumsfeld's performance as a resourceful, get-it-done Congressman prompted President Nixon to appoint Rumsfeld to bring order into the foundering poverty program left behind by President Johnson. Out of respect for Rumsfeld's ability and promise as a future leader, and aware of his interest in foreign policy, Nixon appointed him to NATO.

"Rummy was an excellent Member of the House, and I was disappointed to see him leave in '69," Ford said. "He was energetic. He was ambitious. He was obviously very able. The fact that he was in the Nixon White House and did not get involved in Watergate was testimony to his personal integrity. He was outstanding in his capability. He knew the White House. He was someone I knew I could trust. Rummy was the man I wanted to take charge of the transition."

Next on Ford's agenda: the appointment of a press secretary. Buchen suggested Jerry terHorst—a Grand Rapids reporter who had covered Ford since his early days in the House. "A great idea," Ford said. Hartmann agreed, and Ford made the call. TerHorst immediately accepted.

That accomplished, Ford met at dusk with Navy Secretary William Middendorf and Admiral James Holloway, Chief of Naval Operations. Weeks before, they had asked for a few minutes to present the Vice President with a framed photograph of the USS *Monterey*—the aircraft carrier Lieutenant Ford had served on in the Pacific during World War II.

Missing no opportunity to tell his favorite sea story, Ford recounted how, in 1944, during the worst typhoon the U.S. Navy ever experienced, he had almost lost his life. At the height of the storm a towering wave rolled the carrier twenty-five degrees, hurling him across the carrier deck and almost overboard into the raging sea. Luckily, he told his visitors, he had caught the raised edge of the carrier deck with his foot, vaulted into the catwalk below, and made his way up to the bridge to report for duty as officer of the deck.

There, he learned that the *Monterey* faced disaster. Planes loaded with high-octane gasoline had broken their moorings, and were crashing into each other and burning on the hangar deck. Flames spread fore and aft. Smoke asphyxiated the engine-room crew. With three of the *Monterey*'s four boilers out of operation, the helmsman could no longer steer. The ship, broadside to the sea, could capsize at any moment. Fleet Admiral William Halsey signaled authority to abandon ship. But the executive officer, Commander Pappy Atwood, took command, maneuvered the ship into the wind, restored power, and brought the badly crippled ship to safe harbor in Ulithi. By quick thinking and cool action, Commander Atwood had saved the *Monterey* and the lives of her crew. Ford never forgot that example of what a second-in-command could accomplish in a crisis.

As soon as the Navy visit ended, Ford again summoned Hartmann. He had decided to address a joint session of Congress as soon as possible—on Monday, if Marsh could arrange it. He wanted no oratory, but a working agenda. He would promise to cooperate with Congress, but also meet his new and different responsibility as Chief Executive to initiate solutions to problems too long delayed—inflation, excessive government spending, health care, and the energy crisis.

After looking in on Marsh and Seidman to make sure arrangements were going well for the next day, Ford went back to his office to clear his desk. After returning four phone calls—to Arthur Burns, House Republican Whip Les Arends, California businessman Justin Dart, and General Haig—he looked at his watch: 8:10 p.m. Time to go home, he thought, as he stuffed papers into his battered old briefcase for overnight reading.

On the fifteen-minute ride to the Ford family's comfortable split-level at 514 Crown View Drive in Alexandria, Virginia, Ford reflected on the chain of unforeseen events that had brought him to this momentous passage in his life.

He had never expected to be President. A rarity among Washington's eminent, Ford had never even entertained the notion of running for President. His sole ambition—envisioned and fixed in his freshman term in Congress—was to be Speaker of the House of Representatives. To reach that goal, he challenged his party's old order, won election as House Republican Leader, and for eight years campaigned across the nation to break the Democrats' hold on the majority in the House. Failing, for the fourth time, in the 1972 Congressional elections, Ford decided to retire from public office. He would go home to Grand Rapids, practice law, and play golf.

Events intervened. In less than a year Vice President Spiro Agnew was charged with taking bribes in his White House office; on October 10, 1973, he was forced to resign. That very evening, Ford was asked to consider becoming Vice President under the new Twenty-Fifth Amendment.

At first he hesitated. The title was imposing, but the job mostly ceremonial. Why change, Ford asked himself. He loved the House. For all of his thirteen terms, he had been an enthusiastic and effective player in the give-and-take gamesmanship that intrigues and challenges the practicing legislator. He had never liked being on the sidelines, watching others compete on the field of play. But after talking it over with Betty he accepted, reasoning, "It was not the office I sought, but it would constitute recognition of my long service in Washington."

Ford assumed, as did most Americans at that point, that President Nixon had not been personally involved in Watergate. Soon after he was sworn in as Vice President, on December 6, 1973, Ford reassured his worried party chairman. "When all the facts come out," he told George H. W. Bush, "I believe the President will be cleared." Later, Nixon told Ford face to face, gave his word, that he had nothing to do with the Watergate break in or cover-up. To Ford, when any man in public office gave his word, he must be believed.

Time and testimony changed Ford's mind. Sometime in early 1974, his faith in Nixon began to weaken. In late spring, as the House Judiciary Committee drafted an article of impeachment charging Nixon with obstructing justice, Ford confronted the possibility that Nixon might be forced from office. "That, I knew, would be a national catastrophe," Ford said. "Because of what it would do to the country, I honestly did not want to become President."

Yet his sense of duty drove him to be prepared for the possibility he dreaded. All his life, Ford had been an earnest student, and now, as

Vice President, he systematically brought in the experts—Federal Reserve Chairman Arthur Burns on the economy and monetary policy; OMB Director Roy Ash on Federal spending and the management of programs; Kissinger and his deputy, Brent Scowcroft, on national security. As his own national-security adviser and all-around counselor, Ford recruited a Democrat—his former House colleague, Jack Marsh. A Virginia gentleman, World War II veteran, astute lawyer, and accomplished problem solver, Marsh had served four terms as a Democratic Representative from Virginia, and two years as an Assistant Secretary of Defense.

At the same time, Ford opened his Vice Presidential door to diplomats, governors, and journalists. Often he rode up to Capitol Hill to visit with old friends in the House and to preside over the Senate. He continued to take part in, and learn from, the discussions of former New York Governor Nelson Rockefeller's Commission on Critical Choices—an initiative to analyze and propose solutions for the most pressing problems of the nation, and the world.

Tirelessly, this Vice President traveled the country, speaking wherever invited, for two reasons—to distance himself from Watergate, and to offer the American people some idea of who he was just in case he might become President. Although Ford did not welcome that prospect, he did not fear it. From his seat in the House, he had observed five Presidents—Truman, Eisenhower, Kennedy, Johnson, and Nixon. Working with each, learning from all, he had watched them succeed in some endeavors, fail in others, act in crisis, make mistakes, propose, compromise, and rise and fall in popular opinion. Uncommon men, all had been; but not one was a genius. To Ford, the job required not brilliance but common sense, knowledge of how the Federal government works, the ability to choose capable advisers, the willingness to listen, the sound judgment to know when to say yes, and the courage, when necessary, to say no. In Ford's private opinion, and in fact, not one of the five Presidents, upon first taking the oath of office, had more experience in Washington decision making than he.

It did not concern Ford that he had not been elected President. He would take office on the bedrock foundation of the Constitution and its fortuitous Twenty-Fifth Amendment. As instructed by that amendment, Ford's peers in the House and Senate—the men and women who best knew his ability and his trustworthiness—had confirmed him by a combined vote of 479-38: the equivalent of an electoral landslide. Acting as surrogate for the American people, Congress had met the country's most critical need: to put a qualified man in the White House who was honest.

As circumstance had granted him no mandate by popular vote, Ford resolved to create his own. He would heal the nation, restore comity between the President and Congress, and show Americans they could again trust the word of their President.

Arriving home in Alexandria at 8:25 p.m., Ford found the house strangely quiet. He was concerned about how his becoming President might affect his family. "I knew Betty would have mixed feelings about this change in our lives," he said, but he found that she had, as usual, made up her own mind.

Betty Ford, after twenty-five years as a Congressman's wife, had a sure sense of political realities. "From what I read and saw, I knew things in the White House were coming apart, that President Nixon might have to resign; but I kept denying the fact," she said. "I just had a real empty feeling of 'What now?' I realized the responsibility that was going to fall on Jerry. And my thoughts were toward my responsibility as a woman and a wife and mother—'How was it going to affect the family?'" Practical by nature, Betty Ford also began preparing to accept the responsibilities of First Lady, and resolved to meet them in her own way.

Their two younger children—Steve, 18, and Susan, 17—both still in high school, were awed by the thought of moving into the White House and being guarded by Secret Service. The oldest son—Michael, 24—and Gayle, his bride of a month, were at that moment driving to Gordon Conwell Theological Seminary in Massachusetts. State police stopped them on a highway and delivered the message: get on a plane back to Washington. Jack, 22—a summer forest ranger, was tracked down in a remote part of Yellowstone National Park so he could be helicoptered to the nearest airport.

After dinner, mother, father, and the two teenage Fords turned on the television to watch President Nixon. Delusory to the end, Nixon told the nation that he was resigning because " . . . I no longer have a strong enough political base in the Congress . . ."

Ford was shocked. "I realized that Nixon, by blaming Congress, was out of touch with reality," he said. "It would have been better for him, and for the country, if he had admitted his mistakes, expressed contrition, and asked for forgiveness."

When Nixon's speech ended, Ford went out to his front lawn to speak to reporters and cameramen waiting in the summer drizzle. Of Nixon, he said only that he "has made one of the greatest personal sacrifices for the country." Looking ahead, he announced his first presidential decision: Henry Kissinger would remain as secretary of state.

As always, he and Betty watched the eleven o'clock news, saying little. "We were deeply saddened, Betty and I, that this tragedy would happen to Dick and Pat, our good friends since we first came to Washington. On the other hand, it was a tremendous relief to have the festering crisis resolved. We were prepared to handle our new responsibilities and challenges, and we were confident that we could, and would."

As they retired, they held hands and offered the nightly prayer from Proverbs that Ford had learned in childhood from his mother: "Trust in the Lord with all thine heart; and lean not unto thine own understanding. In all thy ways acknowledge Him, and He shall direct thy paths."

For a time, he lay awake in the dark, thinking about the next day, anticipating his appointment with history. Then he slept soundly, confident that the country was in good hands.

CHAPTER 3

Transformation

On the day he was to become President, Ford rose as usual soon after daybreak. He was rested. He was serenely confident. He was ready to accept the Constitutional responsibility thrust upon him by the mindless error of a President and the prescient wisdom of the legislators who wrote and passed the Twenty-Fifth Amendment.

He was also hungry. Brewing his coffee, toasting his English muffin, Ford contemplated his surpassing objective for that day: to reassure the American people; to show, by his actions and by his words, that the Watergate crisis was over.

At 8:00 a.m., right on time, Phil Buchen and John Byrnes arrived with a four-page transition plan that the team had labored through the night to put together. In the Vice Presidential limousine, Ford methodically read through the document.

> Team Coordinator: We share your view that there should be no Chief of Staff, especially at the outset. However, there should be someone who could rapidly and efficiently organize the new staff organization, but who will not be perceived or be eager to be Chief of Staff.
> Recommendation: Frank Carlucci, Bill Clements, Don Rumsfeld.
> Your choice:

Without hesitation, Ford wrote *Rumsfeld*.

Moving deliberately through the transition document, Ford designated Rogers Morton to be liaison with the Nixon Cabinet, Jack Marsh to work with Congress, governors, business and labor groups, and Bill Scranton to oversee personnel.

Byrnes, wise in the ways of Washington's bureaucracy and mindful of national concern about the long-running crisis, had proposed:

> For public confidence, to keep the executive branch administration intact, and to assure the smoothest, most rapid assumption of the Presidential mantle, you should have a series of meetings the first few days to assert your personal direction and control over the executive branch of the government.

"I agree," Ford said, looking over the list—Congressional leaders, key White House staff, Cabinet, National Security Council, Governors, Diplomatic Corps. In his left-handed scrawl, Ford added: "Mayors, county officials, Joint Chiefs of Staff."

Next came the crucial decision to remove Haig.

> You must walk a delicate line between compassion and consideration for the former President's staff and the rapid assertion of your personal control over the executive branch. . . . Al Haig has done yeoman service for his country. You should meet with him personally as soon as possible and prevail upon him to help you and your transition team, thus completing the holding-together he has done for so long. He will also be needed for liaison with Mr. Nixon and his family. However, he should not be expected, asked, or be given the option to become your Chief of Staff.

Ford nodded. He understood, but said nothing. He had witnessed, from a better vantage point than any other person in the United States, General Haig's meritorious service to the country. For at least a year, Haig had managed the White House and the executive departments, balanced the best interests of his country against loyalty to his commander in chief, counseled and defended Nixon, and at times nullified the worst of Nixonian designs. More often than not, Haig had served the nation as de facto President; for that, he deserved commendation. The problem was that Haig did not intend to give up his prime ministry. In fact, he had convinced himself that he was indispensable; that Ford could not manage the Presidency without him. "Jerry needs me more than he realizes," Haig told a subordinate, "and I can run his White House with the back of my hand."

But Ford had already decided that he, and not Haig or any other minister, would run his White House. In Ford's judgment, Nixon had delegated too much to staff. Consequently, he had made up his mind to demolish the traditional White House staff pyramid. He would replace it with a team of six or so senior aides with equal rank and access, and meet with them daily to discuss issues and reach decisions. That was the way he had operated as House Minority Leader; that was the way he intended to manage the Presidency. In his system there would be no place for a regent, as both Haldeman and Haig had been.

Furthermore, Haig was Nixon's man: he must go. But the deed must be done with care. Ford knew that he must draw on his quarter century of dealing with outsized egos to preserve Haig's high opinion of himself, and at the same time remove him from office. Patience—a prime asset of Ford as House Leader—would serve him now. He decided to wait for the right opportunity to act regarding Haig.

In its concluding recommendation, the transition team suggested Ford ask Members of the House, Senators, governors, and party leaders to recommend candidates for Vice President. To collect suggestions and coordinate that assignment, Ford wrote down Bryce Harlow, the affable sage from Oklahoma; Harlow had counseled President Eisenhower and every President since.

The journey from Ford's house in Virginia to his office took fourteen minutes. In that brief, back-seat limousine session, Ford had not only made decisions that would shape his Presidency, but it also epitomized Ford's way: collect the best available advice, read the memo, ask questions, decide, move on.

Arriving in his Vice Presidential office, he summoned Hartmann to be his audience as he again practiced his speech. This, Ford knew, would be the crucial performance of his public career; it would fix in the public mind the first and perhaps lasting impression of who Ford was and what kind of a President he was likely to be.

Two hundred yards east, in the Lincoln Sitting Room of the White House, President Nixon breakfasted alone, making notes for his farewell to his staff when he heard a knock on the door. General Haig was there with a letter for the President's signature. "This is something that will have to be done, Mr. President, and I thought you would rather do it now."

Addressed to the Secretary of State was one sentence:

I hereby resign the office of President of the United States.

Without a word, Nixon signed the letter.

After Haig left, Nixon sat alone for a time, then sent for a book in his study in the old Executive Office Building. On a page of a biography of Theodore Roosevelt by Noel Busch, Nixon found the quote he wanted—an elegy Roosevelt had written when his first wife died in childbirth.

Nixon marked the place and joined his family, waiting by the elevator to go to the East Room. To the brassy thumping of his final "Hail to the Chief," Nixon stepped to the podium. Arrayed beside him, like figures in a tableaux, were Pat Nixon, daughters Tricia and Julie, and their husbands Edward Cox and David Eisenhower. When the applause faded, Nixon began an unforgettably maudlin, rambling, and dissembling farewell, recounting with welling anguish the failures of his luckless father and the sacrificial devotion of his saintly mother.

In a final effort to rally his followers against despair—and perhaps himself—he read from Roosevelt's diary, "She was beautiful in face and form and lovelier still in spirit. . . . When my heart's dearest died, the light went from my life forever." Putting the book aside Nixon said: "That was T.R. He thought the light had gone from his life forever but he went on and he not only became President but as an ex-President he served his country, always in the arena. Tempestuous, strong, sometimes wrong, sometimes right, but he was a *man.*"

The performance revealed the real Nixon—a Shakespearean figure of greater ambition than character, a paradox of uncommon ability and tectonic fault, and on this, his last day, the personification of ignominious defeat, the loser.

Ford did not watch; to him, it was more important that he focus on what he was preparing to say.

Betty arrived and they waited until they were notified that the Nixons were ready to leave. Hartmann, who had first reported on Nixon for the *Los Angeles Times* in 1950, asked to go with them to the Diplomatic Reception Room. There, a few minutes later, President and Mrs. Nixon arrived, followed by their daughters and their husbands. After soft-spoken words and embraces—the somber quiet exchanges reminded Hartmann of a funeral—Nixon looked at his watch and said to Pat: "Time to go."

As they marched toward to the South Lawn and the waiting helicopter, Nixon and Ford in front, their wives arm in arm behind, Pat Nixon said: "My heavens, they've even rolled out the red carpet for us. Isn't that something?" After a moment she added, bitterly reflecting the gnawing emptiness of many a political wife, "Well, Betty, you'll see many of these red carpets, and you'll get so you hate 'em."

Nixon and Ford shook hands, their faces somber. "Goodbye, Mr. President," Ford said. "Goodbye, Mr. President," Nixon replied.

As the helicopter rose, the Fords walked back toward the White House; Ford took his wife's hand. "We can do it," he said. "We are ready."

Secretary of State Kissinger watched the drama from the South Portico of the White House. Seeing Ford's resolute steps toward the diplomatic entrance, Kissinger reflected, "No one [takes] over the Presidency in more challenging circumstances." He prayed, "For the sake of all of us, that fate would be kind to this good man, that his heart would be stout, and that America under his leadership would again find its faith."

At 11:35 a.m., General Haig entered the West Wing office of Secretary Kissinger and formally presented Richard Nixon's letter of resignation as 37th President of the United States. Kissinger accepted the letter. By that official act, Nixon ceased to be president.

Ford, back in his Vice Presidential office, read through his speech one more time. He was pleased, confident; it was just what he wanted to say. At 11:45 a.m., Marsh came into his office. "It's time to go over." As Ford rose from his desk, Marsh said: "Jerry, this is the last time I can ever call you by that name. From now on it will be 'Mr. President.'"

The remark moved Ford. He had always liked being Jerry. In Grand Rapids, everyone called him Jerry. The customary use of his first name was a leveler—kept him close to the people, one of them. In the House of Representatives, the name Jerry somehow reflected his easy accessibility and affable nature. Now, like it or not, Jerry Ford would be elevated to a title he must honor and enforce. For the rest of his life, except within his family, he would be Mr. President.

The East Room was jammed. All seats were filled; lesser notables stood along the walls. The drone of conversation suggested excitement, anticipation. People were smiling, bantering—a marked difference from the mood of the audience at Nixon's tearful farewell in the same room two hours earlier.

As the loudspeaker heralded "Vice President Ford and Mrs. Ford," they walked together to the podium. There was no resounding "Hail to the Chief"; Ford considered it unsuitable to the occasion, but immediately the crowd stood and delivered long and spirited applause. Ford, somber and serious, waited at the podium for the acclamation to subside. He confessed later that he had a sense of awe as he stood there. "It was almost as if all of America's past Presidents were praying for me to succeed."

Chief Justice Burger stepped forward. "Mr. Vice President, are you prepared to take the oath as President?"

"I am, sir."

With his hand on the Bible, held by his wife and opened to his beloved prayer in Proverbs, Ford recited the Constitutional oath of office, thereby becoming, at 12:03 p.m. on August 9, 1974, the 38th president of the United States.

"Congratulations, Mr. President," the Chief Justice said with warmth and respect.

Burger's words prompted everyone to stand and deliver an even louder ovation. Calmly, with a grave expression on his face, Ford waited. Fully aware that he had no talent for acting, and that television was not always kind to him, he had decided his role today was to play himself—a sturdy, dependable, straightforward midwesterner who had come out of obscurity to lead the most important nation in the world. He did not want to make this a celebration. "The circumstances were so serious that I wanted to get on with what I had to say," he said later.

Finally his guests were back in their seats, and he could begin.

"Mr. Chief Justice, my dear friends, my fellow Americans: The oath that I have taken is the same oath that was taken by George Washington and by every President under the Constitution. But I assume the Presidency under extraordinary circumstances never before experienced by

Americans. This is an hour of history that troubles our minds and hurts our hearts.

"Therefore, I feel it is my first duty to make an unprecedented compact with my countrymen. Not an inaugural address, not a fireside chat, not a campaign speech—just a little straight talk among friends. And I intend it to be the first of many."

"Straight talk" was Ford's nature. Candor and directness had defined him in his growing up and in the House of Representatives; he wanted it to define his Presidency. In his mind, he was on this dais to acknowledge his duty to his country, and to accept that duty with profound humility.

"I am acutely aware that you have not elected me as your President by your ballots, and so I ask you to confirm me as your President with your prayers. And I hope that such prayers will also be the first of many.

"If you have not chosen me by secret ballot, neither have I gained office by any secret promises. I have not campaigned either for the Presidency or the Vice Presidency. I have not subscribed to any partisan platform. I am indebted to no man, and only to one woman—my dear wife—as I begin this very difficult job." There was a catch in his voice as he mentioned Betty Ford.

"I have not sought this enormous responsibility, but I will not shirk it. Those who nominated and confirmed me as Vice President were my friends and are my friends. They were of both parties, elected by all the people and acting under the Constitution in their name. It is only fitting then that I should pledge to them and to you that I will be the President of all the people.

"Thomas Jefferson said the people are the only sure reliance for the preservation of our liberty. And down the years, Abraham Lincoln renewed this American article of faith asking, 'Is there any better way or equal hope in the world?'"

This was Ford the idealist, the optimist. As he had been chosen and confirmed by Democrats and Republicans in surpassing numbers, he hoped to use that bipartisan affirmation to end the partisan differences magnified by Watergate. In fact, Ford initially believed that he could govern as a nonpartisan President.

"I intend, on Monday next, to request of the Speaker of the House of Representatives and the President pro tempore of the Senate the privilege of appearing before the Congress to share with my former colleagues and with you, the American people, my views on the priority business of the Nation and to solicit your views and their views."

Departing from the text, he looked toward the Congressional leaders in the front row and added, "And may I say to the Speaker and the others, if I could meet with you right after these remarks, I would appreciate it.

"Even though this is late in an election year, there is no way we can go forward except together and no way anybody can win except by serving the people's urgent needs. We cannot stand still or slip backwards. We must go forward now together."

No President ever took office with greater respect for the power, egocentricity, and unpredictability of Congress. As a creature of the House, Ford had made up his mind to begin at once to restore comity between the White House and Capitol Hill.

"To the peoples and the governments of all friendly nations, and I hope that could encompass the whole world, I pledge an uninterrupted and sincere search for peace. America will remain strong and united, but its strength will remain dedicated to the safety and sanity of the entire family of man, as well as to our own precious freedom."

After that gesture to the international community, Ford reached the point where he must confront Watergate and the criminal acts of Nixon, then reach beyond: "I believe that truth is the glue that holds government together, not only our government but civilization itself. That bond, though strained, is unbroken at home and abroad. In all my public and private acts as your President, I expect to follow my instincts of openness and candor with full confidence that honesty is always the best policy in the end."

Then, with only the slightest pause, Ford proclaimed the message that, as Hartmann foresaw, Americans were waiting to hear:

"My fellow Americans, our long national nightmare is over.

"Our Constitution works; our great Republic is a government of laws and not of men. Here the people rule."

As a new President, in a new time, Ford hoped to lead the nation beyond the tragedy of Watergate to compassion and forgiveness, as he continued: " . . . There is a higher Power, by whatever name we honor Him, who ordains not only righteousness but love, not only justice but mercy. As we bind up the internal wounds of Watergate, more painful and more poisonous than those of foreign wars, let us restore the golden rule to our political process, and let brotherly love purge our hearts of suspicion and of hate.

"In the beginning, I asked you to pray for me. Before closing, I ask again your prayers, for Richard Nixon and for his family. May our former President, who brought peace to millions, find it for himself. May God bless and comfort his wonderful wife and daughters, whose love and loyalty will forever be a shining legacy to all who bear the lonely burdens of the White House. I can only guess at those burdens, although I have witnessed at close hand the tragedies that befell three Presidents and the lesser trials of others."

It took courage at that hour for anyone in public life to show compassion for a dishonest and disgraced Richard Nixon, but forgiveness was imbedded in Ford's character. He had never turned on a friend who was down.

To conclude his address, Ford made his heartfelt pledge to the country: "With all the strength and all the good sense I have gained from life, with all the confidence my family, my friends, and my dedicated staff impart to me, and with the good will of countless Americans I have encountered in recent visits to forty states, I now solemnly reaffirm my promise I made to you last December 6: to uphold the Constitution, to do what is right as God gives me to see the right, and to do the very best I can for America.

"God helping me, I will not let you down."

At those words, the guests rose and responded in a tremendous and continuing ovation.

Ford's inaugural address took eight minutes. Howard K. Smith, ABC's senior commentator, immediately described it on the air as "a perfect little gem." The *New York Times* bannered a headline the next day: FORD SWORN IN AS PRESIDENT; ASSERTS "NIGHTMARE IS OVER." In the *Washington Post*, which had played a central role in bringing down Nixon, Jules Witcover's story led all editions: "Gerald Rudolph Ford Jr. took the oath of office as 38th President of the United States at noon yesterday and assured a nation torn by the ravages of the Watergate scandal that 'our long national nightmare is over.'" Long after, the eminent Presidential biographer Edmund Morris wrote of Ford's "little straight talk among friends": "Simple, unstudied eloquence—one sentence that both healed and joined."

As the applause mounted, the new President walked briskly from the East Room. He was eager to tackle his new job, and the first order of business: Meeting in the Red Room with the leaders of Congress—the five Democrats and five Republicans who ran the House and Senate. Speaker Carl Albert and Senate Majority Leader Mike Mansfield—both

Democrats, both close friends of Ford—were first to congratulate him and assure him they were ready to cooperate.

As Ford moved about the room, shaking hands and accepting congratulations, the mood was jovial, the good wishes warm and sincere. "A great burden had been lifted from all our shoulders," Speaker Albert said later.

Albert was speaking for all those present, for a profound sense of relief had come to these ten leaders of Congress. For more than two years, the legitimacy of the U.S. government had been theirs to preserve, and they had met their responsibility to the Constitution and to the American people. They, and their Members, had placed the national interest above partisan advantage. Tragically, Watergate destroyed men and damaged institutions, but it brought Congress to reach its finest hour.

From the Red Room, Ford strode across the South Portico to the West Wing, and into the Press Room. He was there to announce that "one of yours," Jerry terHorst, would be his Press Secretary.

Ford, in the House, had never been a reporters' favorite. "He was a tremendously modest man, believable, open, available," according to Joseph R. L. Sterne, then Washington Bureau Chief for the *Baltimore Sun*. "There was no guile about him. He exuded a straight shooting character." Yet his mundane discussions of legislative business rarely made headlines. To television audiences, he was best known for his supporting role in the *Ev and Jerry Show*—the occasional joint press conferences of the Senate and House Republican leaders. There, Ford usually stood silent, grinning in admiration while that master showman—the mellifluous Everett Dirksen—pontificated on people and politics with the wit and precision that merited a front-page feature or a spot on the nightly TV news.

That subordinate role was past. Now, Ford knew, the media would focus on him, and he wanted to get off to a good start. Speaking to the packed room of White House reporters who had battled the secretiveness, deceptions, and outright lies of Nixon and his press secretary, the new President promised: "We will have an open, we will have a candid Administration. I can't change my nature after sixty-one years."

With a compliment to terHorst, "I am just delighted to have Jerry with us," Ford turned over the podium to him. Moments later, terHorst, trying his best to make the quantum leap from White House reporter to White House spokesman, made a grave mistake. Asked if Ford might pardon Nixon, terHorst said no, even though he had not spoken to the new President about the matter. It was a mistake that terHorst and the President would come to regret.

From the Press Room, Ford strode down the hall to the Oval Office. Entering it for first time as President, he planted his speech portfolio on the middle of the Presidential desk, thereby taking possession. His family—Betty, their three sons and daughter, his three half-brothers and their wives—housekeeper Clara Powell, and a few close friends had gathered. After an official photo, Ford proceeded to his next assignment: a meeting with the Nixon senior staff. Haig had made it his highest priority.

The Roosevelt Room, across the hall from the Oval Office, is a conference room smaller than the Cabinet Room, but no less imposing. It is named for the two Roosevelts: President Theodore Roosevelt's portrait on horseback as a Rough Rider hangs above the fireplace; a painting of President Franklin D. Roosevelt dominates the north wall. By custom, a President's senior staff gathered there every morning to brief the Chief of Staff on pressing issues, problems, and opportunities. On this inaugural afternoon, Haig had summoned Nixon's eleven top assistants to hear the new President.

To guide Ford in what he should say to the Nixon staff, Haig gave Ford prepared talking points.

> The main purposes of this meeting are:
> 1. Reassure the staff of your respect, your need for their help, and your regard for President Nixon.
> 2. Inform the staff of the role the transition team will play for the next few weeks and their relation to it.
>
> We suggest that this be a fairly short meeting covering the following general points:
> 1. The stress on the staff in these last few days and indeed the last year.
> 2. How important it is that they stayed in Mr. Nixon's service.
> 3. The special and heroic role of Al Haig.
> 4. Your personal need for the staff to remain intact and in place for a time to help you and the transition team.
> 5. The team members will be in touch with them and General Haig will be actively involved in the transition team's efforts.

DO NOTS—At this time, do not commit yourself to dealing
   directly with anyone but Al Haig.
DO—Ask each staff member to be alert to problems and to
   make suggestions to Al Haig or to transition team members.

Ford entered the Roosevelt Room accompanied by Hartmann,
Marsh, Scranton, and Buchen. For the President, Haig had provided a
big armchair at the head of the conference table; there were no seats for
Ford aides.

Ford did not follow all points in Haig's memo, but he did pay a
high compliment to Haig and reaffirm his authority: "Al has unselfishly
agreed to stay on." He also urged the Nixon staff to remain on their jobs
and pleaded for their help.

Ford's entreaty shocked Hartman, Marsh, and Buchen—all standing
against the wall. Intentionally or not, he had commissioned Haig to be
his Chief of Staff, thereby rejecting his transition team's strongest recommendation. It would, Hartmann felt, be the same old Nixon White
House.

In his mind, Ford was not continuing Haig's authority, but there
were good reasons to keep him temporarily. First, he would not dismiss
a good soldier who had met his duty. "Al deserved a hell of a medal for
keeping the country going during that last year of Nixon," Ford said.
Also, Ford felt a strong obligation to continue the Nixon policies and
programs that the American people had endorsed, by a landslide vote,
less than two years earlier. Haig could help him with that obligation,
and with the transition.

From that first day, Ford was acutely aware of a White House divided. "Many of the Nixon holdovers on the White House staff were
saying, 'Here comes Jerry Ford and his minor leaguers. Once we settle
them down and show them how this game is played, everything will
be all right.'" Ford wrote later. "And my own people were saying, 'As
soon as we get rid of these Nixon appointees, the government will be
legitimate again.'"

Staff division was just one more problem he would deal with in time.
"At that point," Ford said, "the most important thing to me was that I
had the government to run, and that's why I made the decision myself
that I wanted no resignations."

From the Roosevelt Room, Ford hurried on to the Cabinet Room
to confront what he already knew would be his most immediate and

perilous problem: inflation, soaring at an annual rate of 12 percent. At Ford's direction, Seidman had brought together the six most influential watchmen of fiscal and economic affairs: Arthur F. Burns, Chairman of the Federal Reserve and long a friend and confidant of Ford; Secretary of the Treasury William Simon; Kenneth Rush, Nixon's counselor for economic policy; Herbert Stein, retiring Chairman of Nixon's Council of Economic Advisers; Alan Greenspan, incoming CEA Chairman; and Roy Ash, Director of the Office of Management and Budget.

Sitting for the first time in the President's Chair in the Cabinet Room, Ford spent an hour with the group, asking each man for his views, listening, asking questions: what are the causes of inflation? Where is it headed? What is being done now? What can be done to curb inflation? Near the end of the session, he made and proclaimed his first economic policy decision: to cut Federal spending. "I will veto any excessive spending bill Congress sends me," he said.

In closing, Ford instructed Seidman to have the group set forth in writing their analysis of the reasons for inflation and their recommendations for dealing with the problem.

From the Cabinet Room, Ford returned to the Roosevelt Room to meet with thirteen ambassadors from the NATO nations—the first of eight foreign-policy appearances arranged by Secretary of State Kissinger for Ford's first day in office. "Nobody knew anything about the new President," Kissinger said, and he assumed that every ambassador in Washington would need to cable his home government that he had personally met the new President and could report on his impressions. Shuttling between the Roosevelt Room and the Cabinet Room, Ford met with a group of fifteen diplomats from the Middle East, a group of twenty-four ambassadors from Latin America, and individually with representatives from Japan, the USSR, Red China, Israel, and South Vietnam. Each meeting took only five to twenty minutes, with Ford emphasizing that in his Presidency, America would continue to stand strong in its own national defense and remain diligent in its search for peace and order in the world.

At 5:40 p.m., in the Cabinet Room, Ford met for the first time with his transition team. Rumsfeld, who was to take charge, had just arrived. Less than twenty-four hours before, Rumsfeld and his wife, Joyce, were in Italy, having just landed from a ten-day Mediterranean cruise. Driving along the French Riviera to visit a friend in Grimaud, near St. Tropez, they were astonished to learn, from a day-old *International Herald-Tribune,* that Nixon might resign. At the house of their friend, André de Staercke, Belgium's Ambassador to NATO, Rumsfeld telephoned his secretary at NATO in Brussels to find out more. Her evaluation: "It looks as though things are coming apart." Anticipating that Ford might need his help, he told her to make a plane reservation to Washington. When she called back with the flight number, she also relayed an urgent message that had just arrived for Rumsfeld from the Vice President: come to Washington immediately.

The Rumsfelds stayed up until 3:00 a.m. to hear Nixon's resignation speech; then, at 5:00 a.m., Joyce drove him to the Nice Airport. From there, Rumsfeld flew directly to Dulles Airport, to be met by a White House car and his protégé, Richard Cheney, bearing a sealed White House envelope. In it was a letter from Ford: he was to come to the White House at once to head the transition team.

During the meeting of the transition team, Rumsfeld listened and made notes. Ford, it was immediately apparent, had not foreseen how his transition team would work with the holdover Nixon staff. His uncertainty showed when, at the outset, he gave no direction but inquired: "on personnel, Scranton will work with Al, I suppose."

Morton, assigned as Cabinet liaison, asked Ford if the Cabinet should report through him to the President. Haig intervened, noting that he decided when a Cabinet member should see the President. Responding to neither, Ford said, "I'll have an open door to the Cabinet, but when you come, talk about something. Don't waste my time."

Ford did outline his daily routine: He would be in the office at 8:00 a.m., and begin his day with his intelligence briefing. Then, in sequence, he would meet with Hartmann, Marsh and the legislative liaison staff, and his press secretary. At 10:00 a.m., he would be ready for other visitors. "I listen better than I read," he said, "but I like to take papers home to read at night, and I prefer brief papers." And, he emphasized, "I like to see the alternatives."

Griffin asked how and when he planned to choose his Vice President. Ford said he did not have anyone in mind, but would talk with close advisers and decide in a week or ten days. With that, he hurried away to meet with the Latin American ambassadors.

After the inconclusive session, Rumsfeld found a vacant office. "I sat down and thought about the philosophy of what we ought to be doing, and how the transition might be managed. The objective was to move from an illegitimate government in the minds of the American people to a legitimate government, which was fundamentally necessary to governing in a society where you govern by consent. By the time I'd gotten there, two hours after the President was sworn in, he had made the decision to keep Kissinger, keep Haig, keep the Cabinet and keep the White House staff. So the President was emphasizing continuity as opposed to change."

As a counselor in the early Nixon White House, Rumsfeld had observed the constant, cross-departmental issues that confronted every President, so he was convinced that Ford's "spokes of the wheel" staff structure would not work. "There's no way the President could serve as his own filter. There aren't enough hours in the day. He can't decide who's going to be in every meeting, who's going to do all the things that need to be done. But he had made his decisions—and The President is The President. So I said, 'Terrific. Fine. That's that. Now you try to make that work.'"

Late in the day, Rumsfeld went in alone to see the President. Pointing out that conflict would be inevitable between a transition team of Ford newcomers and the still-in-place Nixon staff, Rumsfeld said there could not be "two White House staffs" or "two Administrations." The solution: "Let us get in and help out," he said. "And let's understand that barring some major catastrophe, we'll be out of here in a month. And he agreed with that."

As President Ford prepared to leave for the day, Hartmann came in with a mission. Anticipating the first Cabinet meeting the next morning, Hartmann walked Ford into the Cabinet Room and suggested he might change the portraits to reflect his own favorite presidents. Ford looked at the Nixon choices: Eisenhower in the place of honor above the fireplace; Theodore Roosevelt and Woodrow Wilson on the walls. Keep Eisenhower, Ford said, and replace Roosevelt with Lincoln.

"For a Democrat, how about Andrew Jackson," Hartmann suggested.

"No," Ford said. "Harry Truman."

Truman was President when Ford entered Congress. As a freshman, Representative Ford had been invited by President Truman to tour the White House and see the need for its renovation. From that first meeting, Ford liked this plainspeaking fellow midwesterner, and he also came to admire Truman's courage in making momentous decisions and the way he never let his high position go to his head.

"You're sure?" Hartmann asked.

"Absolutely," Ford said.

At 7:47 p.m., when Ford arrived at the family split level across the Potomac River in Alexandria, Virginia, he found his house full of people and boisterous with laughter. His children, brothers, and close friends were there, and neighbors had brought in ham and salad, lasagna and champagne. For the first time that day, Ford could take off his coat, pour champagne for toasts to the new President, and join the festivities.

When the crowd left, David Kennerly was invited to stay for a while. Kennerly, then 27 years old, was a superb photographer who had won a Pulitzer Prize in 1971 for his dramatic pictures of the Vietnam War—photographs that "capture the loneliness and desolation of war." Assigned by *Time-Life* in 1973 to cover the new Vice President, Kennerly—along with half a dozen reporters—had toured the country with Ford in the shaky old Convair that Haig had assigned the Vice President. Bearded, brash, and endowed with irrepressible good humor, Kennerly had become, by Betty Ford's account, "a kind of member of the family." On the Convair, Kennerly kidded the Vice President: "We've heard that same speech fifty times," and Ford kidded Kennerly about being "a heller and a woman chaser." Beneath the bantering, Ford saw another side of Kennerly. "He had a great sense of humor, but he could be deadly serious," Ford said. "Our views on Vietnam were identical. I absolutely trusted him."

Settled down in their living room, they talked over the highlights of the day. At one point the new President asked Kennerly if he would like to work in the White House. Yes, Kennerly said without hesitation, if he had unlimited access to meetings so that he would produce "a true photographic documentary" of the Ford Presidency. The agreement made, they shook hands, and Ford looked Kennerly in the eye and said: "I just want you to know that you're a really good friend."

At the end of that momentous day—a day like no other in the life of Jerry Ford, or in the history of the country—the new President reflected on his unprecedented inaugural and thought he had made a good start. "I wanted to establish that I was in charge, and I wanted to convey the impression that I was competent, that I knew what I was doing, and that I was acting through strength and not with any apology. And I think that's the way it came out."

PART 2

CHAPTER 4

Challenges

Who was this new President? How did this almost-stranger happen to attain the preeminent office in the world?

Not since Harry Truman succeeded Franklin D. Roosevelt twenty-nine years earlier had the American people known so little about a man who had stepped forward from obscurity to take the oath of office as President of the United States.

Like Truman, Ford was a sturdy, stolid, dependable, hardworking, straightforward midwesterner. The two had more in common. Each had a happy boyhood, growing up in a time and place where life was pleasant, neighborhoods were safe, and material possessions less important. Each had the good fortune to be guided by parents who had to work hard to keep bread on the table, who lived by old-fashioned principles, and who taught their sons precepts they never forgot: Tell the truth. Earn your way. Keep your word. Never forsake a friend. If at first you don't succeed, try, try again. Do what is right, whatever the consequences.

Each had his courage tested and his provincial outlook broadened by war: Truman as a captain of artillery in France; Ford as a lieutenant on the bridge of an aircraft carrier in the Pacific. Both aspired early to public service and became workhorses on Capitol Hill. Neither man expected to be President—or even wanted to be. Both took the oath of office in war and brought about a time of peace.

But there were significant differences, notably in their political beginnings. Truman was the product of a corrupt political boss: Thomas J. Prendergast and his Kansas City machine put Truman in his first elected office, as a courthouse commissioner in Jackson County, Missouri, and

39

elevated him to the U.S. Senate. Democratic Party bosses chose Truman to succeed President Franklin Roosevelt.

Ford fought the bosses, and beat them. He began his political career by challenging and defeating the corrupt Republican boss of western Michigan. Again and again Ford opposed the entrenched political powers. His first vote upon entering the House of Representatives in 1949 was against party leaders scheming to expand their power. Defying the conservative Republican establishment that supported Senator Robert Taft for President in 1952, Ford—with eighteen other young Republicans in the House—signed an open letter urging General Dwight D. Eisenhower to run as "the surest way . . . to promote peace in the world." Their initiative to place peace before party, Eisenhower wrote later, strongly influenced his decision to run.

In 1962, Ford was so dissatisfied with his party's lackluster leadership in the House that he challenged the aging Chairman of the House Republican Conference and won. Two years later, he took on the do-nothing Republican Leader of the House, hard-drinking Charles Halleck, and defeated him.

In his quarter-century as a House Member and Leader, Ford worked with colleagues of both parties, with three Democratic Presidents and two Republican Presidents, but he consistently maintained his independence. Jerry Ford was always his own man.

So he had been taught in childhood. His training began with a mother who was loving, indomitable by nature, spontaneous in spirit, but tempered by an unfortunate first marriage.

When Dorothy Gardner was 20 years old and a student at a women's college in Knoxville, Illinois, she met the blond, handsome, and charming brother of a classmate. He was Leslie King—the only son of an Omaha banker and merchant. She was infatuated; so, at 30 years old, was he. After a whirlwind courtship, King asked Dorothy's father for her hand. He was, he assured Levi Gardner, well established financially. With $35,000 in his bank account and a well-paying job in one of his father's companies, King said he could provide a comfortable life for her. Gardner, aware that the young man's father, Charles Henry King, was a multimillionaire entrepreneur in Omaha, had no reason to doubt Leslie. He consented.

The wedding, on September 12, 1912, was the social event of the season in Harvard, Illinois, where Gardner was a prosperous merchant and former mayor. Joining in the celebration were King's wealthy parents and a score of his Omaha friends. When the bride and groom boarded the Pullman to begin their wedding trip to the West Coast, Adele Gardner had never seen her younger daughter so happy.

Three weeks later, Dorothy's happiness ended. In the lobby of the elegant Multnomah Hotel in Portland, Oregon, Leslie King suddenly became enraged, called his bride vile names, slapped her in the face, and struck her a vicious blow to the head. Reconciled briefly, they entrained for California. On the way he again flew into a rage, beat her, and kicked her.

Dorothy was at first bewildered, then frightened. King's courtship charm had turned to unprovoked anger; his endearing words to curses; his geniality to brutality. When they reached Omaha she discovered her husband was also a liar: he had no money in the bank, but was deep in debt. She found out that he was taking money from the till in his father's warehouse where he worked.

Heartsick, knowing she had been betrayed, she decided to leave King and go home to her parents. Packing her trousseau, she discovered she was pregnant. King's parents pleaded with her to have the baby in Omaha, hoping the presence of a child would persuade their wastrel son to change his ways.

Reluctantly, she agreed, even though it meant that for months she must endure a husband who was a suspicious and unpredictable brute. On July 14, 1913, in the elder Kings' mansion at 3202 Woolworth Avenue, Dorothy Gardner King bore a son. At her husband's insistence, the child was named Leslie L. King Jr. The very next day, King burst into the sickroom and began berating the new mother. Her doctor warned King that she was quite ill and said he must stop abusing her. So concerned was the doctor that he brought in a nurse to care for Dorothy and protect the mother and child. A few days later, King came into the sickroom with a butcher knife and threatened to kill his wife and son. The nurse called the police, who restrained King and took him away.

Uncertain of her legal situation, Dorothy telephoned an Omaha lawyer. His instructions: for the safety of her child and herself, leave the house and the state at once. Taking no time to pack, the new mother wrapped her 16-day-old baby in a blanket, climbed into a public livery carriage, and crossed the bridge over the Missouri River to Council Bluffs, Iowa. There her mother and father were waiting to take her and her son out of King's reach.

In 1913, divorce was uncommon—an invitation to gossip, and often, the presumption of scandal. To avoid any embarrassment to their daughter in their hometown in Illinois, the Gardners moved her and their grandson to Grand Rapids, Michigan, where Levi Gardner had business interests. Through her Omaha lawyer, Dorothy filed for a divorce, which the court granted on December 19, 1913. The judge found King's conduct despicable, granted sole custody of their son to the mother, and ordered King to pay $25 a month in child support.

King refused to pay. The court found that he had no job and was heavily in debt. His father had fired him for mismanaging a warehouse, overdrawing his bank account, and unacceptable personal conduct. The elder King wrote Dorothy that he would pay the court-ordered child support.

In Grand Rapids Dorothy and her son began a new and better life. Her fifteen-month marriage had been a bitter experience, but she came out of it stronger and more resourceful. She kept the winsome ways and brimming optimism of her girlhood and matured into a woman of sound judgment, indomitable will, open generosity, and firm resolution.

By extraordinary good fortune, at an Episcopal church social in her second year in her new city, she met the right man. He was an amiable bachelor, a regular at church, reserved, ruggedly handsome, and only a year older than she was. His name: Gerald R. Ford. He asked if he might call on her.

This time Dorothy was more deliberate. She learned that Ford's trade was selling paint and varnish to the furniture industry—Grand Rapids' biggest at the time. He had quit school at 14 years old to support his widowed mother and sisters; ever since, he had earned a decent living for them and himself. It was well-known in the community that he was an upstanding and well-respected citizen who worked hard and was scrupulously honest—the diametric opposite of Leslie King.

In courtship Ford was kind, thoughtful, and devoted to Dorothy King and to her infant son. She invested a year in getting to know her new suitor—making certain of his character, steadiness of purpose, and evenness of disposition—before she accepted his proposal. They were married, in the church where they met, on February 1, 1916.

From that day on, all went well for Dorothy and her new husband. Theirs was, in every way, a happy, fulfilling, and lasting marriage. As she had taken a new name, she conferred it also on her son. "Junie"—her diminutive for "Junior"—became Junie Ford. Since he was only eighteen months old when she married Ford, the child grew up believing his father was Gerald Ford.

As stepfather, Gerald Ford proved to be the very model of a father—attentive and caring, masculine but gentle. A natural at teaching, he devoted himself to his stepson. He took the boy camping and fishing. He taught him to swim, catch a baseball, and throw a football. He coached him to think for himself and follow his conscience. Remembering him some sixty years later, Ford said: "He was my father, the father I learned from and loved and respected. He was my Dad."

When Junie Ford was 5 years old, his mother gave birth to Tom—the first of her three sons by Gerald Ford. But the bonds between Dorothy's firstborn and second husband never frayed. "We had a tremendous relationship, Dad and I," Ford said. "My stepfather had as much love for me, if not more, than his own three sons."

In Grand Rapids, mother and son had not only found the right man; they had found the right city. In the boom times after World War I, Grand Rapids was America at its best—prosperous, enterprising, clean, well governed, full of opportunity. Most families owned their own homes. Public schools were ranked in a national survey as the best in the nation. The city could boast of good hospitals and convenient parks. Streets were safe. Citizens—Gerald and Dorothy Gardner Ford typified the Grand Rapids community—were thrifty, self-reliant, and active in civic affairs.

The early 1920s brought good times for the Fords. His business was thriving. He bought a house, and later a car. The four boys were growing up, doing well in school, earning their freedom, and learning responsibility. The parents enforced three house rules: tell the truth, work hard, come to dinner on time.

When dinner was over and the dishes washed, the boys buckled down to homework at the dining-room table. School and learning—that was the first priority imposed by Mother and Father. She had experienced the benefits of good schooling; he was determined that the boys would have the education he had missed.

At night, young Jerry would climb into bed with the latest Horatio Alger book. "They were all stories about heroes, poor boys who struggled and eventually succeeded," he said. "They were my favorite reading." For poetry, he chose the homespun truisms of Edgar Guest, published regularly in the *Detroit Free Press*.

After school, the father encouraged the boys to take an active part in competitive sports—football, baseball, basketball, tennis. "He believed sports taught you how to live," Ford said. "Sports taught you how to compete but always by the rules, how to be part of as team, how to win, how to lose and come back to try again."

Dorothy Ford was a generous and loving mother, but a strict disciplinarian. Her son by King had inherited his biological father's bad temper; to help the boy control it, she would reason with him, or make a face to show him how absurd he looked, or send him to his room to cool down. Once, after a particularly angry outburst, she had him memorize Kipling's "If," and recite it over and over until he could control his temper.

At some point in his childhood—Ford was never sure of the year— his mother mentioned in an offhand way that she had been married before, and that he had been born before she met Gerald Ford. "It didn't make a big impression on me at the time," Ford said. "I didn't understand exactly what a stepfather was. Dad and I had the closest, most intimate relationship. We acted alike. We had the same interests. I thought we looked alike. I had never met the man she said was my father. I couldn't have cared less about him, because I was as happy a young boy as you could find."

On his twelfth birthday Jerry Ford joined the Boy Scouts—a significant rite of passage for him. Standing before the Scoutmaster, he raised his hand to take the Scout oath, memorized it, and never forgot it: "To do my duty to God and my country, and to obey the Scout law; to help other people at all times; to keep myself physically strong, mentally awake, and morally straight."

With the coaching of Scoutmaster Chuck Kindel, Ford and five friends who had joined with him moved up in three years to become Eagle Scouts. At summer camp, Ford was assigned to be swimming coach and assistant counselor—his first experience as a leader. Not only did he like being in charge, but he did so well at instructing younger Scouts and earning merit badges that he was chosen to be one of eight Eagle Scouts appointed by Michigan Governor Fred Green to guide visitors at Fort Mackinac during the summer of 1929. For 15-year-old Jerry Ford, it was a great experience: He was on his own. He made friends. He enjoyed meeting the public. He discovered he could speak and hold an audience's attention.

As it came time for Ford to go to high school, the family weighed the choices. Since they lived on a block where district lines met, he could go to Central High, attended by the upper-middle class; Ottawa Hills, a newer school in an elite neighborhood; or South High, which brought together Italians, Greeks, Poles, Lithuanians, blacks, and recent immigrants from Eastern Europe. For advice, Ford's parents turned to a knowledgeable friend—Ralph Conger, a teacher and basketball coach at Central. "Send Jerry to South High," Conger advised. "They have the best teachers. And there he will learn more about people, and about living."

It was a decision of the greatest consequence. South High spanned the formative years of Ford's growing up: years that strengthened his youthful character and set his course in life. In the classroom he responded well to South High's good teachers and began to think about his future. He set his ambition: to go to college and become a lawyer. For that, he realized, he must prepare himself. Diligent in his studies, he learned also by observing his peers, forming an optimistic and lasting personal philosophy: "Look for the good in every person," he told a classmate. "That way, you will never hate anybody."

As an honor student, Ford was earning the respect of classmates and teachers. Beyond the classroom there was more, far more: on South High's football field he came under the influence of Coach Clifford Gettings—a wise and capable leader who implanted enduring principles in the teenage Ford and brought out in him the athletic skill that endowed his education.

On the first day that Ford and a hundred other freshmen assembled on the dirt practice field, Gettings picked out the stocky blond (5'8, 130 pounds) and said, "Hey, whitey, you're a center." Ford did not question the assignment. "Coach saw me. I had white hair, and he needed a center. That's how I became a center."

Fifty years later, Ford's memory of that practice field was still vivid: "Coach Gettings was a stern taskmaster. I spent hours learning from him how to snap the ball back, lead a tailback a step in the direction he was going to run, put it high and soft for a fullback coming into the line, get it on the right hip for the punter. And then after you centered the ball, you had to be quick to block the opposing lineman who had the jump on you."

In Ford's sophomore year the varsity center was injured, so Ford came in off the bench and played the rest of the season. From the first he demonstrated the competitive spirit and joy of brute contact that make a football player. "Jerry was a hard-working kid and totally dependable," Coach Gettings said. "Center was a demanding position. I never saw Jerry make a bad pass. And on defense, he and another kid named Joe Russo made about ninety percent of the tackles. Jerry knew everyone's assignment on every play; having him in the game was like having a coach on the field."

Ford's prowess in football won him a part-time job at a Greek diner across the street from South High. It was owned by Bill Skougis—an ardent football fan who paid Ford $2 a week and his lunch for serving food and washing dishes. One day, as Ford stood at the stove frying hamburgers, a man he had never seen before walked in, stopped near the counter, and stood there staring. For at least fifteen minutes the stranger continued to stand in silence and stare at Ford.

Finally Ford turned from the stove and asked: "Can I help you?"

"Are you Leslie King?" the stranger said.

"No."

After a long pause the man said: "I'm your father. You're Leslie King."

Ford was startled, speechless. He looked at the man.

"I'm in town with my wife," King said, "and I would like to take you out to lunch."

Ford was not afraid of the stranger, but wary. He knew that someone other than "Dad" was his real father, but he did not know that his birth name was Leslie King. He wondered: "Could this stranger be my father?" It took but a moment for him to decide that he had to find out.

"Bill, I've got a crisis," he said to Skougis. "Can you let me go for an hour? I've got to have lunch with this man."

Skougis looked over the visitor, thought he seemed respectable, and said, "Okay."

Waiting in a new Lincoln outside was King's wife of ten years, and a daughter. At a nearby restaurant King said they had taken the train from Wyoming to Detroit to buy their new car, and he had decided to drive through Grand Rapids on the way back to look up his teenage son. Unable to find any Leslie King enrolled at the three high schools, he had asked the principal at South High if he had a boy named Ford. "Oh yes," the principal said. "You mean Jerry Ford. He's at work at Skougis's diner across the street."

During their lunch, King invited Ford to leave Grand Rapids and come out to live with him on his big ranch outside Riverton, Wyoming.

"No, I like it here," his son said.

As they talked, he looked at his father, searching for a resemblance, but found none. He wondered why his father had waited so many years to find him. Was it because he wanted to brag about a son who was a football star? He wanted to ask how his father could boast of buying a new Lincoln, yet had paid nothing for his support or education. "I bit my tongue to stop myself from being impolite," he said.

As King left his son back at Skougis's diner, he said: "Can I help you financially?"

"Well, that would be nice."

King reached into his pocket and handed Ford a twenty-dollar bill—the only aid he ever gave his son.

That day was one that Ford would always remember. "It was a hell of a shock for a 15-year-old kid," he said. "I was not frightened by him but by what I was going to tell my parents that night. And I was really terrified about that."

That evening, after dinner and homework, with his younger brothers in bed, Ford mustered his courage. "Telling Mother and Dad was one of the most difficult experiences of my life. But I did. I told them the whole story, hoping they would understand. And they did. Mother was not visibly upset. She and Dad consoled me, and showed in every way that they loved me."

In bed that night Ford lay sleepless in the darkness. He was confused, troubled. He was not who he thought he was. A stranger had upset his happy life. He wanted to find something good in that person, but could not. "Nothing could erase the image I gained of my real father that day—a carefree, well-to-do man who really didn't give a damn about the hopes and dreams of his son." He wept—not in sorrow, but in anger that his own father cared so little. He drifted into sleep repeating his mother's favorite prayer from Proverbs.

Trust in the Lord with all thine heart; and lean not unto thine own understanding.
In all thy ways acknowledge him; and he shall direct thy paths.

In October 1929, Gerald Ford Sr. was doing so well as a salesman that he bought a paint store. Three weeks later the stock market crashed. In

Grand Rapids, as across the nation, hard times struck. Banks closed. Factories shut down. Workers lost their jobs. Undaunted, the elder Ford resolved to keep his store open. DuPont, in recognition of his honesty and good record for paying his bills, extended unlimited credit. Selling whatever he could, Ford paid his employees, and himself, $5 a week so their families could buy food. He promised to make up the difference in their wages when times got better, and did.

To make things worse for the Fords in that grim autumn, Charles Henry King, Ford's grandfather, died in Omaha. His death terminated the meager child support he had paid for sixteen years to Mrs. Ford. She, knowing that Leslie King would inherit a fortune, filed suit in Omaha, asking the court to require King to pay for his son's college education. The court decided in her favor and ordered King to pay $100 a month until his son finished college. Again King refused to pay. As a resident of Wyoming he was beyond the Nebraska court's jurisdiction.

In his senior year at South High, Ford was elected captain of the football team. "I was proud, honored, because we had a great team and developed wonderful rapport," Ford said. "When the season opened the newspapers looked on us as city champions and even state champions." As it turned out, South High reached the finals, played before 12,000 people, and won the Michigan state championship. Ford was named all-state center and captain of the all-state team. On the sports pages of Grand Rapids newspapers, he was acclaimed as a hero. His mother clipped and saved every line printed about her star player.

For Ford, football was far more than a game. "I learned discipline," he said in later life. "I learned you were part of a team, especially as a lineman, where you worked in the trenches with six other linemen. I learned to have a good attitude—it's infectious and can bring victory. I learned that losing a game was terrible, but you had to go on, prepare for the next game, and the next. I admired my coach. He inspired us. He motivated us. He taught us: 'You play to win. You give it everything you've got, but you always play within the rules.' We believed that. That's the way we played then. I still do."

With the Great Depression continuing to humble Grand Rapids and the nation, there was not a chance that Ford's parents could afford to send him to college. Knowing this, the principal at South High intervened. Without the Fords' knowledge, Arthur Krause wrote the University of Michigan football coach, Harry Kipke, telling him about this fine South High athlete and National Honors student, and suggesting he meet Ford. Kipke drove from Ann Arbor to Grand Rapids, talked to Ford and his parents, and acted. Michigan offered no football scholarships in those days, but Kipke arranged for Ford to meet his biggest expense: he could earn his meals waiting on tables at the University hospital.

Principal Krause, aware that Ford would also need $100 cash for his first year's tuition, stepped in again: he initiated a scholarship fund from South High bookstore profits, and announced that honor student Ford would receive the first award—$100.

From summer jobs Ford saved enough to rent a cheap room. His stepfather's childless sister and her husband volunteered to send Ford $2 every Monday for spending money. "So that's how I got to college," Ford said, "and that was the luckiest break I could have had."

In September 1931, Ford arrived in Ann Arbor to begin his new life, but he never really left Grand Rapids, or his parents. "From Mother he learned self-discipline and to be calm in a crisis," said Dick Ford, younger by eleven years. "From Dad he took on a gregarious nature, a keen interest in politics, and a commitment to civic affairs." They, and others in Grand Rapids, had set down like a granite plinth stone the foundation of young Jerry's character: confidence, trustworthiness, fair play, honesty, loyalty, tolerance, determination, reliance on self. The qualities they instilled would endure for all his days.

As one of 1,188 freshmen entering storied University of Michigan, Ford buckled down to validate the confidence so many had placed in him. Coach Kipke would expect his best; Ford did not disappoint him. Twenty-five freshmen tried out for football that fall; Ford excelled. He played first-string center on the freshman team, and won the school trophy for the first-year player who demonstrated the best attitude and greatest promise for the varsity.

As a sophomore, to Ford's dismay, he sat on the sidelines. Michigan's varsity center was an all-American, and only a junior, which relegated Ford to reserve status for two years as Michigan went undefeated. "Not playing was tough, but I learned a lot sitting on the bench," Ford said. "I learned that there was the potential always that somebody could be better than you. And Chuck Bernard was better overall—twenty-five pounds bigger, and better on defense. I was the better offensive center. But in those days of few substitutions, the coach played one guy on offense and defense."

His demeanor left a lasting impression on Coach Kipke, who told a sports audience in Grand Rapids: "Jerry Ford is one of the finest boys I have ever met. I'm not now talking of football ability, but of character. He's always cheerful, always does the very best that's in him . . . He has never complained, never crabbed, never felt that he wasn't getting a square deal, always boosting for Bernard who was keeping him on the bench . . . Give me eleven boys with the disposition of Jerry Ford."

In his senior year Ford made the first team; but Michigan, weakened by injuries, lost most of its games. Nevertheless, Ford made All Big Ten, and his team voted him their most valuable player—a rare honor for a lineman.

For his academic courses, Ford studied as diligently as he performed on the football field, but with less success. Majoring in history and economics, he made A's and B's, but he struggled in English composition. His best was a C; in French he fell to a D. In his senior year he concentrated on economics and business administration, and earned B's across the board.

With studying, football, and earning his way, he had little time for social life. He did join the Delta Kappa Epsilon fraternity, but had to wait on tables to pay for his board. By his senior year, he was deep in debt. Needing more than $1,000 to pay his bills and graduate, he wrote his birth father in Wyoming and asked for financial help. His letter was never answered.

As graduation approached in the spring of 1935, Ford was more than ever determined to attend Michigan's law school, but he had no way to pay for it. Hopefully, he asked Coach Kipke for a job as an assistant. Kipke, short of funds, had to turn him down. Ford did have other job offers: the Green Bay Packers offered him $110 a game; the Detroit Lions, $200 a game. To both teams Ford said no: professional football would not get him to law school.

Then, out of the blue one morning, Kipke telephoned and invited Ford to have lunch with Ducky Pond, Yale's football coach. Pond was in Ann Arbor scouting for an assistant line coach, and Ford had been highly recommended for the job by Ivan Williamson—Yale's end coach, and captain of the Michigan team during Ford's sophomore year. Kipke agreed, advising Pond that Ford would make an excellent coach.

After interviewing Ford for two hours, Pond confirmed their judgment. Certain that he had found the right man, Pond brought Ford to New Haven to meet the other Yale coaches, then made him an offer: to start in September at $2,400 a year as an assistant line coach.

For Jerry Ford, it was an extraordinary stroke of fortune. Coaching at Yale would be prestigious; and in 1935, $2,400 a year was good pay for a 22-year-old college graduate. He could pay off his debts. Far more important, he knew that once he was working at Yale, he would somehow find a way to go to law school at Yale. "I was," Ford said, "very lucky."

Yet it was not mere luck that brought him to Yale. Again, someone had perceived the promise in young Ford and intervened. As Coach Gettings and Principal Krause had stepped in to get Ford to Ann Arbor, a Michigan teammate and Coach Pond brought him to New Haven. Williamson and Pond not only gave him his first job, which he badly needed; the two advocates also placed him in sight of his goal: law school.

After he graduated from Michigan in June 1935, with a BA in Economics, Ford went home for the summer to help out in Dad's paint store. One evening he sat down with his parents to tell them of a decision he had made. He intended to change his name. Although family, friends, schoolmates, everyone, always called him Jerry Ford, his legal name was still Leslie L. King Jr., as recorded on his birth certificate in Omaha. "I wanted to have Dad's name legally," he said. "I was 21, of age, and could make that decision. It was my initiative, a decision on my part out of respect for Dad and love for him. I was about to begin my first job, and I wanted the record to be clear: So far as I was concerned, Gerald Ford *was* my father."

Dorothy and Gerald were delighted. On December 3, 1935, the Kent County judge of probate declared Dorothy Ford's eldest son to be legally the person that in his heart and mind he had always been—Gerald Rudolph Ford Jr.

From his first days at Yale, Ford liked his job and proved to be good at it. "Players were of a high order of intelligence, for the most part anyway," said William Proxmire, an end on the junior varsity. "They saw in Coach Ford not only diligence, but a first-rate mind." Robert Taft Jr., another junior varsity player, said of Ford: "He didn't shout like some coaches. He was very calm, and spoke to your intelligence. He taught the basics, blocking and tackling. He told you how, and showed you how." Both of these players would go on to serve in the U.S. Senate.

Another walk-on was John Hersey—later a Pulitzer Prize-winning novelist. "Yale was a challenge," he said. "I worked hard. I learned a lot.

I thrived in the atmosphere. I played football because I liked the game, and I learned from Coach Ford how to play my best." Hersey, Ford said, practiced with diligence and great effort, but he lacked the speed to make varsity end.

Like Hersey, Ford also thrived in the atmosphere at Yale. As he taught, he learned. He studied his players, evaluated their strengths and weaknesses, and motivated them. "You had to see each player as an individual, bring out his particular skills, and inspire him to play up to the limit of his capability," Ford said. After two seasons Pond raised his pay to $3,600 a year, promoted him to head coach for the junior varsity and director of all scouting, and sent him out to recruit new players and talk football to gatherings of Yale alumni. "It was a great job, traveling, speaking, meeting people," Ford said. "I loved it."

But he never wavered in his singular ambition. His first application to Yale's law school was summarily rejected. Most entrants, he was coldly informed, were Phi Beta Kappa. To test his own resolve about becoming a lawyer, in the summer of 1937 Ford enrolled in two courses at Michigan's law school. With B's in both, he again applied for admission to Yale. Two professors said no, but another—Professor Myres McDougal—looked him over more carefully. McDougal's verdict: "Very mature, wise person of good judgment, good-looking, well-dressed, plenty of poise, personality excellent. Informational background not the best, but interested, mature, and serious of purpose. I see no reason for not admitting him."

On McDougal's recommendation, Ford was admitted in the spring session of 1938, but only on trial and as a part-time student. He could take only two courses, but earned a B in each. That was convincing. "I knew," Ford said, "I just *knew* I would find a way to go on."

Concentrating, working hard, he did even better during a second trial semester. Finally, in 1939, he was admitted as a full-time student. This meant that in the mornings he attended classes, in the long afternoons he coached undergraduates on the practice fields, and at night he pored over the assigned cases and wrote briefs. Looking back many years later, Ford said: "I found I could handle two full-time jobs at once, but I must say I worked my ass off."

Yet he still found the time and incentive to fill a void in his life. Through a friend, he met a remarkable young woman: Phyllis Brown—a preppie, 17-year-old honors student at Connecticut College for Women. She was fair of face and form, with the verve and vivacious personality of a woman well beyond her youthful years. From her first meeting with Ford, she said, "I knew I wanted to see him again and again." Reflecting on their friendship half a century later, she said, "He was very serious. He had worked all through high school and college, playing football, waiting on tables, studying, managing the fraternity house—he had not had time to have a girl. He had not had time to play. And along comes this player—me! I wanted Jerry to be my playmate. I had a great love of life, of doing things. He too had a lot of energy, a lot of vitality. We both liked to do a lot of things, so we did them together."

Ford, at 23 years old, had found a young woman whose energy, intelligence, love of sports, and zest for life matched his own. "For the first time in my life," he said, "I fell deeply in love."

Their courtship was typical of the well-to-do in the 1930s. He often drove his four-door Ford convertible to New London to see her; she came just as often to New Haven to see him. They played tennis, golf, and bridge. They sailed. They read novels together. Weekends, they skied in Vermont. They could afford the good life: she was wealthy; the daughter of a prosperous merchant in Lewiston, Maine, and Ford, for the first time in his life, had money in his pocket.

At a Dartmouth College winter carnival, Miss Brown's radiant beauty and svelte grace attracted the professional eye of McClelland Barclay—a leading magazine illustrator, and he introduced her to John Robert Powers, head of the top model agency in New York City. Signed up in her initial interview, Phyllis left college and moved to Manhattan. When Ford could break away from coaching and studying, he joined her. Together they saw Broadway shows, attended the opera, applauded the symphony at Carnegie Hall, and visited the Metropolitan and other art museums. They played tennis in Queens, lunched at 21, and danced at the Rainbow Room in Rockefeller Center. To Ford, New York City was exciting and challenging: a place to see and explore; an opportunity to experience bustling, big-city America.

There, Phyllis Brown not only enjoyed his company but saw him grow. Her impressions of Ford in his mid-twenties reflect the early and enduring character of the man. "Jerry was forthright, honest, honorable, a very solid young man," she said. "Everybody liked him, whether we were in New Haven or New London or New York. He was always cheerful, optimistic by temperament. Wherever we went, whatever company we were in, he had an innate awareness of everything going on around him. Sometimes he pretended he was not as smart as he was.

He listened. He learned. He remembered. He put things together. He was not quick, but mulled everything over and came out with the right answer. People he met quickly discovered that he was a very smart man, not brilliant, but very smart. He was not a babbling brook, but a clear stream with depth."

In the summer of 1940 Ford ventured into politics—his first step on the long journey that would lead to the White House. He had been listening to Wendell Willkie on the popular radio program "Information Please," reading about Willkie in *Time* and New York City newspapers, and had come to admire the ideas and bonhomie of Willkie. He strongly supported Willkie's promise to keep the United States out of the war in Europe. So he told his stepfather he wanted to volunteer to work for Willkie in Grand Rapids that summer. His stepfather, active in the Kent County Republican Party, advised him to speak to Frank McKay, the Republican power of western Michigan. But he warned: McKay was arrogant and corrupt; a political boss who ruled by fear, not persuasion. Ford telephoned for an appointment, went to McKay's office, and waited, and waited, and waited. "Finally, after four hours, McKay gave me three minutes," Ford said. "He showed no interest in how I might help the party."

Dismissed in his hometown, Ford drove to New York City to volunteer at Willkie's national headquarters; there he was welcomed. The work was mundane—stuffing envelopes and handing out leaflets—but Ford learned the basics and earned a ticket to the Republican National Convention. In Philadelphia he stood as one of the throng chanting "We Want Willkie": the clarion call from the well-organized amateurs that delivered the nomination.

That November, Willkie's political career ended, but Ford's had just begun. "My participation did not make much difference to Wendell Willkie, but it did to me," he said. "By participating, I learned. Not only did I learn a little about politics, but more important I learned about myself. I liked politics. I liked everything about it."

Returning to New Haven, he took his next significant political stand. In September 1940, he joined, with fellow law students Sargent Shriver and Potter Stewart, the America First Committee. This committee, an initiative started by Douglas Stuart Jr.—another Yale law student—organized public opinion to force President Roosevelt to enforce the 1939 Neutrality Act, and keep America out of war. Ford's action reflected his belief, common in the isolationist Midwest and elsewhere, that neutrality and two oceans would save the United States from being drawn into the proximate war in Europe, or the distant war in Asia.

That autumn, Ford coached his last junior varsity squad and attended his last classes in law school. His performance on the football field and in the classroom was recognized. Coach Pond paid tribute to Ford for his contributions to his fellow coaches and the players on six Yale football teams. His evaluation: "Very intelligent, industrious, conscientious and exceptionally loyal . . . Distinct leadership ability." The Dean of Yale's law professors ranked Ford in the top third of a distinguished class.

The years at Yale were invaluable for Ford. First, Yale broadened his view of the nation; he experienced another America and began to rise above his midwestern provincialism. At Yale his mental capacity and physical stamina were stretched to the limit, but never breached. He saw how much he could undertake, and accomplish. So challenged in responsibilities and interests, he found it necessary to organize his time; never in his life did he lose that useful habit. He succeeded in his first paid job, which for him was far more than a job. Coaching was leadership; lessons learned there would give him an advantage on many fields of competition.

In the classrooms he found his professors able and learned: the best of teachers. Later, in many times of need or crisis, he would turn to and rely on scholars and educators. His fellow Yale students, many of superior intellect, he found not daunting, but bracing. Ever after he sought out those who knew more about a subject: in their company he would question, listen, and draw from their knowledge.

Evenings, poring over the casebooks, Ford learned to consider an array of conflicting fact and opinion, and cut through disorder to make the right choice. It was, Ford said, "thinking and analysis, the application of logic to issues." Instinctive judgment he had always had; Yale turned Ford into a man of informed judgment.

Thus endowed, he mapped out his future. He could join a major law firm in Philadelphia or New York City; his academic record had brought impressive offers. He turned them all down. He was already thinking about a possible future in politics, and the place for that would be his hometown.

There would be personal consequences; that he knew. Going back to Grand Rapids would end his romance with Phyllis Brown. She had no intention of leaving New York City. Flourishing as a model—for *Cos-*

mopolitan covers, fashion magazines, Coca-Cola ads—and enjoying the whirl of café society, she was unwilling to give up her successful career and Manhattan's sophistication for obscurity in western Michigan—even if she had been asked, which she was not.

Looking ahead, Ford had decided that marriage to Phyllis Brown would be a mistake. "With all her wonderful traits, with all her terrific qualities of attractiveness and ability, she had a wandering eye," Ford said. "It was her nature to be, well, gregarious; and somehow I sensed that would not be good for a political wife."

"I was a flirt," Phyllis admitted. "I was a giddy girl with a lot of beaus, playing the field. I thought, when I got around to it, I would marry Jerry."

Consciously, deliberately, Jerry Ford put his career ahead of his personal feelings. Although the love affair ended, the two could look back and see that their four years together had been felicitous and rewarding. Ford, then and thereafter, recognized that Phyllis Brown had influenced his life: she broadened his horizons, introduced him to music, art, and drama, advanced his social graces, and showed him how to get away from the grind of work and study—and just enjoy life. In turn, he encouraged her ambition and professional initiative. "She was a driver, a shaker and mover," he said. He once told her that if she had been a man, she would have risen to the top of the corporate world.

In January 1941, a dozen years after he had set his goal in South High, Ford reached it: graduation from law school. That accomplished, he wasted no time in returning to Grand Rapids to begin his practice. He was twenty-eight, and, "impatient, ambitious, and ready to strike out on my own."

As his partner he chose Philip Buchen, a fraternity brother who had overcome teenage polio to graduate from Michigan law school at the top of his class. Together they took the bar exam in Lansing in March. In June, as soon as they learned they had passed, each put up $1,000—Ford's from savings, Buchen's as a loan from his father—and opened a tiny office: Ford and Buchen. "I still don't know how we had the guts to do it," Ford said long after. "We didn't have a single client—not one client."

On the first day a man walked in and asked for a title search. The fee: $10. Gradually more clients came in; soon they were dealing with labor disputes, pensions, divorces. In their first year the two partners were paying the rent, breaking even, and on the way to success. Ford's initial confidence was confirmed; he had chosen the right profession and the right city.

One day Ford learned that Republican friends of his stepfather were organizing an effort to end the boss rule of Frank McKay. To the leader, Dr. Willard Ver Meulen, ridding the Republican Party of a corrupt political boss was a moral issue. When Ford asked to join, Dr. Ver Meulen warned: "You will lose clients."

Ford laughed. "I don't have that many clients," he said. "Count me in."

The band of rebels not only brought Ford in; they elected him president of the Home Front—the name they had given their enterprise. Their plan was ambitious—to defeat McKay's entrenched lackeys in each of Kent County's 142 precincts, and then turn out the boss. Ford thus began his next lesson in practical politics: recruiting, teaching neophytes how to canvass, and organizing the scattered forces into a unified and effective team. Ford relished the assignment; in Grand Rapids, as at Yale, by teaching, he learned.

On Sunday, December 7, 1941, Ford spent much of the day alone at his office, hard at work on a complex case. Driving home in the late afternoon, he turned on the car radio and first heard the momentous news: the Japanese had attacked Pearl Harbor.

For Ford, as for the vast majority of 132 million other Americans, that unexpected and unreal and infamous event changed everything. Pearl Harbor shattered his hope, and the hope of his fellow America Firsters and most other Americans, that the United States could keep out of the war. It had been a delusion—the notion that America could be neutral in a worldwide conflict between freedom and tyranny.

To Ford, passing through the peaceful streets of that Sunday afternoon in Grand Rapids, there was no doubt about what he must do: answer the call to arms. Law and politics would have to be postponed. Indefinitely.

At home, he walked in and gravely addressed his anxious parents. "Mother, Dad, I am going to volunteer for the Navy tomorrow morning."

And he did.

CHAPTER 5

Advancing

As American forces endured defeat after defeat on land, at sea, and in the air—Manila, Wake Island, Guam, all lost; the USS *Houston* sunk in the Java Sea; eighty-five P-40s and eighteen B-17s destroyed in the Philippines—Ford grew more and more impatient to put on a uniform and join the fight. He persuaded Grand Rapids' leading citizens, fellow lawyers, and Coach Pond to write the Navy and urge that he be called to duty.

Finally, after waiting for months, Ford learned that Tom Hamilton, a former football coach at the U.S. Naval Academy, was organizing the Navy's V-5 preflight training program. Ford and Hamilton had become friends at football conferences, so Ford telephoned Hamilton and asked for his help. Days later, the Navy acted.

On April 16, 1942, Ford was commissioned an ensign, given USNR serial number 141329, immediately promoted to lieutenant (junior grade), and ordered to report to Annapolis for basic training. After a hurry-up month of instruction in drill, saluting, correct dress, and proper conduct for an officer, Ford was ordered to the Navy preflight school in Chapel Hill, North Carolina.

The Navy's preflight training concentrated not only on physical conditioning, calisthenics, and endurance marches, but also on team sports—particularly football. Competition, the Navy reasoned, would develop winning attitudes and group spirit. Ford was one of 83 coaches developing 1,500 cadets in "physical strength, courage, and concentration under pressure." In his brief hours off duty, Ford took lessons in flying from a private instructor. His goal was to be a Navy pilot, but he failed the pilot's physical. He was too old—twenty-nine—and lacked 20/20 vision.

Disappointed, he applied for a berth on a destroyer or a PT boat. Having no luck, he asked influential friends in Grand Rapids and Washington to find him a billet on any warship. In May, 1943, he was rewarded: assignment to a new aircraft carrier, the USS *Monterey*, almost ready to slide off the ways in Camden, New Jersey.

Packing to leave Chapel Hill, Ford received his first fitness report: "An outstanding officer," his commanding officer wrote. "One of the finest in the station, and an excellent shipmate."

The *Monterey* was a hybrid—a light cruiser with a platform welded on top for a flight deck. After Pearl Harbor, the Navy desperately needed carriers. Ford's ship, and other light carriers of the *Independence* class, had two advantages: they were fast at sea—31.5 knots—and fast in construction. From the laying of the keel to commissioning, on June 17, 1943, the *Monterey* was built in only eighteen months.

On her shakedown cruise to Trinidad the *Monterey* carried a crew of 1,500 and 45 aircraft—F6F Hellcat fighters and TBM torpedo bombers. Captain Lester Hundt handed Ford three assignments: Second Division Officer, commanding a deck group of ninety enlisted men and two junior officers responsible for handling lines when docking, anchoring, and fueling at sea; Athletic instructor, keeping the crew physically ready for combat; and Gunnery officer, with his battle station on the fantail, directing the fire of half the ship's 40-mm antiaircraft guns.

Stripped for combat, the *Monterey* left her home port in New Jersey, dodged German submarines along the Atlantic coast and in the Caribbean Sea, and passed through the Panama Canal. After a brief stop in San Diego to bring aboard SBD dive bombers, she embarked for Pearl Harbor and sailed westward at flank speed. On the way, to keep the crew in good physical condition, Ford asked the ship's carpenters to jury-rig a basketball court on a lowered aircraft elevator. Basketball, he persuaded Captain Hundt, was the best sport "for officers and men to get the most exercise in the shortest time."

Quickly fueled and provisioned in Pearl Harbor, the *Monterey* joined another carrier—the USS *Enterprise*—a light cruiser, and six destroyers, and headed for battle. Her first engagement: November 19, 1943, supporting the Army landings at Makin. On Christmas Day, wave after wave of aircraft from the carrier began attacking Japan's port, ships, and air base on Kavieng, New Ireland. For two weeks, the battle raged, and Ford, standing on the fantail directing the ship's quad 40-mm antiaircraft guns, was in the thick of it. "Japanese planes came at us with a vengeance," Ford said "It was as much action as I'd ever hoped to see." The attacks on Kavieng were successful: *Monterey*'s planes were credited with sinking a Japanese cruiser and a destroyer.

Makin and Kavieng were just the beginning. *Monterey* and her sister carriers, cruisers, and destroyers struck the Japanese at Kwajalein and Eniwetok. Next, the task force boldly attacked Japanese land, sea, and air forces at their powerful base at Truk, then moved on to battle the Japanese army and navy at Palau, Hollandia, Saipan, Tinian, and Guam. In the Eastern Philippine Sea, *Monterey*'s bombers sank a Japanese carrier. In a later Japanese counterattack off Formosa, a torpedo narrowly missed Ford's ship and exploded against the cruiser *Canberra*. With two surviving but crippled cruisers in tow, the Navy fought off Japanese planes for twenty-four desperate hours. Once the damaged ships were out of range, the task force turned and launched a series of attacks against the Bonins, Wake, Yap, Luzon, Formosa, and the Ryukus. In her first thirteen months in the Pacific the *Monterey* was in continuous combat—earning eleven battle stars for officers and crew.

To the gunners on the fantail, Ford's calm was impressive. "Nothing ever seemed to rattle him," Seaman Second Class Ronald Smith said. "One day we came under attack and I dived for cover in the hatchway. I looked up and there was Lieutenant Ford. He smiled and asked me, 'Why the hell are you in such a hurry?'"

Though he met his responsibilities as gunnery officer, Ford resolved to learn more. When he heard that the assistant ship's navigator was being transferred, he asked Captain Hundt for the job—and got it. "I didn't have any idea how to take a sighting," Ford said. "But we had a great navigator who had been a former merchant marine skipper, Commander Pappy Atwood, and we had a first-class quartermaster. They taught me navigation, how to take a sighting, and with their help I learned very quickly. As a result, I became the officer of the deck during General Quarters, which meant I was on the bridge with the captain, the navigator, and the air officer during combat. Couldn't have had a better place to be; I was right there where everything was going on. That gave me a whole new appreciation of operations and the fleet in combat, and of the war itself. It was good duty to be at the center of action."

After the typhoon of December 1944—the worst ever recorded by any American fleet—disabled the *Monterey,* she limped into Ulithi, in the Carolines. Her hanger deck was buckled by fire and all her planes had been lost, pushed burning into the sea or damaged beyond repair. "*Monterey* is unfit for service," Navy engineers reported, and ordered her to Bremerton, Washington, for months of repair. Upon learning that, Ford asked to be transferred to another carrier in Admiral Halsey's fleet; he was turned down. The Navy had decided that officers with combat experience should condition future pilots, physically and mentally; Ford was reassigned to the United States.

For his service aboard the *Monterey*, Lieutenant Ford had earned respect and a promotion. "He is steady, reliable, and resourceful," Captain Ingersoll wrote in his fitness report. "His unfailing good humor, pleasing personality, and natural ability as a leader made him well liked and respected by the officers and men. He is an excellent organizer, and can be relied upon for the successful conclusion of any operation which he may undertake."

Every good sailor finds a soul mate in his favorite ship; his love for her never fades; his memories of her never dim. So it was with Lieutenant Ford and the *Monterey*. "I had a great feeling for my ship," he said. "I had started with her before the commissioning. I had been through battles with her. I had two skippers who treated me well. I had a mentor and friend in Pappy Atwood, who saved our ship. I made lots of good friends. I had great jobs. If you are going to be in a war, you might as well be where the action is. And that's where my ship was."

On Christmas Eve 1944, Ford left with mixed feelings of pride and sadness. After his farewell calls on Captain Ingersoll, Commander Atwood, his fellow officers, and crew, he stood at the top of the gangway and saluted the American flag flying at the stern of the *Monterey* for the last time. A Navy transport plane landed him in San Francisco.

Home on leave, Ford spent a few days in Grand Rapids with his parents, then reported to the Navy preflight School at St. Mary's College in Moraga, California—part of the Naval Air Station complex headquartered at Alameda. Three months later, Ford learned that a new carrier, the *Coral Sea*, was being fitted out to join the Pacific fleet. Ford applied for a berth on the new ship, but was turned down. Instead, he was transferred to the Navy Training Command in Glenview, Illinois. Again, he applied for sea duty, and waited. He was still waiting when the Japanese surrendered on August 14, 1945. His promotion to Lieutenant Commander came through in October, and in January he was released from active duty.

War changed Ford, just as it did the United States. He had observed and experienced another world, far from Grand Rapids, or Ann Arbor, or New Haven. Some three decades later he reflected on his transformation. "Before World War II I was, like a lot of Middle Westerners, an isolationist. At Yale I was involved with America First, a very respectable group of people who just thought the U.S. shouldn't get involved in European wars. Four or five of us in law school used to talk about the reasons why the U.S. should stay out of wars, and certainly not get involved in problems between Germany and England and France and the Soviet Union. Well, I went to war, and when I came back I had become a devout, enthusiastic internationalist. I saw the mistakes of this country in staying out of international affairs. In the 20s and 30s we made mistakes in not being a leader among nations to preserve peace and prevent war. In the Pacific I saw firsthand the problems this country faced when we were unprepared and war was thrust on us. So I became not only an internationalist in concept, but in practice. I came out of the war a person who strongly believed that the U.S. must always be well prepared militarily and must always be ready to lead the world in preserving peace."

Back home, Lieutenant Commander Ford, like sixteen million other American veterans, faced the next challenge: To find a civilian job and make a living. He and his prewar law partner, Phil Buchen, exempt from military service because of crippling polio, considered resuming their practice. But Buchen, recruited by the most prestigious law firm in Grand Rapids while Ford was away, and now a partner, had a better idea: why not join him at Butterfield, Keaney, and Amberg?

Eager to get going, Ford talked the next day with Julius Amberg, widely regarded as the outstanding lawyer in Grand Rapids. At Harvard Law School he had exceeded his classmate, Felix Frankfurter, in scholarship. During World War II, Amberg had been one of Washington's wise men, summoned by Secretary of War Henry Stimson to be his deputy.

The interview went well. Amberg invited Ford to join the firm—not as a partner, but with the promise of becoming one if he performed well. When Ford mentioned his interest in business and economics, Amberg said he would assign him to the most challenging cases in that field. Then he added: "Jerry, I'm going to train you to be a good lawyer."

To Ford, that commitment was persuasive. He accepted without hesitating. "I was lucky," Ford said. "To have Julius Amberg teach me the practice of law, well, that was a wonderful break." Not for the first time, Ford had found the right mentor.

All through the war years Ford had maintained his interest in politics. Back home, he became active again, initially, in his words, as "a joiner." He took over as President of the Home Front reform movement. He joined the American Legion, the Veterans of Foreign Wars, and the Amvets. He signed up to help the local chapter of the American Red Cross, the Kent County cancer drive, and the Grand Rapids troop of the Boy Scouts. He joined the Kent County Farm Bureau. Remembering the discrimination against black friends and football players at South High and the University of Michigan, he joined the local chapter of the National Association for the Advancement of Colored People. Since Ford had, as a high-school football star, worked for two leaders in the Greek community, he was invited to become an honorary member of Ahepa, and accepted. All these actions were preparation. He had no plan at that point, in 1946, to be a candidate for public office, but he believed that in time he would be, and he calculated that a broad political base would be useful, if not essential, to winning an election.

Ford was living at home—delighted to be with his parents after fifteen years away. There was plenty of room: the paint business had improved, and the Fords had bought a bigger house. The three younger brothers had all married and were out on their own. Gerald and Dorothy were pleased to have the eldest back in the house, but after some months, his ever attentive mother spoke up: he was, she told him, working so hard at the law firm, and spending so much time with civic organizations that he had overlooked his personal future. "Jerry, you need to find a nice girl and get married and settle down. You're not getting any younger, you know."

Ford listened to his mother. She was right. One evening in the autumn of 1947, when he was working with his friends Frank and Peg Neuman on the Kent County cancer drive, Ford asked: "By the way, do you know Betty Warren?"

"Oh sure," Peg Neuman said. "You know she's getting a divorce."

Ford did know that. Several weeks earlier he had met her at a party, talked with her, and decided he would like to know her better. He also knew that Peg and Betty were close friends. "Would you call her?" he asked. "I'll get on the phone and see if I can convince her to have a drink."

Peg Neuman did call. "Jerry Ford is here, and wants you to come out for a drink."

Betty Warren remembered meeting Ford at the party, and had heard the talk about him: he was a rising young lawyer and the most eligible bachelor in town. "No, Peg," she said. She was managing an important style show the next morning as part of her job at Herpolsheimer's, one of the three big department stores in Grand Rapids. "I'll be up late writing the continuity for that. And, I'm not going out with anyone while I'm waiting for my divorce."

"Talk to him anyway," Peg said, handing Ford the phone.

"Let me pick you up, and we'll go out for an hour, and have a beer," Ford said. "You'll be refreshed when you go back to work. It'll be good for you."

"Thank you, but no," she said. "I'm in the process of getting a divorce, and you're a lawyer, you ought to know better."

Ford persisted, promised to take her to a quiet place where nobody would know them, and she finally agreed. "But I can only be gone twenty minutes."

Knocking at the door of her apartment, Ford expected she would be cool, even distant, but she greeted him with warmth and enthusiasm. In an obscure bar they discussed their jobs, mutual friends, common interests, values, and goals. An hour later, they were still talking.

At work the next day, she wondered if he would call again. "My interest was aroused," she said.

Ford did call a few days later, and they began to go out for dinner, or a movie, or just to be together. "He wanted a companion," she said, "and I filled the bill. He was a person of achievement, and I admired him for his community work, his involvement in civic affairs. We discovered that we both belonged to the Urban League. I found him attractive just to be with, fun to go out with on a date. That was all I was interested in at the time, because I had been so disappointed in marriage. I enjoyed the social part of going places, and you had to have a partner to do this. So our relationship started as good friends."

Ford, from their first date, found Betty Warren a most attractive young lady and excellent company. "But," he said, "I had no idea that someone special had just come into my life." The reality was that Ford had a higher priority—his mounting concern about a political battle in Washington that would change history.

Ford had always been an assiduous reader; in the *Grand Rapids Press* and in the *Herald,* and in the magazine *World Report,* he had been following closely the controversy over rebuilding Europe. Six years of total war had not only ruined great cities—Berlin, Warsaw, Rotterdam, London; far worse, it had destroyed the economy of the British Isles and much of the Continent. Millions of once-comfortable Europeans were homeless, hungry, cold, and in despair. Governments were broke; their leaders desperate. Diplomats, economists, agronomists, sociologists, journalists, all were unanimous in reporting to America that the people of Europe were destitute; their need for help urgent and unprecedented.

President Truman acted. Recognizing that "Europe had to be rescued and quickly," he had his Secretary of State, General George Marshall, set forth a bold and unprecedented plan. In a Harvard commencement speech on June 7, 1947, Marshall proposed that the United States simply finance, unilaterally, the reconstruction of Europe—including defeated Germany and Italy.

It was a magnificent act of humanity. Conquerors punish; they do not redeem a broken enemy. But there was common sense as well as lofty virtue in Truman's Marshall Plan. Our allies who had suffered most deserved our help; our defeated enemies could turn to Communism or collapse into anarchy without it.

Noble and practical it was, but the Marshall Plan was nevertheless opposed by powerful men in Washington. Some Democrats, revenge in their souls, were determined to incapacitate the German people. Conservative Republicans, their heads in the sand, had reverted to isolationism. And they controlled the 80th Congress—both the House and Senate. But one Republican broke with his colleagues. Senator Arthur Vandenberg of Michigan saw the merit in restoring a continent that, historically, had lived by free markets and under democratic governments. As Chairman of the then-powerful Senate Foreign Relations Committee, Vandenberg committed to support the Marshall Plan. Aid to Europe was not only commendable as a good deed, he told the Senate, but "we have a direct self-interest in doing everything within our peaceful power to sustain democratic freedoms, based on self-determination, in other lands . . . This precious thing called Western Civilization is a common asset which we cannot indefinitely preserve alone."

As it happened, Vandenberg was a native of Grand Rapids, the most popular elected official in Michigan, and widely admired for his statesmanlike stand on foreign policy. But the Congressman for Grand Rapids, Bartel Jonkman, also a Republican, vehemently opposed Vandenberg and his commitment to aid for Europe.

A political Neanderthal, Jonkman scorned the Marshall Plan as "a boondoggle," and used his House seniority to push amendments that would gut aid to Greece, Turkey, Hungary, and Poland. On the House floor he argued that America should keep its money at home and tell a bankrupt Europe to solve its own problems. Just before Christmas in 1947, he told reporters: "Let them work to pay off their debts."

Ford was outraged at Jonkman's opposition. "Literally, day after day, he was undercutting Vandenberg's efforts in cooperation with President Truman to get the Marshall Plan through Congress," Ford said.

Initiative was never Ford's greatest asset; he had always been more responsive to a challenge—especially one of principle. And Jonkman's wrongheadedness constituted an open challenge—and not only to Truman's policy and Vandenberg's support of that policy. To Ford, Jonkman did not represent the lend-a-helping-hand character of the people of Grand Rapids. Even more important, Jonkman did not represent Ford's view that the world was one, that Europe's plight was America's plight—a view that he believed he shared with millions of other young Americans who had fought around the world to free people from oppression, injustice, want, and hunger. To Ford, isolationism was the past. Jonkman was the past; his obstruction a threat to future world peace and order.

"I felt somebody ought to run against him," Ford said. He thought it over, carefully, deliberately, as was his way. Sometime in the fall of 1947, he made his decision: if a citizen no more prominent than he would agree to challenge Jonkman, then he would do it. The more Ford thought about it, the more he wanted to be the man to take him on.

Defeating Jonkman would not be easy. He was Dutch, with a Dutch name and a Dutch identity in a Congressional district that was 60 percent Dutch. A former county prosecutor, Jonkman had won his first Congressional race in 1940 with the help of the Republican boss, Frank McKay, narrowly defeating three other Republican candidates in a special election. With McKay's support, Jonkman had won reelection four times, all by overwhelming majorities. In the public mind he was entrenched.

Ford talked first to his mother and stepfather—always his closest advisers. Both encouraged him, and his stepfather repeated the advice offered so many times before: "Jerry, do what you think is right."

Buchen, Ford's longtime friend and law partner, was immediately enthusiastic. Get a manager right away, Buchen counseled. He recommended a Michigan fraternity brother, Jack Stiles. So the two, Stiles—a Grand Rapids businessman and aspiring novelist—and Ford went to work. Though amateurs—Ford had little campaign experience; Stiles, none—they approached the task with professional directness.

To find out how Jonkman might be defeated, they collected the Fifth District election returns for ten years and carefully analyzed them, precinct by precinct. "The contest would be in the primary," Ford said. "No Democrat could win that District in the general election. And we came to the conclusion that Jonkman was beatable in a two-man primary, but not if he had more than one candidate against him. So Jack and I laid out the campaign. There were three people more senior than I who we thought would be good congressmen and who we thought might be willing to run. All were friends of mine, and one by one, in a very deliberate process, I went to see them."

His first call was on Paul Goebel, a former Michigan football captain and well-known civic leader in Grand Rapids. "I think Barney Jonkman ought to be beaten," Ford told Goebel. Citing his political analysis, he outlined the strategy for defeating Jonkman. "I believe you are qualified and I urge you to run," Ford said. "If you will agree to be the candidate, I will do everything I can to help you get elected."

Goebel shook his head. "Nobody can beat Barney," he said. "He is entrenched. If you think he ought to be beaten, why don't you run? If you run, I will support you."

"Well," Ford said later, "that was exactly what I wanted to hear."

He next approached Paul Strawhecker, a prominent lawyer who had lost to Jonkman in the 1940 primary, and then Lynn Clark, the highly regarded former head of the Kent County school system. Neither would run. Neither believed anyone could beat Jonkman; nevertheless, both urged Ford to run against him and offered their support.

Clearing the field was a canny maneuver, not original, but often practiced by political strategists far more experienced than Ford and Stiles—but it was just the beginning. Next, following their plan, they lined up provisional endorsements. To split the Dutch vote, Ford persuaded Dr. Willard Ver Meulen, a Home Front ally, to bring in a group of Dutch reform leaders. To broaden his base, Ford recruited officers of the veterans' organizations, the Farm Bureau, the United Way, and the NAACP—all the organizations he had joined. He formed a willing cadre of anti-McKay Republicans and signed up volunteers for precinct workers.

All this was done quietly. "My one advantage was surprise," Ford said. Jonkman would certainly pick up rumors of opposition, but Ford calculated that he was so accustomed to reelection that he would take it for granted and dismiss whispers of a threat. So Ford worked, planned, and waited. At one point, he visited Senator Vandenberg—a friend and political ally of his stepfather—to inform him that he intended to run against Jonkman. Vandenberg said he could not publicly support Ford, but would do nothing to help Jonkman. Moreover, Ford said, "He told me how very, very pleased he was that I was taking Jonkman on." It was the answer Ford was hoping to hear.

He got another break. His boss at the law firm, Julius Amberg, called him into his office. A strong Democrat, Amberg despised Jonkman. "Jerry, I don't know if you can beat Jonkman, but we want to help you. Why don't you come in to the office for one hour a day, and spend the rest of the time campaigning." Fervently, Ford thanked his boss for such a significant contribution to his pocketbook and his campaign.

The stealth campaign ended on June 17, 1948, just before the filing date, when Ford confirmed to the *Press* and the *Herald* that he was a candidate for the House. By that time, he was well organized and eager to start his public campaign. The first billboard went up, a heroic-size drawing of a jut-jawed Ford with the underline a calculated gibe against Jonkman's reputation for laziness.

To work for YOU in CONGRESS.
Gerald R. FORD Jr.

To remind voters of his wartime service, Ford rented a Navy surplus Quonset hut for his headquarters, painted it red, white, and blue, and set it up on space he leased in the parking lot of Wurzburg's—a popular downtown department store. By design, it was sited below the office window of Frank McKay, the political boss who had put Jonkman in office. As expected, McKay complained to Wurzburg's president: "Get Ford off that property!"

The store's president called the company lawyer: none other than

Julius Amberg. He, in turn, summoned Ford. "Jerry, as you know, Wurzburg's is a good client of this firm, and they are getting complaints about your headquarters on their parking lot. Would you be willing to move your Quonset hut somewhere else?"

"Mr. Amberg, we have a contract for that space and we are not going to move that hut," Ford said.

"Excellent," Amberg said, with a grin. "That's exactly what I was hoping you would say."

Ford broke into a smile and added: "We would welcome a public confrontation with Frank McKay."

The Quonset hut stood in place.

The issue that brought Ford into the race became the central issue of the campaign. He made it so, defining and emphasizing their difference: Jonkman personifying an America withdrawing from the world, *versus* Ford, representing a strong and confident America leading the world.

Ford wrote his own speeches with conviction and delivered them with fervor. In one, he attacked Jonkman's record going back to 1940, contending that his opponent voted "against practically every measure which possibly could have bulwarked America's defenses before World War II . . . We as citizens of this district cannot again place our future and the welfare of the succeeding generations in the hands of a man who was partly to blame for an insufficient number of ships and planes during the early phases of the last war."

Now, Ford said, "This country is in grave danger from totalitarian forces that seek to destroy democracy around the world . . . We cannot convincingly carry the torch for freedom against the Russian bully unless we are adequately prepared." He committed to a stronger military, expanding the Army, Navy, and Air Force to convince "Russia—or any other nation—that tampering with our security is risking destruction and sudden death." He committed to the Marshall Plan, stating that the United States must "continue to bulwark freedom-loving nations in Europe with dollars-and-cents aid in their struggle to remain free."

As part of his plan, Ford challenged Jonkman to public debates. Jonkman, in Washington, did not reply. "He seldom got back to campaign," Ford said. "He took his reelection for granted." Ford got another break: In midsummer, President Truman called an emergency session of Congress, demanding that the Republican majorities deal with rising prices, the housing shortage, and civil rights. The special session began July 26, and kept Jonkman in Washington until mid-August.

In the closing days of the campaign, Ford worked even harder, walking door-to-door in Grand Rapids, shaking hands at factory gates, speaking in rural villages and to growing crowds in Grand Rapids, talking with farmers in the fields. "We worked our tails off," Ford said. "We had the organization, and we developed the momentum."

Ten days before the election, the *Grand Rapids Press*—the afternoon and dominant newspaper—endorsed Ford. An angry Jonkman, back in the district, responded by attacking the *Press* and its editors, then belittling Ford—"a stubborn and willful boy"—and his endorsements by Grand Rapids leaders. As a result of Jonkman's vitriol, reporters and editors gave Ford even better coverage in the *Press* and in the competition, the morning *Herald*.

On September 14, 1948, the day of the Republican primary, Ford soundly defeated Jonkman, winning 23,632 votes to Jonkman's 14,341. It was an impressive victory—almost 2-1—even better than Ford or his most confident advisers had expected.

"Jonkman did everything wrong in the campaign," Ford said. "He got frantic, charging all over and making ridiculous accusations. We hadn't expected that. We had gone to the people, early, and it worked. I tell you it was a lot of fun."

Inwardly, he was proud of his victory, proud of his decision to run, and gratified that he had turned out of office the highest elected official of the corrupt McKay machine. It had taken guts. "I had won a race that no one had given me a chance to win," he said. And in the campaign he had learned the essentials of the great game: motivation, organization, performance. "Politics is basic intuitiveness," he said long after. "Common sense. Knowing how to work with and sell people."

For a year, Ford had been preoccupied with his campaign; nevertheless, he had found or made time for Betty Warren. The more he saw of her, the more he enjoyed being with her. She was a beautiful and stylish woman, personable, intelligent, a figure of innate grace, and more. She was strong, self-reliant, trustworthy. She never boasted of her fidelity, but it was there. Indeed, in the freshness of her twenties she had proved her steadfast character by a singular act of devotion. Betty Bloomer had married, at age 24, Bill Warren, a charming young Grand Rapids man she had known since childhood. He turned out to be a barfly and itinerant who could not hold a job. For three years she endured, realizing she had made a mistake. Finally she decided to write him that she wanted a divorce. In mid-sentence, literally, she got a telephone call from a Boston hospital: Bill was in a diabetic coma and might die. Putting personal feelings aside, she devoted two years to nursing him, postponing her plans for divorce until he could walk again and work again. Only then did she consult a lawyer. "I took $1 in settlement," she wrote, "and it was finished."

It had been a long and bitter experience for a young woman of such a sunny disposition, but her broken marriage did not turn her against the idea. Instead, she became more mature, and in her heart continued to long for a caring and considerate husband, a home and children: the steadiness of life that a good marriage brings.

Then, and thereafter, those who met her would remark on her candor, her quickness in saying what she believed. They would admire her charm and brightness of personality, and reflect on her deft ability to support a political husband, enhance and advance his career, and yet always speak her mind and resolutely advocate her own convictions.

From his first meeting with Betty Warren, Ford liked everything about her. She looked him full in the eyes and spoke in a low but firm voice, and what she said made sense. There was constancy and seriousness in her nature. Her goals and values closely matched his own. He began to think that at age thirty-four, he had finally found the right partner. In a significant gesture, he took her home for Thanksgiving dinner with his parents, brothers, and their families. She liked them, and they liked her.

Together, the two went skiing with mutual friends at Caberfae, in northern Michigan. They drove to Ann Arbor for football games. They played bridge, and discussed books they were reading. At Christmas, he left her for two weeks of skiing in Sun Valley, Idaho. There, despite the variety of attractions schussing down the slopes and lounging beside the fireside, he was lonely. "Suddenly," he said, "it dawned on me that I missed and needed her very much." He wrote her every day.

For her, the fortnight of separation brought her to realize that she had fallen in love with him. One evening in February 1947, he came to her apartment and, sitting on her couch, said: "I'd like to marry you, but we can't get married until next fall, and I can't tell you why."

She didn't ask. "I took him up on it instantly, before he could change his mind."

Ford was putting politics first. He was concerned that marriage in mid-campaign to a divorcée might be an issue that would hurt him with the conservative Dutch voters he was counting on to defeat Jonkman. After his victory in the primary, they set the wedding date: Friday, October 15, 1948—eighteen days before the general election. The political risk was manageable. The Fifth District had not elected a Democrat to Congress since 1910.

After the wedding in Grace Episcopal Church in Grand Rapids, Janet Packer Ford, brother Tom's wife, presciently told the bride: "Betty, Jerry's mistress will not be a woman. It will be his work." Their honeymoon previewed their life. After driving to Ann Arbor to celebrate with friends, they attended the Michigan-Northwestern football game on Saturday, then drove sixty-five miles to Owosso to hear Governor Thomas Dewey, the Republican nominee for President, address a political rally in his home town. They left Owosso at midnight for Detroit, arrived at the Book Cadillac Hotel at 3:00 a.m., and headed back to Grand Rapids on Sunday afternoon. The bride was looking forward to a quiet evening at her apartment when, as they reached the outskirts of the city, he said: "I've got a very important political meeting at 7:30. Do you suppose you could fix me a bowl of soup and a sandwich before I leave?"

From that moment on, Betty Ford said, "I knew what it was going to be like."

The Ford campaign never stopped—even though the Democratic nominee, Fred Barr, a friend of both Jerry and Betty Ford, virtually conceded by contributing to Ford's campaign. For the last six weeks, Ford worked as diligently as he had before the primary. On Tuesday, November 2, 1948, President Truman defeated Governor Dewey and the Democrats recaptured the House and Senate. Despite the national trend, Ford carried the Fifth District of Michigan with 74,191 votes, by a margin of 60.5 percent.

Two months later, with his bride and his parents beaming with pride from the gallery, Ford stood in the Chamber of the House of Representatives to be sworn in as a new Member. By that act, he set his course for the long and unprecedented voyage through public life. Although he could not have foreseen how far he would go in that journey, his swearing-in was for him something of an epiphany. "From that first day on," he said, "I knew I wanted the House to be my career."

Moments after he had taken the oath, another young House Member came up to shake his hand. "I'm Dick Nixon, from California. I heard about your big win in Michigan, and I want to say hello and welcome you to the House." By chance, a few days later, Ford was assigned an office across the hall from a young Democrat from Massachusetts: John F. Kennedy. They got acquainted walking from their distant offices to the House floor to vote.

As he had not been elected by the party establishment in Michigan, Ford felt no obligation to the party establishment in Congress. Before his first vote, an organizational maneuver to empower House leaders over members, he listened to the arguments of the Republican leaders, Joseph Martin and Charles Halleck, and then voted against them. "I thought I was right, and I told them so," Ford said.

Like all freshmen, he was assigned to a low-choice committee—in his case, Public Works. As the junior member of the minority, he had neither power nor prestige, but Ford saw it as opportunity, a place to learn. Trading is the common currency of democratic government, and, Ford said, "I found out on that committee how deals were made, how the House really worked."

That apprentice assignment brought him his first visit to 1600 Pennsylvania Avenue. President Truman, needing money to repair the White House, brought the committee members in to see the broken plaster and sagging floor where Margaret Truman's grand piano had almost fallen through. In the Oval Office, Ford noticed the sign on the Presidential desk: The Buck Stops Here. "Well," he said to himself, "that's a good description of a President's job."

Early on, some Michigan Republicans shunned Ford because he had defeated their fellow isolationist; but one Republican, Earl Michener, took a liking to Ford. That was significant, for Michener was an important member of the bipartisan hierarchy that controlled the House. He had served there for thirty years, and was dean of the Michigan delegation.

Sitting beside Michener in the chamber, listening and observing, Ford began to absorb the arcane and specialized procedures of the House. "Jerry," Michener said, "you can become one of two kinds of Members in the House. You can either be a floor man, and learn how to handle debate, rules, procedures; or you can become a committee expert. If it's the latter, pick an area of your committee on which you want to be an expert. Learn more about that subject than anyone else in the House of Representatives, so that when you speak on it, people listen."

Michener introduced Ford to John Taber—a stocky, crusty, upstate New Yorker who also took a liking to Ford. This too was significant, for

Taber was the senior, and by far the most influential, Republican on the House Appropriations Committee. Ford learned from Taber; he sat at his side for hours, listening to his counsel and coming to understand the comparative powers of House committees. The three most important: Rules, which dictated the floor agenda; Ways and Means, which held sole authority over raising money; and Appropriations, which held the ultimate power in government: spending public money. Members on lesser committees would plead and plot for years to win a place on one of the three.

Ford knew which committee he wanted, and by fortuitous circumstance, opportunity came early. In 1950, Albert Engel, Michigan's Republican on Appropriations, decided to leave the House to run for governor. Ford asked his new friend and mentor for the seat. "Jerry," Taber replied, "if the Michigan delegation will vote for you, I want you on the committee."

But Ford had a problem with his delegation. They had made a deal for a major public-works project in the state, and Ford opposed it as wasteful and unnecessary. At home with Betty, he discussed his dilemma: ambition versus principle. Betty, as always, spoke her mind. "Frankly, Jerry, if you're not going to vote your conscience, you're no good as a Congressman, and you might as well quit. You always say you've got to vote for what you think is right, and if that means you have to sacrifice getting on the Appropriations Committee, that's too bad."

Ford listened. His resolve stiffened; he continued to oppose the project. Yet, with Michener's help, he managed to win his delegation's support to succeed Engel on Appropriations. "And that," he said, "was the greatest break in the world—to get on one of the three best committees in the House before the end of my first term," Ford said. "Appropriations was where the power was, and I said to myself, 'That's going to be my specialty: How the government spends money.'"

It was more than a break for Ford; it was a momentous step forward. But it was not pure luck. There was a consistent pattern to Ford's advancement in life. Elders saw something in the boy and the young man—promise, earnestness, character, good nature, readiness to listen and learn; it was never precisely defined—that moved each to become a mentor. After his stepfather, an exemplar of trustworthiness and values and the dominant force in shaping Ford's early and enduring character, there had been Scoutmaster Kindel, Coach Gettings, Principal Krause, Coach Kipke, teammate Williamson, Coach Pond, Professor McDougal,

Captain Hundt, Commander Atwood, Julius Amberg, and then, in the House, Earl Michener and John Taber.

Ford was forthright in recognizing and using his talent for making the right connections. "I have always been able to develop allegiances with good people," he said. "I don't know how to define it, or why I have it, but I have a capability of getting people to like to work with me. I am very proud of it. I know I have had a lot of good luck. But I have always believed what my Dad used to say, 'The harder you work, the better your luck.'"

CHAPTER 6

Advancing

Ford first joined the House Appropriations Committee at a special session of Congress on November 27, 1950. The date is significant, for the arc of Ford's ascent to the Presidency began with that event.

It was on Appropriations that the 37-year-old Congressman first made his mark. His performance there persuaded his fellow Republicans to elect him Leader. His performance as Leader persuaded his colleagues in Congress—in both parties—to make Ford Vice President. As they did, most Members of the House and Senate believed they were in fact making Ford the next President.

For all its power, in the 1950's, the House Appropriations Committee received little coverage from the press, and even less attention from the public. Members—thirty Democrats and twenty Republicans when Ford joined—were divided into thirteen subcommittees, with each assigned a fiefdom such as Agriculture, Foreign Operations, Interior, or National Security. Group by group, members spent hours, days, weeks, examining and discussing and evaluating hundreds of Federal programs. They sat through endless hearings; they listened to interminable appeals for money; they discussed, argued, bargained. Finally, they made their decisions and allotted to petitioners the millions and billions of dollars that financed the Federal government.

The match between Ford and Appropriations was a natural. He loved the job and he was good at it. In his first weeks he displayed to committee seniors his readiness to probe into programs and costs, his grasp of telling detail, his deftness in negotiating. After the Republicans won control of Congress in 1952, Taber appointed him to the Defense

Subcommittee: it was exactly what Ford wanted. Ever since Pearl Harbor he had been a tireless advocate of a strong Army, Navy, and Air Force; indeed, he had been elected on the issue of national security. Now he would be in a place of power where he could act on his campaign commitment.

Taber brought him in. "Jerry, there will be three groups—one for the Army, one for the Navy, one for the Air Force. I'm going to make you chairman of the Army panel."

"Why, Mr. Chairman? I know more about the Navy."

"You've got too many friends in the Navy," Taber said. "All those damn admirals will be after you, and you won't resist them. But if you're with the Army, you will tell those generals to go to hell."

Instead, Ford asked questions. At that he excelled, according to Melvin Laird—the Wisconsin Republican who served with him on Appropriations. Regularly, the Defense Subcommittee would summon the Secretary of Defense; the Joint Chiefs; the Secretaries of the Army, Navy, and Air Force; and their uniformed and civilian subordinates. When each appeared, Laird remembered, Ford would begin and follow a logical sequence of questioning: what is the purpose of this new weapon you propose? How will it benefit our troops? How much will it cost? Give us, in writing, your schedule for research, development, production, and deployment. Ford kept notes, and would come back the next year to match their results against expectations.

In his time, Ford questioned six Defense Secretaries—George Marshall, Robert Lovett, Charles Wilson, Neil McElroy, Thomas Gates, and Robert McNamara—and scores of generals and admirals, secretaries, and assistants. He remembered those years with relish. "We went through the documentation page by page, making them prove the need for a weapons program, requiring the best figures on costs. The eleven of us on that subcommittee knew more about the military and its programs than most admirals and generals. The brass changed, but there was almost no turnover on the committee. One Democrat on the Committee used to say, 'Generals and admirals come and go like Greyhound buses, but we stay in place.' That's the way it was."

To observe U.S forces in the field, Ford flew to Korea during the August recess of 1953. Accompanied by General George Hannan, the Army controller, Ford was at the border to see the first American prisoners returned from North Korea. He inspected South Korean infantry troops and concluded their officers could train and field a fine army with U.S. aid. With General Hannan he flew on to Vietnam; his committee was financing military advisers to the French. "Spit and polish uniforms, and a strategy on paper," he noted after a session with the French high command. He had no doubt about the end: the French would lose their colony to Ho Chi Minh and his insurgents. Returning through Formosa, Ford talked with General and Madam Chiang Kai-shek and other officials. Formosa-China, he observed, had barely adequate forces for its defense, but a real chance to build a strong economy. After a round of briefings in Japan, he inspected military hospitals in Hawaii and San Francisco, then returned to Washington. He greeted his family, unpacked, and headed to the office to draft his report to his Defense Subcommittee.

Of his first Asian tour, Ford said: "I became absolutely convinced that we had an important stake in preventing Soviet or Chinese domination of that part of Asia. I saw that Secretary of State Dean Acheson had made an error when he in effect invited the North Koreans to march into South Korea. I learned to appreciate the strength of President Truman in forthrightly committing our forces to stop the North Koreans. I became convinced that in the long run the United States had a massive interest and obligation in the Pacific Basin." Later, he flew to Europe to report on the readiness of U.S. forces defending the Western democracies, and on to Moscow to judge the Soviet threat.

In the jargon of the day, Ford was a hawk—committed and outspoken. He took a stand and never moved: the United States must always be ready to stop the expansion of the Russian and Chinese empires. To make that position credible, he argued, the United States must maintain a strong and well-trained Army, Navy, and Air Force, and equip each with powerful and up-to-date weapons. In his time he voted for the H-bomb, the first nuclear submarine, the first supercarriers, the B-1 bomber, and the volunteer Army. His record in the annals of Congress is clear: "Consistent support for . . . the strategic doctrine of nuclear deterrence vis-à-vis the Soviet Union and China and involving reliance on the 'triad' concept of intercontinental ballistic missiles, sea-launched missiles, and strategic bombers. At the same time he has advocated the maintenance of strong and balanced conventional forces and air defense capabilities."

The Ford record in the House shows no significant bill bearing his name; Appropriations bills did not carry names. His work was rarely mentioned in the press; but in the Defense Subcommittee's tiny, clubby conference room in the Capitol his observations and judgments were listened to and respected. George Mahon, the austere, no-nonsense Texas Democrat who for twenty years chaired the subcommittee, described Ford as diligent, hardworking, and never partisan. He "always takes a national view," Mahon said. "I was impressed with his calm judgment and steady hand. [He even understood] the intricacies of nuclear strategic capabilities and the effect this has on international relationships."

In Ford's first term, his mentor Earl Michener had advised, "Learn more than anyone else on the subject, so when you speak, people listen." By his sixth term, Members listened to Ford on the House floor, and scholars recognized his merit off the floor. The American Political Association awarded Ford its Congressional Distinguished Service Award with the citation: "A moderate conservative who is highly respected by his colleagues of both parties, he symbolizes the hard-working competent legislator who eschews the more colorful publicity seeking roles in favor of a solid record of achievement in the real work of the House: Committee work." To the Association, as in the House, Ford was not a show horse but a workhorse; not a thoroughbred racing on the downs but a Clydesdale pulling a heavy load.

One day in 1956, on the House floor, the taciturn veteran Clarence Cannon, Chairman of the full House Appropriations Committee, summoned Ford to his desk. He gave Ford a room number and said cryptically: "Be there at 10 o'clock tomorrow morning."

"What for, Mr. Chairman?"

"Just be there," Cannon said, "and mention it to no one."

Ford showed up as instructed and was met by three armed Capitol police officers. They asked for his credentials, carefully reviewed them, and opened the door. "Inside," he said, "I found that I was about to become a member of the Intelligence Subcommittee of Appropriations." Five men—Cannon and two other senior Democrats, as well as Republicans Taber and Ford—made up the clandestine brotherhood that controlled all the intelligence-based spending. Allen Dulles, then director of the CIA, and every director thereafter would appear before the five to testify on all secret actions—planting agents, arming revolutionaries, bringing down hostile governments, eavesdropping on enemies, building satellites to spot a threat anywhere in the world—and ask for the money to support these operations. No House staff was present; no transcripts were made. Ford never spoke to anyone outside the secret group about what he learned and endorsed during his eight years on the subcommittee; neither did the other members. It was the way Congressional business could be accomplished, and secrets kept, in that era.

Ford was chosen for that unique responsibility in part because he was well-informed, dependable, and could be trusted, but also because his seat was safe. Cannon and Taber wanted no transients.

Ford's seat was indeed safe; he worked to make it so. He kept in close touch with the people of the Fifth District. He typed out his own Congressional letter, telling his communities what he was doing and what was happening in Washington that was important to Grand Rapids. He, with his staff, answered all letters and telephone calls. Regularly, he recorded messages for hometown radio stations. On weekends and during recesses he would drive or fly to Grand Rapids and, at his insistence, follow a full schedule—addressing a civic luncheon, visiting constituents, marching in a parade, listening to factory owners and workers, sitting down with editors and reporters from the *Press* and *Herald*. He won his first reelection with two-thirds of the vote.

Ford faced one brief but serious threat in 1952. After he came out for Eisenhower, Taft conservatives in his district denounced Ford and his action. Some proposed recruiting a pro-Taft Republican to oppose him in the primary that year. Ford flew home to deal with his problem. "It took a lot of explaining to people back in the district," he said, "but I had to make my own judgment about what to do. And I did." He avoided a primary and was reelected, again carrying the district by two-thirds of the vote. Ten more times he was reelected—by margins never below 60 percent.

Over time, his winning record and increasing popularity throughout Michigan prompted the state's Republican leaders to press Ford to run for Governor or Senator. He always turned them down. The House was where he wanted to be; that he had known from his first day there. Moreover, he had set for himself, early on, a specific and higher goal: to become Speaker of the House. To Ford, the Speaker held the most responsible position in the most important branch of the American government. Ford was inspired in part by Speaker Sam Rayburn—an outstanding boss of the House who ruled with dispatch, firmness, magisterial calm, and fairness to all. Ford decided that if, and when, he should become Speaker, Rayburn would be his model.

As Ford prospered on Capitol Hill, so also was everything going well at home. Betty Ford was enjoying Washington life. "Our marriage was going beautifully," she wrote. Their first child, a son, was born on March 14, 1950. Betty wanted to name him Gerald R. Ford, but Ford said no. In his childhood he had never liked being called Junior, and he would not inflict the nickname on any son. The compromise: Michael Gerald Ford, and they would call him Mike. Two years later, John Gardner Ford was born.

In the mid-1950s, after Ford's third election, Betty Ford concluded they were in Washington to stay. Therefore, she insisted, they needed to get out of their small, rented apartment and into a home of their own. So they bought a lot across the Potomac in Alexandria, Virginia, at 514 Crown View Drive, and built a brick and wood-siding house with four bedrooms, a playroom, living room, and small den. It cost about $40,000, which the Fords financed with a 7 percent mortgage. They moved into their new home in time for the birth of their third son, Steven Meigs Ford, in 1956, and their daughter, Susan Elizabeth Ford, the next year.

In October 1957 Ford was summoned to the office of the Speaker one day. He had been called, Rayburn told him, to be given a new and urgent assignment. Days earlier the USSR had launched a missile—the Sputnik—into space. Americans were surprised, even astonished, at this feat of Soviet technology; military strategists realized that the Soviets' achievement could give them an ominous advantage in delivering nuclear weapons. To meet that threat, Rayburn told Ford, President Eisenhower had brought him and Senate Majority Leader Lyndon Johnson to the White House, and proposed that they immediately create a new government agency to explore and conquer space. Such a major undertaking would require complex legislation, so he and Johnson were forming a bipartisan House-Senate Special Committee to establish the National Aeronautics and Space Administration (NASA). Ford, Rayburn said, would be a member of that committee; Ford accepted at once. It was a singular honor to have been chosen by Speaker Rayburn to help meet the national emergency, just the kind of challenge Ford liked.

With Johnson as self-appointed chairman, the committee immediately went to work. And Ford, for his first time, experienced this master at making something happen. "Johnson knew exactly what he wanted," Ford said. "To get it, he would work on each and every person. He knew how far he could push, how to cajole, how to threaten. He wouldn't shout. But he could be very firm. He would be hardline, and then he would give just enough to get what he wanted."

Johnson got precisely what he wanted. NASA was created, financed, and operating in less than a year—with its headquarters, by Johnson's forceful persuasion, in Houston. Ford also gained from the experience: he learned how to deal with the formidable Johnson. Moreover, he saw firsthand how U.S. space-related research would advance national security and in time affect everyday life—in medical care, communications, industry, and the coming age of electronics.

As the Eisenhower era ended and the 1960 Presidential campaign began, Ford had no doubt about his choice: Richard Nixon. From their first meeting, Nixon and Ford had become good friends and political allies. They talked often and found much in common: both were survivors of the Great Depression, veterans of the Navy in the Pacific, believers in strong military forces and U.S. leadership in the world. In Ford's second term he had invited Nixon, just elected to the Senate, to address the Lincoln Day dinner in Grand Rapids. Turnout was a record, and after the dinner Nixon spoke in a private home to twenty local party leaders. "For an hour and a half, Nixon very articulately answered all their questions," Ford said. "That visit to Grand Rapids was where I first really got to know Nixon. That day and a half convinced me that he was going to play a significant role in the American political scene."

After Nixon became Vice President they continued to talk often, with Nixon describing to his eager junior his observations about the leaders and nations he was meeting as he traveled the continents representing President Eisenhower. Ford was impressed with the way Nixon was systematically preparing himself to succeed Eisenhower in the White House. "I thought then," Ford said, "that Nixon had the prospect of becoming a great President."

At the 1960 Republican National Convention in Chicago, Nixon passed the word that Ford was on his short list for Vice President, as the man who "would get on better with Congress than anyone in sight." But President Eisenhower came to Chicago and imposed on Nixon another choice: former Senator Henry Cabot Lodge.

In November, Ford carried the Fifth District for Nixon, but his friend lost Michigan and the election. Ford was disappointed, but not dismayed. "I knew Kennedy, and his ability, and I had no apprehension at all about the future of the country."

Just before Nixon left office in January, he invited Ford and other close allies to his Capitol office for a farewell gathering. Watching, Ford found Nixon downhearted but resolute. "I said to myself, 'He'll be around.'"

Ford was working in his office on January 26, 1962, when he received a call from Janet Ford, his sister-in-law: his stepfather had died. He had slipped on the ice and suffered a fatal concussion.

A tide of memories swept over Ford as he put down the phone. When he was a small boy, there had been "Dad," towering and muscular, taking him to the lake on a fishing trip, walking him to the park to play catch or toss a football. The father had instilled in the Ford boys his love of sports, persuading them that competition, teamwork, and playing by the rules, would train them for life. During the Depression, the bank had foreclosed and "Dad" lost their house, but he never gave up. "Well," he had said when he came home, "I'll just have to work harder." By diligence and fair dealing he rebuilt his paint business, and prospered.

His stepson would never forget the cardinal instructions for life: "You are a person of your word. Rich or poor, famous or insignificant, the integrity of your word, your veracity, is a tremendous possession of great value. Keep it. Never lose it."

For the funeral, all of Grand Rapids seemed to turn out to mourn the loss of a popular civic leader. Ford would always remember that tribute to his stepfather. "Here was a man who never got past the eighth grade, but he was widely recognized as an outstanding citizen and good businessman, a man with an impeccable record of integrity and honesty."

In the midterm elections of 1962 the Republicans gained only one House seat—provoking a handful of disappointed young Republican activists to rebel against their older, out-of-touch leaders. Three Members—Melvin Laird of Wisconsin, Charles Goodell of New York, and Robert Griffin of Michigan—and one former House staffer who had just been elected, 30-year-old Donald Rumsfeld of Illinois, came to Ford's office with a proposal: he should challenge and defeat Charles Hoeven for Chairman of the House Republican Conference. In theory, the Conference transformed party policy into legislation to advance Republican principles and create campaign issues. In practice, Hoeven, an aged and ineffective Iowan, had allowed the conference to drift into impotence.

"We chose Ford," Rumsfeld said, "because he was a workman and well-liked." Earlier they had considered Laird, who was more enterprising but too controversial. Ford was not only respected for his work on Appropriations and his effectiveness in House debate; he had no enemies.

Take the Chairmanship, the four rebels told Ford. We will get you elected. Use the Conference to initiate and brand Republican legislation. Give us alternatives to Democratic bills. Generate good Republican issues that will attract voters.

Ford, cautious as ever, promised to think it over. "Before I make any commitment, I want to talk to Betty."

In truth he also wanted to pause, get a fix on his position, and chart his course ahead. He was 49 years old, in his seventh term in the House, and enjoyed the prospect of remaining. He had the perfect assignment: Defense Appropriations. There, more than once, he had made a difference. He could keep that job indefinitely, acquiring more knowledge, influencing more decisions, and steadily gaining in seniority. But if he was ever going to become Speaker—which was his goal and his dream—he must begin. The four rebels were offering an opportunity. Ford was a pro, and pros know that in politics, opportunity never waits, and rarely comes again. So he reasoned: "By itself the Conference Chairman was of little importance. But if I defeated Charlie Hoeven, and I felt I could, I would get a head start on the possibility of becoming Leader, and that could lead to becoming Speaker of the House."

When Ford spoke with Betty, she agreed. She realized that as Conference Chairman he would spend even more time at work and less with his family, but this was what he wanted to do. The next day, Ford called the group in and said he would run. Rumsfeld, expecting that answer, was ready. He immediately brought out the campaign plan he had already prepared, listing the most likely prospects for support, and handing out assignments for telephone calls and personal visits.

The election was a rough battle: The fusty but determined Old Guard versus the young Turks committed to change. Ford won 86-78—a first step on the ladder to Speaker.

Like millions of other Americans, Ford would never forget where he was early in the afternoon of November 22, 1963. He and Betty were in the family Ford, returning from a conference with Jack's teacher about his performance in class, when a voice over the car radio reported that President Kennedy had been shot in Dallas. Ford quickly drove Betty home and raced to the office to get more information. The first report was true: President Kennedy was dead.

In his heart and in his head, Ford was staggered by the news. He and Kennedy had been corridor friends—never close but well acquainted and mutually respectful. They had talked about their wartime Navy service in the Pacific and what prompted them, after the war, to run for Congress. Ford admired Kennedy's gregarious charm and political savvy, and his speaking skill. He considered Kennedy's soaring inaugural address to be "one of the best speeches I ever heard, or read." Upon his death, Ford and his family joined the nation in mourning the tragic end of a President of memorable charisma and lofty promise.

Two days later, President Johnson called Ford at home. He was creating a high-level bipartisan commission to investigate the Kennedy assassination and deliver a comprehensive report to the American people on what had happened. Chief Justice Earl Warren had agreed to chair the commission, Johnson said. He named the members—Allen Dulles and John McCloy from the peerage of public service; Richard Russell and John Sherman Cooper from the Senate; Majority Leader Hale Boggs and Ford from the House. Ford accepted, believing that America and the world needed to know the truth about the assassination. He felt highly complimented that he had been chosen to serve with leaders of such probity and reputation.

He had been appointed, Ford learned later, because Defense Secretary Robert McNamara had urged President Johnson to do so. McNamara, who had often appeared before Ford's Defense Appropriations Subcommittee, told the President: "Ford is always fair and reliable. Where national security is important, he is always nonpartisan."

For ten months the Warren Commission and six teams of lawyers and investigators collected evidence, studied film, reenacted the crime, and questioned participants and witnesses. Warren and Ford traveled to Dallas to examine the building and window where the assassin stood to fire the fatal shots. They retraced the route of the Kennedy motorcade and the assassin's flight. They questioned Jack Ruby, pressing for the reason he shot and killed Lee Harvey Oswald. Ruby's repeated response: to spare Jacqueline Kennedy from having to come back to Dallas to testify.

After their deliberations, the commission published twenty-six volumes of evidence, testimony, and conclusions. The most important finding was unanimous: Lee Harvey Oswald alone killed President Kennedy.

The staff proposed that the commission also state: "There was no conspiracy, foreign or domestic." Russell, Boggs, and Ford objected, and changed the wording: "The Commission has found no evidence that either Lee Harvey Oswald or Jack Ruby was part of any conspiracy, domestic or foreign, to assassinate President Kennedy."

That was more precise, Ford said. "To prove that a conspiracy did not exist in this case was almost impossible."

As the commission member who lived the longest, Ford was often asked about fictional recreations of the Kennedy assassination. He never wavered in his judgment: "Oswald alone killed Kennedy," he said. However, he took care to add, "I recognize that not all questions will ever be answered."

At the 1964 Republican National Convention in San Francisco, Ford and Nixon shared a VIP box. Together they watched a well-organized confederacy of conservative delegates jeer and taunt three moderate Eastern governors—Nelson Rockefeller, William Scranton, and George Romney. Not as participants, but as deeply interested observers, Ford and Nixon saw conservatives dictate the platform, control the agenda, turn on and off the clangor of the delegates, and choose the nominee. A coup, the press reported; but this was no sudden revolution. Over many months, a master strategist, Clifton White, had systematically elected, through state conventions and primaries, delegates committed to the conservative cause and Senator Barry Goldwater. By convention time White had organized them into an unstoppable political force. The result, as he planned and predicted: Goldwater nominated on the first ballot.

Ford was familiar with conservative Republicans. They were a major force in his district, and he was himself strongly committed to the then conservative principles of balanced budgets and limited government. He had often worked with Goldwater on defense spending, and liked him. "Even though he was much more conservative than I was, I thought he was a fine guy and effective Senator," Ford said. But he was dismayed by Goldwater's extremist oratory, the incivility of his delegates, and the convention's rejection of moderate Republicans. Out of loyalty Ford campaigned for Goldwater, but spent more time campaigning for Republican candidates for the House.

In Grand Rapids, on election night, Ford watched the Goldwater campaign end in disaster—losing forty-four states and costing Republicans a staggering thirty-six seats in the House. Ford was so infuriated that near midnight he got in his Ford Falcon and, stopping only for fuel, drove fourteen hours to Washington.

A day or so later, three Republicans who had survived the Goldwater debacle—Griffin, Goodell, and Rumsfeld—came to see Ford in his office. The party must change, the three demanded, and change must begin by electing a new leader. Bluntly, they proposed that Ford challenge Charles Halleck, the House Republican Leader. "Halleck is too old, a bad image," Griffin said. Actually Halleck was worse: lazy, ineffective, and sometimes drunk on the House floor. "We need imagination, ideas, positive alternatives," Griffin said. "We need a new leader. We are talking to two or three others, but we want to know your views. If we get behind you, would you want to do it?"

Ford, still incensed at the loss of thirty-six seats, responded at once: "I agree with you that something must be done. I am interested." He asked for a day to think it over.

He faced a difficult choice: if he were elected Leader, he must give up his seat on Appropriations—that was the House rule. But it would be hard for him to leave his place on that committee. In his first term, Ford had decided he would become an expert on how the Federal government spends money, and for fourteen years, that had been his career. His original campaign promise was to build and maintain the military forces; Appropriations had provided the opportunity to keep that promise. He had made a difference; of that he had no doubt. He, with his colleagues, had improved the weapons and safety and well-being of the man in uniform. They had saved public money. But there was much more work to be done, and Ford wanted to be part of it. His decision was made even more difficult by the fact that the two Republicans senior to him on Appropriations had lost in the Goldwater rout, so, in the new Congress, he would become the ranking Republican on Appropriations—a position of prestige and enormous power.

But Ford was ambitious. If he defeated Halleck for Leader, he would be only one political move from becoming Speaker—which was, and would continue to be, his highest goal.

After deliberating in his own cautious way, Ford decided to run for Leader. If he defeated Halleck, he would lead his party in the House to better times; if he could elect enough Republicans, he would become Speaker. If he lost to Halleck, he would still move up to ranking Republican on Appropriations. Either way he would win.

His mind made up, Ford called in Griffin, Goodell, and Rumsfeld, and told them of his decision. The four agreed that Halleck, though aging, was still a crafty and resourceful infighter, so the race would be close.

Rumsfeld, always prepared, brought out his plan: "Politics is addition, not subtraction," Rumsfeld said. "The Republican Party was a minority in Congress and a minority in the country, therefore the task was to use the base of Republicans in Congress to build the party. We needed something Republicans could vote for that was different from what was being proposed by Johnson, some of which was put together with baling wire and chewing gum. We set out to develop more private enterprise oriented alternatives that Members could vote for, a place to go instead of blind negativism." Halleck's image was opposition to change, so Ford's supporters made the race a contest between the old order and a new generation.

Over the next weeks and through the Christmas holidays, Ford and his team lined up commitments, one by one by one. On the day the 89th Congress opened, on January 4, 1965, all 140 surviving Republicans met in the Longworth Building to choose their Leader. On the first tally, clerks counted 141 ballots—one too many. Someone had voted twice. On the second ballot, the judges required each Member to drop his ballot in the box as his name was called. As the votes were tallied the lead switched back and forth, but at the end Ford won: 73-67. Five members claimed they delivered the last crucial votes for Ford. He credited a young third-term Congressman from Kansas, Bob Dole, who persuaded three other Kansans to vote for Ford. Ford never forgot his political debt: "Bob's four votes saved the day."

The first-among-equals titles of Majority Leader and Minority Leader were first established in the House either in 1899 or 1911 (records differ), primarily to bring order and direction to the process of legislation. By Ford's time, the Leader had become the honest broker—the one who brought together the interests of the many to support the party's policy or program. The job's first requirement is a retentive mind. A Leader must know—for each member of his party—the voting record, philosophy, ego, aspiration, weakness, and political makeup of his or her district. The Leader must excel at counting votes. He must be trusted. Members must know that once the Leader gives his word, he will keep it. He must be fair to all, open to every Member of his party; firm but reasonable, in dealing with the Democratic hierarchy.

Ford, not surprisingly, found that serving as Leader was much like coaching—instructing, motivating, developing a strategy for the next big contest. To give his fellow Republicans a sense of purpose and direction, he told Laird, Goodell, and John Rhodes: "Come forward with proposals that will broaden our political base. We must begin to rebuild our party and bring younger Republicans into the House."

It was a formidable task. President Johnson, believing his forty-four-state reelection constituted a compelling mandate for action, inundated Capitol Hill with bills to create his Great Society: War on Poverty, Federal Aid to Education, the Job Corps, Medicare, Medicaid, and a series of civil-rights proposals.

Ford, leading the responsible opposition, proposed alternatives: Federal Revenue Sharing, a plan for economic growth, and extending voting rights protection to all states. But they paled in comparison to Johnson's bold initiatives. Wielding the great power of the White House, bearing down hard on Democrats in the House and Senate, Johnson controlled Congress as few Presidents ever have. To Ford, he was a driven man who felt that time was short if he was to make sure his greatness would be recognized. "He moved too fast on a whole raft of broad-based social legislation," Ford said. "He put the pressure on his two-to-one majorities in the House and Senate to enact legislative programs hook, line, and sinker without thorough hearings and debate." As a result, Ford said, Congress passed loose laws and handed off far too much power to the Federal bureaucracy. "The Eighty-Ninth Congress was a disgrace," Ford said. "It was not an independent branch of the government, but a tool of Johnson's White House."

While he opposed President Johnson on most domestic issues, Ford supported him on stopping Communists in Vietnam. He had been there, seen the mistakes of the French colonialists, and formed a conviction: The Vietnamese people should choose their own government and not be subjected to Communist rule. In a private meeting with President Johnson in 1965, Ford said: "We must do what we have to do to win." He warned Johnson that permitting the Vietnam War to drag on would, in time, cause the public and Congress to turn against it. America must win in Asia, Ford said; he promised to support Johnson publicly if he would order the bombing of Hanoi and send U.S. troops into Cambodia to deny Communist sanctuaries. Johnson refused, contending that he would not risk action that might provoke Red China to come into Vietnam, as had happened in Korea.

When Ford went public, criticizing Johnson for not doing enough to win the war in Vietnam, Johnson hit back. Using the most formidable

weapon in the Capital—humor—Johnson ridiculed Ford, telling reporters that Ford was dumb, played football without a helmet, and was so
clumsy he could not chew gum and walk at the same time.

Ford refused the advice of aides who urged him to retaliate. "I knew
the President was wounded by his failure in Vietnam, and was taking
out his anger on me. I knew he was wrong. I made up my mind I was
not going to let it bother me."

In Ford's first year as Leader, Richard Nixon came to Washington for
what would turn out to be a mutually advantageous visit. The two met,
at Nixon's request, to discuss the future of the Republican Party. It was
less than a year after the Goldwater defeat, and Nixon, who had moved
to New York City, was plotting his restoration.

On September 15, 1965, at breakfast in Washington's Mayflower
Hotel, Nixon unfolded his plan: To campaign in 1966 for Republicans
running for the House or Senate all across America. He did not mention
to Ford that this was to be his first step in another Presidential campaign. Ford, who knew Nixon well, considered that obvious. Evidently,
Nixon did not. Years later, he disclosed in his *Memoirs:* "It was prag-
matism more than altruism that led me to take on (the job), because I
believed that whoever did would gain a significant advantage in the race
for the 1968 Presidential nomination . . . I did not reveal to my family
or anyone else that this was what I had in mind. I knew that Pat and the
girls would again be disappointed."

With complementing goals, Ford and Nixon toured the country in
1966, recruiting candidates, raising money, and encouraging Republicans to go out and vote. That year, the party surpassed expectations—
electing three new Senators and forty-seven new Members to the House.
Among them: George H. W. Bush. Ford had not only campaigned for
Bush; he also promised influential Texans that if they got behind Bush
and elected him, he would see that Bush was appointed in his first term
to the House Ways and Means Committee—preserver of the oil industry's tax breaks. Ford kept his commitment.

The major gains by Republicans in 1966 could be credited in some
part to Nixon and Ford, but far more significant was the popular condemnation of the Vietnam War and what it was costing in American
lives, money, and standing in the world.

As the 90th Congress opened in January 1967, Ford would be leading 187 Republicans—only 31 short of a majority. Looking ahead, he

calculated that if Nixon should be nominated in 1968, and ran a strong and successful campaign, then together they might bring in enough new Members to form the majority that would elect him Speaker.

On Sunday, September 17, 1967, Ford returned home from golfing to a tearful Betty. His mother had died that morning, in her pew at Grace Church in Grand Rapids. She had often said she wanted to die "with my boots on," and she got her wish. At seventy-five, she was a resolute survivor—of a bad first marriage; of the Great Depression of the thirties; of two heart attacks, diabetes, a splenectomy, and a double mastectomy. Yet she never faltered. With a deeply ingrained spirit of caring, she served her community, baking bread for the poor, aiding her church, and volunteering to help patients at the hospital. Most important of all, she counted some forty years of a good second marriage, during which time she raised and educated her four sons—all of them successful. To each she had given unbounded love, wise counsel, and inspiration; on all she had bestowed her abiding faith, her sense of fairness, and her readiness to forgive.

At her funeral Ford could not hold back the tears. "It was the first time I ever saw my father cry," said Michael Ford, then seventeen. "I cried for him, for I knew he was in pain."

CHAPTER 7

Passage

The Republican National Convention of 1968 opened in Miami on August 5, 1968, to choose the party's candidate for President. Richard Nixon, who had assiduously collected and banked the most delegates, was back, after eight years, as the near-certain nominee. Still competing, but far behind in the delegate count was the ever-hopeful Nelson Rockefeller, Governor of New York. Further behind, with only a handful of delegates but making a lasting impression, was a first-time candidate, Ronald Reagan, Governor of California.

The three personified the evolving Republican Party: Nixon, the heir to the old order of National Committee, state and county chairmen, and party workers; Rockefeller, the symbol of the once dominant, almost extinct East Coast Republican establishment; Reagan, the rising star of the new order, then a small but soon-to-proliferate cadre of conservative Republicans.

By long tradition, the Republican Leader in the House is Convention Chairman, so Jerry Ford stood at the podium to gavel the delegates to order.

As Chairman, Ford was officially neutral. In fact he was committed: "I was a Nixon man even before the 1968 campaign began. No equivocation. No question. He knew that, and so did everyone else."

When Nixon was nominated on the first ballot, he invited ten party leaders to a midnight session in his hotel suite at to discuss his choice for Vice President. Opening the discussion, Nixon turned to Ford: "Jerry, I know you've thought about being VP in the past. Would you take it now?"

Ford, taken aback because he had never wanted to be or even contemplated being Vice President, stated his first and only priority: "Dick, I am totally dedicated to being Speaker of the House. If we do well in this election, and I believe we will, we can get the necessary 218 we need to have a majority."

Ford was complimented by Nixon's offer, but learned the next day that Nixon was, at best, just being courteous. Nixon had already decided that Governor Spiro Agnew of Maryland would be his nominee for Vice President, and made it public only hours later.

The Presidential Campaign of 1968 was base, mean, and violent, marked by race riots, bloody street battles between police and youth protesting the Vietnam War, the assassination of Martin Luther King Jr., and the assassination of Robert Kennedy—each a tragedy that left a permanent scar on the soul of America. On Election Day the nation repudiated President Johnson, his lost war, and the Democratic nominee, Vice President Hubert Humphrey.

The election was not a victory for Nixon; it was instead what Theodore White, the Homer of Presidential campaigns, aptly termed "a negative landslide." Of the 43 million Americans who had voted for Johnson in 1964, 12 million rejected his party and his successor. To White, it was the most sweeping repudiation of a President since the country rejected Herbert Hoover forty years earlier. So Nixon was elected, but by a wafer-thin plurality: 43.4 percent to Humphrey's 42.7 percent. In that ignoble year, George Wallace, the openly racist candidate, took 13.5 percent and carried five Southern states.

Ford, watching the returns in Grand Rapids, was gratified by Nixon's election, but disappointed by the House results. So close was the election that Republicans had picked up only five seats, leaving him twenty-six short of the number that would make him Speaker. Nevertheless, he looked ahead with optimism. "I had tremendous faith in Dick's ability," he said. "He was intelligent, knew the issues, and understood how politics worked. I thought he would be a great President. I was confident that with Nixon in the White House we would build a good Republican record by 1972. I believed we would have a good chance to win the House with his reelection."

With Nixon's inaugural, Ford expected that the new President would immediately summon him and Senate Republican Leader Everett Dirksen to the White House to outline his programs and priorities. They heard nothing. "Incredibly," Ford said, "Ev and I had trouble finding anyone on the White House staff who was interested in consulting with us on domestic legislative priorities."

To Ford, it quickly became obvious that Nixon had other priorities: the Vietnam War and foreign policy. In his first month as President, Nixon flew to Europe for consultations with Allied leaders; Ford thought he would have been better off to consult with the bipartisan leaders of Congress.

As Republican Leader in the House, Ford had a mixed view of the President's men. Some he liked—notably, his friend Mel Laird at Defense; George Romney at Housing and Urban Development (HUD); William Rogers at the State Department. All met his pass-fail test: they got along with Congress. Ford continued his long friendship with Henry Kissinger, now the President's National Security Adviser. On his visits to the White House, Ford would stop by Kissinger's office to continue the talk of their trade. Ford would exchange the mood of Congress for a foreign-policy briefing.

To Ford's astonishment, three men closest to Nixon—Attorney General John Mitchell, Chief of Staff Bob Haldeman, and Domestic Policy Assistant John Ehrlichman—scorned Congress. Once, when Ford asked Ehrlichman to come to the Capitol to take part in a policy discussion, Ehrlichman fell asleep during the meeting. Ford never asked him back.

"Haldeman and Ehrlichman seemed to believe that we existed only to follow their instructions," Ford said, "and we had no right to behave as if we were a coequal branch of government." In particular, he said, "They were obnoxious when it came to their dealings with Congress."

Both reflected the President's state of mind. From his first days in the White House, Nixon saw Congress as the enemy. He did have a domestic agenda, he wrote ten years later, "but it didn't take long to discover that enthusiasm and determination could not overcome the reality that I was still the first President in 120 years to begin his term with both Houses of Congress controlled by the opposition party." By his own account, Nixon's pessimism bordered on paranoia. He warned Ehrlichman that Washington was dominated by liberal Democrats who had planted activists in the bureaucracy, and there they were aided and abetted by the liberal *Washington Post*.

Ford, more adept in the ways of Washington, worked around Nixon's staff. "When it was a matter of great importance," Ford said, "I just went to see Dick. Or called him."

From his first days in the House, Ford had been a model of comity. He was, by nature, friendly, agreeable, and courteous. When debating on the floor he would argue with spirit and partisan conviction, but immediately after, he made a point of going up to his opponent to shake hands and show his respect. His differences were political and philosophical, but never personal: with one exception.

For reasons that he could never explain, to others or himself, on April 15, 1970, Ford took the floor to make a personal attack on Supreme Court Justice William O. Douglas. He had a good case in law and ethics. Douglas, it had been revealed by the *Los Angeles Times*, had for ten years been paid $12,000 a year in legal fees by Alvin Parvin, a wealthy businessman with connections to organized crime. Clearly, this was a potential conflict of interest. Moreover, under Federal law, a Federal judge could not accept legal fees from any source.

But Ford did not press his valid arguments. Instead, he attacked Douglas personally, suggesting the Justice's "fractious behavior as the first sign of senility." Ford was outraged that Douglas had written an article for *Eros*, a pornographic magazine. For that, Ford argued, "He is unfit and should be removed."

Ford's move against Douglas failed. In his three decades on the court, Douglas had become a popular figure, particularly with liberal Democrats. His small army of supporters mobilized, inside and outside the House, to defeat and ridicule Ford. John Osborn wrote in the liberal *New Republic:* Ford's action was "the shoddiest enterprise on his record."

For Ford, it was an important lesson. "I let my emotion get the better of the facts," he said. "I made a mistake. A costly mistake."

Preparing for the midterm House elections of 1970, Ford and the Republican Party faced a bleak prospect. In the public mind, Vietnam had become Nixon's war—impossible to win, dishonorable to lose. Challenging the odds against him, Ford traveled more extensively, spoke more frequently, and raised more money than ever before, hoping to pick up at least a few seats; instead, he lost twelve. This put him thirty-eight seats short of the number that would make him Speaker.

Nevertheless, Ford saw his prospects brighten at the beginning of the 92nd Congress. President Nixon, in his 1971 State of the Union address, advanced an impressive domestic agenda. He proposed the Family Assistance Plan to provide money and job training to the poor and unemployed. He initiated measures to protect the environment, to broaden health care, and to improve the production and distribution of energy. As part of his "New Federalism," Nixon advocated Federal Revenue Sharing: a measure designed to give $5 billion annually—no strings attached—to state and local governments. Most of Nixon's initiatives were needed; all were designed to bring him votes.

Then, a political masterstroke: nine months before the 1972 election, the President surprised the nation and the world by a bold and timely act of statesmanship—he reopened U.S. relations with Red China. Before Nixon, four U.S. Presidents had distanced the United States from the Chinese government and the Chinese people. But Nixon, the politician who had made a career of fighting Communists, reversed himself and U.S. policy. He initiated an historic journey to Beijing, Hangzhou, and Shanghai to meet with Mao Zedong and Zhou Enlai: two of the most powerful and bloodstained Communist dictators in the world. There the American President and the Communist leaders talked, dined sumptuously, negotiated, and agreed to pursue a common goal: countering Soviet expansion.

Nixon's opening to China was an extraordinary accomplishment—personally, diplomatically, and politically. To Ford, that visit, plus Nixon's record of domestic actions, virtually guaranteed a second term as President. With a resounding Nixon victory, and a promising lineup of Republican challengers for House seats, Ford could realistically look ahead to a Republican majority that would make him Speaker of the House.

As Nixon prospered, in early 1972 the aspiring princes of the Democratic Party plotted fratricide—and carried it out. First to go down was the heir presumptive to the nomination—Senator Edmund Muskie of Maine. A man of the center, a conscientious and diligent performer in the Senate, Muskie had delivered a sterling performance four years before as the Vice Presidential nominee. Now he was endorsed by governors, senators, and party professionals. More important, he matched President Nixon in the early, popular polls.

But Muskie was done in at the beginning, and by his own mistakes. He spent so much time campaigning in other states that he neglected New Hampshire, so voters turned away. Then, a week before the primary, he committed a fatal act of imagery. During the campaign, the systemically toxic *Manchester Union-Leader* accused Muskie's outspoken wife, Jane, of drinking to excess and telling dirty jokes. To defend her, Muskie climbed on the bed of a flatbed truck outside the *Union-Leader,* began to speak, and lost control of his emotions. His voice broke and he started crying. New Hampshire voters—indeed, all Americans—expect strength in their leaders; they had never seen a Presidential candidate cry in public before. Muskie was finished.

The bloodletting continued, with Florida destroying both the charismatic Mayor of New York City, John Lindsay, and the able and highly respected Senator Henry Jackson of Washington. In Maryland, at a shopping-center rally in May, the backwoods favorite, George Wallace, was shot five times in the chest and stomach by a glory-seeking loner, Arthur Bremer. Wallace survived, paralyzed by a bullet lodged in his spine, his political life ended.

After Wallace was shot, two candidates were left standing: former Vice President Hubert Humphrey, who had won Ohio, and Senator George McGovern, who had swept Wisconsin and Massachusetts. The winner-take-all primary in California was sure to bring one down.

Humphrey, behind and desperate, made an uncharacteristic but necessary decision. He would attack McGovern—show his weakness on issues; paint him as unfit and unready to be President. So he lured McGovern into a televised debate, and there he accused his friend and protégé of being "wrong on Vietnam . . . wrong on labor law . . . wrong on unemployment compensation . . . contradictory and inconsistent on taxation . . ." Ridiculing McGovern's position on defense, Humphrey charged that McGovern would reduce American forces "66,000 below what we had pre-Pearl Harbor." Humphrey was right: McGovern was shallow on the issues.

Yet McGovern won California, and went on to win New York and the Democratic nomination. But in the process he had sundered the coalition of political entities that elected Democrats. His amateurs had ousted the party's old reliable professionals. Labor was gone; McGovern had broken his word with their leaders. He had offended and dismissed ethnic minorities. To the astonishment of Republicans, the Democratic Party had dismissed its most capable leaders and nominated its weakest and least qualified candidate for President.

Ford, who had come to know McGovern during his four years in the House, watched the Democratic debacle and the coming election with personal and political interest. "George was a typical farm state liberal, anti-military, believing money is the solution to all problems,"

Ford said. "I thought the country would see that George did not have the experience or preparation to be President. I was sure that Nixon, with his record, and on the crest of his popularity, would win the election by a huge margin."

Ford was confident. The Republican Party was confident. President Nixon had every reason to be confident. Given the circumstances—his standing in public opinion was his highest ever, and his prospects for reelection were excellent—the political event that happened next became all the more inexplicable.

On the morning of Sunday, June 18, 1972, Congressman Ford was driving through Grand Rapids when he heard on the car radio a news report from Washington: five men had broken into Democratic National Headquarters in the Watergate office building. All five had been caught in the act, arrested, and charged with attempting to bug the Democrats' office—a Federal crime. "I was flabbergasted," he said. "Who could be so stupid? What could anyone gain by breaking into the Democrats' Headquarters?"

Back in Washington on Monday morning, Ford read in the *Washington Post* that one of the five burglars, James McCord, was on the Nixon campaign payroll, nominally as a security expert. Four others were former CIA operatives; two had been involved in the failed Bay of Pigs invasion under President Kennedy. Two other men, E. Howard Hunt and G. Gordon Liddy, who had supervised the break-in from a motel across the street, were also arrested.

By chance, Ford was meeting that morning with Jack Marsh, a close friend then practicing law in Washington.

"Jack," Ford asked, "do you suppose that anyone in the White House might have been involved in the Watergate burglary?"

"Jerry, I know this fellow McCord, and I know he works closely with John Mitchell."

Marsh explained: His office was on the eleventh floor of the Olmstead Building, across from the White House complex. Nixon campaign headquarters occupied lower floors. Some weeks before, McCord had come to Marsh's office, and introduced himself as director of security for the Nixon campaign. He was opening an office on that floor for Martha Mitchell, the garrulous and uninhibited wife of the campaign chairman. Marsh, hospitable by nature, permitted McCord to use the telephone and copier in his office.

"In light of McCord's position, and who he works for," Marsh said, "it seems to me that someone at a very high level was bound to have had some knowledge or association with this break-in at the Watergate."

"Well," Ford said, "Dick Nixon is much too smart a politician to have been involved in anything like that. If anyone in the White House was involved, Nixon ought to fire them, and I don't care how high it would go. If he does that, it will be the end of it."

As it happened, Ford was scheduled to see Mitchell that day. He, Senate Republican Leader Hugh Scott, and the chairmen of the Senate and House Campaign Committees were meeting Mitchell and his deputy, Jeb Magruder, to coordinate their campaigns with the President's.

Ford deliberately arrived early and went in to see Mitchell. "John, did you or anyone at the Nixon Campaign Committee have anything to do with the break-in at Democratic National Headquarters?"

"Absolutely not," Mitchell replied, looking Ford in the eye.

"Did the President have anything to do with it?" Ford asked.

"Absolutely not," Mitchell replied, shaking his head to emphasize the point.

Mitchell had given his word. Ford accepted it.

A week later, at 8:00 a.m. on the morning of Friday, June 23, 1972, Ford and Hale Boggs, Majority Leader in the House, met with President Nixon at the White House to be briefed on Red China. Nixon, on his visit four months earlier, had encouraged Mao and Zhou to get to know other American political leaders. So, the Chinese rulers had invited the two House leaders to make an official, highest-level visit. That morning, Ford and Boggs were to hear Nixon's brief on China before they set out on their journey.

The President was at the top of his game; relishing the opportunity to assess China's leaders, share the highlights of his trip, and offer suggestions for discussing problems between the United States and China.

For Ford, it was a memorable briefing. "The President was knowledgeable, told us what to expect, what to look for. He was justifiably proud of what he had accomplished. He was riding high, at his pinnacle." The three talked for ninety minutes before Ford and Boggs climbed into the limousine that would take them to Andrews Air Force Base to take off, with their wives and staff, for China.

China—Nixon's initiative, his successful mission, his grasp of foreign leaders and affairs, and his mastery in summarizing another nation's political situation—reflected the best of the 37th President of the United

States. Yet, within the hour after demonstrating that skill to Ford and Boggs, Richard Nixon showed the worst of himself.

At 10:04 a.m., his chief of staff, Bob Haldeman, came in to the Oval Office to deliver an ominous report on Watergate. The FBI had traced serial numbers on hundred-dollar bills in the pockets of the Watergate burglars. They led directly to the Nixon campaign committee. Soon, Haldeman warned, the FBI investigation might lead from the campaign into the White House.

To prevent that, Haldeman continued, Mitchell and White House Counsel John Dean proposed to stop the FBI investigation. That could be done only by the CIA, which could claim it interfered with intelligence activities. So the plan, Haldeman said, was this: he and Ehrlichman would summon Richard Helms, Director of the CIA, to the White House and instruct him to tell the FBI to stop the investigation because it affects their work.

Nixon listened, and said: "All right."

To make sure the President understood and approved, Haldeman said: "And you seem to think the thing to do is to get them to stop."

"Right, fine," Nixon said.

"They [Mitchell and Dean] say the only way to do that is from White House instructions," Haldeman said. "And the proposal would be that Ehrlichman and I call them in and say, ah . . ."

Nixon interrupted. "All right, fine . . . We protected Helms from a hell of a lot of things."

The two then discussed what the FBI investigation might find out, whether Mitchell knew about the break-in beforehand, and what role Nixon's obsequious political aide, Charles Colson, might have played. Nixon then restated his instructions. "You call them in . . . Play it tough. That's the way they play it, and that's the way we are going to play it."

"Okay," Haldeman said.

Again Nixon reviewed the plan. "When you get the [CIA] people in, say, 'Look, the problem is that this will open the whole Bay of Pigs thing' . . . They should call the FBI in and [tell them] don't go any further into this thing, period!"

Three hours later, with Helms and his deputy, Vernon Walters, on their way to the White House, Nixon sent for Haldeman. "Just say, it is likely to blow the whole Bay of Pigs thing, which we think would be very unfortunate, both for the CIA and for the country . . . Just tell him to lay off."

The Nixon-Haldeman conversations took place in the most private and secure of places—the White House Oval Office. Both spoke as if confident their plotting was secret and would remain secret. Yet both Nixon and Haldeman knew, but took no account of, the fact that they were conspiring before open microphones connected to a central taping mechanism that was recording every word of their attempt to stop the FBI's investigation of a crime.

For Jerry Ford, the two-week visit to China was a memorable experience. He and Boggs toured steel factories and art museums, saw rice fields in Manchuria, observed surgery under acupuncture, and gained a sense of the culture and the people. Fascinated by all he saw, Ford asked questions, and learned. One night, Premier Zhou Enlai invited Boggs, Ford, and their wives for dinner. After greeting them in a chamber of the Great Hall, Zhou seated visitors in a semicircle; Boggs on his right, Ford on his left, and their wives next. After tea was served they talked, and Ford appraised his host. "He was of medium height, trim build, and firm facial features, a strikingly handsome Chinese appearance," Ford said. "He had sharp, steely eyes, and short black hair, showing a little gray. It was amazing that Mao Zedong and Zhou Enlai, who had gone on the long march under the most horrendously adverse conditions, could live that long and be so healthy."

After chatting about their tour, Zhou led them into another room for what Ford remembered as "a delicious dinner, beautifully served. We got up about midnight and Zhou Enlai very graciously turned to Lindy Boggs and Betty Ford and said how nice it was to have had them for dinner and he knew they were tired and had a long day ahead." Of course Lindy and Betty got the word that they were being excused. "I was impressed, it was so properly, discreetly done," Ford said.

With that, Zhou, Boggs, and Ford and their interpreters moved into another room and sat down about 12:30 a.m. "Zhou was very pleasant in conversation but probing. Very businesslike—alert to what you say in every word, every phrase," Ford said. "Zhou reminded us of his snub by John Foster Dulles at Geneva in 1954, and criticized the U.S. for Vietnam and Korea. He was very well informed about domestic as well as foreign policies of the United States. He wondered why we were not strengthening NATO. He asked whether Congress would accept McGovern's proposed $30 billion cut in defense expenditures."

Frankly, Zhou told them, "We don't believe you can reduce your military spendings. With the Soviet Union increasing their own defenses, how can you reduce yours?"

At all times, Ford said, Zhou was anti-Soviet. "He wanted the United States to be in power in the Pacific mainly against the Soviet Union being a power in the Pacific. He felt the U.S. had an obligation to oppose the Soviet Union threat in Europe, Asia, everywhere in the world." At one point, Ford asked him if China might in the future realign his country with the Soviet Union. Without waiting for the interpreter, Zhou replied in perfect English: "Never! Never!"

Ford would never forget Zhou. "I never had a more interesting political discussion," he said. "Zhou Enlai was one of the most able intellectual political figures I ever met—imposing in his intelligence and knowledge, and fluent in discussing issues. He was well-informed, realistic, foresighted. I would certainly put him at the very top of those I ever met in international politics."

Back in the United States, Ford watched the Democratic National Convention ratify the nomination of McGovern, then flew to Miami in August for the Republican National Convention. There, he presided over the staged jubilance that culminated in the renomination of President Nixon. Republicans had reason to celebrate. A post-conventions Gallup poll showed the President with 64 percent of the popular vote, against 30 percent for McGovern.

Nixon's lead held. Through September, then October, it was never in doubt. To Republicans, independents, and even some Democrats, he had been a front-rank President, evidenced by a record of accomplishment. He had made a strategic ally of China and eased nuclear tensions with the Soviet Union. U.S. casualties in Vietnam were down, and negotiations to end the war seemed promising. Kissinger declared "Peace is at hand." At home the economy was strong. Inflation was down. Employment and the gross national product were up. Midwestern grain was selling. Wall Street was confident.

Bad luck had often dogged Dick Nixon, but not in 1972. For the first time in his political life, he had drawn an inept and ineffective opponent. McGovern lacked presence. Before a crowd he wavered and seemed uncertain. On television, he appeared to be wan, muddled. In private, with his advisers, he was more student than leader. At briefings he took copious notes, but was slow to make decisions. When he did, as in choosing Senator Tom Eagleton to be his nominee for vice president, he had to reverse himself. He did not delegate, nor ever appoint one person to run his campaign. As a result, his headquarters was mired in dissension and confusion. Without direction, his comanagers could not produce a central theme and strategy. Gary Hart, his most experienced professional, said that McGovern was outright opposed to organization. He wanted to answer every phone call himself. Richard Dougherty, the gifted New Yorker who served as McGovern's press secretary, considered McGovern a dreamer—"a creature out of Tolstoy, a Levin, I'd think, full of dreams for the betterment of society, at one time awash with affection for the common man and at another irritated by his ignorance and cupidity . . ."

Even so dedicated a Democrat as former President Lyndon Johnson gave up on McGovern. Through Billy Graham, Johnson passed a message to Nixon: "Ignore McGovern . . . Stay above the campaign, like I did with Goldwater . . . The McGovern people are going to defeat themselves."

Watergate, which could have been a disaster for Nixon, was contained for almost five months. From the perspective of later events, that is hard to believe; but, it happened. It happened in great part because Nixon used the power of the office and the prestige of the Presidency to cover up the crime. The ruse to stop the FBI investigation failed; Helms refused to intervene. But Nixon had and used a great advantage. Dean was getting regular reports from FBI director Gray on the progress of investigators and prosecutors, so Nixon could counter every move. One day, with indictments of the burglars near, Nixon told Haldeman to slip them hush money. Another time, just before deputy campaign chairman Magruder appeared before the grand jury, the President told Ehrlichman: get word to Magruder that he can expect money for lawyers for his defense, and a pardon—after the election.

Without hesitation, Nixon also used the authority of the Presidential pulpit to cover his crime. Even as he, Haldeman, Ehrlichman, and Dean were obstructing the investigation, the President stated at a press conference that on the basis of an investigation by White House Counsel Dean, "I can say categorically that his investigation indicates that no one in the White House staff, no one in this administration presently employed, was involved in this very bizarre incident."

As Nixon conspired to hide the truth, five blocks away, the *Washington Post* was doing its best to discover and disclose the truth. Two star reporters—Bob Woodward and Carl Bernstein—were relentless, disclosing hard evidence connecting the break-in and the Nixon campaign. They revealed that a $25,000 check to the Nixon campaign had been deposited in the bank account of one of the burglars. They reported that John Mitchell, while still Attorney General, had authorized spying on the Democrats. They published a story that Nixon's personal-appointments secretary had hired a friend to sabotage the Democratic campaign.

The stories were all true, for Woodard had an astonishing secret source: Mark Felt, deputy director of the FBI. As the FBI's number two, Felt had full and regular knowledge of every aspect of the ongoing Watergate investigation. His motive for passing information to Woodward was twofold. He was disgruntled at having been passed over for director of the FBI, and he believed that someone in the White House was involved in the break-in and should be exposed.

The *Post* was diligent, indefatigable. Ben Bradlee, its best-ever editor, pushed and protected his reporters, and put their stories on the front page. But after the first weeks of dramatic revelations, new information was hard to come by. "We had a long dry spell," Bradlee said. "It was hard to find out, and verify, what was going on." Moreover, most Washington reporters, lacking the *Post's* sources and spirit, tended to accept the White House official line, that nobody in the Nixon administration had ordered or even knew about the break-in. Except for two solid segments on CBS, the television networks skimmed or skipped the story.

Consequently, the President himself escaped the taint of Watergate when it counted—before the election. He escaped by conspiracy, luck, and in part because Americans did not want to believe their President was involved in the break-in. The office commands such respect that a President is by definition upright, honest, and truthful. Nobody wants to believe he is a liar. Or a crook. And Nixon, of all people, was presumed to be too experienced, too practiced a political hand, to have been involved in an escapade concocted by amateurs. Even his Democratic opponent thought so. When McGovern first heard of the burglary, from the press traveling with him, he dismissed the suggestion that Nixon or the Republican Party had been involved.

In mid-September, Nixon's Attorney General Richard Kleindienst informed him that a Federal grand jury would indict the Watergate burglars, six hired hands, and only one campaign employee. Nixon was elated: none was connected to the White House. Dean, discussing the limited indictments in the Oval Office that day, gloated that the grand jury had been dismissed, so the threat to the President's reelection was over. Haldeman was also delighted: "It has been kept away from the White House and of course completely from the President."

Early on the morning of Election Day, November 7, 1972, Congressman Jerry Ford stood in line at the redbrick schoolhouse that was his polling place in East Grand Rapids, Michigan. This was the thirteenth time he had asked the voters of the Fifth District of Michigan to send him to Congress as their Representative; in his mind, it could be the last.

After he voted, Ford visited with constituents through the morning, displaying his usual good cheer and confidence. At noon, he joined Walter Russell, his close friend and campaign manager, for lunch in the Finial Restaurant on top of the Union Bank Building. They talked about their expectation of Nixon's reelection by a landslide, and how that might affect Ford's future. Ford's hopes were high, but realistic. "Walt, this election is my last chance to be Speaker," he said. "If we don't gain enough seats today to control the House, I'm going to get out of politics."

Russell was sympathetic; he did not object. Like Ford's other friends, in Grand Rapids and elsewhere, Russell knew that Ford's pride in serving the people of western Michigan had been at a cost: House business had come before time with Betty, their three sons, and daughter. Money had always been tight; it had not been easy to provide for the family, educate the children, and support two homes on government pay. His net worth was skimpy; nothing like what it could have been for a lawyer of his education, legal ability, and negotiating skills.

After the afternoon flight from Grand Rapids, Ford settled down before the TV in the den at Crown View Drive in Alexandria. Betty, well aware that the evening could change their lives, had set up TV tables for his favorite dinner—steak, baked potato, and butter pecan ice cream.

Together they watched the returns unfold. The first scattered results in Connecticut put Nixon in the lead with 60 percent. Then a flood of reports: Florida, Nixon ahead by 2-1 in the early count; Nixon sweeping the South; Nixon leading in New England, except in Massachusetts; Nixon winning the Midwest. At 8:51 p.m. EST, Walter Cronkite, the most authoritative and trusted public man in America, officially declared the President's reelection: "Michigan has put Nixon over the top."

For Nixon, it was his greatest victory. He won 61.8 percent of the popular vote, carried every state except Massachusetts, and could count on 520 of 538 electoral votes. For Ford, however, the election was a stunning defeat. His party had not won the House; had not even come close. Republicans had gained not the 38 seats that would make him Speaker, but only 12. In the new Congress, Democrats would hold 242 seats, to his 192.

In the quiet of his den that election night, Ford said to Betty: "If we can't get a majority against McGovern, with a Republican President winning virtually every state, when can we? Maybe it's time for us to get out of politics and have another life."

For Betty Ford it was a revelation. "I had never expected to hear those words," she said, "though for years I had been waiting and waiting for the day when we could have a life together." As she had so many times before, she said, "Jerry, I will support whatever you decide to do."

Ford made his decision that evening, but not before deliberate and logical examination. Looking back on his career, he was filled with pride that he had given twenty-four years to public service. They were the best years of his life, and they had been good, challenging, and rewarding. By hard work, by patience, by endurance, he knew he had served his district and the nation. But it had not been easy. As Leader there had been the necessary long hours in the office and on the House floor, the endless traveling to support his colleagues. One year he had flown 138,000 miles campaigning for incumbents and challengers. Being away so often was hard on the family, and especially on Betty, who suffered with arthritis and a pinched nerve. There was also the frustration of being in the minority, of lacking the votes to prevail on important legislation. He respected his good friend Dick Nixon, and thought the President would have another four years of accomplishment, but he did not like having to deal with the President's men. Haldeman, Ehrlichman, and Colson, in particular, "seemed to think that we in Congress were their patsies."

He was only 59 years old—young enough to practice law, or go into business. Perhaps it was time. There were opportunities at home in Grand Rapids, and in Washington. He would of course serve out the thirteenth term to which he had been elected. With one more, he would have served Michigan's Fifth in Congress longer than anyone in history: that would be a political record. So that night he decided: "After one more campaign and one more term in the House, Betty and I would have a new life."

Two days later he and Betty left for ten days at the resort of Try-all, near Montego Bay in Jamaica. They were vacationing with favorite friends—Rod and Annabel Markley, Bill and Peggy Whyte, and Congressman John and Mary Lou Jarman, of Oklahoma. Markley was Washington Vice President for Ford Motor Company; Whyte had a comparable position with U.S. Steel. On the golf course one day Ford told his friends of his plan to leave the House. He knew that Whyte and Markley had discussed retiring and setting up a lobbying firm for major corporate clients. Would they, Ford asked, consider him as a partner in their firm? Both were enthusiastic; both knew why Ford needed to change. "It was money," Whyte said. "Jerry never had any money."

Back in Washington, Ford told his staff of his plans, and suggested they begin to think of finding other jobs. He had made up his mind. He would leave the House at the end of 1976 and begin a new life.

CHAPTER 8

Revelations

The 93rd Congress opened on January 3, 1973, and elected Carl Albert of Oklahoma to his second term as Speaker, and Jerry Ford to his fifth term as Minority Leader. The speeches were unexceptionable. In the Senate, Majority Leader Mike Mansfield called for "complete disinvolvement" from Vietnam. Speaker Albert, with more prescience than he could have known, affirmed that the House of Representatives must "safeguard its Constitutional role as a strong and influential branch of our national government." Ford, invited to escort Albert to the chair, ruefully mentioned his disappointment in not becoming Speaker himself. "But after five defeats," he acknowledged to his House colleagues, "you learn to grit your teeth and smile."

It was business as usual for the first days of the new Congress, and then Washington, always ready to revel in the latest bad news, turned its attention to the next big story: the trial of seven Watergate burglars. It began on January 8, 1973, in U.S. District Court three blocks west of the Capitol, in the courtroom of Judge John J. Sirica.

Sirica was no scholar of jurisprudence. In four decades of practice he had climbed through the ranks, sitting alone in a small law office waiting for clients and wondering how to pay the rent, finding a patron and mentor, demonstrating his ability as one of the best trial lawyers in the Washington courts, and reaching his goal to serve on the Federal bench. Through the years he had learned about courts and the practical application of the law and a great deal about the nature and motivation of humans, felonious and otherwise.

In his court, Judge Sirica was intense, feisty, and always totally engaged in the play of words and evidence before him. Trying a case, he was a participant, not a referee; less an august presence than a combatant. He believed with Edmund Burke that a judge is not "merely a passive instrument of parties. He has a duty of his own, independent of them, and that duty is to investigate the truth." If, in his judgment, a prosecuting attorney was not aggressive enough in questioning a witness, Sirica took over, interrogating, probing, sometimes harassing the victimized witness to bring forth the facts that would reveal the full story of what had happened. His juries rarely came back with questions about evidence or testimony. Once the verdict was in, Sirica never hesitated to hand down a severe sentence. Defense attorneys called him, for good reason, "Maximum John."

His was a story made in the United States: a poor boy struggling to find his way and eventually reaching his lofty status. The firstborn son of immigrants from Italy, Sirica grew up rootless as his itinerant father looked for work—moving from Connecticut to Ohio, to Florida, to Virginia, to Washington. Ferdinand Sirica, handicapped by having no schooling beyond the third grade, pushed his indolent son to learn and achieve, insisting the boy finish high school and go on to law school. John Sirica did enter law school, but he found legal terms as incomprehensible as a foreign language and dropped out. Idle, he starting going to the YMCA, and there he learned to box. After a brief professional career as a 5 foot 6 inch welterweight, he went back to the classroom. "Because I had seen my father disappointed and frustrated so many times," Sirica wrote, "I had made up my mind to stick with law school." He did, graduating from Georgetown Law School in 1926, and passing the District of Columbia bar on his first try.

With no clients and ample time, he began working out at the Knights of Columbus gym, sparring, and coaching young businessmen and lawyers who wanted to keep fit. "Boxing," he wrote, "had become more than a sport for me. It gave me confidence and courage and introduced me to people who became good friends." Through one of those friends, Sirica landed a job with Bert Emerson, then one of Washington's outstanding criminal lawyers. Emerson, by instruction and example, turned Sirica into a lawyer. The acolyte's performance in court led to his appointment as an assistant in the U.S. Attorney's office, and in turn to the staff of a Senate committee as chief counsel, and then to partnership at Hogan and Hartson—an old and distinguished Washington firm.

Sirica had always liked politics. He had campaigned before Italian-

American groups for Willkie, and Dewey, and twice for the Eisenhower-Nixon ticket. In 1957, on the recommendation of Deputy Attorney General William Rogers, a friend from their service as counsels for Senate committees, President Eisenhower appointed Sirica to the U.S. District Court.

By the time the Watergate indictments reached him, he had served on the bench for fifteen years. He was experienced, wise beyond his 69 years, and fully aware of both the political sensitivity and public importance of the Watergate case; so much so that he took very seriously his responsibility as Chief Judge to assign the Watergate case. Thinking it over, he decided he would not turn it over to one of his fourteen fellow judges; he would instead preside over the trial himself.

To Sirica, there were compelling reasons. First, he was a Republican. If the trial of Republicans were to be conducted by a judge appointed by a Democrat, charges of partisanship would be certain to follow. Sirica consulted with fellow judges, Democrats and Republicans; they agreed he should conduct the trial. Second, it was such an important and unusual case—the crime political, the defendants perhaps of consequence—that it would attract major press and public attention and so require special handling. Since newspaper accounts had already convicted the seven defendants, it was all the more important that they have a fair trial. Sirica felt that he had the experience and temperament to ensure that.

Finally, and not least, Sirica wanted to try the case. From the beginning, on that Saturday morning in June when he read in the *Washington Post* that five men had broken into Democratic headquarters and been arrested in the act of placing a bug on the chairman's telephone, Sirica had suspected that the burglars were acting for higher officials. When he read the indictments of the five and their two handlers, he was certain that the accused were hirelings, brought in for a dirty job by someone on the Nixon campaign staff, or even in the White House. As presiding judge, Sirica intended to use the trial not merely to determine whether the seven were guilty of the break-in, but—far more important—to determine who hired them to do it. And why.

"I didn't really know what I was getting into," Sirica wrote later. He was right. He could not have known that in the next five years he would preside over not just one Watergate trial but three historic legal proceedings that, over time, would send senior White House officials to jail, force President Nixon from office, and validate the U.S. Constitution.

As he prepared to open the first Watergate trial, Judge Sirica was clear about his objective. He was less sure about the prosecutor, Earl Silbert, the Assistant U.S. Attorney assigned the case. In a pretrial session, Sirica asked Silbert if he planned to trace the hundred-dollar bills found on the defendants. Dissatisfied with Silbert's circumlocutions, Sirica put the issue bluntly: "This jury is going to want to know somewhere along the line what did these men go into the headquarters for? What was their purpose? . . . Who hired them to go in there? Who started this thing?"

As soon as the jury was selected and the trial underway, Sirica leaned forward with anticipation to hear the prosecution's opening statement. Silbert, he felt sure, would lay out the theory of the case and outline the evidence and testimony that would answer the unanswered questions about Watergate. Instead, Silbert simply recounted the break-in events and suggested that Liddy had thought up the caper and carried it off without authority. All seven, Silbert contended, were motivated by the need for money. Sirica was disappointed. Whether by incompetence or fear of his superiors in Nixon's Justice Department, Silbert had no plan to ask who ordered the break-in, or who supplied the big money in the burglars' pockets.

Vexing Sirica more, as soon as the defense attorneys completed their opening statements, Hunt pleaded guilty and thereby avoided testifying. When Sirica brought Hunt forward to explain to the jury how he got into the conspiracy, Hunt's lawyer stopped him from answering. Four days later, the four Miamians pleaded guilty. When Sirica questioned them, all said they had been motivated not by money but by Hunt telling them it was an anti-Castro operation. "Where did this money come from, these hundred dollar bills," the cash to pay your fellow burglars? Sirica asked defendant Bernard Barker.

"Your Honor, I got that money in the mail in a blank envelope," Barker replied. He insisted he did not know who sent it.

Sirica asked the four if they had been promised clemency, or money for their families. All said no.

Sirica shook his head in disbelief. In the privacy of his office he had confided to his principal clerk, Todd Christofferson, "Someone will talk. *Someone* will talk." But no one was talking. Their collective silence made Sirica even more suspicious that they were pawns for higher officials, but in his courtroom the prosecution produced no evidence connecting the break-in to the Nixon campaign. With five of the accused pleading guilty, and McCord and Liddy not about to take the stand and risk cross-examination, Sirica was becoming more concerned. He told Christofferson that if all seven being prosecuted simply accepted their prison sentences and remained silent, then the truth about Watergate might never come out.

For a fortnight, the trial of Liddy and McCord continued; the former brazen; the latter stoic, as, one after another, Nixon campaign executives put all the blame on them. Their common line: Liddy was a rogue chieftain who thought up and carried out the break-in, and McCord was his accomplice for money. Exonerating himself, Jeb Magruder, campaign deputy, denied under oath that he had authorized Liddy to undertake the break-in and bugging. Hugh Sloan, campaign treasurer, testified that he carried out Magruder's order to turn over $199,000 in cash to Liddy, but he had no idea what the money was for. On the bench, Sirica was impassive; in chambers, his anger mounted. "I just didn't believe these people," Sirica said. "The whole case looked more and more like a big cover-up."

So it seemed to the trial's end. In his concluding argument to the jury, Chief Prosecutor Silbert stated as fact that the break-in was Liddy's idea, and that McCord joined in for the money. "He and Liddy were off on an enterprise of their own," Silbert told the court. Defense attorneys, with clients caught red-handed, argued as best they could with the little they had. On the afternoon of January 30, the jury retired, and in less than two hours delivered its verdict: Liddy and McCord, both guilty, on all eight counts of burglary, conspiracy, and violating Federal laws against wiretapping.

With the verdict in, Judge Sirica set March 23 as the day for sentencing. He had already decided to hand down stiff sentences, but wanted to spend some weeks in deciding the length of jail terms, and his reasoning. Disappointed that the truth had not come out in his court, he was nevertheless encouraged that other legal entities and the press were probing for answers to the Watergate mystery. The grand jury that indicted the seven was still sitting, still interrogating witnesses; not only the convicted burglars, but also high-ranking Nixon campaign officials. The *Washington Post* and other newspapers, profiting from nonstop leaks from the FBI and other investigators, raised more and more suspicions with their headlines and well-sourced articles. Of even greater consequence, one week after Liddy and McCord were found guilty, the U.S. Senate acted, voting 77-0 to create a select committee to investigate Watergate.

Fortuitously, Senate leaders appointed wise and folksy Sam Ervin of North Carolina as Chairman, and the astute but little-known Howard Baker of Tennessee as Vice Chairman. Both were experienced trial lawyers. Both were men of character, perseverance, infectious humor, and instinctive good judgment. Moving promptly, Senators Ervin and Baker commissioned highly qualified lawyers and investigators to question White House and Nixon campaign officials, and scheduled hearings to begin in May.

Anticipating the wider investigations to come, Sirica searched for a way to euchre the Watergate witnesses into breaking the closed ring of silence. Studying the precedents, he found a statute that would authorize him to postpone sentencing until, as he put it, "I could see just how well the defendants cooperated in the pending investigations . . . I had already decided that in one last attempt to get the truth out, I was going to impose provisional sentences on the five defendants who had pleaded guilty. I planned to tell them that one factor in determining their final sentences would be their cooperation with the Senate committee, the grand jury, and the prosecutors. I had given up on Liddy, who had napped and grinned his way throughout his own trial. I was prepared to give McCord a substantial sentence."

Three days before he was to bring the seven into his courtroom to hand down the sentences, Sirica was in his office, drafting his order, when his clerk knocked on his door. A probation officer was there to deliver a sealed white envelope. The officer told the judge it was from one of the convicted burglars, James McCord.

Hoping, but wary, Sirica brought in witnesses and opened the envelope. Looking at the letterhead, he saw that indeed it was from McCord. Typed neatly, it was addressed: "To Judge Sirica." Wondering what to expect, Sirica read the letter in silence, disciplining himself to keep the poker face he tried to show in court. Halfway through, with a flush of excitement that he could not conceal, he grasped the momentous significance of the letter he held in his hand. McCord, the Nixon campaign security chief who had been so impassive in court, was now ready to talk. This is it, he said to himself. This is it; this is the break I've been hoping for.

Reading on, Sirica's first reaction was quickly confirmed. McCord had put on paper that he and his fellow defendants were under White House pressure to remain silent; that campaign officials had lied and committed perjury; that higher-ups were involved in the Watergate

break-in, and had conspired to cover up their crime. McCord had decided to talk, he wrote Sirica, after weeks of agonizing: he feared long
years in prison; but if he talked, he and his family knew he might be
killed for doing so. He had decided to accept that risk and write to
Judge Sirica, emphasizing that he did not trust the FBI or the prosecutors or the Nixon Justice Department. Looking at the signature—James
W. McCord Jr.—Sirica knew there was no longer any doubt: the Watergate case was broken.

Calming his emotions, Sirica read the letter aloud to his witnesses,
two clerks, and the court reporter, then ordered them to say nothing to
anyone until the day of sentencing. Minutes later, alone with Christofferson, his clerk, Sirica was beaming, exultant. He noted that McCord
had written on March 19, Sirica's birthday. "This is the best damned
birthday present I've ever gotten," he told Christofferson. "I always told
you someone would talk. This is going to break this case wide open."

Break the Watergate case it did. On March 23, 1973, Sirica read Mc-
Cord's letter to a packed courtroom. Sam Dash, attending as the newly
appointed chief counsel of the Senate Watergate Committee, confronted
McCord in the corridor and began questioning him that afternoon. By
the next day, Silbert and his fellow prosecutors had turned from lan-
guor to zeal. They directed the grand jury to reopen its investigation of
Watergate and move at once to bring in the President's closest aides to
be questioned.

Thirteen days after McCord broke the Nixonians' tight ring of conspiracy, Dean ended his silence. Fearful of a long term in jail, Dean
decided to talk in exchange for leniency, and instructed his lawyers to
ask prosecutors for a deal. Talk he did, revealing to the grand jury in
secret testimony his own part in the break-in and cover-up, and naming
Haldeman, Ehrlichman, Mitchell, Colson, and President Nixon himself
as accomplices in crime. Magruder turned. With McCord and Dean cooperating to reduce their sentences, Magruder agreed to become one of
the prosecutors' chief witnesses in exchange for their agreement to drop
all but one charge against him. Colson's lawyers began exploring a deal
with the prosecutors. Fred LaRue, assistant to Campaign Chairman
Mitchell, walked into Silbert's office, confessed, and offered to testify
against his superiors in exchange for a light sentence.

Thus McCord's letter to Judge Sirica breached the wall of silence—
opening the gates for the flood of witnesses and evidence to come. It had
been a near thing. Long after, Senator Sam Ervin reflected on the Wa-

tergate scandal and observed of the Nixon conspirators: "They almost got away with it."

Like most experienced politicians in Washington, House Republican Leader Jerry Ford was astonished at the hard-to-believe evidence that men close to his friend President Nixon had actually been involved in such a witless folly as Watergate. With his usual direct approach to a problem, Ford told an audience in his Michigan district: "The way to clear up Watergate is for John Mitchell, Bob Haldeman, John Dean, and any others who have said they were not involved in, and had no information on Watergate, to go before the Senate Committee, take an oath, and deny it publicly. They say they're innocent. They say they were not involved. Say it under oath."

His proposal, picked up by United Press International and read back in the White House, alarmed President Nixon. A few days later he invited his old friend and loyal supporter in Congress to the White House for a chat. With just the two of them in the quiet of the Oval Office, Nixon assured Ford that he had in no way been involved with the Watergate incident. The controversy, he said, was nothing more than political charges by Democrats, and he did not foresee any serious problem. With some embarrassment, Nixon added that he had been so involved in negotiations with China and the USSR that he had paid no attention to "inconsequential political things."

Ford rode back to his office in the Capitol convinced that the President was telling the truth. "You have to believe the President," he said, "and I did believe him. He had never lied to me."

In the spring of 1973 most Americans, like Congressman Ford, could not accept the possibility that their President had conspired in the Oval Office to commit a crime.

That would change over the next fifteen months, as witness by witness, revelation by revelation, the full story of Watergate began to unfold. Never before had the nation's capital witnessed, and endured, such a concatenation of events.

First, the grand jury, acting on evidence from Dean, Magruder, McCord, and other campaign officials cooperating as witnesses for the prosecution, indicted Haldeman, Ehrlichman, Mitchell, and Dean, among others. Consequently, Haldeman and Ehrlichman, the two men closest to President Nixon and best known to the public, were forced to resign in humiliation. At the same time, Dean was fired and Attorney General Kleindienst was compelled to resign. His own assistants had informed him that he was too closely connected personally and professionally with Mitchell to continue as Attorney General.

In a move to regain credibility, Nixon appointed a pillar of rectitude and integrity to be his new Attorney General. Elliott Richardson, then serving as Secretary of Defense, had outstanding credentials—former Attorney General of Massachusetts, former deputy Secretary of State, former HEW Secretary. He was reluctant to accept the appointment at first, and agreed only after a frank one-on-one discussion with Nixon. "I'm innocent," the President told Richardson. "If you don't believe I'm innocent, don't take the job." Richardson concluded Nixon was indeed innocent, or he would not have given him full control over the investigation. For public consumption, Nixon announced to the nation that he had commissioned the new Attorney General "to pursue this case wherever it leads." As for his part, Nixon pledged: "I will do everything in my power to ensure that the guilty are brought to justice."

Unconvinced, the Senate intervened. By voice vote on May 1, the Senate passed a bipartisan resolution calling on Nixon to appoint a "Special Prosecutor . . . from outside the Executive Branch" to handle the investigation and prosecution of Watergate. It was initiated by a Republican, Senator Charles Percy of Illinois, who said: "Should the executive branch investigate itself? I do not think so." To make sure of the Special Prosecutor's merit and independence, the appointee would require Senate confirmation.

At the time, Nixon raised no objection to the creation of an independent prosecutor. In fact, on May 9, he told a Republican gathering that Attorney General Richardson, and "the special prosecutor that he will appoint in this case will have the total cooperation of the Executive branch . . . [and] see to it that all those who are guilty will be prosecuted and are brought to justice. This is the pledge I make tonight."

On the surface, Nixon's public commitments seem curious. He knew he was guilty. Ehrlichman and Dean had told him that they, and he, could be indicted for obstructing justice. Why then would Nixon make a pledge that, if carried out, would invite his own prosecution? The answer was that the President was conflicted, deeply; and his actions reflect the nature of the man. He knew he was doomed, yet he kept clinging to the irrational hope that if he publicly affirmed and reaffirmed his innocence, somehow he might survive.

Logic told him he was finished. He said so. In despair on the day he terminated Haldeman and Ehrlichman at Camp David, he confided to Ron Ziegler, his loyal press secretary. "It's all over, Ron. Do you know that? . . . Well, it is. It's all over." Later that afternoon, as he worked on his first public address about Watergate with his trusted speechwriter, Ray Price, he suddenly turned to Price. "If you feel I should resign, I am ready to do so . . . Just put it in the next draft." Price said later that he became "very concerned about his state of mind."

But Nixon had no intention of resigning. Or admitting his own entanglement in Watergate. In *The Memoirs of Richard Nixon,* he wrote that all through that crucial day, April 30, 1973, he agonized over his dilemma and debated with himself about what he should do. "We recognized that we were marching headlong into a trap with no exits," he wrote. Yet he could not bring himself to surrender to his enemies, in "Congress, the bureaucracy, the media, the Washington Establishment . . . I felt that if in this speech I admitted any vulnerabilities, my opponents would savage me with them." So, he said, "I decided to answer no to the question whether I was also involved in Watergate." In politics as in life, a lie, once told, must be repeated; so with Nixon. From that point on, Nixon knew he must continue to lie, and he did, saying in private and in public what he knew to be untrue.

He misled his new Chief of Staff, General Alexander Haig. To replace Haldeman, Nixon had brought in a highly qualified man well known to him. Haig had served as Kissinger's deputy before returning to the Army as Vice Chief of Staff. Working with Haig, Nixon had found him to be a good soldier—confident and decisive, with a steely toughness and readiness to carry out Presidential decisions. Most importantly, he could count on Haig's loyalty.

When he asked Haig to accept the appointment, Nixon emphasized that he wanted Haig to manage the White House staff and operations; he and his lawyers would handle Watergate. Within days, Haig realized that this was not the President or the White House he had experienced in Nixon's first term; now, Watergate dominated. The scandal consumed the President's time, attention, and energy. When Haig saw that he too must deal with Watergate and its consequences, he acted to make sure he did not end up indicted like his predecessor. Haig brought in Fred Buzhardt, his friend and fellow West Point graduate, then serving as Counsel to the Defense Department, as his legal adviser. Both soldiers would see their courage and resolve tested in the momentous battles to come.

Late that spring of 1973, Ford became concerned that President Nixon was no longer making decisions on legislation and other issues critical to Congress and the administration. As House Republican Leader, he felt a responsibility to act, so he talked it over with Hugh Scott, his counterpart in the Senate. "We need to get some reliable people to go down there and straighten out the White House staff," he told Scott. Their first choices were Mel Laird and Bryce Harlow, who had left government to go into lucrative business life. Ford invited them to his Capitol office and made his appeal. "The President needs help. He needs your help. We need to end this desperate situation, and get him back on track. You two can do that. It's in his interest and the party's interest and the country's interest that he have the expertise and assistance you can bring him. Frankly, if you don't do this, we may have a catastrophe . . ."

Laird said no. "That's a jungle down there now, and that would not be a happy situation for me," he told Ford. To overcome Laird's reluctance, Ford enlisted the Democratic Leaders of Congress—Senator Mike Mansfield and Speaker Carl Albert. They too insisted to Laird and Harlow that the national interest required order and stability in the White House. "The government was at a standstill, they told me," Laird said. "No action from the White House on important bills, agriculture, health, among others. So Bryce and I agreed to go, on the condition that Nixon convinced us he had in no way been involved in Watergate."

They met with Nixon, who persuaded them he was innocent. On June 6, each was formally appointed a Counselor to the President. "It was a rough period," Laird said. "You would go in and see the President, and he was not really with you. It was like he was in a cocoon. So Bryce and I just made the decisions, yes on this bill, no on that one. Kissinger had a free hand to make foreign policy decisions in Nixon's name, and we made domestic decisions in his name. And he never challenged us."

Within a month, Laird said, "I found out that the President had lied to me about Watergate. I found out he had been involved from the beginning. But I couldn't just walk out. I had made a commitment to Albert and Mansfield as well as to Ford and Scott. And I realized that Bryce and I had to keep things going at least through December and the preparation of the next budget. Turned out a lot more happened than we expected."

The sequence of Watergate events quickened in early summer 1973; for the first time, the hard evidence of crime in the White House entered the public record. John Dean—by now notorious for having turned on the President—was expected to serve as a star witness before the Senate Watergate Committee. On June 25, he took the oath and matched his press notices. On his first day, he read a 245-page prepared statement, including the charge that President Nixon personally and repeatedly took part in the cover-up. Specifically, he said, the President discussed raising $1 million to meet the burglars' demands for money to remain silent. On another occasion, he testified, the President discussed clemency for the burglars if they refused to talk. He told how Nixon had sent for him on the day McCord's letter was read in court, and instructed him to analyze their situation and recommend actions to counter McCord's disclosures. He also described in detail how Haldeman, Ehrlichman, Colson, and Mitchell had taken part in the cover-up.

Calm, self-assured, articulate, the 34-year-old Dean mentioned briefly that he suspected the President may have taped one of their cover-up conversations. If it existed, he said, that tape would corroborate that part of his testimony. He also revealed to the Senate Committee the beginning of the Watergate break-in. In January 1972, he testified, he attended a meeting in Mitchell's office at the Justice Department where Liddy proposed a plan for bugging, mugging, entrapping, and kidnapping Democrats at their convention. After Mitchell told Liddy to revise the plan, Liddy came back a month later with a scaled-down version—a new scheme to spy on and disrupt the Democratic party, campaign, and candidate.

By the middle of the fourth day of Dean's testimony, the seven members of the Senate Committee had questioned Dean on a broad range of subjects. Most related to Watergate; others were random, often irrelevant—about demonstrators in Lafayette Park, tapping a columnist's phone, surveillance on critics. To Senator Baker, the committee cochairman, they were missing the central point of the Senate hearings. He was sure he knew the right question to ask Dean and any other witness. So, when it was his turn at the microphone at the afternoon session, Baker looked Dean in the eye and put this question about the Watergate burglary and cover-up: what did the President know, and when did he know it?

It was the essence of discovery. It was exactly what the Senate Committee and much of America wanted to know. Consequently, Baker's question marked the next turning point in Watergate. Dean did not have the answer to what Nixon knew about Watergate and when he knew it—but another witness did.

On Friday, July 13, 1973, a staff investigator for the Republicans on the Senate Committee, Don Sanders, spent part of a sultry afternoon in a tiny Senate office interrogating Alexander Butterfield, a retired Air Force colonel responsible for White House communications and records. Sanders had been wondering who was telling the truth: President Nixon in his denials of any involvement in Watergate, or Dean under oath on the witness stand. Remembering that Dean had testified that he suspected one of his discussions with the President might have been taped, Sanders asked Butterfield: "Is it possible that Dean knew what he was talking about?"

For a long moment Butterfield was silent. Then he said quietly: "There is tape in each of the President's offices. It is kept by the Secret Service, and only four other men know about it. Dean had no way of knowing about it. He was just guessing."

Sanders was stunned. He immediately telephoned Fred Thompson, Baker's chief counsel, and Thompson notified Baker. This new break in the case could not wait; Butterfield was called to the stand on Monday, July 16. Questioned by Thompson, Butterfield revealed that President Nixon had, since 1971, recorded all conversations and telephone calls in the Oval Office, the Nixon hideaway in the Old Executive Office Building, the Cabinet Room, and the Nixon study in the Aspen Lodge at Camp David.

The secret was out: the President had taped himself.

Rarely had Washington been so surprised. To people across the country, many of whom had watched the Senate hearings on live television, the news was puzzling, baffling, or intriguing. Why would a President tape-record everything he said? Ego? To document history? To write books? There was no precise answer, but for more than two years, President Nixon had recorded both his statesmanlike views on world affairs and the scheming to win in 1972 by whatever actions, lawful or not, were necessary.

In the pivotal moment when Butterfield exposed the Nixon tapes, Watergate was transformed. From that time on, the tapes were the prize to be sought—by prosecutors and press, and by a curious and somewhat bemused public.

To President Nixon, in Bethesda Naval Hospital being treated for viral pneumonia, Butterfield's disclosure was a disaster. Destroy the tapes, Vice President Agnew advised. Keep them to show you are innocent, lawyers Garment and Buzhardt counseled; and let us listen to them to organize your defense. "No! Never!" Nixon replied. "No, no, no!" His aides had never seen him so vehement. Haig began to wonder if the president was concerned about Constitutional separation of powers, or had something to hide.

The legal battle over the White House tapes began three days after Butterfield had revealed the secret. To begin, Ervin and Baker wrote the President formally requesting that he provide their Senate Committee with tapes and documents relevant to their investigation. That same day, Special Prosecutor Cox also wrote to ask the President for tapes he needed for his investigation.

Nixon, back in the White House, having been released from the hospital, debated with himself about what he should do. In an act of self-serving reasoning, he wrote a memo to himself: "If I had discussed illegal action, I would not have taped." But he was not certain. On one hand, the tapes could disprove Dean's testimony that he conspired in obstruction of justice. Yet other discussions, particularly with Haldeman, would be hard to explain. He decided he would not destroy the tapes; Haig had persuaded him that destroying the tapes would convince everyone—the courts, Congress, the public—that the President was guilty.

In the end, Nixon wrote, "I simply was not sure what was on the tapes." Fear determined his course; fear of offering "a tantalizing lure" to his Democratic enemies; fear that the tapes might show evidence of his collusion in Watergate. On his bedside notepad he wrote with grim prescience: "Tapes—once start, no stopping."

So Nixon claimed executive privilege, recognizing that "most people [would] think executive privilege was just a cloak that I drew around me to protect myself from the disclosure of my wrongdoing."

To the letters from Ervin and Baker and the Senate Watergate Committee, and from Special Prosecutor Cox, Nixon said no. "I cannot and will not consent to giving any investigative body private Presidential papers."

Their polite request refused, the Senate Committee voted unanimously to subpoena the tapes and documents it needed. By the legal act of subpoenaing the President, as Senator Baker observed, the two sides had "come to the brink of a Constitutional confrontation . . . between the Congress and the White House." That same day, Cox—for himself and a new Watergate grand jury—asked Judge Sirica to sign a subpoena for the tapes. Thus, for the second time, the Watergate scandal reached Sirica's Court. He signed the subpoena and two Cox assistants served it on White House lawyers.

Nixon, informed by Haig of the subpoenas, was outraged. Not only was the Democratic Congress out to destroy him, he said, but the Special Prosecutor appointed by his own Attorney General had turned against him. Inform Richardson, he instructed Haig, that if Cox continues to make such demands, then Richardson might have to dismiss him. Furthermore, he made clear, he would not comply with either subpoena. Affirming his position in a formal reply to Judge Sirica, Nixon wrote: "The President is not subject to compulsory process from the courts."

By Nixon's action, at the end of July 1973, the three Constitutional branches of the U.S. government had reached an impasse. Not for a tumultuous year would it be resolved.

On Saturday, August 4, 1973, Ford, Laird, and twenty House Members flew to Groton, Connecticut, to attend the laying of the keel for the nuclear submarine, *Glennard Lipscomb*. Before his death two years earlier, Lipscomb had been a House colleague and close friend of Ford and Laird.

On the flight back to Washington, the two talked about Watergate, Nixon, and his predicament. "You think things are bad now," Laird said grimly. "They're going to get worse." Vice President Agnew, he hinted, had a serious legal problem of his own.

The facts, known to few inside the White House, were ominous. A month before, George Beall, U.S. Attorney in Baltimore, had driven to Washington to inform Attorney General Richardson that he had witnesses and evidence sufficient to prosecute Agnew for extortion and taking bribes, and he intended to do so. Agnew had committed crimes as Governor of Maryland, Beall said, and had even taken envelopes of cash in the office of the Vice President. Richardson informed the President, who said he would do nothing to intervene, and left the problem in Richardson's hands.

Richardson, on his own and in the privacy of his office, weighed the situation in his own logical way. First, the President himself might be forced from office; Richardson had seen enough evidence of Nixon's involvement in Watergate to believe he might well be impeached. Second, the Vice President is a felon, and would soon be indicted, and probably convicted. Third, the country could not accept the risk of a felon succeeding a dishonored President. Therefore, Agnew must be forced to leave office before Congress acts on Nixon. Richardson felt it would be his responsibility, as Attorney General, to persuade the Vice President to resign. He decided to arrange a plea bargain for Agnew: resignation in exchange for no prosecution.

With Nixon's approval of a deal, Richardson approached Agnew; but Agnew resisted, stubbornly, angrily. He insisted he was innocent, and claimed the charges were politically motivated. Richardson, in his methodical way, did his best to persuade the Vice President that he should accept a plea bargain, but Agnew held out. After two months of wrangling, it was Haig who made it happen. Very simply, he threatened Agnew, sending the explicit message: "the President has a lot of power—don't forget that."

Agnew did not want to go; but he did want to live. "His remark sent a chill through my body," Agnew wrote later. "I feared for my life. If a decision had been made to eliminate me—through an automobile accident, a fake suicide, or whatever—the order would not have been traced back to the White House any more than the 'get Castro' orders were ever traced to their source." He did not doubt that Haig could have him killed.

Agnew's strong sense of Greek fatalism told him he must accept the inevitable. So he sent his lawyers back to his prosecutors to negotiate a deal. He agreed to resign and plead no contest to a felony charge that he had not paid income taxes. For the record, the prosecution placed before the Court a forty-page document, detailing the charges against Agnew and evidence that over the previous six years he had taken bribes and kickbacks of more than $100,000. Agnew could have been indicted and brought to trial, Richardson pointed out to the Court, but the greater national interest was not to prosecute Agnew but to remove him from the Vice Presidency.

So Agnew resigned, in a one-sentence letter, delivered at 2:05 p.m. on October 10, 1973, to Secretary of State Kissinger.

At that moment the country had no Vice President. At the beginning of the Republic, and for almost 200 years, there had been no way to fill a vacancy in the second office. Fifteen Presidents before Nixon—James Madison, Andrew Jackson, John Tyler, Millard Fillmore, Franklin Pierce, Andrew Johnson, Ulysses S. Grant, Chester Arthur, Grover Cleveland, William McKinley, Theodore Roosevelt, William Howard

Taft, Calvin Coolidge, Harry Truman, and Lyndon Johnson—governed at some point without a Vice President. Over the years, Congress kept changing the line of succession: at first it was the President pro tempore of the Senate; later, the Secretary of State; from 1947 on, the next in line was the Speaker of the House.

After the death of President Kennedy, Senator Birch Bayh led Congress in passing the Twenty-Fifth Amendment to the Constitution. Ratified in 1967, it provided that the President would nominate a person to fill a vacancy in the Vice Presidency, with the requirement that he or she be confirmed by both the House and Senate before taking office. In concept, Bayh testified, a President should nominate a member of his own party, "compatible in temperament and view with the President." Since a nominee would not be elected by the people, Bayh said, the two Houses of Congress "would represent all of the people in our country, in what can accurately be called a Congressional election of the new Vice President." Congress, representing the electorate, would judge the nominee's character and qualifications to succeed to the Presidency, Bayh said, "acting as a surrogate electoral body for the people."

Thus, on October 10, 1973, for the first time, a President and Congress would turn to the Constitution's Twenty-Fifth Amendment to elect the person next in line to become President.

Well before Agnew agreed to resign, Nixon had made his choice for his new Vice President: John Connally. Nixon had long been infatuated—politically and personally—with the former Democratic governor of Texas and political ally of President Johnson. And Connally was an impressive public figure. Tall and charismatic, he exuded confidence, strength, and authority. So impressed was Nixon by Connally that in 1971 he made him Secretary of the Treasury, and privy counselor. The next year, Nixon secretly schemed to dump Agnew from the ticket and, at the 1972 Republican National Convention, name Connally as the nominee for Vice President.

Mitchell stopped him, pointing out to Nixon that it would be a wrong political move, damaging to his own chances to be reelected. Agnew, by bombastic speeches that amused and agitated Republican audiences, had become a folk hero to Republican conservatives. In fact, polls indicated Agnew was their favorite for nomination in 1976, well ahead of Ronald Reagan. Consequently, Nixon accepted Mitchell's judgment that he could not replace Agnew in 1972, but he continued to harbor the idea.

With Agnew on the way out early in 1973—either by Nixon's design or Agnew's own proclivities, or both—Nixon saw a new opportunity to bring in Connally as his Vice President. On May 1, Nixon persuaded Connally to switch to the Republican Party, and in September arranged for him to make a campaign tour of Republican leaders around the country. Questioned by *Newsweek*'s Hal Bruno as to whether he would accept the Vice Presidency, Connally replied: "Yes, but only on my terms. That is, I would . . . [take] charge of the entire economic scene. Then I would ride into the '76 Convention as the Vice President who saved the economy." Upon returning from his campaign swing, Connally opened an office in the Mayflower Hotel in Washington to await his nomination.

When Richardson informed the President on October 9 that Agnew had agreed to resign, Nixon was ready to carry out his plan. He summoned Laird and Harlow, informed them that he intended to nominate Connally to be the new Vice President, and instructed them to meet with Congressional leaders as the first step in preparing for his confirmation by Congress.

Laird and Harlow, anticipating Nixon's intent to nominate Connally, had already tested the idea on Capitol Hill. Never one to suppress his views, Laird was blunt: "Mr. President, we cannot get Connally confirmed. It will be a disaster."

"I disagree with you," Nixon said. "Connally is the best qualified, and he is my choice."

"Mr. President," Harlow said, "John's qualifications are not in question. Your Presidency is our concern. With Congress already antagonistic over Watergate, we consider it unwise for you to risk a second battle over Connally."

The President persisted. He told his counselors he intended to nominate Connally.

"We cannot help," Laird insisted. "It is an impossible assignment."

Nixon would not give up. He insisted that Laird and Harlow go back to the Capitol to talk to the leaders of Congress. They agreed, but only if Nixon would agree to bring in the Democratic and Republican leaders of the House and Senate before he sent up a name for confirmation.

Determined to have his way, Nixon dispatched Tom Korologos—his most knowledgeable assistant dealing with the Senate—to inform Senator Robert Byrd, Deputy Minority Leader, that he intended to nominate Connally. Korologos met Byrd by the Ohio Clock in the south corridor outside the Senate chamber, and asked the Democratic leader to evaluate Connally's chances of confirmation in the Senate.

Byrd pointed toward the chamber. "Tom," he said, "tell my friend Dick Nixon that if he sends Connally's name to the Senate, blood will be running out from under that Senate door."

At the same time, across the Capitol dome and just off the House floor, Harlow met with Speaker Albert. Harlow told Albert of Nixon's plan to nominate Connally. "Bryce," Albert replied, "John Connally is my friend. But the Democrats in the House don't think much of him changing his colors. The House will not confirm Connally, and you can tell the President that."

After a pause he added: "If the President wants to know who would be the first choice of the House, it would be Jerry Ford."

Harlow reported his conversation with Albert to Nixon, and added that House Republicans were enthusiastically signing a petition, drafted by John Byrnes and Barber Conable, supporting Ford for Vice President.

With great reluctance Nixon accepted Congress's rejection of his choice and instructed Haig to telephone Connally at the Mayflower Hotel. "Tell him that, while he still remained my first choice, I was very seriously concerned whether he could survive a confirmation battle." Connally accepted his rejection with grace. He told Haig his Democratic friends in the House had already informed him that he could not be confirmed.

For all their political acumen, neither Connally nor Nixon had anticipated the reaction among professional politicians to Connally's party switch. To Congressional Democrats he was a turncoat, renegade, traitor. To Republicans Connally was an intruder, uninvited and unwelcome, a usurper who had no record in their party and no place in their party.

Denied his first choice, Nixon instructed Haig to telephone Ford and invite him to come at once to the White House. On the ride down Pennsylvania Avenue to the White House, Ford assumed that the President wanted to update him on the Yom Kippur War, with Israel defending against a two-front attack by Egypt and Syria, or maybe he had an urgent legislative problem. The two met, at Nixon's invitation, in the President's hideaway office in the Executive Office Building (EOB) where he read, meditated, and set down his thoughts on yellow legal pads. Ford walked in to find Nixon completely at ease in sport coat and slacks, smoking a pipe, with his feet propped up on an ottoman.

Ford mentioned that he had never before seen Nixon smoking a pipe. "Well, Jerry, I do it when I'm alone, or want to relax, or I'm talking to someone like you—an old friend."

As Ford took a big chair opposite and lit his pipe, Nixon asked about Betty and the Ford children. Ford, in turn, asked about Pat and the Nixon daughters. After family talk, Nixon got to the point. "Jerry, we've got a serious problem. The Vice President is in serious difficulty." At length Nixon described Agnew's plight: as Baltimore County Executive, his first public office, Agnew had taken bribes from contractors doing business with the county. As Governor of Maryland, he had continued taking bribes and kickbacks; even as Vice President, he had accepted an envelope of money in the Vice President's office in the EOB. Ford knew some of the story, but as Nixon talked on and on about Agnew's crimes, he began to wonder why Nixon was investing so much time in telling him about them. At one point Ford thought he was wasting the President's time and stood up to go. Nixon waved him back to the chair, and Ford concluded that the Vice President's criminality was deeply troubling to the President and he needed to unburden himself by sharing his concern with an old friend.

After what seemed like hours, a White House aide brought Ford a message: A House vote was about to begin. With a warm handshake, Nixon thanked Ford for coming and listening. Ford rode back to the Capitol, puzzled about why Nixon had spent hours telling him about Agnew's dismal record of corruption and legal difficulties. He hurried to the floor to vote, and was watching the tally from the Minority Leader's seat when a fellow Michigan Republican raced up to say: "Jerry, have you heard? Agnew resigned."

Suddenly the morning meeting was clear to Ford: Nixon had been evaluating him as a candidate for Vice President, testing their friendship and assuring himself of Ford's loyalty.

Moments later, Joe Waggoner, a Democrat from Louisiana, walked over to Ford's chair. "Jerry, how would you like to be Vice President?" Ford considered the question and the questioner. Waggoner, a leader of

Southern conservatives who often supported Nixon, had considerable influence in the White House. "Well, Joe, it would be a good way to end my political career."

"I'm going to call the President," Waggoner said.

"Go ahead," Ford said.

In the White House later that day, Nixon followed the advice of Laird and Harlow, and talked to the Congressional leaders. First to arrive were Republicans: from the Senate, Minority Leader Hugh Scott and Minority Whip Robert Griffin; from the House, Minority Whip Leslie Arends, and Ford—there for the second time that day. The President told them he wanted every Republican in the House and Senate to submit three names, ranked in order, for the nomination. He had already asked George H. W. Bush, Chairman of the Republican National Committee, to collect recommendations from all members of the Republican National Committee (RNC), he said. All suggestions were to be delivered to Rose Mary Woods, his trusted secretary, in the White House by 6:00 p.m. the next day.

In mid-afternoon Nixon personally telephoned Senate Majority Leader Mike Mansfield, then Speaker Albert, and asked them to come to the White House to discuss prospective choices for Vice President and the Congressional process of confirmation. The three—each a ruler of a realm of the whole, met in the Oval Office at 6:07 p.m. After customary handshakes and greetings, they moved to the couches at the rear, and President Nixon brought forth the serious business at hand. "The Vice President has resigned," Nixon said, "and under the Twenty-Fifth Amendment it is my responsibility to move quickly to nominate a Vice President. I believe it is my right to select someone of my own party, and I have asked for Republican leaders in Congress and across the country to suggest names for consideration, and I would be glad to consider any suggestions you may have." Turning to the Speaker, he said: "Carl, are you interested in it?"

Albert was surprised. He thought the President was either trying to flatter him, or making a comment about his well-advertised dislike of being constantly watched and guarded by a cadre of thirty-six Secret Service agents—assigned to him as next in line of succession. With a chuckle, the Speaker replied: "No, no, Mr. President. Not at all. I came to Washington to be a Congressman."

"As far as I am concerned, Carl, you would be a fine nominee except for political considerations. Is there somebody who you think would be a good choice?"

"No, that's your job, Mr. President."

"I do," Mansfield broke in. "I can name two persons who would be good. One is Bill Rogers [former Secretary of State], and the other is [Senator] John Sherman Cooper."

"If Mike is going to make a suggestion," Albert said, "then I'm going to make a suggestion."

"Who is it?" Nixon asked. "Jerry Ford?"

"Yes sir, Jerry Ford," Albert said. "And I'm going to tell you something, Mr. President. He will be the easiest man that I know of to confirm in the House of Representatives. There just isn't any question in my mind but that he will be confirmed. And it would not be a long, drawn-out matter."

Nixon turned to Mansfield. With an affirmative nod, he said: "Ford would be a good choice." Would he be confirmed in the Senate? Another affirmative nod. "Yes."

Nixon made no commitment but said he would act promptly to send up the nomination. "As I study the Twenty-Fifth Amendment, I believe it contemplates that the country should have a Vice President at all times, that the security and stability of the government demands it," he said. "I would like your assurance that Congress will move as expeditiously as possible." Mansfield and Albert committed to do so. The three briefly discussed Congress' responsibility to proceed for the first time under this part of the Constitution: committees would examine the nominee's qualifications, hold hearings on his views of policy and governing, and decide by vote whether he should become Vice President.

The meeting ended after twenty-three minutes. In that brief session, the two leaders of Congress—both Democrats—made an historic decision. By advising Nixon on the one person Congress would confirm quickly, they made Gerald Ford the next Vice President.

Ford was Albert's first and only choice. Albert considered Mansfield's suggested nominees to be acceptable candidates, but in his opinion, neither was as well qualified as Ford. And he was not sure that either had the merit or the standing in the House to be confirmed. Confirming a Presidential appointment would be a new and unprecedented challenge to the House, and Albert had been thinking about how to handle it since he first learned from Elliot Richardson, weeks earlier, that Agnew would be indicted. With Watergate a threat to the President, Albert was convinced that a vacancy in the line of succession imperiled the stability of the Federal establishment, so he had decided well before Agnew's resignation—and this meeting with the President—that he, as House leader, would do his best to fill that void as quickly as possible.

Facing the President in the Oval Office, Albert had not expected to be asked to suggest a nominee, and was surprised when Mansfield did. In that instant, Albert decided he must propose his better qualified and certain-to-be-confirmed man. Sitting there with the President, he thought of the growing number of Democrats coming into his office to demand the impeachment of this President, and the thought of their pressure reaffirmed his earlier conviction that the country could not afford an extended confirmation battle or, even worse, a rejection of the President's nominee; therefore, he made a point of emphasizing that Ford was the House's choice. He knew how much House Members of both parties respected Ford for his ability, integrity, and trustworthiness; he was certain they would be eager to confirm one of their own. Once Mansfield gave his approval, Albert was sure he had done the right thing in suggesting Ford.

Both Albert and Mansfield said later that they became aware during their meeting with the President that afternoon that they were giving Nixon no choice but Ford. Neither planned it. Circumstances brought it about. Yet both had more in mind. Each said later that he had already seen enough Watergate evidence against the President to believe he would be forced from office; consequently, and separately, Albert and Mansfield knew at the time that they were in fact deciding that Ford would become the next President.

"It wasn't a case of Ford being picked by Nixon," Mansfield said of the momentous discussion he and Albert had with the President. "It was a case of keeping the institution of the Congress, both bodies, in mind as to what its reaction would be. In fact, Ford was *elected* to the Vice Presidency, by the House and Senate."

"We gave Nixon no choice but Ford," Albert said. "Congress made Jerry Ford President."

In his own circuitous way, Nixon affirmed that reality. Looking back eighteen years later, Nixon remembered that party leaders recommended to him—in order—Nelson Rockefeller, Ronald Reagan, John Connally, and Gerald Ford. "Ford, however, was first choice among members of Congress," he wrote, "and they were the ones who would have to approve the man I nominated . . . In view of my own weak political position at that time, confirmability had to be a major consideration in my decision . . . Ford's confirmability gave him an edge which the others could not match and was the decisive factor in my final decision."

Nixon also acknowledged that at the time of his meeting with Albert and Mansfield, he was well aware that the candidate they recommended might take his place. With evidence of his complicity in Watergate mounting, and his support in Congress disintegrating, Nixon said, "I felt that as a political realist there was at least a fifty percent chance that Ford might become President."

As soon as the President's meeting with the Democratic leaders ended, Laird and Harlow went in to the Oval Office to find out who the Democrats had recommended. Nixon told them their choice was Ford, but asked: "How do you know Ford would accept?"

Laird volunteered to ask Ford, and assumed he would accept. "I know we can get Ford through both the House and Senate," Laird said, "and, Mr. President, we need to get this over with."

Nixon turned to Harlow. "Mr. President," Harlow said, "I agree with Mel. We must get this done."

Ford, after his busy day on the Hill and two trips to the White House, was relaxing at home with Betty, having a quiet drink, and discussing the day's events when Laird telephoned.

"Jerry, I am calling to find out if you were asked, would you accept the Vice Presidency. I need your answer tonight. So talk to Betty and call me back. Tonight."

Betty Ford thought first of their children, and how it might affect them. Mike, then 23, was doing well at Gordon Conwell Seminary. Jack, 21, was at Utah State studying forestry. Steve, 17, and Susan, 16, were still in high school. "Not one of them would like being watched by the Secret Service," she said.

Ford initially thought he should say no. "I was reluctant to give up my role in influencing major legislation to take a job that was largely ceremonial," he said. "I was used to working at a fast pace, and I knew that most of the time, a Vice President is idle."

As the two talked for a couple of hours, Ford's loyalty to President Nixon and to his beloved Republican Party changed his mind. He had never turned down a Presidential assignment, Democratic or Republican: this was a call to duty. Furthermore, Ford decided, it would be an honor; recognition by his peers of his service to the party and the country. "Since I'm not ever going to be Speaker, it would be a nice cap for my career," he told Betty. She agreed. But both were skeptical that he would be asked.

With his mind made up, Ford telephoned Laird. "Mel, Betty and I have talked. If I am asked, I will accept. I will do what the President asks, but I will not conduct a campaign for the job. You know that Betty and I have already decided that we will get out of politics in January of 1977, and we are looking forward to that time and a new life."

Laird thanked Ford and called the President. "I talked to Jerry and he will accept," Laird said. "You should also know that Jerry has promised Betty he will get out of politics after January 1977."

That last point was not lost on Nixon. Before he made an announcement, Nixon invited Ford back to the Oval Office, this time for one firm understanding. "Jerry, I'm going to nominate you for Vice President," he said. "But there is one thing I want you to know. Come '76, I am going to campaign to nominate John Connally to be President."

"Mr. President, that's no problem for me," Ford said. "I have no further political ambitions." In fact, he added, he and Betty had firm plans to quit politics at the end of the President's term. Furthermore, Ford said, "I think John Connally would be a first-class candidate. We met at a golf tournament in Palm Springs four or five months ago, and I urged him to run and said I might support him."

Nixon, delighted to hear that, told Ford that after confirmation, he wanted him to concentrate on domestic legislation, energy policy, and Republican politics.

Ford readily agreed. "That sounds fine to me."

In his limousine riding back to the Hill, Ford wondered what Nixon's reaction might have been if he had said he intended to run for President in 1976. Bemused, he thought: "Would he have changed his mind?"

President Nixon staged the announcement of Ford's nomination as a political show produced for live, prime-time television. Into the East Room he brought the Cabinet, the leadership and committee chairman and ranking members of the Senate and House, the expanded White House staff, and other powers in Washington for a state occasion. After a full display of self-serving oratory—"It is vital that we turn away from the obsessions of the past and turn to the great challenges of the future . . ."—Nixon reverted to a hoary "man-who" convention cliché: "My nominee is a man who has served for twenty five years in the House . . ." When everyone turned to Ford and began applauding, Nixon raised his hands to stop the demonstration. "Ladies and gentlemen," he said with mock sternness, "please don't be premature. There are several here who have served twenty-five years in the House." After more minutes of lame attempts at suspense, Nixon proclaimed: "Our distinguished guests and my fellow Americans, I proudly present to you . . . Congressman Gerald Ford of Michigan."

A standing ovation brought Ford to the podium, and for the first time, Americans saw and heard his plain words and flat midwestern voice. He had written his brief remarks in longhand late that afternoon. "Mr. President, . . . I pledge to you and I pledge to my colleagues in the Congress, and I pledge to the American people, that to the best of my ability—if confirmed by my colleagues in the Congress—that I will do my utmost to the best of my ability to serve this country well and to perform those duties that will be my new assignment as effectively and as efficiently and with as much accomplishment as possible . . ." It was pure Ford—earnest, redundant, gravely responsive to the call of duty.

Riding home with Betty, driven and protected by the Secret Service for the first time, Ford was puzzled. How strange it was, he said, that the President turned the occasion of naming a substitute for a felonious Vice President into such a celebration. Not once had Agnew's name been mentioned. "The ceremony was oddly exuberant," he said to his wife. "It had all the trappings and the hoopla of a political convention."

Back in his split-level house, Ford learned that two former Vice Presidents had called and left messages of congratulation. Hubert Humphrey had long been a good Democratic friend, and Ford thanked him. Out of compassion for a fallen and disgraced fellow politician, Ford also telephoned Agnew: "I want you to know how sorry I am that events worked out this way."

CHAPTER 9

Confirmation

With Ford's nomination, events moved swiftly on three parallel courses. In the House, on the morning after Nixon made the announcement, Bella Abzug, a splenetic New Yorker representing lower Manhattan, barged into the office of Speaker Albert. "Get off your goddamned ass," she yelled, "We can take this Presidency." Towering over the five-foot Speaker, she punched him in the chest to emphasize the force of her words: "Why in the hell are you going to let Ford get this thing? We can get control and keep control!"

Abzug—an accomplished lawyer as well as an irascible termagant, had appointed herself the leader of a score and more of Far Left Democratic Members who were plotting a Constitutional coup. Their scheme was to delay Ford's confirmation until after Nixon's impeachment, thereby making Speaker Albert the President.

Abzug was serious. She advanced her polemic in an op-ed article in the *New York Times:* "Under the Succession Act of 1947, we already have an elected official designated to replace the President in the absence of a Vice President. The Speaker of the House is just as well qualified to stand around and wait as is House Minority Leader Ford . . . Does anyone seriously think the American people would select Gerald Ford as their President, if they had a chance?" Dismissing the clear purpose of the Twenty-Fifth Amendment, she wrote: "Only after the House Judiciary Committee [decides] whether a bill of impeachment should be returned against the President would it be proper for the committee to take up the question of who shall be Vice President."

Abzug was not alone in her determination to take over the government. Two doctrinaire liberal Members from California—wily Philip

Burton and ambitious Jerome Waldie—were plotting on their own to block Ford's appointment. An eastern faction, led by Joseph Moakley of Massachusetts, signed a petition to postpone confirming Ford until Nixon released the tapes. Others—Elizabeth Holtzman, Charles Rangel, John Conyers, Robert Drinan, John Seiberling—pressed the House investigating team to find something in Ford's record or character or competence to block his confirmation.

To Albert, a coup was unthinkable. He did not want to be President; he had never wanted the job, and did not want it now. More importantly, in his political judgment, the people of the United States would not accept a Democratic takeover of the White House. "The country had re-elected Nixon by a landslide less than a year before, and we could not veto an election," he said. "This faction of my party—too few to carry the House but too many and too vocal to ignore—could do irreparable damage to the United States. If I let them get out of hand, it would cause a permanent division in the country."

The insurgents also confronted Peter Rodino, Chairman of the House Judiciary Committee. Rodino's committee would be responsible for both Ford's confirmation and, if it came to that, the impeachment of President Nixon. "There was pressure, heavy pressure, some of it from my own committee members," Rodino said. "They wanted to delay the confirmation so that if we went ahead with impeaching Nixon there would be a vacancy and the Democratic Speaker would take over."

Rodino consulted Speaker Albert about how to prevent an open revolt. He found Albert adamant. "Taking over the Presidency was the furthest thing from the Speaker's mind," Rodino said. "He told me: 'Move as fast as you can. Proceed in a proper way, but move as fast as you can.'"

To deal with the insurgents, they agreed to Abzug's demand that the question of which would take priority—confirmation or impeachment—be brought before the full caucus of House Democrats. There, in an impassioned speech, Rodino appealed to his fellow Members' sense of responsibility. "How wrong it would be for us to go down the road that some are advocating," he said. "We must not stand in the way of the Constitutional process. The President, whether we like it or not, has the right—even if he is under a cloud—the right and the power to make the nomination, and we have a responsibility to evaluate it and judge it and reach a conclusion. The responsible thing for us to do is to proceed with the confirmation."

Since the House had never before undertaken a confirmation, Rodino told his caucus: "We must establish a precedent. First, we will undertake a complete investigation of the nominee. Then we will hold hearings. We will complete a fair proceeding and come out with a resolution to place before the full House for a vote. That is our responsibility, and we must go forward and meet our obligation under the Constitution."

Rodino won the support of the Democrats' caucus, by a strong margin, but only after accepting the insurgents' compromise: hearings on Ford would not begin until after the FBI had completed its full field investigation of his background. That meant that for six weeks or longer, Albert would remain next in line to become President.

In the White House, Nixon raged at his enemies as he battled to repel the powers demanding his tapes. He had defied subpoenas from the Senate Watergate Committee. He had defied Judge Sirica's order to turn over tapes to Special Prosecutor Cox, but his wall of executive privilege was crumbling. The Court of Appeals upheld Sirica, ruling that the President must give nine Watergate tapes to Cox.

To Nixon, that would be a disaster. He had listened to enough of the tapes to know that they contained indisputable evidence that he was personally involved in the Watergate cover-up. He would not even permit his own lawyers, Leonard Garment and Fred Buzhardt, to listen to them; he was afraid they might feel it their legal duty to report evidence to the court. In a dilemma, Nixon asked for options. Buzhardt suggested three: reject the Circuit Court decision on grounds of separation of powers, permit his attorneys to negotiate with Cox, or fire Cox as Special Prosecutor.

To make his decision, Nixon flew to Camp David. There, debating with himself, he listed his choices on a yellow legal pad. If he refused the court order it would cost him heavily in public support, and the polls already showed that one in three Americans thought he should resign. If he accepted the court order, and released the nine tapes to Cox, then surely Cox would only demand more. Cox was the problem, he decided; therefore, Cox must go. "Firing him seemed to be the only way to rid the administration of the partisan viper we had planted in our bosom," Nixon wrote.

In Aspen Lodge, scribbling on his pad, Nixon devised his plan: First, he would order Richardson to fire Cox and have the Justice Department manage the investigation of Watergate. If there were no Cox, he rationalized, there would be no more subpoenas for tapes. Second, he would not reject the court order, but provide Sirica summaries—not transcripts—of the subpoenaed tapes. His lawyers would draft the summaries and submit them to a highly respected Senator—John Stennis of Mississippi, a Democrat and former judge, to evaluate and certify to be accurate.

From the first, Nixon's plan went awry. On Friday, October 19, 1973, Haig told Richardson that the President wanted him to fire Cox. Richardson replied that he would have to resign too, as he had pledged under oath during his Senate confirmation that Cox would be fired only for "extraordinary improprieties." Informed of Richardson's response, Nixon backed off. He could not afford to lose Richardson, so he told Haig to ask Richardson to persuade Cox to accept the Stennis compromise. Cox refused, stating that as Special Prosecutor he could accept no limits in seeking evidence of criminal acts resulting from Watergate.

The next day, Nixon decided to force Cox's hand. He told Haig to have the press office announce the Stennis plan and state that he had ordered Cox to ask for no more tapes or documents. As soon as this news reached Cox, he invited reporters to his office. "I cannot be a party to such an agreement," he announced. "Will you resign?" one reporter asked. "Hell, no!" Cox said. He told reporters he might even ask the court to hold Nixon "guilty of contempt."

Nixon, enraged by Cox's defiance and open threat, told Haig to call Richardson at once and order him to fire Cox. "I can't do that," Richardson replied. He said he must see the President at once.

Arriving at the White House, he was swiftly escorted to the Oval Office. There, President Nixon emphasized the danger that the United States might be drawn into the open warfare in the Middle East, and he pleaded: "Delay [your] resignation in order not to trigger a domestic crisis at such a critical time for us abroad."

Richardson was moved. He was deeply concerned about Israel's battle against Egypt and Syria, and the risk that the United States and the USSR might be brought into direct military confrontation. But he gravely reminded President Nixon that he had accepted the responsibility to be Attorney General only after Nixon had given his word that he would have independence of judgment and action, and so would the Special Prosecutor he appointed. As that commitment was not being honored, he said to Nixon: "I feel I have no choice but to go forward with this."

"Be it on your head," Nixon replied in anger, evoking Pontius Pilate, and accused Richardson of acting "on a purely personal commitment rather than the national interest."

In reply, Richardson said that justice was also in the national interest, and left the Oval Office.

As Richardson headed back to the Justice Department to turn in his resignation, Haig telephoned William Ruckelshaus, the Deputy Attorney General. The President orders you to fire Cox, Haig said. Ruckleshaus refused, said he would resign, and suggested that Haig hand the assignment to the next in line of authority—Solicitor General Robert Bork.

Put Bork on the phone, Haig ordered. Bork agreed to perform the deed. Brought to the White House and brevetted Acting Attorney General, Bork fired Cox.

At 8:25 that Saturday evening, Press Secretary Ron Ziegler summoned the press to an extraordinary press conference and handed out four banner headlines: Cox fired. Richardson resigns. Ruckleshaus fired. The office of Special Prosecutor abolished.

Ford, at home that Saturday night, was shocked by what Nixon had done. "I assumed the President was innocent," he said. "He had told me so and I believed him. But I could not understand why he would not turn over the documents that proved his innocence. Why had he precipitated another crisis? I thought it was just politically dumb."

On Sunday morning Haig telephoned Ford to relay Nixon's side of the story: the President was so concerned about the war in the Middle East that he thought Richardson and Ruckelshaus had let him down by causing an unnecessary domestic crisis. Haig said Nixon had to dismiss Cox, who had rejected a reasonable compromise that preserved Executive Privilege.

As Ford hung up the phone he began to wonder: Is it possible that the documents Cox wanted contain evidence against the President? If so, that would explain why he had to fire Cox.

The "Saturday Night Massacre"—as the avid Washington press corps called the stunning news of that evening—ended any chance Nixon might ever have had of surviving Watergate. Until then, with the tapes still locked in a room in the basement of the EOB, he could count on a loose but loyal alliance in the House and Senate to protect him. They considered his involvement in Watergate, whatever it was, embarrassing and dumb, but not impeachable. But Nixon's decapitation of the Justice Department left little doubt about his guilt. Senator Robert Byrd, Deputy Democratic Leader, articulated the obvious: "There is no way to avoid the assumption that the President is trying to conceal evidence."

In the House, the reaction was unprecedented. From Sunday morning on, telephone calls jammed the Capitol switchboard. Telegrams overloaded and then choked Western Union's lines. By the best count, three million Americans telephoned, telegraphed, or wrote their Representatives to condemn the President's action. Members responded to their constituents and their consciences. Tip O'Neill spent two nights and all day Sunday taking calls from his Democratic Members demanding impeachment. John Anderson, Chairman of the Republican Conference, said that impeachment resolutions "were raining down like hailstones" from the staunchest of Republicans.

By Monday, Speaker Albert confronted the inevitable. "I had hoped to save the country the trauma of impeachment," he said. "But after Cox was fired, this was no longer possible. Members would not be restrained. The situation the President created had taken the matter out of my hands."

As Speaker, Albert had already decided that the House must confirm Ford as Vice President before acting to impeach the President. After the Saturday Night Massacre, Albert realized that might not be possible. "If someone could find a way to bring impeachment to a vote on the House floor that first day, it might pass," Albert said.

For an ally, he brought to his office his counterpart, the Minority Leader. He and Ford agreed: First, they would use their parliamentary power as leaders to block any immediate impeachment vote. Second, Ford would mobilize his Republican Members to support the Speaker's plan to assign the impeachment inquiry to the Judiciary Committee rather than to an ad hoc committee loaded against Nixon—as many Democrats were insisting.

This joint action of principle by the Leader of the majority and the Leader of the opposition was not uncommon in that time. A Democrat next in line to become President, and a Republican nominated to become next in line, were as one in making certain that a flawed and embattled President would have a fair trial.

When the House opened its session on Tuesday, October 23, 1973, Members were standing in line, resolutions in hand, speeches ready, impatient to impeach President Nixon. Their words varied, but the theme was consistent: "The President . . . has disgraced the country and himself," "The President is obstructing justice," "President Nixon has broken the people's trust . . ." "This country is in mortal danger." Throughout the day the attacks on Nixon continued, vengeful, unrelenting, with Republicans as well as Democrats demanding that the House use its power to force Nixon out of office.

Down the corridor from the House floor, Albert listened, hearing no one come to Nixon's defense. Sometime late in the day, he said to himself: the House must examine the President, and in the process the American people will examine the House of Representatives. The matter resolved in his mind, Albert strode to the floor and took the Speaker's Chair. Confident that his action would be right for the House and for history, Albert directed Chairman Rodino and the House Judiciary Committee to begin the investigation that would lead to the impeachment of the President. "I did not put it to a vote," Albert said. "But I knew that no decision I could ever make would be more significant for my country."

It was a fateful autumn afternoon for Richard Nixon. Until then, he had successfully secured his tapes under the persistent claim of Executive Privilege. No such claim would hold against impeachment. Under the Constitution, the House has sole and unlimited power to impeach a President. By inference, in an action to impeach, the House claims and can enforce the right to demand evidence from anyone, including a President.

Ford was present in the House Chamber that day, ready to respond to any surprise move or disguised parliamentary maneuver. Like the Speaker, he observed that the mood of the House was to impeach, and it could not be put down. Let it go forward, he thought. As he believed Nixon innocent of any wrongdoing, the House Judiciary investigation would exonerate the President, and the crisis would end.

To Ford, there was an immediate and collateral responsibility—to win confirmation as Vice President. That meant he must prepare for an examination that neither he nor anyone else in public life had ever faced. He assumed that the Senate and House committees, in judging his worthiness to be Vice President, would investigate his personal life, his finances, his health, his beliefs, his record as a legislator—and as a man.

For a brief but meaningful time, he judged, he would be a witness before Congress and the country, and he must perform at his best.

It would be a new experience, and he was excited about the challenge. Nine years earlier, he had voted for the Twenty-Fifth Amendment, believing it to be a logical act of executive continuity and therefore in the best interest of the country. Now the responsibility to validate that part of the Constitution would fall to him. So he had decided the best course to follow was simply to be himself—to demonstrate the candor and openness that had been central to his political career.

"Hold nothing back," he told his chief of staff, Bob Hartmann. "Give them everything. I want them to see I am clean as a whistle." Ford personally telephoned his banker, accountant, doctor, lawyer, his friends and his brothers, and told them to keep nothing secret. He had his staff go back through twenty-three years of District records and disclose everything: check stubs for every expense, personal and household; campaign contributions and expenditures; every request to Federal departments and agencies; every record of assistance to a constituent. "Any question about anything," he instructed Hartmann, "see me and we will clear it up."

The Senate and House—matching Ford's resolve for full disclosure— ordered the most extensive and the most invasive investigation of any public figure in history. The FBI dispatched more than 350 agents in 33 field offices to conduct more than 1,000 interviews, and filed 1,700 pages exposing every facet of Ford's life—from childhood on. In Grand Rapids, Ann Arbor, and New Haven, FBI agents questioned his elementary and high school teachers, his Scoutmaster, coaches, classmates and football teammates, fraternity brothers, landlords, professors, employers, and in-laws. One agent, upon finding out that Ford had once been penalized on the football field for unsportsmanlike conduct, tracked down the referee and heard the explanation: Ford had tackled an opponent after the play stopped because he had not heard the whistle. Agents found and questioned Lieutenant Ford's fellow officers and crew on the *Monterey*. They talked to his campaign opponents; all said he was fair and honorable. They talked to contributors, searching for political deals or conflicts of interest.

As part of this comprehensive investigation, the IRS audited Ford's tax returns for the previous seven years. Revenue agents found one inappropriate entry in that time: Ford had deducted as a business expense two new suits he bought for his television appearances at the 1972 Republican Convention. That, IRS ruled, was not an acceptable deduction, so Ford paid $435.77 in back taxes.

A team of historians at the Library of Congress searched through twenty-four years of the Congressional Record, and compiled an analysis of every vote Ford had cast and every word he had spoken in the House during his career. In his summary of the 144-page Ford record, Dr. Joseph Gorman, the senior historian who supervised the study, identified a consistent fiscal conservative: "From the earliest days of his Congressional career, Congressman Ford can be placed with the reasonably balanced budget school of fiscal policy. Virtually without deviation, he has favored reduced spending and balancing the budget. He has resisted increasing the share of the public sector at the expense of the private sector and frequently has advocated cutting taxes within the structure of a balanced budget."

Some fifty House and Senate investigators conducted more than a hundred interviews in fourteen states, inquiring into Ford's dealings with twenty-three departments and agencies. They reviewed all Federal contracts of $50,000 or more in his district to determine if any had benefited Ford his family, or his campaign contributors: none had. They examined his children's savings accounts; all were meager. They talked to his doctors, who reported that he was in excellent physical condition for a man of sixty. They searched the records of the Michigan Bar Association; there had never been a complaint about Ford. They questioned his law partners in Grand Rapids, matching his fees against work accomplished. They interviewed his fellow members of the Warren Commission; all commended his regard for evidence, his perseverance in exploring alternate theories, and his concern for precision in the wording of the report.

The agencies—the FBI, IRS, GAO, Secret Service, special investigators hired by Congress—did their utmost to answer every question about the character and conduct and affairs of Ford. Never before, or since, had so much information been placed on the public record about a candidate for public office. "Not one public day nor one issue nor one vote nor one public statement of [Ford] went unexamined," the House Committee report stated.

On November 1, 1973, twenty days after his nomination, Ford faced the nine members of the Senate Committee on Rules and Administration—the Senate entity that dealt with Presidential elections, inaugurals, and succession. Chairman Howard Cannon, a staunch Democrat and former Nevada prosecutor, opened the hearings with a pointed charge to his colleagues: "We are here," he said, "to judge the nominee's qualifications to be Vice President"; but, he emphasized, "this committee should view its obligations as no less important than the selection of a potential President of the United States."

With an explicit reference to the growing evidence of Nixon's collusion in the Watergate cover-up, Cannon observed that some in the Senate proposed that "the nomination of Mr. Ford be made hostage to the domestic political warfare currently under way . . . I believe I speak for the Committee when I say that we see no merit—but only danger—in such an approach."

Chairman Cannon directed his fellow committeemen to a dual responsibility: To examine the nominee before them, and in doing so, to make a record for the future. "This is the first time in the history of our country that any nominee for either of its two top posts has been subjected to such an exhaustive investigation," he said. "It is for the members of this committee to establish a precedent—a solid, Constitutional precedent—by pursuing an orderly, logical, thorough, and honest inquiry into the nominee's qualifications . . . so that the results will be accepted as just and honorable."

To Senator Claiborne Pell, there was little doubt that Ford would replace Nixon as President. Observing that "because of domestic events"—a euphemism for Nixon's plight—Pell predicted that Ford "may not only be the Vice President of tomorrow but could be the President of next year." Therefore, he said, "We should concentrate on the qualifications, views, and abilities of the nominee" to become President "in the event history continues to unravel itself along the present sad path."

After the preliminaries, Ford began his twenty-seven-minute opening statement. He testified that he had thought through what he would do as Vice President if confirmed, and decided that his first objective would be to restore comity between Congress and the President. Only one year before, he observed, America's voters had split their choices for governing, delivering "a reelection mandate of the Republican President and an equally emphatic mandate of the Democratic 93rd Congress." Both must work together, he said, for "the American people never intended to paralyze and cripple government in Washington."

As to his qualifications to become Vice President at a time of deep division in Washington, Ford said: "I believe I can be a ready conciliator and calm communicator between the White House and Capitol Hill . . . I believe I can do this, not because I know much about the Vice Presidency, but because I know both the Congress of the United States and the President of the United States as well and as intimately as anybody who has known both for a quarter century."

The words expressed Ford's deepest conviction. He pointed out that he had served in the House with three Democratic Presidents and two Republican Presidents—supporting all when he believed they were right; opposing all when he considered them wrong. From experience, he said: "I know these men and women can work together because I have worked together with them the very best years of my life."

From his first day in Congress, Ford said, openness and honesty had been his way, and he pledged that would continue to be his way in the Vice Presidency if Congress should confirm him. "Truth is the glue on the bond that holds government together, and not only government, but civilization itself," he said. Intentionally or not, he had pointed up a contrast in principle and practice to Nixon.

To the nine Senators, a priority consideration was how Ford would differ from Nixon. To make the point, Senator Pell said the American people are "yearning for character, honesty, and integrity" in their leaders, and asked: should a President lie?

Ford's answer: "I do not think a President under any circumstances that I can envision ought to lie to the American people."

Senator Robert Byrd, noting that Nixon had repeatedly refused to surrender tapes and documents relating to Watergate criminal investigations, asked: should executive privilege be invoked to avoid releasing evidence of crime in the Presidential office in compliance with a court order?

"The best interest of the country would be that they should be made available," Ford said. He added that he had said publicly weeks before that President Nixon should turn over White House tapes and documents to the courts, and to the Senate Watergate Committee.

As a general rule, Ford volunteered, a President does not have unlimited authority to withhold information, but Congress and the public do not have unlimited right to the confidential conversations between a President and his advisers.

Senator Byrd reminded Ford that in 1963 he had condemned President Kennedy for ordering General Maxwell Taylor to refuse a Congressional request for information about the disastrous Bay of Pigs invasion. At that time, Ford declared in the House that too often a President claimed executive privilege "to cover up dishonestly, stupidity, and failure of all kinds."

"Would you say that this statement still represents your thinking on this subject?" Byrd said.

"Yes, I would, Senator Byrd."

"Can you conceive of any justification for a President to disobey a court order?" Byrd asked.

"I do not think any person in this country is above the law," Ford answered. "I would strongly say that any person, including the President, where a determination has been made by the highest court in the land, ought to obey the court order."

Byrd contended that the firing of Special Prosecutor Cox and the resignations of Richardson and Ruckelshaus had provoked unprecedented national outrage, and asked Ford if he would support a move in Congress to have Judge Sirica appoint an independent Special Prosecutor.

"I personally recommend and firmly believe that there ought to be a Special Prosecutor in the Department of Justice," Ford said. "To place a prosecutor under the judiciary conflicts with the Constitutional separation of powers," he added.

Then, Byrd asked, "how do you guarantee the independence of the Special Prosecutor, and prevent his dismissal by a President?"

"I don't think you can really do it by law," Ford said. "I think you have to have faith in the man who appointed him, faith in the person who is appointed, and good faith between Congress and the Chief Executive."

Senator Mark Hatfield told the witness and committee that many people in Oregon and elsewhere were saying "they have lost confidence in the Administration's ability to govern, and therefore have called for the resignation of the President . . . I feel that this whole matter of impeachment is really paramount in the public's mind today." How would you, he asked, meet "this great emotional, passionate issue that we face today?"

Ford replied that the House should go forward with the impeachment process. "I think it would be very helpful in clearing the air," he said. "I do not believe there are grounds—but that is a personal judgment—but I think it would be very helpful in the minds of the American people if they knew that such an inquiry is being conducted."

If he were confirmed, Hatfield asked, what could he do as Vice President to avoid "the unpleasant political experiences we are in and perhaps restore confidence" in the Presidency?

"I have always felt that I could speak very directly to the President, whether I agreed or disagreed with him," Ford said. To make his point, he said that during floor debate on a recent bill terminating U.S. troop presence in Vietnam, the President opposed the bill. From the cloakroom, Ford telephoned the President and said: "Mr. President, number one, I think you ought to accept it. Number two, it is going to happen anyhow. Number three, I think it is the best thing for the country to end this slaughter. He agreed."

"I assume," Hatfield continued, "that within the councils of the White House, that you will have honest differences and disagreements, and that you will express them freely and forthrightly as your best counsel to the President."

"I certainly will, Senator Hatfield, to him and to his advisers," Ford said. "You have to have that right to have an input. And I will have it. I know. I have had it before and I think it had an impact."

"Mr. Ford," Chairman Cannon said, "the Presidency itself is in trouble . . . How do you see your potential Vice Presidency as strengthening the administration in its ability to govern?"

"It seems to me," Ford said, "that in light of the experience I have had in Congress, and my personal relationship with the President and many of his advisers, that I can be a helpful bridge between the executive and the legislative branch."

How, Hatfield asked, can you help "bind up some of these deep-seated wounds, political and otherwise?"

First, Ford said, "Work with the Members of the Congress on both sides of the Capitol and both sides of the aisle." Second, he would travel the country, speaking "to calm the waters."

With his promise to do his best to bind up the nation's wounds, Ford made an unexpected public commitment: he would not use the Vice Presidency as a platform to run for President. "I [have] no intention of seeking any public office in 1976," he said emphatically.

"Do you think you might be subject to a draft?" Senator Allen asked.

"Well, the answer is still 'no!'" Ford said. "I have no intention to run, and I can foresee no circumstances where I would change my mind."

Does your decision not to be a candidate for President in 1976 "give you greater freedom, greater flexibility to play this peacemaker role?" Hatfield asked.

"It certainly does," Ford said. "Nobody can accuse me of seeking personal political aggrandizement."

Might he then, as Vice President, be "an ombudsman to carry complaints to the President?" Senator Marlow Cook asked. "Do you feel that this is an integral part of your position?"

"I certainly do, Senator Cook. I believe a Vice President, if he maintains a close association with Members of the House and Senate, on both sides of the political aisles, if he keeps his contacts with people generally throughout the United States, people from all walks of life, he can come back and report to the President, views that the President ought to have."

As most of the nine Senators on the Committee—like Cannon and Pell—fully expected that Ford would become President, they interrogated him on the broad range of issues that he would confront in that event.

"How would you state your understanding of Presidential leadership?" Hatfield asked.

"I believe that the President . . . has to give the kind of leadership to the American people that gets their strong basic support. He must have policies, domestic and foreign, that bring support from the people that elected him. Therefore, it is performance on the job, achieving peace around the world, to the degree that our country can effect it, achieving a kind of equity and prosperity at home domestically, those policies are . . . the most important role of the President."

"Can he be right on the basics and policies," Hatfield asked, "and yet be unpopular?"

"Yes, during a short term interval," Ford said. As an example, he cited President Truman. "His popularity in the polls plunged very badly, but he stuck doggedly to decisions he had made, and in retrospect the decisions were right, and today I feel, and I think most Americans feel, that he was a first-class President."

"What personal characteristics are important to Presidential leadership?" Hatfield asked.

"I think the President has to be a person of great truth, and the American people have to believe that he is truthful," Ford said. "I believe the President has to be a man of thought, and not impetuous . . . I believe that a President has to exemplify by his personal life, the standards—morally, ethically, and otherwise—by which most Americans live their lives."

"Can he live in that exalted environment of the White House and still be humble?" Hatfield asked.

"Humbled by the responsibilities," Ford said, "but he could not go out and wear that on his sleeve . . . The President has to appear forceful and strong, and if you appear to be too humble, you undercut the other necessary ingredients."

"Can a President admit mistakes and not appear weak?" Hatfield asked.

"Oh, sure," Ford said. "The American people realize that Presidents, like the rest of us, can and do make mistakes. They hope they are not too frequent, however."

Pell set forth his view that next to Watergate, America's principal concern was inflation, and asked Ford what he would do about it.

"I agree the greatest domestic problem we have today is inflation," Ford said. "First, you have to identify where the major areas of inflation are. Number 1 is food. Number 2 is petroleum." Pending legislation, Ford predicted, would increase food supplies. In petroleum, he said, "We face a different situation . . . Today the United States gets about ten percent of its petroleum from the Middle Eastern countries, and we have no real choice there—if they want to increase the price or reduce the supply . . . What we have to do is expedite other sources of energy in this country," increase gas and oil exploration in the U.S., build nuclear power plants, and provide more Federal funds for research in burning coal in a cleaner way. Third, he said, the Federal Reserve Board must pursue an intelligent monetary policy, and fourth, "We have to have a reasonable budget policy, a responsible fiscal policy. That is the responsibility of the Congress and the President. And I think for a temporary period we have to have wage and price control."

Responding to questions, Ford put himself on record in support of affirmative action, but opposed to forced busing of school children to promote integration, in favor of Federal aid to elementary and secondary education but with limits, against public financing of elections and against an Attorney General being involved in politics. He said he would be reluctant to change the Federal tax system because, he pointed out, one critic's loophole is another taxpayer's equity. He defended a President's right to refuse to spend all the money appropriated by Congress.

"A President has to look at the big picture for the husbandry of our resources so that we just do not spend money on unjustified programs that may be out of date, that are no longer necessary, despite Congressional support."

Senator Robert Griffin, observing that some commentators had expressed doubts about Ford's experience in foreign policy and national-security affairs, asked him to cite his record. Actually, Ford replied, he had specialized in national security since his first term. As a Member of the House Subcommittee on Defense Appropriations for twelve years, he had discussed and debated defense policy and commitments with six Secretaries of Defense, and uncounted Joint Chiefs, generals, admirals, and service secretaries. Secretaries of State and their assistants had come before him to explain foreign policy and their need for foreign aid money. The director of the CIA and his top staff had appeared before him to review their record and plans, and to appeal for money for future operations. As part of his responsibilities on Appropriations and as Leader, Ford had traveled on official missions to Europe and Asia. He described his seven-hour conversation with Zhou Enlai when he and House Majority Leader Hale Boggs undertook their official mission to China.

Earlier, he remembered, both President Kennedy and President Johnson had often invited him to the White House to discuss military objectives and international affairs. In all, he suggested, he had been deeply engaged in U.S. national security and foreign policy for more than twenty years.

"Do you," Byrd asked, "favor any kind of exploratory review of current United States policy toward Cuba?"

Yes, Ford said. "If a policy is not working, or can be improved, certainly the top strategists" in the State Department and the White House "ought to be working on it."

"Has NATO outlived its usefulness?" Byrd asked.

"In my judgment, NATO is a very important part of our foreign policy—for the United States and for the free world," Ford said. But he considered it time for our now prospering allies to contribute their share. "The pressure should come from the United States that they should do more."

Referring to the recent attack by Egypt and Syria against Israel, Byrd asked: "Should the U.S. guarantee the State of Israel its independence in case of attack by another country?"

"I do not think the United States should enter into such an agreement," Ford said.

Ford's beliefs, record, character, competence—all were scrutinized and most commended by the nine Senators. But there were also negatives—turned up by the press and Congressional investigators. The most difficult connection Ford had to explain was with a lobbyist, Robert Winter-Berger. In *The Washington Payoff*—a book about corruption in Washington, Winter-Berger claimed he had loaned and given money to many government officials, including Ford. To assess the accusation, the Senate Rules Committee and staff had interrogated Winter-Berger behind closed doors, and found he lacked credibility as a witness and could produce no evidence to support his claim. But Ford had met the man and had, on one occasion, followed his advice.

"How is it," Senator James Allen asked, "that a man of this sort is able to ingratiate himself into the good offices of an outstanding Member of the Congress, when he is not a constituent of the Congressman?"

"I am delighted that you asked that question," Ford said, "because I think it shows how any one of us, certainly including myself, can be duped. And here is the story."

Two friends from his high school days—Pete and Alice Boter—had written Ford that a disgruntled Democrat they knew wanted to help the Republican Party, he said. Could they bring him in for an introduction? Ford agreed, and Ms. Boter brought in Winter-Berger for a brief meeting in his Washington office. After that, Winter-Berger began waiting in the corridors outside the House Chamber and Ford's office to walk with him and talk. The man soon became a nuisance, Ford said, but he did not want to offend a friend of his Michigan friends. At some point, Winter-Berger began insisting that Ford visit Dr. Arnold Hutschnecker, a New York City psychiatrist who was an authority on leadership. To placate Winter-Berger, Ford agreed that on his next trip to New York City he would stop by Dr. Hutschnecker's office for a brief visit, and did.

"Were you treated as a patient?" Cook asked.

No, Ford said. "I never visited Dr. Hutschnecker for any treatment. I visited [him] for approximately fifteen minutes . . . He gave me a lecture on leadership." In support of his response, Ford placed on the record a quote from a statement by Dr. Hutschnecker to the Associated Press on October 17, 1973: "Gerald Ford never came to my office as a patient."

Had Ford ever received money from Winter-Berger? The lobbyist claimed in an affidavit he had given to the committee: "Between 1966 and September of 1979, I personally loaned Gerald Ford in the neighborhood of $15,000."

No, Ford said. "I want to, at this time, categorically, unqualifiably, and unreservedly say that is a lie."

"If your relationship with Mr. Winter-Berger was as casual as your statement to us indicated," Chairman Cannon asked, "why did you visit Dr. Hutschnecker only because he insisted?"

"It finally got to be such a persistent request, and such a pain, to be frank, that I said, while I am going to be in New York to make a speech, between the end of my speech and the flight back to Washington, I would stop to see Dr. Hutschnecker for a limited period of time, just to get the request out of the way," Ford said. In their visit, Ford said, "We talked about the role of leadership in the American political system . . . I saw no harm in having a conversation of that nature with him."

Cannon asked Ford about a report that he had once assisted Winter-Berger in an immigration case.

Yes, Ford said, he had assisted Dr. Albert A. Buytendorp, a Dutch national, in becoming a resident of the United States. "About sixty percent of my constituency has a Dutch heritage, so I am particularly interested in any matters of this sort where there are individuals who have a Dutch background." He stated that physicians from five medical schools—including Harvard, Albert Einstein, and the University of Maryland—had commended Dr. Buytendorp's unique qualifications in obstetrics and gynecology, so he had his staff shepherd the application through the HEW review process so that Dr. Buytendorp's immigration status could be changed.

"When did you end Winter-Berger's imposition on your time?" Senator Harrison "Pete" Williams asked.

"Early in the 1970s," Ford said, "I heard indirectly that he was being investigated by the Justice Department. When I heard that, I told my staff no longer will he be permitted in the office."

If Winter-Berger's book is "so packed with lies," Griffin asked, "why is it that there have been no libel suits filed?"

"Unfortunately," Ford said, "a recent decision of the Supreme Court makes it virtually impossible for a person in public life to collect anything from individuals who write that kind of trash . . . One of the extra burdens people in public life have to carry is that the courts say most anybody can say anything or write anything they want to about you, whether it is true or untrue."

In fact, Senator Griffin added, alluding to the vexation of many in public life, "In the interest of freedom of the press," the Supreme Court has ruled that "a public figure who has been maligned cannot recover unless he can prove in court, not only that the statement printed was false, but that the writer knew it to be false, and that he wrote it with a malicious intent." Moreover, Byrd added, the public figure must prove injury from that malice.

Ford had given the committee a detailed account of his net worth: $256,378. In addition to $1,282 in the bank, and a $9,000 investment in the Ford Paint Company, he had a $49,414 House retirement fund, an $82,000 family house in Virginia, a $70,000 condominium in Vail, Colorado, and a $27,000 house he rented in Grand Rapids.

"I noticed an absence of any mortgage hanging over you," Williams said. "Is that accurate or not?"

"That is entirely accurate," Ford said. "I have borrowed a very limited amount for immediate cash obligations," such as income-tax payments, "but I have no mortgage on any one of the three pieces of real estate we have." His accountant provided the details: They bought the Alexandria house in 1955, and paid off the mortgage eleven years later. They bought the house in Grand Rapids with a GI loan, and paid that off in 1964. They bought the Vail condominium with a modest inheritance, a loan on life insurance, children's savings, and a short-term bank loan.

The committee closed its interrogation with questions relating to Watergate. Allen asked: "Would you comment on newspaper stories that you helped Mr. Gordon Liddy, convicted in the Watergate break-in, get a job in the Treasury Department four years ago, and were responsible for him being brought to Washington?"

"Here are the facts," Ford said. "In 1968, in my capacity as Minority Leader, I traveled that year, as I have in the past and subsequently, around the country trying to help Republican candidates. I went up to Dutchess County in New York State. We had Ham Fish Jr. running for that House seat. In a very controversial primary, Mr. Liddy and Mr. Fish battled it out, and Mr. Fish won." Liddy, Ford was told, still planned to run as the Conservative Party candidate, and that would take votes from Fish and cost Republicans the seat. To keep Liddy out of the contest, Dutchess County party leaders said: "If Nixon wins, and if we ask you, will you put in a good word for Mr. Liddy?"

Yes, Ford said, he would. After Fish won the House seat and Nixon won the Presidency, the Dutchess County party leaders came to Washington and asked Ford to endorse Liddy for a job at Treasury. Liddy's background, Ford said, "was very impressive"—a good record in the Dutchess County prosecutor's office and a former FBI agent. Ford called Gene Rossides, an Assistant Secretary of the Treasury, and said: "If you can help out, I would appreciate it. That is all I did. He got the job. What happened to him afterward, I have no responsibility for."

In his Watergate testimony, John Dean had charged that House Republican leaders, "at the request of the White House," had in October 1972, blocked the House Banking and Currency Committee and its Chairman, Wright Patman, from investigating illegal transfers of Nixon campaign money. Byrd asked Ford: What was "your role, if any," in blocking that investigation?

Ford said that he had met with Republican members of that committee to discuss whether to grant Patman subpoena power. They believed Patman was seeking publicity—as he often did—eager to set out on a fishing expedition. Consequently, Ford testified, he encouraged them to be present when the vote was to be taken. The fifteen Republicans on the committee and five Democratic members, voted down the chairman's request.

Did you, Byrd asked, "during that period of August–October" talk to the President, Haldeman, Ehrlichman, or Dean "about the proposed investigation by the Patman committee?"

"I can say categorically, Senator Byrd, I never talked with the President about it, or with Mr. Haldeman, Mr. Ehrlichman, or Mr. Dean." Ford volunteered that he met almost daily with William Timmons, of the White House Legislative Liaison Office, "but even in this case I do not recall any conversations concerning this particular matter."

With the probability of Nixon's impeachment and possible resignation in mind, Chairman Cannon asked: "Do you believe that a President is immune from prosecution for a crime so long as he holds office?"

"That is my understanding under the Constitution," Ford said, "that before a President can be charged and convicted of a crime, he must be impeached and convicted."

"If," Cannon continued, "a President resigned from office before his term expired, would his successor have the power to prevent or to terminate any investigation or criminal prosecution charges against the former President?"

"I do not think the public would stand for it," Ford said. "Whether he has the technical authority or not, I cannot give you a categorical answer." Chairman Cannon had not mentioned the word "pardon." Nor did Ford.

After the final round of questions and answers, with Ford still seated before the committee, there were compliments all around. Senator Byrd, the most relentless interrogator, set the tone: "Your answers have been open, forthright, and frank. You have met some tough questions head on, and I commend you." Pell reiterated what had become self-evident: that Ford was being examined not just for Vice President, but perhaps as President, and said: "I believe you have the qualities of character, honesty, and integrity . . . our country is really searching and yearning for." It was both high praise from Democrats, and an example of the comity systemic in Congress in that era.

In the witness chair, Ford had answered questions for nine hours and thirteen minutes, without notes, without any need to confer with an aide or attorney. His responses were full and specific, spoken with confidence. Not once did he hesitate or evade. In his ready answers to the nine Senators, Ford had placed on the public record what he believed and exactly where he stood on national security, international affairs, social policy, economic affairs, energy, taxes, and budget and fiscal policy. To anyone observing, there was no mistaking his mastery of substance or the breadth of his experience in the arcane art and science of governing. He had, moreover, demonstrated the qualities of temperament, honesty, and sound judgment critical to high office, but not always found there. He had spoken plainly about his ambition—not for the Vice Presidency, but to be Speaker of the House—and accepted the lesser office out of his lifelong sense of duty. He readily professed loyalty to his party and to President Nixon, but it was clear that his higher loyalty was to principle. He was his own man.

At the outset Chairman Cannon had said, "Usually, the press functions as the investigator of the candidates for President and Vice President." Substituting, under the Twenty-Fifth Amendment, the nine Senators performed well. In two days they brought out more relevant and specific information about the merit and qualifications, and the probable actions of a prospective President, than the best political reporters ever had in any Presidential campaign. As a result, Jerry Ford revealed to the American people more about his character, his record in office, and what he would do if he should become President than any other candidate for the office in U.S. history.

The difference was in objective: to the reporters who cover Presidential campaigns it is the contest that counts. They call a race, judging whether a candidate has the popularity, stamina, and money to survive a haphazard itinerary of travel and scrutiny, win a party nomination, and then win election. In Ford's case, the Senators focused on whether the candidate had the knowledge and ability to handle the job. By their knowledge of issues and practical experience in governing, they knew what questions to ask.

The distinction is self-evident: One entity—the press—speculates on which candidate *may* become President; the other judged whether this candidate *should* be President.

After hearing more witnesses—twelve in favor, four opposed—and interrogating Dr. Hutschnecker and Winter-Berger to validate Ford's account of events, the Senate Rules Committee voted unanimously to recommend that Ford be confirmed. On November 27, 1973, the full Senate voted 92-3 to confirm Ford to be Vice President.

The House Judiciary Committee, lacking experience in confirmations, took longer to question Ford, and turned up less relevant information. Of the twenty-one Democrats on the committee, most were avowed liberals. Eight opposed Ford from the beginning and raised a point of order to stop the proceeding. Chairman Rodino overruled them. Undaunted, they plotted to block Ford's confirmation. They searched the stacks of FBI and IRS reports for something they could charge as wrongdoing. They faulted Ford for his votes on civil rights. They harried him on the stand, looking for a sinister motive in his move four years earlier to impeach a liberal hero: Supreme Court Justice William Douglas.

Ford stood his ground, pointing out an obvious breach of judicial ethics: Douglas had voted on a Supreme Court case when he was on the payroll of a litigant. Ford reminded the committee that he was not alone in questioning Douglas's conduct: 111 other House members had signed the resolution to consider whether there were grounds for impeaching Douglas. But the pro-Douglas faction on the committee argued that Ford's move against Douglas was a bald political act and therefore grounds for disqualification.

Even worse, to this faction, Ford was a Nixon man; Ford had left no doubt about his loyalty. "Of course I support the President," he said. "He is my friend of a quarter century. His political philosophy is very close to my own. He is the head of my party and the Constitutional

Chief Executive of the nation. He was chosen quite emphatically by the people a year ago." Ford pointed out that he had also supported three Democratic presidents, guided always by what he believed to be in the national interest.

The eight liberals were not persuaded. Scholarly Robert Kastenmeier reasoned that "the President has a form of disability" because of Watergate; therefore, "this nomination is a tainted appointment." Ford, he contended, was demonstrably "loyal to a President whose moral authority to govern has diminished to unacceptable levels."

Yet, even Ford's opponents commended his openness. Jerome Waldie, his most insidious interrogator, said at the end: "Mr. Ford, I am not going to vote for you, but I am terribly impressed with the honesty and the candor that you have revealed to the committee." Another opponent, Charles Rangel, reflecting on the nominee's quarter-century in politics, looked directly at Ford and said: "The FBI reports . . . run like a testimonial to the way you conducted yourself."

After all witnesses had been heard, and all evidence reviewed, Rodino counted the committee votes and saw that Ford had a clear majority. As Chairman, he had met his responsibility. He had carried out his commitment to conduct a prompt, thorough, and fair inquiry. But he himself could not vote to confirm the nominee. He could not accept Ford's action against Justice Douglas. So he telephoned Ford. "Jerry, you have the votes for the Committee to report out your nomination, but I want you to know that I am not going to support you."

"Peter, I understand," Ford said. "Don't you be concerned about that at all."

In the Committee room the roll was called: twenty-eight to confirm Ford, eight against, one present.

On December 6, 1973, Speaker Albert brought the nomination to the floor. Ford's colleagues in the House—the men and women who knew him best—voted 387-35 to confirm him to be Vice President of the United States.

From Nixon came the request that Ford be sworn in at the White House. Both Ford and Speaker Albert rejected the idea; Ford wanted to be sworn in where he had served for twenty-four years; Albert decided to emphasize Congress' role in this circumstance and set a precedent. Under the Twenty-Fifth Amendment, Albert said, it was the 535 Members of Congress, representing the American electorate, who had elected Ford to be Vice President. Consequently, it was most fitting that the new

Vice President be sworn in at the Capitol, and in his case, on the floor of the House.

At 6:10 p.m., on December 6, 1973, with Supreme Court Justice Warren Burger conducting the ceremony and Betty Ford holding a Bible given them by their minister son, Gerald R. Ford took the oath of office as Vice President of the United States.

The process that flowed from the Twenty-Fifth Amendment, not by accident, was close to the founders' creation of the Electoral College. In March 1788 Alexander Hamilton published *Federalist Paper* No. 68, in the *New York Packet,* advocating the Electoral College. Its purpose, Hamilton explained, was to assign the election of the Chief Magistrate to select and well-informed electors who would know best the qualities needed in the Chief Magistrate and would then, with deliberation and judiciousness, name and elect the best person to fill the office.

Hamilton commended it as best for "The mode of appointment of the Chief Magistrate of the United States . . ." The choice should be made not by "the mass," he wrote, but by "a small number of persons . . . , men most capable of analyzing the qualities adapted to the station, and acting under circumstances favorable to deliberation, and to a judicious combination of all the reasons and inducements which were proper to govern their choice . . . [They] will be most likely to possess the information and discernment requisite . . ."

In effect and in fact, the 479 Members of the House and Senate who voted to confirm Ford had acted as Hamilton proposed. They knew the qualities required of the Chief Magistrate. They were deliberate and discerning. They knew they were choosing the next President. They knew Ford. They knew the record, the temperament, and the character of the man. They knew he had "the qualities adapted to the station."

CHAPTER 10

Conflicted

Ford liked his new job at first. Always comfortable with his fortune in life, his sunny outlook and buoyant spirits were lifted even higher by his election to the Vice Presidency. He was grateful that he had come into the office by such a commanding majority of his colleagues. To him, if to nobody else, it was the equivalent of an electoral landslide. In accepting the nomination two months before, he had hoped the honor would be in recognition of his service to the country; and so it had turned out to be.

His hopes were high. "I thought I had been selected for two reasons: One, I would be most easily confirmed, and that was proven. Two, I was sure that the President thought that my nomination going through so easily, showing my popularity on the Hill, that I could be very helpful in Congress' relations with the White House. So did I."

Ford's new job also brought a gift of freedom. For the first time in a quarter century, he had time to do what he chose to do. No longer ruled by a House schedule set by the Democratic majority, he could decide for himself how to invest his days and hours. Time, he had discovered in law school, was his most precious resource, to be used most carefully. Now he could set his pace and priorities.

The first priority: national security. As international affairs and military readiness had prompted him to make his first bid for public office, now—some twenty-six years later—he was delighted to be on the inside for information and decisions. In the guarded basement sanctum of the White House where the National Security Council (NSC) met, he listened attentively to Kissinger and his experts, to CIA Director William Colby, to the Joint Chiefs, to the President. When asked, he offered Congress' viewpoint of international problems and proposals.

Determined to keep up-to-date on international developments, Ford called for regular one-on-one briefings by Kissinger or Scowcroft on the trouble spots of the world. Kissinger had been Ford's friend and mentor for a decade; Scowcroft swiftly became a new friend and, in time, a lifelong confidant. "He was thin and spare, and an intellectual," Ford said. "He was a West Point graduate and had taught there. I knew he was a Mormon, didn't smoke or drink. He was all business. He would come in with a list of things he thought we should talk about and go through them factually and briskly. He had a fantastic memory, of both military and diplomatic history." Ford concluded that Scowcroft matched Kissinger in brains but not in ego.

For an update on national-security issues, Ford arranged a breakfast meeting at the Pentagon with Defense Secretary James Schlesinger—not as a courtesy call, but as a working session. With a list of twelve tough questions about military procurement and planning he had written out early that morning, Ford brought himself up-to-date on the state of weapons and forces. Schlesinger, he concluded, knew military concept and theory but was too arrogant to listen to the Members of Congress who, after all, controlled the money for Defense.

Ford's new job also gave him time to examine and study one of his specialties: the Federal budget. Twelve years on Appropriations had implanted in him a strong and continuing interest in the functioning of the vast and complex machinery of the Federal government. Then and thereafter, he had been one of the few persons—inside or outside of government—who actually read the entire Federal budget. More important, he actually understood the import of the numbers and commentary. So Vice President Ford called in Roy Ash, Director of the Office of Management and Budget (OMB), and his deputy, Fred Malek, to learn the details of actual and projected spending. To Ford's dismay, the next budget, for fiscal 1975, would soar to $300 billion—a huge amount for its time—and the deficit was projected at $6 billion.

Ford had always been a learner, a reader, a listener. He realized that his new status as Vice President offered unlimited opportunities to learn, and he was eager to take advantage of every opportunity. He pored over a catalog OMB's four associate directors had put together for him that identified the most important problems the nation faced, and the status of each. He visited the departments; asked for briefings by secretaries and their senior experts at Treasury, Agriculture, Labor, Health Education and Welfare (HEW), Housing and Urban Development (HUD).

He studied a book given him by Marjorie Hunter, a reporter for the *New York Times*: *The Twilight of the Presidency*, by George Reedy, a writer and press secretary for President Lyndon Johnson. Ford found it instructive—a short course in proper conduct and attitude. "It was about how people moved into the White House and became all of a sudden enamored with power," Ford said. "I read it at least twice while I was Vice President and gave it to Bob Hartmann to read. The Nixon staff should have read it and used it."

Ford liked his new offices in the Old Executive Office Building—the five-story, fifteen-acre, granite and iron mass President Grant ordered built after the Civil War to house the State, War, and Navy Departments. There on the second floor Ford had a spacious and handsomely furnished room for himself, with a carved oak desk ample for working on papers, and a comfortable chair for reading. For meetings there was a conference table for eight in the corner.

Through a private door was the office of Bob Hartmann—Ford's chief assistant, a man for all purposes and all seasons. A former political reporter for the *Los Angeles Times*, Hartmann had joined Ford in 1965, proved his worth, and become counselor, speechwriter, and press adviser. Ford once described him as "not lovable, but wise and reliable."

Space was limited, doled out stingily by a Nixon functionary; but there were desks for Mildred Leonard, his appointments secretary, press secretary Paul Miltich, and assistants to answer the flood of mail—500 invitations weekly—generated by his new prominence. Initially Ford decided not to expand his staff. "I didn't expect to be in the political arena after I was Vice President," he said, "so why bring in a person for two years?"

As President of the Senate, Ford took that new duty seriously, appearing often in the chair to preside, even during routine sessions. It was a promise he had made to the Senate Rules nine, and he kept it.

On Tuesdays he joined the forty-three Republican Senators and George Bush, the party chairman, for their weekly policy lunch in an ornate room across the hall from the Senate chamber. He listened to the discussions of floor action, scheduling, politics, finding them much like those he had led in the House.

After one Tuesday lunch, Ford invited Bush to his ceremonial office off the Senate floor for an update on Republican Party affairs. The two were longtime allies. In 1966, Ford had flown to Houston to encourage the young and aspiring Bush to make his first run for the House, and

•

tendered a significant offer: he would help him land a choice committee assignment if he won. Bush did win, and Ford managed to get the freshman assigned to Ways and Means—the committee that preserved the depletion allowance for Texas oil. Then and after, Ford became something of a mentor to Bush.

With the door closed in Ford's private Senate office, Bush confided that their beloved party was in trouble, with polls indicating that the combined scandals—Agnew and Watergate—would cost Republicans heavily in the 1974 Senate and House elections. Ford recognized the possibility, but assured Bush that Nixon was innocent. "When the facts all come out, I believe the President will be cleared," he said.

One unexpected perquisite of Ford's new office was his own airplane. For all his public life, Ford had campaigned for fellow Republicans by flying commercially, or, at times, in small private planes with a weekend pilot in the cockpit. As Vice President, he could have demanded the sleek Air Force jet formerly assigned to Agnew, but Ford chose a smaller, slower plane because it burned less fuel. It was an Air Force Convair 580—a twin-engine propjet, slow and creaky, and the cabin noisy—but Ford was delighted with it.

So was Ford's family. For Christmas, they brought their ski boots, hooded jackets, and presents aboard Air Force Two and, in great excitement, took off for Vail—with Ford paying first-class fare for each member of his family. Christmas had always been the family's favorite holiday, and Ford remembered 1973 as one of their best. The Colorado mountain weather was bracing, the skiing excellent, the condo warm and inviting. Gathered around the fire on Christmas Day, he was not Mr. Vice President but Jerry, and "Dad," husband and father; filled with pride and joy at his own success and his expectations for the children. He had a beautiful wife, an equally beautiful daughter, and three fine, well-brought-up sons on the threshold of independence. Susan Ford would never forget the good time they had that year. "It was our last private Christmas," she said. "It was the last one where we could just be ourselves."

In January, reality intruded. Back in Washington and appearing on NBC's *Meet the Press*, Ford replied to a question about Nixon's refusal to turn over tapes to the Senate Watergate Committee by answering, "There may be, and I underline may be, some area of compromise." It was typical Ford—the legislator searching for middle ground between opposing viewpoints. Logically, he observed, "the relevant material on those tapes ought to be released. Stonewalling or hoping the issue would fade away was an exercise in futility."

He met a quick rebuff. Gerry Warren, Nixon's communications aide, immediately dismissed the possibility of any compromise on the tapes, telling the White House press corps: the Vice President is speaking for himself. Ford realized he had made a mistake. "It was a suggestion on my part aimed at trying to prod the Administration to find a better answer than pure stonewall," Ford said. "It seemed to me that that there must be some information on those tapes that would be helpful to Nixon if what I was being told was accurate." His public intervention provoked resentment all the way into the Oval Office, and right away Ford observed "a chill in my relations with the White House."

A few days later Ford made a second mistake. Asked by Haig to substitute for the President in speaking to the American Farm Bureau Federation in Atlantic City, Ford agreed. The President's writers sent over the speech written for Nixon. Ford, feeling it his duty, delivered the speech—a Nixonian attack on his Watergate accusers, calling it a plot by liberals and labor and including the line, "a few extreme partisans . . . bent on stretching out the ordeal of Watergate for their own purposes . . ."

Returning to Washington, Ford realized he had gone too far; that he did not believe what he had said. Already embarrassed, he was shocked when told later that day that FBI electronic experts had discovered that one crucial, eighteen-and-a-half minute segment of a White House tape turned over to Judge Sirica for private review had been deliberately erased.

Ford learned from his Atlantic City mistake. "It was," he said, "one tough job to maintain support for a President under siege, with conditions deteriorating virtually every day, and at the same time trying to maintain my own personal integrity. Because the deeper the Nixon White House got into trouble, the more easily it could have been for me to get engulfed in that swamp. And yet, I didn't want to appear disloyal. So I had the problem of trying to maintain my own personal integrity without seeming to undercut the boss. And of course I was always under scrutiny. If I said anything the wrong way, people would say you're just trying to become President. So it was a very narrow path. Not a very pleasant one."

To correct his Atlantic City mistake, Ford called in Hartmann. "We can't go on getting our speeches from the White House," he said. "My credibility will erode overnight. We're going to have to do it on our own. So get whatever help you need; but from now on, you're in charge of speeches." Furthermore, Ford said: "I intend to make more public appearances and on my own. Accept every invitation you possibly can."

Hartmann was relieved. Long before his boss, Hartmann had recognized that the White House staff intended to exploit Ford's good nature and reputation for integrity in any way they could. Now the Vice President would show his independence. "He deliberately fled Washington," Hartmann said. "I am sure the thought crossed his mind that he was a lot safer out on the road than he was in his Washington office. The best way to show he was not Nixon's boy was to go out in the country and express thoughts that were vaguely at variance." Within the hour, Hartmann was negotiating with two prospective speechwriters and planning the schedule that would distance Ford from the White House staff, from Nixon, and especially from Watergate.

Ford first took the Vice President's chair in the Cabinet Room on January 21, 1974. The occasion: President Nixon's meeting with the bipartisan leaders of the second session of the 93rd Congress, which had just opened. The room buzzed with good wishes from Ford's friends—Carl Albert; Mike Mansfield; Hugh Scott; John Rhodes, who had succeeded Ford as House Republican Leader; Bob Griffin; John Anderson. Their bantering stilled when the President entered.

The agenda was full, with Nixon dominating the discussion, raising domestic issues, prospective legislation, the upcoming Federal budget—everything except Watergate. After the session ended, Nixon asked Ford to join him in the Oval Office.

With Haig taking notes, Nixon brought up Watergate, insisting once more that he was innocent. "He told me that there was material that would clear him of involvement in Watergate and he volunteered to show me some of it." Ford declined. He remembered having been warned, only days earlier, by Barber Conable, John Anderson, and other close friends in the House: "Don't get sucked in and destroyed as Agnew was," Conable said. "Stay at arm's length from Nixon on Watergate." So Ford told the President he did not need to look at the evidence; he accepted his word that he was innocent.

From Watergate, Ford said, Nixon "turned to foreign policy, giving me his impressions of world affairs. He went over his reactions to what was happening on Capitol Hill. Then he began to ramble about the political history of our time and the things we had done together in Congress years before. He touched on a number of irrelevancies. It was embarrassing. I had a lot of appointments on my agenda that day. I knew that he had work to do and I felt I ought to leave. But you just don't get up and walk out on the President while he is still talking." After almost two hours, the President let his Vice President go.

Ford felt sorry for his friend. "Here was a man who had been elected by an overwhelming majority, 49 out of 50 states, done some outstanding things in foreign policy; yet he couldn't leave the White House. Couldn't go to college campuses. Couldn't make public appearances. Couldn't make a speech before any group. He was a prisoner of the White House. He just wanted to talk. So he used me as a person to unload himself on."

The next day, at a press conference in the Capitol, reporters asked Ford about his meeting with the President. The President looked just fine and spoke well, Ford said. He made a point of telling the press that Nixon had assured him he was innocent of any part in the cover-up and had the evidence to prove it.

After Atlantic City, Ford began gradually to point out the difference between himself and his imperiled President. Ford opened his door to all—deliberately contrasting his easy accessibility to Nixon's isolation. On successive days he gave press interviews to three widely syndicated columnists: Mark Childs, Rowland Evans, and Charles Bartlett. He talked business and economics with reporters from *Fortune* and the *Economist*. He discussed policy and politics with Nancy Dickerson, an independent television commentator, and with Marvin Arrowsmith, of the Associated Press. He met with the editors of *Time*, and spent two hours with Tom DeFrank for a *Newsweek* cover story.

Ambassadors presented themselves—Lord Cromer from the United Kingdom, Jacques Kosciusko-Morizet from France. Ford dined privately with Anatoly Dobrynin, Ambassador to the United States from the USSR. Helmut Kohl, leader of the German opposition, called on him. Fellow politicians sought him out—Richard Lugar, mayor of Indianapolis; Jake Garn, mayor of Salt Lake City; Ralph Perk, mayor of Cleveland; Bob Ray, governor of Iowa; Meldrim Thompson, governor of New Hampshire; Ronald Reagan, governor of California; Dick Herman, Republican National Committeeman from Nebraska; Clarke Reed, party boss in Mississippi. By circumstance, but not by Ford's design, the office of the Vice President had become the lifeboat for the Republican Party.

Then he was off in his Convair. He flew to Omaha for a briefing at the Strategic Air Command and lunch with the editors of the *Omaha World-Herald*; to Grand Rapids for Gerald Ford Day; to Columbus, Ohio, for the Touchdown Club; to Kentucky and Ohio for Republican Congressmen. Then to Oregon for a fundraiser; to Cincinnati for his House colleague Willis Radison; to New York City to receive an American-Israel Friendship Award, and lunch with the editors of the *New York Times*.

He set for himself a killer schedule. He flew to Hawaii for a day of eleven events, with no time off for golf or the beach. He flew from Washington, D.C., to Seattle and back in a day; to Hartford and Charlotte, Boston and Birmingham, Phoenix and Palm Beach; to Denver, St. Petersburg, Atlanta, Kansas City. Altogether, he traveled 130,000 miles as Vice President, and visited forty-one states. Most weeks, he flew coast to coast and back at least once.

The compact cabin of the Convair was a boon to the seven press representatives who traveled regularly with Ford (Marjorie Hunter, *New York Times;* Phil Jones, CBS; Ron Nessen, NBC; Bill Zimmerman, ABC; Tom DeFrank, *Newsweek;* Bob Leonard, Voice of America; David Kennerly, *Time-Life* photographer). Confined for so many hours, seated so closely together, they swiftly became well acquainted, then friends. Walking aboard and back to his place in the rear, the Vice President kidded their weariness, answered their loaded questions with as much candor as he considered prudent, and waited patiently if they fell behind. They, in turn, were gleefully critical of his performances. One night, having a martini aboard with the press, Ford retold the story of how Nixon had telephoned him to ask that he accept the Vice Presidency, and he had to ask the President to call him back. "Hey," *Time-Life*'s irrepressible photographer David Kennerly called from the rear, "After the twelfth time we've heard that story, we wish the President hadn't called you back."

Proximity offered the reporters a special opportunity to measure the man. At one point, DeFrank wrote for *Newsweek*: "He is basically the poor man's Dwight D. Eisenhower, an earnest plodder whose intellect will never be described as scintillating. He exudes about as much flair and charisma as Calvin Coolidge. He is a terrible orator, one of the worst in recent memory . . . Major chunks of his speeches fail to hang together and trail off into dead ends. [He has] a soporific delivery so deadly it could put an insomniac to sleep, and probably has . . . Why then, all the popular adulation? The answer is deceptively simple: Jerry Ford is a human being cum laude, a down-to-earth, earnest, genuinely likable guy with an infectious laugh and not the slightest hint of pretentiousness. He is a politician of great and genuine sincerity . . . And in a time when virtuous pols seem as scarce as gasoline, Jerry Ford sticks out as a man of abundant decency."

Traveling gave Ford time to evaluate his situation—to look ahead. Early on he remembered and followed his Scout motto: Be prepared. Returning to Washington in early February, he talked to Hartmann. "Bob, we better think about bringing in some more good people to work with us. I want a national security adviser, not someone in uniform but who has military and foreign policy knowledge, who understands that I spent some years on Appropriations in that area myself, and he ought to be able to work with Congress."

"Would you consider Jack Marsh?" Hartmann asked.

Ford had previously ruled out former Members of Congress for his staff; but Marsh, a former Democratic Congressman from Virginia, then serving as Assistant Secretary of Defense for Legislative Affairs, was worthy of an exception. Marsh had served four terms in the House— from 1963 through 1970—and during those years, Ford and Marsh had become friends and allies on Appropriations. Both were strong supporters of defense; both were firmly committed to U.S. leadership in international affairs. In Marsh, Ford saw wisdom, judgment, independence, integrity, plus the courage to stand for and speak out on matters of principle.

"Jack would be excellent," Ford told Hartmann. "Would you get him in here?"

Marsh arrived, assuming that Vice President Ford wanted to talk about defense matters. "Jack," Ford said, "I want you to come to work for me."

Marsh was surprised, and delighted. "The answer is yes, Jerry. Just let me tell Schlesinger and I'll be here."

On Ford's staff, Hartmann and Marsh complemented each other. Hartmann was closer to Ford, more knowledgeable about the press, but abrupt and irascible. Marsh was a soft-spoken diplomat, gifted at persuading. Like his eighteenth-century Virginia forebears, he was both practical and idealistic, exemplifying Thomas Jefferson's "natural aristocracy among men" grounded by "virtue and talents." Of Marsh, Ford said: "I knew I could rely on his judgment. Jack was very bright, with a shrewd understanding of people and problems. He was also an indefatigable worker, and tough. He would speak up against five or ten people if he thought I was doing the wrong thing."

Ford came to rely on Hartmann and Marsh for guidance in navigating his narrow path. "In light of my situation, I consulted with Bob and Jack, and we decided that as the person who would succeed Nixon, I should not be an active participant in trying to get him out of office. The public would have looked at me with some reservations. If I did become President, we wanted to make certain that there was no accusation possible that I had sought the job by getting rid of him."

The policy: Ford would defend President Nixon in public, within limits, but speak plainly to him in private. In mid-February, Michigan held a special election to fill Ford's Fifth District Congressional seat, and—for the first time in sixty years—the Democratic candidate won. Ford was shocked. Nixon invited him in to talk about the political upset, and suggested that inflation had cost Republicans the seat.

"No, Mr. President," Ford said. "It is Watergate that is responsible." He reminded him that as the Presidential candidate in 1960, 1968, and 1972, Nixon had won Michigan's Fifth District handily, but "this election reflects the district's verdict now, and it's not good." He urged the President to make public "as quickly as possible" the evidence that would prove his innocence. "The [Michigan] election result is a signal that if you don't clear up Watergate soon, we're going to face disaster in November."

Nixon assured Ford that he had the documents that show he had not been involved in Watergate, and would "at the proper time," make them public. "I left the Oval Office with the sinking feeling that I had heard the story before."

As Vice President, Ford could not criticize the President, but he could attack the amateurs who ran the Committee to Reelect the President in 1972. During the campaign, Nixon's lieutenants had disdained state and county party leaders and ignored local Republican candidates. To a March gathering of 1,000 midwestern Republicans in Chicago, Ford proclaimed: "Never again must Americans allow an arrogant elite guard of political adolescents like 'Creep' to by-pass the regular party organizations and dictate the terms of a national election. The fatal defect of 'Creep' was that it made its own rules and thus made its own ruin. It violated the historic concept of the two-party system in America and ran roughshod over the seasoned political judgment and experience of the party organizations in the fifty states." Even before he finished the carefully crafted sentences, the party faithful rose from their seats, cheering, applauding, calling for more.

Ford had struck a raw political nerve. "Bob and I wrote that speech personally," Ford said. They deliberately did not clear it with the White House.

Ford was changing, and the press picked up the change. "The Vice President has all but abandoned earlier efforts to improve the President's image," Marjorie Hunter wrote in the *New York Times* in March. "The man has changed, too. He appears more sure of himself. He frequently tosses away prepared speeches and speaks whatever happens to be on his mind. He breaks into a smile when confronted with even the toughest, most politically embarrassing questions at news conferences." On one night flight, Ford told Hunter: "I'm doing everything I can to put the party back together."

In talking about Nixon and Watergate, Ford had no choice but to be deliberately inconsistent. In Pensacola he told an audience, "President Nixon is innocent." In Delaware he said Nixon should turn over to the House Judiciary Committee all relevant information: "He should get it out, the sooner the better." In Birmingham he said he understood "the President's current reluctance to turn over more information . . . until the Committee digests what it has." In Philadelphia he said President Nixon "is innocent," but then qualified his opinion by saying, "Time will tell." At one point, Ford confided to his ever-present squad of reporters that he was deeply concerned that President Nixon had been so weakened by Watergate that he would be unable to negotiate a meaningful nuclear arms agreement with the Russians.

In Honolulu, Phil Jones, the CBS reporter traveling on Air Force Two, observed and broadcast that Ford was "finding a variety of views—hard core Republicans supporting the President, others saying, 'Jerry be your own man,' and still others who say the country has to come ahead of the party. Says Ford: 'It's a hard job to go down the straight path.' He admits he's not sure his is a very straight path." With his customary blunt incisiveness, Jones suggested to Ford that he was "zigging and zagging on the question of the President." Ford denied that, at least most of the time; but once told Jones, "A zig-zagger makes touchdowns."

A quarter century later, Ford told a new Vice President, Richard

Cheney, that his Vice Presidency was "the most unhappy eight months of my life." It was so because in that time Ford not only witnessed the ravaging of his friend, Dick Nixon, and not only because he had to stand by and see the honor of the country inexorably diminished, but also because Ford was forced out of character. For all his political career—indeed, all his life—he had been straightforward, candid, truthful. Dissembling was not his nature. Yet, as Vice President to Richard Nixon, Ford could not be as frank and honest with the press and the American public as he wanted to be, and, sometimes, he could not be true to himself.

February 1974 marked the beginning of the end of Richard Nixon's Presidency. In the first week, the House voted 410-4 to authorize its Judiciary Committee to investigate anything and everything Nixon had done as President, and to collect evidence for his possible impeachment. The Senate Watergate Committee voted unanimously to end its public interrogations, handing its volumes of testimony, bundles of evidence, and the responsibility for prosecuting Nixon to Chairman Rodino and the House Judiciary Committee. A grand jury indicted Haldeman, Ehrlichman, Mitchell, Colson, and three other close advisers to Nixon for perjury and obstruction of justice—and named the President himself as a coconspirator. With the indictments, the grand jury delivered a sealed packet of evidence against Nixon to Judge Sirica, which he promptly dispatched to Chairman Rodino for the impeachment proceedings.

Formidable as these problems were, to Nixon the more immediate was the Special Prosecutor, Leon Jaworski. When the President ordered Acting Attorney General Bork to fire Cox, Nixon contrived an implausible plan: he would appoint no successor, and thereby avoid further prosecutorial demands for tapes. Bork informed him otherwise, insisting that as Attorney General he bore the responsibility to appoint a new Special Prosecutor to carry on the Watergate investigation. Nixon yielded, concluding he would be better off to make his own choice rather than have Judge Sirica or Congress appoint an open enemy.

Bork recommended, among others, Leon Jaworski, an eminent Houston lawyer. Jaworski had prosecuted German war criminals after World War II, established the legal basis for Lyndon Johnson to run for both Vice President and Senator in 1960, and later served as president of the American Bar Association. For advice Nixon turned once again to his favorite, John Connally. Without hesitation, Connally recommended Jaworksi, assuring Nixon that Jaworski was no Cox.

This was true. Jaworski was, by nature, less interested in publicity than Cox, but he was no less committed in his determination to bring criminals to justice. When first asked by Haig to take the job, Jaworski—reminding Haig of what had happened to Cox—was reluctant. To persuade him, Haig offered Jaworski the President's guarantee of full independence—a guarantee to be backed up by the bipartisan leaders of Congress. Let it be understood, Jaworski told Haig: "I feel that every person criminally involved [in Watergate] should be prosecuted. If I take this job, I'm going to work this way."

Haig, who may or may not have realized the import of what he was saying, replied: "You've got the right to take the President to court."

Jaworski, after reviewing the case, did take the President to court. He asked Judge Sirica to subpoena tapes and documents covering Nixon conversations with Haldeman, Ehrlichmann, Dean, and Colson—the same evidence that triggered Cox's dismissal. Nixon refused, claiming executive privilege. Undeterred, Jaworski promptly appealed to the Supreme Court, asking the court to rule on a clear and simple question: can a President withhold evidence of a crime? In going directly to the highest court, Jaworski advanced the argument that the issue was too important to risk the procedural delays of the normal chain of appeals. The Supreme Court accepted Jaworski's direct appeal, and set the date for oral arguments: July 8, 1974.

While Jaworski pressed his case against Nixon, the House Judiciary Committee proceeded on a parallel and equally deliberate course. To buttress the evidence already in his committee's hands, Rodino initiated a series of subpoenas to Nixon, in one, demanding forty-five tapes and documents of his conversations about Watergate and the cover-up. Nixon stalled. Advised by his lawyers that refusing a House subpoena would inevitably provoke impeachment, he contrived to send the Judiciary Committee no tapes, but his own selection of altered transcripts. Not acceptable, Rodino informed the President. He ordered Nixon to turn over every tape and document the committee demanded—intact, unaltered. Nixon's response to Rodino: I will not comply.

Isolated inside the White House, Nixon blundered on. One day he invited House Republican Leader John Rhodes to the Oval Office to discuss his standing in the House. Would Rhodes's fellow Republicans support him if he refused to turn over the tapes subpoenaed by the Judiciary Committee? Nixon asked.

Absolutely not, Rhodes replied. In fact, he added, if Nixon continued to reject the House subpoenas, then Republicans would join Democrats in voting Nixon to be in contempt of Congress—grounds for impeachment. Late that night, alone in the Lincoln Sitting Room, Nixon faced his doom. "Lowest day," he wrote on his yellow legal pad. "Contempt equals impeachment."

On the afternoon of May 6, 1974, by his account, Nixon secluded himself in his EOB hideaway to listen to the tape of his June 23, 1972, discussion with Haldeman. He heard the two of them conspiring to have CIA Director Helms stop the FBI investigation of Watergate. In *The Memoirs of Richard Nixon,* he wrote that at first he did not recognize this tape "as the 'smoking gun' it turned out to be." If so, it was a surprising confession of Nixon's ignorance of basic criminal law. Yet in the next sentence of his book he contradicted himself, admitting that the June 23 tape was so incriminating that he would not permit his lawyers or anyone else to listen to that or any other tape "and have to be answerable for what they heard." Consequently, Buzhardt and James St. Clair—a Boston trial lawyer nominally heading Nixon's defense team— were put in the position of good lawyers defending a client who concealed the facts about his crime.

As he was losing the legal battles to keep his job that spring, Nixon was also losing his political savvy. For reasons he never explained, he had convinced himself that Ford protected him against impeachment. To his staff, Nixon disdained Ford, seething at Congress for rejecting his choice of John Connally and imposing Ford as Vice President. After he signed the formal document nominating Ford, Nixon sent the pen to Buzhardt with a note: "Here's the damn pen I signed Jerry Ford's nomination with."

More than once Nixon scorned Ford to Kissinger, confiding that the Vice President lacked foreign policy skills. One day, as Nixon met in the Oval Office with Governor Nelson Rockefeller, he placed his hands on the arms of his chair, and asked sarcastically: "Can you imagine Jerry Ford sitting in this chair?"

It was a fatal misread for Nixon; it was Agnew who had guaranteed him against impeachment. As Speaker Albert said, "Whatever Nixon had done, we would never have turned over the country to Agnew. Unthinkable." Once Agnew was out, and Congress had put in place the man Members had chosen to succeed Nixon, the outcome was inevitable.

In fact, early on, responsible leaders of the President's own party began calling on Nixon to resign and hand the Presidency to Ford. The most telling came from Senator James Buckley, a scholarly New York Conservative and brother to the theoretician of the Conservative movement that had been a major force in Nixon's 1968 election and reelection. Watergate, Senator Buckley declared, had "plunged our country into what historians call a 'crisis of the regime.'" The seamy affair was no longer a "troublesome episode," Buckley said. "Rather it reflects a cumulative loss of faith that has eroded [the President's] credibility and moral authority, a loss that, in my judgment, is beyond repair . . . Richard Nixon must resign as President."

A more moderate Republican, Massachusetts Governor Francis Sargent, proposed that Nixon leave office for the good of the government and the country. Weeks later, John Rhodes, the Republican Leader of the House, told the press that Nixon should consider resigning. For Nixon, that was a particularly heavy blow; he had counted on Rhodes to lead his defense in the House against impeachment.

Powerful Democrats spoke up. House Majority Leader Tip O'Neill declared that Nixon's resignation "would be in the best interest of the nation." One former Supreme Court Justice and onetime adviser to President Lyndon Johnson offered an incentive: if Nixon would resign, Abe Fortas proposed, he could be immunized from prosecution. O'Neill, and Ways and Means Chairman Wilbur Mills, announced they would support legislation to guarantee Nixon against prosecution—if he would just get out.

To Buckley, to Rhodes, to the Democrats, to all such proposals, Nixon was defiant. Over and over he insisted: I will not resign.

For Ford, there was no one day, no single event, no legal maneuver by Nixon that moved him to question Nixon's innocence. When he became Vice President in December 1973, Ford was certain that his politically astute old friend Dick Nixon could not have done anything illegal; John Mitchell had told him so; as had Nixon, who promised documentary proof of his innocence. "As things developed, my mind began to think differently," Ford said. "It was an evolutionary process. Plus the fact that I didn't want it to be. So that was a roadblock in my mind. But as more evidence turned up, the roadblock began to evaporate."

Sometime over the next months, Ford started to wonder; wonder became doubt; and doubt turned into suspicion. "Since the documents that I had been promised to be turned over, had not been turned over, I began to have some subjective reservations," he said. "Yet, in everything Nixon ever indicated to me, he was implying—if not saying directly—that he knew nothing about Watergate, and he had nothing to apologize for or disclose. Now, he either fully believed he was innocent, which is one understandable position for him to take, despite the reality of the circumstances. Or, the alternative could be, that despite his knowledge of Watergate, he decided that in the interest of his Administration and the country, both domestic and internationally, that he had to maintain his innocence, hoping to get through his term and then get out. My impression was the first. But I couldn't rule the other out. One, he didn't really think he was guilty. Two, Even if there were a shade of guilt, the end justified the means."

Ford never asked Nixon point-blank if he were involved in Watergate, and he was always ambivalent about whether he should have. He had thought through the precise questions: Mr. President, did you know in advance about the Watergate break-in? Were you involved in the cover-up? In his one-on-one meetings with Nixon, Ford wanted to put those two questions to Nixon but never did. "Maybe I should have," he said later, "but if I had asked him after I became Vice President, then it might seem that I was suggesting I ought to be President."

Looking back long after, Ford realized that he had been "in a state of denial." He did not want Nixon to be guilty. He did not want Nixon to be impeached, much less convicted in the Senate. In Ford's judgment, for this President or any other to be forced from office would overturn the expressed will of the American people, undermine the legitimacy of the Federal government, and sunder the highest principles of democracy.

Ford was a rarity in Washington: he could and did separate the national interest from his own. He had never aspired to become President. He had never even thought of being President. Above all else, he did not want Nixon to be turned out of office. Despite the ominous circumstances that loomed in early summer of 1974, Ford kept hoping it would not happen. Profoundly, he believed that neither he, nor any other responsible person in public office, would want to see the Presidency and the nation so dishonored. "I knew it would be a catastrophe for the country to have a President impeached, or forced to resign," he said. "Because of what it would do to the country, I honestly did not want to be President."

As it happened, Ford was in Washington on July 24, 1974—a momentous day for him, for Nixon, and in the life of the nation. On that morning, a few minutes after 11:00 a.m., Chief Justice Warren Burger delivered the Supreme Court's unanimous decision, directing President Nixon to make public the White House tapes. Neither a President nor anyone else may withhold information about a crime, the court ruled, upholding Judge Sirica's decision directing the President to turn over sixty-four White House tapes and documents to Special Prosecutor Jaworski. That decision marked the penultimate break in the Watergate case.

Ford heard the news after a prayer breakfast in the Capitol with House friends—Laird, Rhodes, Quie, and others. All prayed for the country. All asked divine guidance for the Vice President. Ford made no change in his day's schedule, walking over to Republican headquarters to deliver a pep talk to Republican candidates for the House and record radio ads for two Senate candidates. At midday he left the Capitol for lunch at the *Washington Post*. "The appointment to meet with the editorial board of the *Post* was on my schedule," he said. "If I had cancelled, that would have been a distinct signal. So I went."

On the way, he thought about the Court's decision. "At first I was surprised that it was unanimous," he said, "but then I understood: It had to be unanimous. Whether the Justices agreed or not on the law, from the point of view of public relations—and that's a factor. They are not immune to what they hear and read, not immune to public opinion. Nor should they be. If the Justices had not been unanimous, the minority would have been accused, rightly or wrongly—and especially any Justice appointed by Nixon—of being part of the conspiracy. A partisan split on the Court would have been horrendous."

The lunch with Katharine Graham, Benjamin Bradlee, and other senior editors at the *Post* was somber, restrained. Bradlee asked if Nixon would comply with the Supreme Court order. Ford said he did not know.

It was the right question. Fifteen days earlier, after the President's chief lawyer, St. Clair, and Special Prosecutor Jaworski had argued the case before the court, St. Clair told the press that Nixon might simply defy any order the court handed down. In a city already rubbed raw with dread and doubt, it had been an ominous threat. Nobody in authority in Washington had expected Nixon would go that far; nobody could calculate what might happen if he did.

In fact, Nixon did come close to rejecting the court decision. His initial reaction to the news that morning was anger, then defiance. Haig had telephoned about 8:30 a.m. to the President's bedroom in the Nixon compound in San Clemente, California, told him the court had ruled against him, unanimously. How, Nixon raged, could Burger, Blackmun, and Powell, three Justices he had appointed to the court, have turned on him? He would not release any tapes until he could assess the risk. Minutes later, he stormed into his San Clemente office, to find Haig talking to Buzhardt in Washington. Nixon grabbed the phone. "There might be a problem with the June 23 tape, Fred. Get right on it," he ordered. "And get back to Al."

At that point Nixon himself was the only lawyer who had heard the tape. He suspected that his June 23 discussion with Haldeman could be seen as obstructing justice, and he had been worrying about it. "Now," he wrote, "I would find out just how much of a problem."

Nixon affirmed in his memoirs that he considered defying the court. By his much later and self-serving account it was only "for a few minutes." Actually it was some eight hours before he accepted the decision. During those hours he agonized, debated with himself, and searched for a way out. Nothing was to go to Sirica right away, he ordered Haig at one point; he must first listen to any tape before it could leave the White House. At another point he told Haig and St. Clair he would refuse the order. Or he might destroy all the tapes and resign.

In his White House office Buzhardt had the Secret Service bring the June 23 tape from the vault in the EOB. Making sure the erase button was blocked, he threaded the tape into his machine, and listened. Making notes in longhand on a yellow legal pad, he heard—clearly and unmistakably—President Nixon approve Haldeman's recommendation that they carry out the Mitchell-Dean plan to direct the CIA to stop the FBI investigation of Watergate. The four, Buzhardt realized, were conspiring to obstruct justice. To make certain of what he had heard, Buzhardt listened a second time. He then put aside the earphones and sat for a moment, stunned and silent. The President, Buzhardt realized, is guilty. He called Haig.

"Well, we've found the smoking pistol," Buzhardt said.

"Are you sure?" Haig asked.

"Yes," Buzhardt said, and told Haig that the President's deliberate act to stop the FBI investigation was at the least an abuse of executive power for a political purpose, and probably an obstruction of justice.

Haig walked to Nixon's office in his residence to report on Buzhardt's finding and conclusion. Again Nixon exploded. Buzhardt was wrong, Nixon said; probably too tired, still recovering from a heart attack; incapable of making a considered judgment. He insisted to Haig that he was innocent, that the order to the CIA was for national security. After venting his anger he asked: what did St. Clair say?

Haig summoned St. Clair, who had just talked at length with Buzhardt. The tape could not be defended, St. Clair said, and advised Nixon to comply with the court order. No, the President said, insisting he had a Constitutional duty as President to protect the power of the President and reject the intrusion of the Supreme Court.

Defying the Supreme Court would unquestionably bring impeachment, St. Clair said.

Then let the House go ahead with impeachment, Nixon said. He insisted he had a duty to protect the power of the Presidency. The three continued the discussion, considering options and legal consequences. As the hours passed, Nixon began to waver. Sometime in the afternoon Nixon instructed St. Clair: tell Sirica that the President must first review all the tapes for national security material and that will take weeks, possibly longer.

"I can't get that," St. Clair said and pointed out that Sirica will insist on an immediate turnover, and he will rule on any national security information. Nixon was bitter, resentful: The Supreme Court was telling the President of the United States what to do; a lower court judge was telling him when to do it. That was unacceptable, offensive to the dignity of a President. Get the delay, he ordered St. Clair.

As the discussions went on through the day and Nixon continued to look for a way out, Haig and St. Clair realized that at some point, without saying so, Nixon had agreed to accept the Supreme Court order. With a Ray Price draft, and multiple revisions, St. Clair, Haig, and Ziegler produced a statement that Nixon reluctantly accepted. About 4:00 p.m. Pacific time, St. Clair met with the press to deliver Nixon's concession: "While I am of course disappointed in the result, I respect and accept the Court's decision, and I have instructed Mr. St. Clair to take whatever measures are necessary to comply with that decision in all respects." With those words Nixon accepted defeat, knowing that surrendering the tapes would end his Presidency.

Three days later, on Saturday, July 27, 1974, the House Judiciary Committee voted 27-11 for Article I to impeach President Nixon. The charge: "To delay, impede, and obstruct the investigation of the [Watergate break-in]; to cover-up, conceal and protect those responsible . . ." The following Monday, the committee voted 21-17 for Article II, charging Nixon with abusing Presidential power by using the FBI, IRS, and CIA against political opponents. The next day, the committee passed Article III by 21-17, charging the President with contempt of Congress by refusing to comply with the committee's subpoenas for Watergate tapes and documents.

The Judiciary Committee's proceedings had never been easy, nor the outcome certain. Initially, politics divided the thirty-eight members into eighteen Democrats determined to impeach Nixon, and ten Republicans equally determined to exonerate Nixon. With the balance undecided, the decision fell to a fragile coalition of seven—four Republicans: Tom Railsback of Illinois, Hamilton Fish of New York, William Cohen of Maine, Caldwell Butler of Virginia, and three Democrats: James Mann of South Carolina, Walter Flowers of Alabama, Ray Thornton of Arkansas.

Each was motivated by his conviction that he must act with honor and in the national interest. If the facts warranted, Nixon must be judged and punished. The proceedings must be fair and bound by legal process. A vote split along party lines of the full committee would dishonor the Members, the House, the Constitution, and taint the action in history. Moreover, in practical terms, if no Republican on judiciary voted to impeach, Nixon would go free, for the Senate would not vote the necessary two-thirds to convict on Articles of Impeachment supported only by Democrats.

With Railsback as their leader, and Mann as their liaison to the eighteen Democrats overanxious to impeach Nixon, the coalition of seven labored from morning to night, discussing Constitutional philosophy, reviewing the evidence, drafting and redrafting. Collectively they came to agree that the essential basis for impeachment must be that Nixon intervened to stop an official investigation of his own people—a clear case of obstructing justice. With some editing by the drafting subcommittee of the full Committee, this became Impeachment Article I.

The seven had broken an impasse. One participant said later: "If this group had met and disbanded, or decided against impeaching Nixon, Nixon would never have been impeached."

In that time and circumstance, it was not uncommon for a cadre of seven Representatives of both parties to act in what they believed to be the national interest, even though all knew it would almost certainly cost them at the next election, only ninety days away. Recognizing their common responsibility, Flowers told his colleagues: "We have an awesome task to do that no one else can do for us."

For Ford, July 1974 was the month of high ambivalence. He could no longer deny to himself that impeachment of Nixon was possible, but he must continue to pretend otherwise. One incident that month forced Ford to acknowledge reality. Alan Greenspan asked to see Ford; Greenspan had just been appointed by President Nixon to succeed Herbert Stein as Chairman of the Council of Economic Advisors in White House, but had not yet been confirmed by the Senate. When Ford and Greenspan met in the Vice President's ceremonial office off the Senate floor, it was mutual high regard at first sight. "He was self-effacing, almost shy," Ford said. "He talked to me from what I knew, and what he knew, and what he was thinking. He spoke in a soft, well-disciplined voice, as one who is trying to get me to understand the background, the interactions in the economic world, and what he thinks is going to be the outcome."

When Greenspan asked Ford whether he should accept Nixon's appointment, Ford decided on the spot he could trust his visitor to keep a confidence. "I believe you should proceed with your confirmation," Ford said. "If I do become President, I want you to be my chief economic adviser." It was the first time Ford confided to another person that he knew Nixon would not survive.

In the last week of July, Ford traveled to Muncie, Indiana, to speak for a House member; to Chicago for a Republican rally; to Canton, Ohio, for lunch with the board of the Football Hall of Fame; to San Francisco to address the Urban League; to Las Vegas and Reno to speak at party fundraising events; to San Diego to meet with the Copley editors, and then be the guest of honor at a San Diego County Republican dinner. After the dinner he boarded Air Force Two for an overnight flight to Washington, arriving home at 4:50 a.m.

Up early, after sleeping for a couple of hours, Ford attended a retirement ceremony for his friend Army General John C. Meyer, then committed the rest of the day to the diversion he most enjoyed. He had been invited to play in a benefit pro-am golf tournament in Worcester, Massachusetts, and boarded his Convair with his good friend Tip O'Neill and other House leaders. After takeoff, House Republican Whip Les Arends confided to Ford: "Jesus, Jerry, do you have any idea how serious this thing is? Tip's been counting votes, and he says, Nixon has no more than forty votes in the House, and twenty-four in the Senate."

Ford was well aware of O'Neill's skill in counting votes, but even with his closest Congressional friends he would not risk a single comment that might leak and suggest disloyalty toward the President, or reflect his mounting dread that Nixon could not survive. As best he could with Arends, Ford bluffed: "Oh, Tip doesn't know what he's talking about."

Golf, not Nixon, was the preoccupation of the day. Ford and O'Neill rode a cart side by side, enjoying their spirited, high-scoring game, and cheerfully posing for cameras. Neither mentioned the looming crisis. A drink, tall stories, good fellowship marked the flight back to Washington. When Ford arrived at home that evening, he found that Hartmann had left him an ominous message: Haig must see him the next morning.

CHAPTER II

Proposition

Ford, in his EOB office by 8:00 a.m. on Thursday, August 1, was still studying the CIA morning intelligence report when Haig telephoned.

"It is urgent that I see you as soon as possible," Haig said. "Come over now," Ford said. Hartmann, who neither liked nor trusted Haig, suggested that either he or Marsh be present as a witness to whatever Haig might tell Ford, or ask of him.

Ford agreed. "Okay, Bob. You sit in."

Haig entered Ford's office prepared to deliver a message directly from the President. Very early that morning Nixon had summoned Haig to the Oval Office. "Al," he said, "it's over. We've done our best. We haven't got the votes. I can't govern. Impeachment would drag on for six months. For the sake of the country, the process must be ended. I will resign on Monday night in a speech to the nation. Tell Ford to be ready. Tell him I am thinking of resigning without indicating when. And impress on him the need for absolute secrecy. This is a decision I must make for and by myself—right up to the end."

But when Haig saw Hartmann sitting there with Ford, he held back. Haig neither liked nor trusted Hartmann, often warning White House staff that Hartmann leaked everything to the press. So in Hartmann's presence Haig said only that the President's situation was deteriorating. Looking Ford in the eye he added: "You'd better start thinking about a change in your life, for one tape is very damaging."

"How bad is it?" Ford asked.

Haig replied that he had not listened to the tape, but St. Clair and Buzhardt had. Both lawyers considered it to be indisputable evidence that would bring about Nixon's impeachment.

"How is the President holding up?" Ford asked.

Conflicted, Haig said. At times, he says he will resign; at others, he resolves to fight for his job, defend himself to the end against impeachment in the House and conviction in the Senate. Haig reiterated that he did not know whether the President would finally decide to resign or fight. Moreover, he said, he believed the President himself did not yet know what he would do.

Ford, scheduled for an appointment at the Senate, ended the discussion with the suggestion that he and Haig keep in close touch. As Ford rode to the Capitol with Hartmann, he said nothing more about the Haig meeting. He had just sat down at his desk in his office off the Senate floor when Haig telephoned. Listening, his face grave, he murmured an occasional cryptic response. As he somberly put the phone down, he said: "Al wants to see me this afternoon. Alone. I will meet him at three thirty, in the EOB."

Hartmann suggested there be a witness. "Never mind," Ford said. "I'll fill you in."

At the appointed time that afternoon, Ford waited in his EOB office, dreading what Haig might tell him. When Haig arrived, Ford studied him, looking for a clue. It was evident in Haig's mien and bearing that the news was grim: "Al looked even more beaten and harassed than he had that morning."

As soon as they were seated, Haig looked Ford in the eye. "Are you ready, Mr. Vice President, to assume the Presidency in a short period of time?"

"If it happens, Al, I am prepared."

With military briskness, Haig delivered an ominous report: He had now read the transcript of a tape of Nixon and Haldeman scheming to obstruct the FBI investigation of Watergate. The transcript showed that the President was involved in the Watergate cover-up only six days after the break-in. Tape and transcript must be turned over to Judge Sirica next week. As evidence, it is damning and cannot be explained. When that transcript becomes public, as it will, it will end Nixon's Presidency. His voice solemn, Haig concluded: "Either the President must resign or face certain impeachment in the House and conviction in the Senate."

Ford said nothing, silenced in part because he was so shocked at learning that Nixon was guilty; in part because he was mentally absorbing the stark reality that he would become President. He never forgot his reaction at that moment, that turning point in his life: "Number one, I felt secure that I was prepared to do the job. I wasn't terrified. I wasn't scared. I felt I was prepared to be President. So I had no qualms. Two, I was sad because I never wanted it to happen. I just didn't think it was in the country's interest to have a President thrown out of office, even for good reasons. But that was beyond my control. The tapes would come out; after that, it was going to happen."

Haig continued his briefing with a caution: "Under no circumstances can you assume the President is going to resign until he tells you himself. As close as I am to the President and the situation, I don't know."

After a pause, Haig's manner changed. The President, Haig said, would like to have the Vice President's current assessment of Nixon's situation in Congress. Ford did not hesitate. "My assessment is that if he fights this through, he will be impeached in the House and the odds are overwhelming that he will be convicted in the Senate," he said. "If the tapes are as bad as the President's own lawyers say, there will be a groundswell of a demand for resignation."

Haig, good soldier that he was, pressed on with his mission. "White House lawyers"—he used the words carefully—had drawn up options for possible action by Nixon. Haig emphasized that he had not been involved in designing or drafting the options but had been ordered to present them to Ford and get his reaction. The President's choices, as Haig stated them: He might step aside temporarily under the Twenty-Fifth Amendment and declare Ford Acting President until after the Senate voted on impeachment. He might postpone any decision, hoping some international crisis or other event would turn up to save him. He might appeal to the House for a censure vote instead of impeachment. He could pardon himself, then resign. He could pardon all the Watergate defendants, pardon himself, then resign.

Then there was the sixth option. As Ford put it: "Haig said that according to some on the White House staff, Nixon could agree to leave in return for an agreement that the new President—Gerald Ford—would pardon him."

The first five choices were actions that Nixon could carry out unilaterally, so Ford decided he should not respond. "Al," he said, "I don't think it would be proper for me to make any recommendations at all. I am an interested party."

As for the sixth option, which would require his action as the new

President, Ford asked: "What is the extent of a President's pardon power?"

Haig was prepared. "It's my understanding from a White House lawyer that a President does have authority to grant a pardon even before criminal action has been taken against an individual," Haig said. With that he handed Ford two sheets from a yellow legal pad, both handwritten. Ford read both, carefully. The first was a one-page legal brief of a President's power to pardon; the second, a draft of the proper and precise language that a President would use in granting a pardon. In the latter the lawyer had not presumed to write in Nixon's name, but had left a blank space for it.

Ford was not shocked by Haig's proposal. "No, I was not," he said. "Because I focused on what I felt was the more important thing Haig had told me: 'The smoking gun tape is going to come out on Monday. And when that comes out, the ball game is over. I cannot guarantee that he will resign, but the odds are in my judgment that he will. So you must be prepared to be President.'"

This was Ford. In fact, no incident in Ford's career portrayed the man so well—at his best and worst—as his reaction and response to the Nixonian "sixth option." Ford's naïveté, his ingrained trust in others blocked any thought that Haig was proposing an unconscionable deal. From childhood, Ford had looked for and almost always found the best in everyone; his most basic instincts were Panglossian. Lacking guile himself, he rarely saw it in others; it did not occur to Ford that "White House lawyers" would propose anything improper or unethical. More important to him at that moment was his struggle to comprehend the enormity of Haig's message: President Nixon was guilty. His friend was a crook. He would be forced from office. The consequence would be a tragedy for the nation. Concomitantly, he, Jerry Ford, who had accepted the Vice Presidency primarily as an honorific, would become the new President of the United States. His life, his responsibilities, his duty to his fellow citizens and to the country—all would change.

As to a pardon for Nixon, Ford did not dismiss it out of hand, or from his mind. He could not—believed he should not—if by a stroke of the pen he could end the anguish and destabilization that Watergate had provoked. His primary concern—in truth, his only concern was: what was best for the country? He knew that Nixon must go. For six weeks, perhaps longer, Ford had recognized—but kept it to himself—that the legitimacy of this Presidency had vanished. Ford also knew the fighter in Nixon; his enraged defiance when cornered; his instinct to battle for survival whatever the consequences to himself, to others, to the country.

Since this President could no longer govern, should he, as Vice President, ease Nixon's way out? Spare the nation the weeks, even months, of the agonizing, demeaning process of impeachment in the House and conviction in the Senate? Prevent the spectacle of a U.S. President in the dock? What was the right thing to do? Ford had vowed to himself—soon after becoming Vice President—that he would do nothing, *nothing*, to undercut Nixon or try to take the Presidency. Now he was being asked, by the President himself through his most credible emissary, to facilitate a resignation that would bring Washington back to its senses and its proper business of governing.

Compromise was an everyday occurrence in Congress, where Ford had served for a quarter of a century. Compromise was essential to the functioning of democracy. If a compromise with Nixon could bring an end to this Constitutional crisis, why would that not be in the public interest? Ford did not think of how prosecutors and courts, the press and public might view the proposed pardon as an undeserved gift to Nixon, and an infamous act on his part. To him, the first, foremost, and only question was: what would be best for the country?

Throughout his life, when Ford faced an important decision, he would demur, deliberate, consult with those he trusted most. Now, as Vice President, as the one person who could assure Nixon's immediate exit from office, he must not decide in a moment. So he said to Haig: "Al, I will need some time to think about this. I want to talk to St. Clair. I want to talk to my wife before giving any response."

Ford rose, grasped Haig's hand firmly, then impulsively clapped his left hand on Haig's shoulder. Both were conscious of sharing a turning point in history.

The Vice Presidential log showed 4:20 p.m. They had talked for fifty minutes.

Ford folded the two handwritten pages Haig had given him, put them in his pocket, and sat back in his chair. Well, Ford said to himself, it's going to happen. One way or the other, Dick Nixon will be forced out of office. I will become President. Not for a moment was he concerned about taking over the responsibility. What preoccupied him was not fear of the future but dismay at events past. Dick Nixon—a good friend and political ally of twenty-five years, had lied to him, lied to Congress, lied to the press, lied to the American people. Ford had trusted Nixon's word, and that trust was broken, never to be restored. "I was angry that Nixon had not told me the truth," Ford said. "The hurt was very deep. I wanted time to think, and I wanted to be alone."

From a side door Marsh came in quietly, interrupting Ford's rumination to say that Mrs. Ford was waiting in the reception room. She was there to join her husband for their long-scheduled tour of what was to become the Vice Presidential residence. A rambling Victorian manse on Massachusetts Avenue had been taken from the Navy Chief of Naval Operations by Congressional order and renovated; the Fords would be the first occupants. Ford nodded to Marsh but said nothing. Marsh left the office, thinking that Ford looked like a man "who had been thunderstruck."

Alone again, Ford summoned Hartmann. When Hartmann came in, he found Ford staring at the ceiling. "His face was grim," Hartmann remembered. "He looked as if a two-hundred-pound blocker had just hit him in the stomach."

Ford first swore Hartmann to secrecy, then summarized Haig's report: the June 23 tape would end Nixon's Presidency. It would show that, from the beginning the President had been a conspirator in the cover-up. He recounted Haig's list of the options Nixon was considering. When he reached the sixth option—that Nixon would resign with the agreement that Ford would pardon him, Hartman exploded: "Jesus! What did you tell him?"

"I didn't tell him anything," Ford said. "I told him I needed time to think about it."

"You WHAT?" Hartmann responded. That answer, he said to Ford, was almost the worst he could have given. "You told Haig you are willing to entertain the idea of a pardon if he resigns. That's probably all Haig and Nixon want to know."

"But Bob, Al wasn't suggesting that. It was just one of the ideas that he said were being kicked around by people at the White house."

Hartmann was adamant. He had known Nixon for decades; as a political reporter for the *Los Angeles Times*, Hartmann had covered Nixon's first political campaigns in California. He knew Nixon's wiliness and the machinations of his White House. To Hartmann there was no doubt: that proposed deal was almost surely made on Nixon's initiative—certainly with his knowledge. Haig was wrong to present it. "You should have taken Haig by the scruff of his neck and the seat of his pants and thrown him the hell out of your office," he said to Ford.

"Bob, you're overreacting," Ford said. "You're making a mountain out of a molehill."

Recognizing that Ford still did not see the danger, Hartmann said: "I think you ought to get Jack Marsh's judgment on this."

"All right, I'll talk to Jack," Ford said. "But later." He was already late for his appointment to inspect the new residence for the Vice President. Although Haig's briefing made it certain that he and Betty would never live there, Ford decided he should not cancel the visit and risk questions by Congress or the press about why he had done so.

An hour later, when Ford returned to his office, Hartmann reminded Ford that he had agreed to consult with Marsh. Not now, Ford said, he was already behind schedule. "Boss, I know you're rushed, but you just can't get involved with this thing in any way," Hartman pleaded. "You are going to be President. But you won't be able to run the country if you have anything to do with the way Nixon leaves office. You can't let anybody ever say you lifted one finger to make yourself President, or the job won't be worth having."

Ford listened, but impatiently. "I want to sleep on it," he said. He wanted to talk to Betty that night, and in the morning to St. Clair. With a grateful smile he added: "Thanks, Bob. I'll talk to Jack then too."

He left his office to attend, with Betty Ford, a dinner hosted by Betty Beale, society columnist for the *Washington Star*. He believed it would be a mistake to cancel; he had accepted the invitation and there would be reporters there, asking questions, and speculating if he and Betty did not show up. Throughout the evening, he was not preoccupied with the plight of a doomed President or the coming transformation of his life, but conversed freely with, among others, ABC's Barbara Walters and the *New York Times* Washington Bureau Chief Clifton Daniel. Not one, Ford said later, asked him a question about Nixon or what was about to happen at the White House.

Back home after the dinner, Ford mixed a drink for himself and Betty in the family room. He told her what Haig had said about Nixon's complicity in Watergate, and for the first time informed her that he would become President. "Either we will go to the White House next week," he said, "or we'll be dangling for six months while the impeachment process takes place in the House and a trial goes through the Senate." He described the "White House lawyers'" six options, and she read the two pages of handwritten notes.

When she put down the documents Betty Ford spoke, as was her way, with candor and from her conscience. She told her husband he should not make that trade to become President. He, in turn, in a lengthy discussion, pointed out the damage to the United States at home and abroad if the American people had to endure another six months of Watergate. "This just has to stop," he said. "It's tearing the country to pieces."

There was no doubt about that, she agreed. After an hour of discussing the pros and cons, she said: "Jerry, do whatever you think is right."

"I am going to go ahead and get this over with," Ford said, and telephoned Haig at 1:30 a.m. They talked, but exactly what Ford said, and what Haig understood Ford to have said, has never been clear.

At 8:00 a.m. the next morning, Ford met in his EOB office with James St. Clair, nominally the President's lead lawyer. For Ford the first question was, lawyer to lawyer: "Is the new evidence enough, in your best judgment, to impeach and convict the President?"

In answering, St. Clair first took care to point out that he had been informed of the criminal evidence on the June 23 tape only four days earlier, and was shocked not only by the extent of Nixon's guilt but also by Nixon's decision to withhold that evidence from his own defense lawyers. It placed him, he told Ford, in an ethically uncomfortable situation.

"What is your assessment now?" Ford asked.

"Unquestionably, this will lead the House to impeach the President and the Senate to convict him," St. Clair said. "The question now is: Will he resign or fight it through?"

Ford reviewed the six options Haig had presented, concluding with the "White House lawyers'" proposal that Nixon would resign in exchange for a pardon by Ford. St. Clair responded quietly: "I was not the source of any White House legal opinion about a President's power to issue pardons."

Ford was shocked. Not only had the President's lead attorney not been involved in the sixth option, but he was deliberately distancing himself from the idea. Ford wondered: who, then, was the White House lawyer who had drafted the two documents?

As soon as St. Clair left, Ford brought in Marsh and Hartmann and motioned them to chairs. For Marsh he recounted in detail the meeting with Haig the afternoon before, the evidence of Nixon's conspiracy in the cover-up, and the six options. Marsh asked to see the two documents Ford had been handed. Looking at them, Marsh immediately recognized the handwriting. It was the work of Fred Buzhardt, with whom Marsh had worked closely at the Pentagon.

The first paper, Marsh saw, was a concise, well-crafted brief of a President's power to pardon, reflecting the quality of legal expertise Marsh had observed in Buzhardt at the Department of Defense. The second was a ready-made grant of a pardon; only the name was missing. A typist could copy the draft, include a name, and have it ready for a new President's signature in minutes.

To Marsh, the scheme was self-evident. Nixon, knowing he could not survive, had concocted a deal: he would offer to end the crisis by resigning in exchange for a guarantee against prosecution. The best guarantee would be a pardon by the new President. Nixon would not use his outside lawyer, St. Clair, as agent; St. Clair might reject the idea and even resign in protest. The inside lawyer Nixon did trust, to a degree, was Buzhardt, so Nixon chose Buzhardt to execute the plan. Both Nixon and Buzhardt foresaw that Ford would not be familiar with a Presidential power to pardon, or the proper form for a pardon, so Buzhardt would provide the Vice President with a legal brief and a legal form: the first to inform him of the power to pardon; the second to make it easy for him to grant the pardon. Nixon calculated that Buzhardt would not be the best negotiator; Ford did not know him. But Nixon was well aware that Ford had come to admire and trust Haig, so Nixon instructed Buzhardt to have Haig propose the deal to Ford. Haig, military to the core, followed orders. Years later, Haig said, "I had no choice, I was told to raise the question of a pardon." To make it easier for Ford to accept, the raw deal was thinly disguised as one of six possibilities "under discussion." Given Ford's naïveté, he might agree on the spot.

Marsh was speculating, putting the pieces together. He did not know that only a day or so before, Nixon, in desperation, had telephoned his close friend and most pragmatic counselor, John Mitchell, and asked for advice. Mitchell was blunt: "Dick, make the best deal you can and resign."

Marsh, in the middle of Ford's account of the Haig meeting, saw the peril to Ford. Haig had jeopardized the Vice President the moment he spoke the word *pardon,* Marsh thought. Putting the deal in writing made it even worse. This had to be stopped. Now. "I am in strong agreement with Bob," Marsh said to Ford. "You can't be involved in anything that might at some point sound like some kind of deal."

Ford was defensive. "Haig was not suggesting a deal, Jack. These options hadn't even originated with him." Then he said something that alarmed his two aides even more. "Betty and I talked it over last night. We felt we were ready. This just has to stop. It's tearing the country to pieces. I decided to go ahead and get it over with, so I called Haig and told him they should do whatever they decided to do; it was all right with me."

That revelation struck the two aides like a body blow. A call to Haig in the middle of the night! Hartmann was outraged: Hadn't the boss promised to consult Marsh before he talked with anyone? Why had he telephoned Haig on so sensitive and crucial a subject at such an hour? "What was said about a pardon?" Marsh asked.

"Nothing that I can recall," Ford said.

That response alarmed Marsh even more. To Ford, he said: "Then Haig might conclude on the basis of your earlier talk, that a future pardon was still a viable option as an inducement to get Nixon to resign."

"Of course not!" Ford said, his voice and anger rising. "Haig knows better than that. There was no commitment, just conversation—and in strict confidence."

It was a tense and perilous moment for all three men. The two aides knew that such a secret would never keep. Nixon, Haig, Buzhardt, St. Clair, and possibly others knew about the deal, and this was a White House that leaked like a sieve. The deal had been put in writing; somewhere there were copies. Ford's telephone call had been logged by a White House phone operator; such a high-level call at that hour would surely cause suspicion. The log was subject to subpoena. Here they were, some eighteen hours after Haig had offered this monstrous deal, and Ford had not turned it down. In fact, it was clear to Marsh and Hartmann that Ford did not yet see, much less accept, the risk of considering the deal. Moreover, Ford was getting angry—the worst time to try to change his mind. As diplomatically as he could, Marsh said: "Jerry, if you don't believe Bob and me, talk to someone else whose advice you value."

"Who do you suggest?" Ford said.

Hartmann had composed a short list for just this situation. Marsh looked it over. "Bryce Harlow," he suggested.

"Fine," Ford said.

Bryce Harlow was graced with the trust of many in public life. Short, almost elfin, bright of eye and affable by nature, he had counseled Dwight D. Eisenhower, every President since, and countless others high in government and industry. All had learned to respect his wisdom and plainspeaking. Ford knew him well, liked his wiry athleticism, his cheerfulness. "Bryce," he once said, "can summarize a complex issue in the fewest words with brutal facts and lay out difficult alternatives very succinctly, in a soft, modulated voice, with crisp use of words and phrases. He never dodges the realities." Ford had often turned to Harlow for "his unbelievably good judgment and capacity to stay out of the headlines." Clearly, Marsh had chosen well. Hartmann telephoned Harlow. He could be there in mid-afternoon.

Sticking to his schedule, Ford rode up to the Capitol to meet with Senate Majority Leader Mansfield and Minority Leader Scott. They wanted to inform him of the procedures they were setting up to conduct the Senate trial of Nixon if the House, as all three expected, voted to impeach him. Ford would have no role in the proceedings—it would be chaired by Chief Justice Warren Burger—but the two Senate leaders wanted Ford to know the plan. Ford said nothing about Haig's disclosure of new evidence against Nixon.

During lunch in the Vice President's office off the Senate floor with his close friend and fellow Michigander, Senator Robert Griffin told Ford that for the first time he doubted Nixon's innocence. He had seen House Judiciary Committee evidence that clearly pointed to Nixon's collusion in the Watergate cover-up. "Jerry," Griffin said, "you might think about toning down your public statements supporting Nixon."

Ford, determined to reveal nothing of what he knew, said, "Well, I'll think about it."

Back in his EOB office, Ford kept an appointment with James Reston, reporter-in-chief for the *New York Times,* and widely acknowledged to be the best-informed newsman in Washington. None was more accurate or gifted with greater insight. Of Ford that day, Reston wrote: "He is the same open, unspoiled character. He is calm and fatalistic about his place in the current drama, as if he were an accidental player in some large inevitable script beyond his control . . ."

After Reston left, Ford closed his door and asked not be disturbed. He wanted time to think, to decide what he should do. Ford was not as naïve as Nixon thought; yet, for a professional politician, he had a minimal sense of popular opinion and public relations. Driven by duty, he believed that nothing—not Nixon's benefit nor his own reputation—was more important than restoring stability to Washington and bringing calm and confidence back to the nation. Ford was a public man who would become a rarity in Washington; he consistently, invariably, put the national interest ahead of personal ambition or partisan advantage. In this, Ford was not alone in his time; a score or more of others were peers of this realm of honor, but none exceeded Ford.

Alone in his office, Ford weighed the facts and the probabilities. If he should turn down the proposal, he must assume that there was an even chance that Nixon would claim his Constitutional right to hold fast to the Presidency unless impeached and convicted. Had not Haig, only yesterday, said he simply did not know whether Nixon would resign or fight? St. Clair had also made a point of saying he did not know whether the President would resign or fight. In the latter event, that would mean more months of Watergate. That would bring unacceptable harm at home and abroad. In Ford's mind there was no doubt: the public spectacle of a President on trial would further destabilize the government, demoralize leaders, shatter the confidence of the American people, and damage the reputation of the United States among the free people of the world. What if, during this time, the USSR or Red China should take advantage of a perceived American weakness to occupy territory vital to U.S. interests? If Watergate dragged on, what would happen to the U.S. economy, already in recession? Certainly it would worsen. It could even turn into a depression if business leaders and private citizens continued to lose confidence in their government. Why were Hartmann and Marsh so adamant? The plea bargain to persuade Agnew to resign had been negotiated by a most conscientious and practical Attorney General, approved by a foresighted Federal judge, and accepted by the press and almost everyone else as being in the best interest of the government and the American people. Was this so different?

At 3:30 p.m., Ford was still deliberating when Harlow arrived. For him, Ford recounted Haig's two visits and their discussions, including the six options, the proposal that he agree to pardon Nixon if he would resign, and the late-night call to Haig. "I told Bryce everything that had happened," Ford said. "He listened, his expression betraying no emotion at all. Only after I finished did he let me know in no uncertain terms that he agreed with Bob and Jack."

Hartmann, still the careful reporter, made notes, and in his inside account of his years with Ford, recorded Harlow's wise and prescient counsel:

"Well, Mr. Vice President," Harlow said, "I cannot for a moment believe that all this was Haig's idea or that the matters he discussed originated with 'the White House staff.' It is inconceivable that he was not carrying out a mission for the President, with precise instructions, and that it is the President who wants to hear your recommendations and test your reaction to the pardon question.

"But the President knows that he must be able to swear under oath that he never discussed this with you and that you must be able to swear that you never discussed it with him. Therefore he sends Haig, and therefore I would not advise you to try to clarify the matter with the President himself. That would only make matters worse, if that's possible.

"Bob and Jack are absolutely right, however, that there is grave danger here of compromising your future independence, because there is bound to be suspicion and bitterness when you take the place of the man who nominated you. You are going to be President for nearly three and hopefully seven years. Whether Nixon resigns or is convicted, the probability is that the question of a pardon will come before you sometime before you leave office.

"There must not be any cause for anyone to cry 'deal' if you have to make that decision, or any mystery about your position now that you know what Haig and St. Clair have told you. But the most urgent thing, Mr. Vice President, is to tell Al Haig, straight out and unequivocally, that whatever discussion you and he had yesterday and last night were purely hypothetical and conversational, that you will in no manner, affirmatively or negatively, advise him or the President as to his future course, and nothing you may have said is to be represented to the President, or to anyone else, to the contrary."

Throughout Harlow's soliloquy Ford listened, his chin resting on interlocked fingers, concentrating on every word. It did not take long for him to realize, he said later, that Harlow was unquestionably right. A deal was not merely unwise but would taint a new Administration. It would not end the Watergate crisis but extend it. The right thing to do was to turn down the proposition and stand free of Nixon's final decision.

"All right," Ford said. "I'll call Haig right now." He wrote out a script to follow, adopting Harlow's words, and delivered them in the presence of the three witnesses. At the end he put down the phone and said: "Al agrees."

Haig, in his White House office, guessed correctly what had happened: Ford's staff had persuaded him to reply "no deal." "That," Ford said later, "was what I wanted Nixon and Haig to know."

That night, after Nixon was informed of Ford's decision, he telephoned Haig at home: "Let them impeach me. We'll fight it out to the end." He told Haig to have Price draft a speech declaring it to be a President's duty to carry out the Constitutional procedure for impeachment and trial.

Ford, committed to his schedule, boarded his Convair the next day, a Saturday, and flew to Mississippi to campaign for three House candidates: Ben Hilbun, Thad Cochran, and Trent Lott. Cochran, a new House member, told Ford he was concerned that he might have to vote to impeach Nixon, still very popular in his District. Attempting to reassure Cochran, Ford confided: "Thad, you may not ever have to cast that vote." It was the first time Ford implied to anyone that he thought Nixon might resign.

Flying on to New Orleans, Ford golfed on Sunday morning, his concentration steady, his score in his customary upper 80s. That evening he attended a small dinner hosted by a House friend, David Treen, and Monday morning, holding to his schedule, he addressed the national convention of the Disabled American Veterans. By mid-afternoon, Ford was back in his EOB office.

Haig immediately came over to give Ford an update: the White House would release the June 23 and other incriminating tapes late that afternoon. The President continued to equivocate; one hour saying he would resign, the next, that he would fight on. Tricia, Julie, and their husbands, Edward Cox and David Eisenhower, continued to plead for him to hold fast, insisting it was not only his duty but it would be best for the country. Buzhardt and St. Clair thought Nixon's case hopeless, and were insisting that any White House comment on the tapes make it clear that this evidence of Presidential conspiracy had been hidden from them. Both were concerned about preserving their reputations.

Haig had brought into his White House office Charles Wiggins, the respected Congressman and astute California lawyer on whom Nixon was counting to lead his defense on the House Judiciary Committee. Handed the transcript of the June 23rd tape, Wiggins read it and told Haig: "The Presidency of Richard Nixon has effectively been destroyed. He should resign." He asked Haig to so inform the President. Yet Nixon continued to vacillate. Again Haig told Ford that he did not know what Nixon would do. "It could go either way," he said.

To Ford it was all too evident that the crisis was leaving its mark on this loyal soldier. "Haig looked even more haggard than before," Ford said. "I had never seen a man so physically and emotionally drained."

Uncertainty was also leaving its mark on Ford. "It was the wait," Ford said later. "Nixon was finished. No longer was there any doubt in my mind about that. The only question was when he would realize this and what he would do about it. I was tired. I had not seen Betty or the children for several days." He called for his car, went home, and had a long swim in his pool and a quiet dinner with Betty, Steve, and Susan.

Just as they finished, Major George Joulwan, Haig's deputy, telephoned to say the President would hold a Cabinet meeting the next morning. Probably, Ford thought, he plans to tell us he will resign. After he hung up the phone, Ford said: "Betty, tomorrow morning I am going to tell the President face to face at the Cabinet meeting that I can no longer support him."

She was relieved. "I was surprised he had gone along with it as long as he had," she said. She had been worried that he was hurting his own reputation, but had held back from telling him so.

On the way to the office the next morning, Ford opened the *Washington Post,* and for the first time read the transcript of the June 23rd White House tape. The evidence was unmistakable: This President had ordered a government agency, the CIA, to stop a legitimate FBI investigation. No doubt about it: this was obstruction of justice, a serious crime.

At Cabinet meetings during the Nixon Administration it was customary for Members to arrive early, take their seats, and—when the President entered—rise and applaud. This time, the Cabinet rose but stood in silence. Ford, seated directly across the table from Nixon, thought he looked tired, drawn, his mind far away.

Affecting firmness and authority, the President opened the session: "I would like to discuss the most important issue confronting the nation and confronting us internationally too—inflation."

Ford was stunned, disbelieving. My God! he said to himself, wondering if events had weighed so heavily on Nixon that he had lost his sense of reality. How, he asked himself, could Nixon not come out and acknowledge that he himself was the issue? How could he not know the question on every mind in the room: what is he going to do? "His words were totally irrelevant to the circumstances that confronted him and the nation," Ford said.

Finally, Nixon brought up Watergate, defending his decision to have the CIA stop the FBI investigation as necessary to national security. "That is ludicrous," Ford thought. Nixon went on to say he "thought it proper" to make the tapes and transcripts public before impeachment proceedings began. That too was denial. Every Member of the Cabinet was well aware that Nixon had surrendered the incriminating documents only after he was ordered to do so by the Supreme Court.

After rambling on for a time, Nixon finally answered the crucial question: He would not resign. He had considered it, but rejected it. To do so, he argued, would set a precedent that a President could remain in office only with the approval of Congress.

His words and rationale provoked a long silence. Not one person in the room offered a word of support.

In that awkward interval Ford spoke up: "Everyone here recognizes the difficult position I'm in. No one regrets more than I do this whole tragic episode. I have deep personal sympathy for you, Mr. President, and your fine family. But I wish to emphasize that had I known what has been discussed in reference to Watergate in the last twenty-four hours, I would not have made a number of the statements I made either as Minority Leader or Vice President.

"I came to a decision yesterday . . . I'll have no further comment on the issue because I'm a party in interest. I'm sure there will be impeachment in the House. I can't predict the Senate outcome . . . Mr. President, you have given us the finest foreign policy this country has ever had. Let me assure you that I expect to continue to support the Administration foreign policy and the fight against inflation."

Nixon looked startled at first, then said, "I think your position is exactly correct," and resumed his discussion of inflation. He told the Cabinet he would support a summit meeting of business and government leaders to address the country's economic problems.

"Mr. President!" a voice interrupted. "I don't think we ought to have a summit conference. We ought to be sure you have the ability to govern." The speaker was William Saxbe, a new Cabinet Member, appointed Attorney General from the Senate because he could be easily confirmed. Saxbe had said what others thought but could not bring themselves to say to a President.

"Bill," Nixon said coldly, "I have the ability just as I have had for the last five and a half years."

After Saxbe's blunt interruption, Republican National Chairman George H. W. Bush spoke out. He told Nixon their party was in turmoil, facing heavy losses in the Congressional elections three months away. "Watergate," Bush said to Nixon, "must be brought to an end." Nixon stared at Bush but said nothing.

Before anyone else could speak, Kissinger intervened. In the sonorous voice that seemed to validate the authority of the highest-ranking Cabinet member, he said: "We are here to do the nation's business . . . We must demonstrate that the country can go through its Constitutional processes. For the sake of foreign policy we must act with assurance and total unity."

It had been a Cabinet meeting like no other, with Nixon's own appointees turning on him, rejecting him. "It was vintage Nixon," Kissinger wrote later. "Fearing individual rejection, he had assembled the largest possible forum. Hoping for a vote of confidence, he sought to confront them with a *fait accompli,* and thereby triggered their near-rebellion."

From the Cabinet meeting Ford rode to the Capitol for his regular Tuesday lunch with Republican senators. Most knew he had just met with Nixon, so he faced a barrage of questions: What's going on at the White House? Will he resign or not? Ford did not know, and said so. Senators Jacob Javits and Bill Brock proposed that Ford deliver a warning to Nixon that he was losing the Senate. "As a party at interest," Ford said, "I can't be a conduit." As Senator Norris Cotton and others spoke up to advocate sending a delegation to inform Nixon of his bleak outlook in the Senate, Ford rose and asked to be excused. "I don't think I should be part of this discussion," he said firmly. As he walked from the room the Senators rose and applauded.

Riding back along Pennsylvania Avenue to his EOB office, Ford thought over the openly expressed hostility of Republican senators and inferred from those voices the Senate verdict to come. The June 23 transcript was fatal. The President, he calculated, could no longer count on one-third of the Senate to stand by him. Therefore, Nixon would be convicted and forced out of office. If the White House legislative staff gave Nixon an accurate count of the Senate vote, then, by all logic, he should resign. Still, only three hours earlier he had told the Cabinet he would not resign.

From his car Ford walked quickly up the stairs to his EOB office, summoned Hartmann immediately, and motioned for him to close the door. "Bob, I think you'd better start thinking about what I should say after the swearing in. I don't want anything fancy, but think about it."

"How much time do we have?" Hartmann asked.

"Well, two or three days, maybe less."

If it happened that soon—and it could—Ford knew he must be prepared.

After the Cabinet meeting, Kissinger returned to the Oval Office to meet alone with Nixon. On his own initiative Kissinger told President Nixon he felt it is duty to advise "that his best service to the country now would be to resign." Impeachment and trial, Kissinger said, would "paralyze our foreign policy . . . [be] too dangerous for our country, and too demeaning to the Presidency." Nixon listened, said he would seriously consider Kissinger's observations, but nothing more. To Kissinger, Nixon appeared still to be at war with himself.

For almost an hour Nixon brooded alone in the Oval Office. At 1:30 p.m., he sent for his chief legislative assistant, William Timmons. Motioning Timmons to the chair to his right, Nixon said: "Bill, where do we stand in the Senate?"

"Mr. President, we can count on only seven Members of the Senate," Timmons said. Roster in hand, Nixon went over the names one by one, mentioning how he had campaigned for this Senator, approved a major project for that Member. One by one, the President and his chief emissary to Congress struck off the names of once-loyal Members on whom they could no longer count. Nixon did not question his assistant's individual or summary judgments. Timmons accuracy was legendary; he and Tom Korogolos, his indefatigable deputy working the Senate, had been updating the count through the night and all morning. Twenty-seven votes had been lost in less than twenty-four hours—all because of the June 23 transcript. The Members they could count on were down to seven: Republicans Wallace Bennett, Norris Cotton, Carl

Curtis, and Roman Hruska; Democrats James Allen, John Stennis, and James Eastland.

The President held the verdict in his hand: Guilty. Defeated.

As Nixon handed the roster back, Timmons mentioned that the Senate Republicans had designated Senator Barry Goldwater as the man to deliver to the President the assessment of his situation in the Senate.

"Bill," Nixon said quietly, "set up a meeting with Goldwater tomorrow afternoon. Scott and Rhodes should come too."

From the meeting with Timmons in the Oval Office, Nixon walked over to his hideaway in the EOB, and there for some time he sat alone, thinking. Late that afternoon, Tuesday, August 6, 1974, he made his final decision: he would resign. He had lost. To be the President of the United States had been the supreme goal of Richard Nixon's life, the pinnacle of a public career—and he had blundered it away.

So, at 3:30 p.m., Nixon telephoned Rose Mary Woods and asked for her help in convincing the family that he must end the agony. "Tell them that the whole bunch is deserting now."

Taking up his yellow legal pad, he wrote down a heading—Resignation Speech—sketched an outline and made notes for Ray Price, his favorite and best speechwriter. He then summoned Haig and Ziegler and informed them of his plan. On Thursday night he would go on television to announce his decision to resign at noon the next day. On Friday morning he would leave the White House, board Air Force One for California, and be somewhere over mid-America when his Presidency ended.

His decision was to remain secret until he announced it himself, he told the two, and he wanted no leaks. On Thursday morning he would personally inform Ford of his decision. In the meantime, Nixon instructed Haig, tell Ford to be ready to take over on short notice, but nothing more.

After a brief silence he added—evidently with an attempt at gallows humor—"Well, I screwed up good, real good, didn't I?"

The truth at last.

From the after-midnight burglary of the Watergate office building on June 17, 1972, to the resignation of President Nixon at noon on August 9, 1974, the infamy of Watergate spanned two years and fifty-four days. Over that course of time, the principal institutions of Washington carried out their duties with skill, integrity, and courage. The press—specifically the *Washington Post*—revealed the crime and provoked the investigations by the courts, prosecutors, and Congress. These entities of the Federal government then acted, in a sort of legal relay, with the baton handed from a Federal Court to the Senate Watergate Committee, to the Special Prosecutor, to the House Judiciary Committee, to the Supreme Court, with these institutions each being led by men whose names shall live in honor: John Sirica, Archibald Cox, Leon Jaworski, Sam Ervin, Howard Baker, Peter Rodino, Warren Burger.

1971. House Minority Leader Gerald Ford, Senate Minority Leader Hugh Scott, and Representative John Rhodes (seated behind Scott) meet with President Nixon in the Cabinet Room. (Courtesy of the Gerald R. Ford Library.)

August 8, 1974. Vice President Ford waits just outside the
Oval Office to see President Nixon. (Nixon Presidential Papers.)

August 8, 1974. Vice President Ford sits at Nixon's right at the Presidential Desk in the Oval Office as Nixon says he will resign the next day, and Ford will become President. (Nixon Presidential Papers.)

August 20, 1974. 10:00 a.m. Ford nominates Nelson Rockefeller to be Vice President. (Courtesy of the Gerald R. Ford Library.)

August 28, 1974. 2:30 p.m. Ford holds his first press conference and gives conflicting answers on what he will do about Nixon. (Courtesy of the Gerald R. Ford Library.)

September 26, 1974. Ford learns Betty may have breast cancer.
(Courtesy of the Gerald R. Ford Library.)

November 19, 1974. Ford in Japan, the first U.S. President to visit Japan. (Courtesy of the Gerald R. Ford Library.)

April 28, 1975. In the Roosevelt Room, Ford meets with the
National Security Council on pulling out Americans from Vietnam.
" . . . saddest day of my life . . ." (Courtesy of the Gerald R. Ford
Library.)

November 3, 1975. Rockefeller dumped. Schlesinger fired;
Rumsfeld to Defense. Colby fired; George H. W. Bush to the CIA.
Kissinger loses National Security Council; Scowcroft takes over.
Rogers Morton resigns from Commerce; Elliott Richardson
succeeds. In the White House, Cheney moves up to Chief of Staff.
Here, the author (*left*) meets with Vice President Rockefeller in the
White House during that time of sweeping changes. (Courtesy of
the Gerald R. Ford Library.)

December 1975. Ford meets with Vice Premier Teng Hsiao-p'ing in Peking. (Courtesy of the Gerald R. Ford Library.)

July 7, 1976. Queen Elizabeth II visits the Fords. (Courtesy of the Gerald R. Ford Library.)

August 19, 1976. Ford wins Republican nomination, calls on
Reagan. (Courtesy of the Gerald R. Ford Library.)

August 20, 1976. Ford chooses Dole for Vice President and begins campaign in Russell, Kansas. (Courtesy of the Gerald R. Ford Library.)

October 6, 1976. Second debate with Carter, and the mistake regarding Poland. (Courtesy of the Gerald R. Ford Library.)

November 3, 1976. The Ford family gathers to hear Betty read President Ford's concession speech, as Ford is too hoarse from the final days of campaigning. (Courtesy of the Gerald R. Ford Library.)

January 20, 1977. President Ford and Betty and Vice President Rockefeller and Mrs. Rockefeller board the helicopter to fly around the Capitol for one last look. (Courtesy of the Gerald R. Ford Library.)

PART 3

Taking Charge

In the first hour of his first full day in the Oval Office, Ford faced his first problem as President: Al Haig.

Haig, assuming he would continue to wield the authority with Ford that he had in the Nixon White House, was waiting at the Oval Office door when Ford arrived at 8:30 a.m. that Saturday. On the previous afternoon, hours after Ford had taken the oath of office, Haig had denigrated Ford's ability, telling Jerry Jones, White House Staff Secretary, that the new President would not know how to govern on his own. "We have to rescue Ford from his own inexperience," he said, and instructed Jones to put together a detailed document instructing Ford on how the White House worked. Greeting Ford the next morning, Haig handed President Ford the ten pages to read, and informed him he would remain as Chief of Staff only on his own terms; that is, he must control all hiring and firing of White House staff, "and the first guy to go will be Hartmann."

Ford, who had come to respect Haig for the way he had kept the Executive departments functioning as Nixon lost his capacity to govern, was astonished at Haig's arrogance. New to the office he was, but Ford had no intention of permitting a hired hand to tell him how to do his job. Ford supposed that the strain on Haig had warped his judgment, so he listened patiently and said nothing.

"Think about it," Haig said abruptly, "and I'll see you in two days."

As Haig turned to go, Ford said quietly: "Al, Bob Hartmann is someone I will handle."

Haig had accelerated his own exit. Ford had already decided there would be no autocrat as chief of staff in his Administration. From the first, he had disliked Haldeman's imperious manner, and he believed that Nixon's downfall was caused in part by giving too much authority to his staff. It was Ford's idea to be his own chief of staff. He would manage the Presidency by a process that he called "spokes of the wheel"; that is, he—the hub of the wheel—would meet daily and separately with senior assistants responsible for domestic policy, foreign policy, Congressional liaison, legal affairs, press, and personnel. Each would bring in the developments and problems of the day; after a discussion, Ford would make his decisions and the assistant would carry them out. One-on-one meetings with Members and staff were the way he had managed his leadership office in the House; he saw no reason to change.

In his hub-and-spokes organization there would be no Nixonian chief of staff. So Haig must go. His presumptuousness that Saturday morning made it easy. Nevertheless, Ford calculated that he could use Haig in the transition, so he decided to keep him around for a few weeks. Ford also recognized that Haig's meritorious performance for the country warranted an honorable exit; he made a mental note to find an appropriate new assignment for Haig.

The next problem for the new President was of greater consequence. At the morning intelligence briefing, Scowcroft asked: "Mr. President, do you remember a briefing on the *Glomar Explorer*?" Ford did remember. In fact, he had not only known about this top secret CIA enterprise, but had been involved in appropriating $300 million for this project to obtain vital information about the Soviet Navy.

In the spring of 1968, U.S. Navy intelligence in Hawaii had tracked a Soviet Golf-II submarine, loaded with ballistic nuclear missiles and moving eastward out of Vladivostok across the Pacific Ocean. Some 750 miles northwest of Hawaii the hull evidently ruptured and the Russian submarine sank 17,000 feet to the bottom of the ocean. The Navy's underwater listening devices heard it go down. Soviet surface vessels searched for the sub, but apparently never found it. The U.S. Navy did know its exact location, and considered it a major prize of intelligence. Almost certainly it contained the Soviets' latest propulsion system, weapons, codes, and systems of communication and command.

Responding to the Navy, the CIA turned to the audacious entrepreneur Howard Hughes, and contracted with him to build a ship that could pick up the Soviet submarine from the bottom of the sea, bring it up into its huge belly, and deliver it to the U.S. Navy. The cover story was that the *Glomar Explorer* was a deep-sea mining vessel that would extract valuable ores—manganese and cobalt—from the ocean floor.

On that August morning, Scowcroft reported to Ford that the *Glomar Explorer* was in position, hovering over the Soviet submarine, and ready to lower the huge claws that would grapple and lift it. But the "mining vessel" was not alone. A Soviet trawler had been trailing and photographing the *Glomar Explorer* for days, and was now circling it. If armed Russians attempted to board the unarmed *Glomar Explorer* to intervene, no U.S. Navy ship was close enough to protect the CIA's spy vessel. President Ford must decide: should the attempt to raise the Soviet submarine go forward?

Ford listened, told Scowcroft he wanted to hear the views of the national security officials involved, and instructed him to convene an NSC meeting as soon as possible.

Moving briskly through the morning, Ford met at 10:00 a.m. with the Cabinet he had inherited from Nixon. Deliberately changing from the stiff formality of Nixon's Cabinet sessions, Ford walked around the coffin-shaped table, shook hands and had a word with each Member before he took his seat. He had prepared his message: "I do not want and will not accept any resignation at this point. We need continuity and stability. I am looking forward to working with each and every one of you." Continuity, not change, was Ford's prime objective at the beginning of his Presidency.

From the Cabinet Room Ford took Kissinger into the Oval Office. He had a political decision in mind, and he wanted advice about it. "Henry," he said, "during my confirmation as Vice President I made a commitment to the Senate that I would not be a candidate for President in 1976. I believe my role as President will be enhanced if I make a public announcement to that effect. I believe I will strengthen myself in the Congress, and in the country, by making it clear that the decisions I make as President have no relation to my political future because I have no intention of being a candidate."

Kissinger was astonished. For a long moment he thought about the best way he could tell a new President, diplomatically, that he was wrong. He decided to speak plainly: "Mr. President, in my judgment that would be a mistake. A very serious mistake, especially as it relates to foreign policy. It would mean that for more than two years foreign governments—both Allies and adversaries—would know that they were dealing with a lame duck President and therefore our foreign policy initiatives would be in a stalemate."

Ford listened, impressed by Kissinger's reasoning. His intentions had been good, but out of political ingenuousness Ford had totally misread the realities of political power and public opinion. He assumed that Congress and the American people would welcome a President who was not running for office; it had not occurred to Ford that the authority of a President is as prospective as it is current. Had he volunteered that he was in the White House merely to serve out the balance of Nixon's term, he would have been scorned as a caretaker. Moreover, he would have raised questions about his capacity for the job, thereby weakening, perhaps irreparably, his new Administration. So, Ford took Kissinger's advice. He remained convinced that during his time as President he should base his decisions not on political advantage but on the public interest, but he accepted Kissinger's advice and withheld an announcement that would have made him a political neuter.

After his talk with Kissinger, the two walked together to the Cabinet room for a full meeting of the National Security Council. The central issue: whether to authorize the *Glomar Explorer* to proceed with the operation to raise the Soviet sub. Going around the room, Ford asked each Member for his assessment of the risks and possible gains from the operation. One by one, they responded—Kissinger, Defense Secretary James Schlesinger, Deputy Defense Secretary Bill Clements, CIA Director William Colby, Chairman of the Joint Chiefs George Brown, Deputy Secretary of State Robert Ingersoll. At the end, Ford asked if anyone had more to say; he wanted to make sure that all opinions had been fully and fairly considered. When all had been heard, Ford made his decision: "Having progressed as far as we have, he said, we should gamble and proceed."

The operation was successful—not as fully as the CIA hoped but more than they admitted. The official report stated that the submarine broke up as it was being lifted, and so only parts were brought up. Actually the haul was significant: the *Glomar Explorer* recovered three Soviet nuclear missiles, two nuclear torpedoes, the submarine's code machine, and code books. Also in the wreckage were the bodies of six Russian sailors, which were respectfully buried at sea.

For the balance of his first full day in office, Ford initiated and followed his spokes-of-the-wheel plan—meeting separately with Hartmann, his senior counselor and chief of speech writing; Marsh, his counselor and chief of Congressional liaison; Buchen, his lawyer; Haig, his holdover for operations; terHorst, his press secretary; and David Kennerly, his chosen White House photographer. With each, he listened and gave directions, then brought in the next man. Twice he summoned Donald Rumsfeld to discuss his next moves in the transition. To close the business of the day, Ford walked over to his Vice Presidential office in the EOB, cleared the desk that he would no longer use, and at 6:02 p.m. left for his house in Alexandria. In his mind, it had been a productive day. "I felt I was off to a good start," he said.

From this first day the formidable challenge to Ford was to learn how to perform as President while climbing out of the debris left by Nixon: a demoralized Washington establishment, a White House staffed by Nixon loyalists who doubted his capability, and a suspicious press that would not and could not let go of Nixon and Watergate.

Ford was well aware that he must learn on the job, as all new Presidents must. He, better than anyone else in Washington, also recognized the problems he confronted. "In that environment, caused by Watergate on the one hand and the tragedy of Vietnam on the other, there was a tension of public feeling that nobody could understand unless they were there," he said long after. "So my first responsibility was to restore public confidence in the Federal government, and with that heal the wounds the country suffered by those two tragedies, Vietnam and Watergate.

"Secondly, I inherited a terrible economic situation—interest at an all-time high, inflation at a postwar high. We were on the brink of an economic recession.

"Third, we had to deal with the last Titan of the Stalinist era, Brezhnev. He was tough. Those who followed were minor leaguers."

These were problems that Ford understood and stood ready to address; but there was another problem, and it would prove to be the most intractable of all. It was a problem he had not anticipated and did not yet grasp: Richard Nixon.

A couple of hours after Ford left the White House that Saturday, Benton Becker, a lawyer temporarily assisting Buchen with the transition, happened to look out the window of the Vice Presidential Suite where he was working. On West Executive Avenue, the closed-to-the-public street between the Executive Office Building and the White House, he witnessed something strange. Trucks with U.S. Air Force markings were lined up on the street, and men were carting file cabinets and sealed boxes out of the Executive Office Building, and loading them into the trucks. Why, Becker wondered, were official documents being spirited out of the White House in the dark on a Saturday night? Outside, he learned that the trucks were loading Nixon's papers. An airman told him they were transporting them to Andrews Air Force Base to be flown to California and delivered to Nixon in San Clemente. Becker found the officer in charge and asked: "Who authorized this shipment?"

"I answer to General Haig," the officer said.

Becker, unable to find any Ford person in the White House with the authority to stop the movement, made an urgent appeal to the Secret Service. The chief agent on duty acted. Confronting the Air Force officer in charge, he ordered the trucks unloaded and the files and boxes returned to the Executive Office Building.

By good fortune, President Ford had escaped—barely—a certain legal problem, and an unexplainable public-relations disaster.

On Sunday, Ford attended church and returned to the Oval Office. Eager to tackle his new responsibilities, he brought in an array of favorite counselors, mostly close friends from the House—mentor Mel Laird, fellow Michigander Al Cederburg, brainy Barber Conable, Republication National Committee chairman George H. W. Bush, House Whip Les Arends, and House Republican Leader John Rhodes. From the Senate he met with Bob Griffin, Barry Goldwater, John Tower, and Hugh Scott. Investing twenty-five to thirty minutes with each man, Ford asked about legislative strategy, military capabilities, topics for his speech to Congress the next day, the state of the Republican Party, the state of the nation, and possible choices for his Vice President. To Bryce Harlow, Ford assigned the job of identifying the best prospects for Vice President and delivering a written evaluation of the merits and disadvantages of each candidate. That busy Sunday afternoon exemplified Ford's way: meet face-to-face, ask questions, listen, make a judgment, assign a task, move on to the next issue.

In his formal televised address to Congress on Monday evening, Ford opened with a typical down-to-earth admonition: "My former colleagues, you and I have a lot of work to do. Let's get on with it." Looking ahead, he added, "I do not want a honeymoon with you. I want a good marriage."

The relationship defined, President Ford set forth his priorities: First, "to work with you to bring inflation under control. Inflation is domestic enemy number one." To that end, he had instructed his Cabinet members "to make fiscal restraint their first order of business." Congress, he admonished, must do its part; he would not hesitate to use the veto to curb excessive Congressional spending. He accepted Senator Majority Leader Mansfield's proposal for a summit conference of government and business leaders to devise a bipartisan plan to stabilize and expand the U.S. economy.

Taking his stand on national security and international relations, Ford reminded Congress, "Over the past five and a half years in Congress and as Vice President, I have fully supported the outstanding foreign policy of President Nixon." As President, Ford said firmly: "This policy I intend to continue." He reaffirmed his conviction, based on his twenty-five years of experience in dealing with military strategy and defense appropriations, that "a strong defense is the surest way to peace . . . Just as America's will for peace is second to none, so will America's strength be second to none." He restated America's commitment to allies in Europe and Asia and to the Paris agreement on Vietnam, and offered his hand of friendship and cooperation to the Soviet Union and the People's Republic of China.

The speech was not an oration, nor was it inspiring, but the words of a public man who spoke plainly and directly. It was exactly what Ford intended it to be: a wide-ranging statement that specified the new President's immediate interests and longer-range objectives. At the speech's end, the Members of the House and Senate stood as one to applaud the man they had chosen to lead the country. In his mind, Ford was pleased with his performance. "I tried to project a calmness and a steady hand," he said later. "A President asserts leadership by communicating with the public and the Congress what the problems are. He has to go to the people with one hand and pull Congress along with the other. He can't get Congress to move unless he has the people with him."

To the press, it was a success. Hedley Donovan, editor-in-chief of *Time*, watched from the press gallery and wrote: "This was perhaps the most moving Presidential speech I have ever heard." The *New York Times*' Washington Bureau Chief, Clifton Daniel, found more sympathy than substance: "They interrupted him with applause 32 times, and they probably would have cheered if he had read them a page from the telephone book. They were that anxious to show their approval of him, and their hopes for his Administration."

The next day, Ford, acting on a backlog of legislation left over from Nixon's inaction, carried out his promise for fiscal restraint. He vetoed a bill from Congress that would have raised the pay of U.S. Marshals as unfair to other Federal employees. He vetoed a second bill—this one for animal-health research—as unnecessary and inflationary. He signed another that provided Federal planning to manage and preserve "our priceless natural legacy of forests and rangelands." This reflected Ford the conservationist; strong views he had held since the summer of 1936, when he had worked as a forest ranger in Yellowstone National Park. For the rest of his life, Ford maintained a special interest in and regard for America's national parks and forests.

In his first full week in office, Ford also kept his predecessor's commitment to host a state visit for King Hussein of Jordan. Dispensing with the stuffy formality of Nixon's state dinners, Ford and Betty invited a cross section of notables for an evening that concluded with music and dancing until 1:00 a.m. At dinner, President Ford toasted King Hussein: "On a very personal note it is a great honor and privilege for me to have you as the first chief of state to visit our country during the new Administration." The dinner also gave Ford an opportunity to show his appreciation to the seven reporters who had ridden the old Convair and covered his peregrinations as Vice President. Another guest was an old friend from Michigan, former Defense Secretary Robert McNamara. As he left the White House, McNamara remarked to Ford: "Boy, what a change."

Bryce Harlow came in to the Oval Office to present his analysis of sixteen possible candidates for Ford to consider. In an example of Harlow's excellent staff work, he had graded each candidate on experience, geography, standing in the Republican Party, clean image, selfless support of the President, competence, national stature, age, capability to broaden Ford's political base, and any taint from too close an association with Nixon. Rating all on qualification and merit, Harlow had narrowed the choice to George H. W. Bush and Nelson Rockefeller. Of Bush, Harlow wrote: "Strongest across the board; greatest weakness— regarded as intellectually 'light' by many top leaders in the country."

Harlow's appraisal of Rockefeller was: "Professionally the best qualified, by far, with added strengths of (a) proving President's self-confidence in bringing in a towering Number Two, (b) making available superb manpower resources to staff the new Administration, and (c) broadening the Ford political base. Greatest weaknesses—age, serious conservative irritation (in both parties), and acute discomfort functioning as Number Two to anyone."

Offering his best judgment, Harlow wrote: "In sum, it would appear that the choice narrows to Bush and Rockefeller. For party harmony, plainly it should be Bush, but generally that would be construed as a weak and depressingly conventional act, foretelling a Presidential hesitance to move boldly in face of known controversy. A Rockefeller choice would be hailed by the media normally most hostile to Republicans, would encourage estranged groups to return to the party, and would signal that this new President will not be a captive of any political faction. As for 1976, a Ford-Rockefeller ticket should be an extremely formidable combination against any opponents the Democrats should offer. Therefore, the best choice—Rockefeller."

Ford listened, studied the grades Harlow had assigned to each candidate, and reflected on Harlow's conclusion. He consulted other advisers—Laird, Conable, Kissinger. "I had a lot of pressure," Ford said. "Pressure from George Bush, who had all the political power, the state chairmen, national committeeman. He had all that group. Ronald Reagan had the California mafia and the hard line right wing. Nelson did not come out first in popularity, but in government experience. I had the feeling that in my own situation as President, my background, the way I came in, I needed the strongest possible, the most highly effective person at my side. That immediately eliminated Reagan. It didn't rule out George Bush, but when you compared his experience to what I needed, he didn't equal Nelson Rockefeller.

"Rockefeller will overshadow you, some told me, but I had no apprehension about that. Too often nominees for President pick a weak guy for a running mate. I think it's a sign of insecurity."

In practical terms, the combination of Ford and Rockefeller was a fusion of political philosophies. Ford was a fiscal conservative, sparing of the taxpayer; Rockefeller was a progressive Republican, an enthusiastic initiator of government programs that cost big money. In other ways, the two were close. Both were internationalists, one-world conceptualizers, believing the United States should maintain and advance a dynamic foreign policy, convinced the United States can and must lead the world. Both advocated and worked toward maintaining strong military defense forces. Both believed strongly in the three-tier Federal system of American government, and worked together to advance that idea. In 1972, for example, Rockefeller had delivered more votes than anyone outside Congress in the successful campaign that Ford—then House Republican Leader—had led for the Federal Revenue Sharing program that delivered financial aid to hard-pressed state and local governments.

On Saturday morning, August 17, Ford made his decision. Methodically, he wrote out nine issues to discuss with Rockefeller and telephoned him in Maine. Rockefeller, who rarely vacationed, was there with Happy and their two sons—Nelson, then 10, and Mark, 7—at their serene retreat overlooking the cold blue waters and verdant islands of Seal Harbor, Maine.

"Nelson, I want you to be the Vice President and I'll tell you why," Ford said. "I think the country needs you, a person of your stature, both domestically and internationally. I think it will strengthen my Administration at a traumatic time. We have worked together before and I know we can work together very well."

Aware that Rockefeller had often said, "I never wanted to be vice president of *anything*," Ford assured him: "I will give you meaningful assignments. I do not intend that you would just preside over the Senate and go on ceremonial trips. We have tremendous problems, both at home and abroad, and I believe your input, whether in the Cabinet or in the National Security Council, will be invaluable."

For both their benefit, Ford carefully addressed the other points he had written out for discussion, asking first about Rockefeller's health. Next, would any of Rockefeller's huge expenditures in politics be embarrassing? If he accepted, Ford warned, the FBI and the IRS would probe into every aspect of his personal life, wealth, and career in politics and public service. Nothing would be overlooked.

As a commitment to Congress, Ford said: "I put down one mandatory requirement: Nelson, you and Happy must live in the new Vice President's house. I know you have your own fine house in Washington, but Senators Byrd, Griffin, and others have broken their ass to take Admiral's House from the Navy and make it the permanent home for the Vice President." Later, Ford said, "Nelson agreed, though I am not sure he knew what I was talking about."

Ford defined their responsibilities: he would handle foreign policy; Rockefeller would manage domestic policy. Rockefeller would be assigned most of the traveling for the Republican Party, but Ford made it plain that he would be barred from using the Vice Presidency to run for

President. "I will run in '76," Ford said, "and I will expect your loyalty and support."

As Ford talked through his offer and set the conditions, Rockefeller listened carefully and at the end said: "I am honored, Mr. President, but I need a day to think it over."

Rockefeller had already been thinking it over. Mel Laird, either on his own initiative or acting for the President, had telephoned several days earlier to find out if Rockefeller would accept if asked. After that call, Rockefeller summoned his most-listened-to-adviser, William Ronan. An astute political scientist and executive, with a quick mind that combined philosophy and practicality, Ronan had been the architect for Rockefeller's first election to New York's highest state office. In Albany, Ronan had served as chief of staff, helping to create, initiate, and execute Rockefeller's programs and policies as New York's most innovative Governor.

"I think you're going to do this, but in my judgment it's not a good thing for you to do," Ronan said. He reminded Rockefeller of how unhappy he had been as a subordinate in the Eisenhower Administration, and now, after being elected four terms as Governor, how much more difficult it would be for him to endure a subordinate status in Washington. Furthermore, Ronan said, "You will lose your independence as an advocate of public policy and your leadership of the moderate wing of the Republican Party, whatever is left of it."

Rockefeller carefully weighed Ronan's counsel. He had long regarded the Vice Presidency as "standby equipment," and that was a role he disdained. Twice—in 1960 and 1968—he had turned it down. From Henry Wallace through Spiro Agnew, Rockefeller had personally known every Vice President; all suffered from the emptiness and sham of the position. Moreover, Rockefeller had conducted a study for President Eisenhower to determine what use could be made of the Vice Presidency. The conclusion: nothing.

Yet, after Ford's call, Rockefeller was inclined to take the job. So he next consulted with the two most important members of his family—Laurance, his closest brother, and Happy. Both thought he should accept. "It sounded very exciting," Happy said, "and I believed it was a good way to end his public career."

Again, Rockefeller talked with Ronan. "What will be your responsibility?" Ronan asked. Foreign policy is Kissinger's domain, he pointed out. Presciently, he suggested, Ford's promise that as Vice President he would oversee domestic policy, while undoubtedly well-intentioned, was unrealistic. Any Rockefeller initiative would inevitably contest with OMB, the Cabinet secretaries, Congressional relations staff, and the President's own domestic philosophy and priorities. In sum, Ronan believed Rockefeller could never accept being in a position so near, and yet so far, from the pinnacle of political power and responsibility.

But with Nixon and Watergate having provoked a national crisis that demanded the best of national leaders, how—Rockefeller asked himself—could he say no? In his head and in his heart Rockefeller had no doubt about it: this new President, taking over in such troubled times, needed him. If he accepted, Rockefeller—ever the optimist— assumed that he would break all precedents and make his Vice Presidency a strong voice and constructive force in the new Administration. In the end, Rockefeller accepted the Vice Presidency out of his sense of duty. To one close New York City friend he said: "I will go to Washington to help President Ford, and through him, the country." Ford, certain that he had made the right choice, was delighted that Rockefeller would be his partner in governing.

Vietnam rose next to the top of Ford's brimming in-box. Determined to heal his country's wounds from the War in Vietnam, Ford followed his compassionate but practical instincts, and listened to his sons.

From his seat in the House of Representatives, Ford had watched three Presidents lose the war in Vietnam. After President Kennedy's initial intervention, President Johnson's mismanagement of the war, and President Nixon's failure to negotiate his "honorable end" to the war, Ford was left with the consequences: More than 53,000 of America's young men and women had been killed in action, and more than 300,000 wounded. All these precious lives had been lost in a war that most Americans had come to believe was without purpose or end. And another 50,000 young Americans had fled to Canada or Sweden or some other foreign country to avoid combat. Most were draft dodgers but many had deserted from the Army.

No one of Ford's three sons—Mike, 24; Jack, 22; or Steve, 18—had been drafted, but classmates and friends had been shipped off to fight and die, or demonstrated their opposition by leaving the country. At the dinner table and in the family living room, the outspoken Ford boys did not hesitate to offer their strong views about the futility of the war. Dad had listened. He also remembered that President Lincoln had offered to restore to Confederate soldiers their rights as citizens if they swore allegiance to the United States.

In his first week as President, Ford told Hartmann, his chief speechwriter and confidante, that he wanted to find a way to offer conditional amnesty to draft dodgers and deserters, and announce it publicly. Deliberately, it would be a complete break from Nixon policy, which had been to prosecute draft dodgers and deserters. Since reaching out to those who had fled the country would be controversial, Ford told Hartmann they must keep it secret until a public announcement.

Hartmann, an experienced hand at converting Ford's wishes into words, drafted a speech that would offer the young émigrés an opportunity to return to the United States, and earn their freedom and rights as citizens. Ford expected that his decision would outrage many who had served honorably in Vietnam, but he was sure it was the right thing to do. Looking at his travel schedule for the best place to announce his new policy, he saw that his choices were a college audience at Ohio State University or a national convention of the Veterans of Foreign Wars in Chicago.

To Hartmann, Ford said: "Bob, I have decided that the place to make my announcement about a conditional amnesty—no, it's really not amnesty, let's call it earned re-entry—is right there in front of three thousand tough Veterans of Foreign Wars, most of whom are against the whole idea."

At Ohio State, Hartmann countered, the student body would roar approval.

"No," Ford said, "it's much better to go to the VFW and lay it on the line."

As Ford wanted his decision to reverse Nixon policy to come as a surprise, Hartmann wrote the speech but withheld the key paragraph from copies distributed in advance to the press. On the flight to Chicago, Ford showed the paragraph to Haig, who became angry, strongly advised against it, and predicted: "They'll boo you."

When Ford entered the ballroom at the Conrad Hilton, the audience of veterans rose to their feet and delivered a rousing ovation in welcome. The speech went well until he reached the critical point: the draft dodgers and deserters are, like those who gave their lives, also casualties of Vietnam, Ford said. "I want them to come home if they want to *work* their way back . . . In my judgment these young Americans should have a second chance . . . So I am throwing the weight of my Presidency into the scales of justice on the side of leniency. I foresee their earned re-entry—*earned* re-entry—into a new atmosphere of hope, hard work, and mutual trust. As I reject amnesty, so do I reject revenge."

The veterans responded in silence. They did not boo. They did not applaud. But at the end of the speech, they delivered another standing ovation, indicating they may have disagreed with his offer to those who had refused to serve, but they applauded the courage of a new President who had been honest and forthcoming with a hard, but necessary, course of action. Ford was relieved. "I knew I wouldn't satisfy liberals, who wanted me to give general amnesty. Nor would it please conservatives, who wanted harsher punishment. Still, I thought it was fair."

By Executive order, Ford created a Clemency Board with specific guidelines: Draft dodgers could return without being prosecuted by reporting to a U.S. Attorney, pledging allegiance to the U.S., and giving two years of alternate civic service. Deserters would also have to pledge allegiance and serve for two years in the military service from which they deserted. At the end they would receive a clemency discharge but not be eligible for any veteran benefits.

Once announced, Ford's clemency program floundered. As he had kept it secret from the White House staff, Ford had not appointed anyone to carry out his proposal. Neither he nor Hartmann had thought through how the board would be organized, who would serve on the board, and how it would carry out its mission. Ford's next mistake was to appoint—on the advice of Hartmann—an old and close friend from the House, Charles Goodell, to head the program.

Goodell was not a manager but a legislator. Even worse, he had become a political pariah. An upstate New Yorker, Goodell had been appointed to the Senate after the assassination of Senator Robert Kennedy in 1968. As a Senator, to the astonishment of everyone who knew him, Goodell metamorphosed from solid Republican conservative to woolly liberal, constant critic of President Nixon, and vocal opponent of the Vietnam War. Consequently, he angered and lost his Republican political base and gained nothing. In the three-way race for the Senate in 1970, Goodell lost to New York Conservative James Buckley, ending up an ignominious third behind the Democratic candidate.

As chairman of the Clemency Board, Goodell was injudicious and inept; his open hostility to the war clashed with military members. As it turned out, the operation was a disaster.

Ford's amnesty proposition was a prime example of the contrast between high purpose and inexperience that he displayed in his first weeks as President: the best intentions, a sound and courageous proposal; poor execution. He was still following the way of Congress—to write a law and trust someone else—the Executive departments principally—to administer it. Now Ford was the Chief Executive, but he had not yet learned how to convert his concept into results, how to direct the waiting and ready instruments of governing—the White House staff, OMB, the Cabinet, the bureaucracy—to carry out his decisions.

Like a ghost from the past, the specter of Richard Nixon continued to haunt Ford's White House. Though disgraced and exiled on the other side of the continent, Nixon remained a presence. His younger daughter was still in the residence; Julie Nixon was packing up. In the West Wing the major offices were occupied by Nixon loyalists. In the White House press room, Nixon was still the main story. After Haig's failed attempt to spirit Nixon's papers and tapes to California on a dark Saturday night, reporters besieged terHorst at every briefing with questions: Who blocked the move? Where are the Nixon tapes? Does Nixon own them? Did Nixon telephone Ford and ask for them? A suspicious reporter for the *Washington Post* demanded: how do we know Julie is not packing evidence in there with Pat Nixon's dresses?

Haig, alerted by the probing of a relentless press, knew he must act swiftly. He had promised Nixon he would deliver his papers and tapes, and he was determined to get it done. He instructed Fred Buzhardt, the holdover White House Counsel, to see that they were prepared for shipment. Buzhardt telephoned Jerry Jones, the Presidential assistant to whom Haig had given the only key to the Executive Office Building stockroom where the tapes were sequestered. Go box all the tapes, Buzhardt told Jones. An Air Force truck will pick up the boxes, he said, and transport them to an Air Force plane that will take the tapes to Nixon in California.

Key in hand, Jones walked from his West Wing basement office across East Executive Avenue, entered the room where the tapes were stacked, and locked the door behind him. "It was hotter than hell," Jones said. "An August afternoon in an office that had no air-conditioning." As he put the tapes into cardboard boxes for shipment, he carefully made an inventory of each box. "For hours I worked there," he said, "and I was just finishing up when Fred came in. He was ashen."

"Jerry, we just can't do this," Buzhardt said. "If we let these tapes out of here, all hell is going to break loose. You and I may go to jail."

"What do you want me to do, Fred?"

"Lock them back up," Buzhardt said.

Jones locked the room and returned to his office. Crossing West Executive Avenue, he saw the Air Force truck that had been waiting there to load the tapes to be flown to California. "It was close," Jones said. "Had Fred not come in to reverse himself, in ten more minutes the tapes would have been in the truck and gone."

Thwarted for the second time, Haig arranged for St. Clair, still serving as senior White House lawyer, to announce his formal opinion that, by precedent, President's Nixon's papers and tapes were his property, clearing a legal path for their shipment. When Ford heard about it, he was furious: St. Clair's public announcement had not been cleared with him. So provoked was Ford that he called in Philip Buchen, appointed him White House Counsel and told terHorst to announce at once that St. Clair was out.

Ford also summoned Attorney General Saxbe. "Bill, who owns these documents?" he asked. "I need you to give me an official opinion before we do anything." Saxbe's opinion was that by law and by precedent, they belonged to Nixon.

Still concerned, Ford consulted with Hartmann and Marsh. Whatever the precedents, Marsh pointed out, President Ford would be held responsible to protect evidence that might be subpoenaed by the Special Prosecutor or the Federal Court for the trials of Mitchell and the other Watergate defendants, and Nixon himself if and when indicted. Ford agreed, and ordered that the Nixon documents and tapes remain under lock and key in the Executive Office Building. He also told Buchen to draft a Presidential order stating that only Nixon's personal clothing could be removed from White House premises.

At the same time, Ford told Haig that he would no longer have the responsibility for liaison with Nixon. Buchen would take custody of Nixon's papers and tapes; Marsh would serve as liaison with Nixon and his staff in California.

Haig ruefully accepted the curtailment of his power. "I lost that battle," he confided to Jerry Jones, "but I will stay long enough to get Nixon the pardon."

On Capitol Hill, the long-running story of Nixon and Watergate finally came to an official end. On August 20, 1974, the House of Representatives voted 412-3 to accept the Judiciary Committee finding that Nixon's actions during Watergate warranted three Articles of Impeachment: obstructing justice, abuse of power, contempt of Congress. The report included a formal resolution recommending impeachment, a verdict Nixon escaped only by his resignation. The committee's document, 528 pages long, detailed the evidence of Nixon's crimes against the state. In voting with near-unanimity to accept the Judiciary Committee report, the House had carried out its Constitutional responsibility and found President Nixon guilty.

To Ford, it was time to move on; he had won the nation's respect and support. The White House press was uniformly kind, commending Ford's candor and humility, his openness and plain speaking. With their penchant for the trivial, some reporters made much of Ford brewing his own coffee and toasting his own English muffin for breakfast. A new Gallup poll indicated 71 percent of the American people approved Ford's first ten days in office. He had succeeded in maintaining his warm and close relations with Congress. He had cleaned out the in-box loaded with business unattended by his distracted predecessor. He was convinced that the wounds of Watergate were beginning to heal.

Eager to share his optimism and his plans for the future with the country, Ford summoned Hartmann and told him to schedule his first press conference, and to arrange for it to be broadcast live on radio and television.

The date was set: Wednesday, August 28, 1974, 2:30 p.m., in the East Room.

CHAPTER 13

Reaction

If circumstances permit, a President never faces the White House press without careful preparation. Typically, he is drilled by his most aggressive press aides and best-informed senior staff, often on a mock stage. There he composes and rehearses his answers to the most contentious questions his aides expect that reporters will ask.

To prepare Ford for his first press conference, Hartmann enlisted a cadre of Ford loyalists: press secretary terHorst and his assistants, Paul Miltich and Paul Theis; counselor Jack Marsh; counsel Phil Buchen; national security adviser Brent Scowcroft; and economists Bill Seidman and Alan Greenspan. All gathered around the President's desk in the Oval Office and began to badger him with their toughest questions: Are you going to send Nixon his tapes and papers? Do you agree with the public statements by Governor Nelson Rockefeller and Senate Republican Leader Hugh Scott that Nixon has suffered enough? Have you talked with Nixon personally about immunity from prosecution? Will you put a stop to all the press questions about whether you will pardon Nixon and the other Watergate defendants?

Their questions were sure to be asked; although Nixon was gone, Washington could not stop talking about him. Ford disagreed. He doubted that he would be asked about Nixon; he thought that reporters would share his concerns about more important issues: how he intended to improve the imperiled economy, changes he planned to make in the Cabinet, the legislative program he was developing, the crisis in Cyprus, the threat of war in the Middle East, his plans for negotiations on strategic arms with Brezhnev. Hartmann and others thought Ford mistaken, and persisted with more questions about Nixon.

After half an hour of their badgering, an annoyed President told his staff: "You're wasting my time. No more questions about Nixon." If he were asked about Nixon, he said, he would not comment, but say any action would be up to the Special Prosecutor and the courts.

To his staff, Ford had dismissed talk of Nixon, but to the Nixon loyalists who were still running the White House, the threat of prosecution of the exiled former President was their prime concern. One even had a plan for the new President to absolve their former boss.

Leonard Garment, Nixon's longtime friend still serving as White House special counsel, had been talking with outsiders—Eric Sevareid of CBS, John Osborne of the *New Republic*, and former Supreme Court Justice Abe Fortas—about a Presidential pardon for Nixon. Each encouraged Garment. Fortas said "the convulsion of a trial of Richard Nixon was the last thing the country needed."

Returning to the White House, Garment reported his conversations to Haig, and asked Haig whether he should propose that President Ford use his first press conference as the occasion to pardon Nixon. Yes, Haig replied, "Time to get something in." Working into the night, Garment wrote a legal brief justifying the pardon. Early the next morning he and Ray Price, a holdover Nixon speechwriter, drafted a statement that Ford might use in announcing the pardon at the press conference that afternoon. When they finished, Garment delivered the brief and draft statement to Buchen to give to Ford, and gave a copy to Haig.

In his regular morning meeting with Ford, Haig briefed the President on Garment's proposal that he pardon Nixon. Immediately after, Haig telephoned Garment. He said he had just spent forty-three minutes alone with the President, and reported that Ford would announce the pardon that day. "It's all set," Haig said. "Don't leave. Hang around."

An hour later Haig again called Garment and assured him: "It's on track."

"Clearly," Garment wrote later, "Haig's expectation at that point was that President Ford was going to do it that day."

After his meeting with Haig, Ford held his regular morning meeting with Hartmann and terHorst. Updating him on the morning news and plans for the afternoon press conference, they affirmed that he would be careful in responding to any questions about Nixon and firm in his decision not to comment on matters before the courts. Ford then saw

Buchen, who suggested that Ford respond to Nixon questions with the simple answers they had worked out: I'm not going to decide this now, and I have nothing more to say about this.

In his hand Buchen also had the Garment memo. In that document, Buchen said, Garment "eloquently pleaded that the President go out and announce to the world at the press conference that he was going to pardon Nixon." Buchen mentioned the Garment proposal to Ford and said, "You don't want to read this, but Garment thinks you ought to say, yes, you're going to pardon him. Whether you say yes or no, Garment believes you ought to. He's given some reasons. One, he supports your legal right to do so. Secondly, he has given the reasons you ought to do it. But I think it's premature, don't you?"

"Yes," Ford said. "I'm going to say we'll let the matter go on for a while."

After Buchen, Ford spent thirty minutes with the Reverend Billy Zeoli, a born-again Christian from Grand Rapids who had befriended and counseled Ford since his early days in the House. Zeoli had become Ford's spiritual adviser, sending him a weekly letter composed of a verse of Scripture and Zeoli's ten-line homily. These epistles, Ford wrote, deeply affected him. "Some served as inspiration, some as guidance, some to assuage the fear and foreboding in the making of important decisions." On this morning, as always, Ford and his chaplain read a passage from the Bible, prayed together, and talked about forgiveness.

By the time he stood on the podium before the White House correspondents that afternoon, Ford had listened to a full morning of conflicting advice about Nixon: Haig urging a pardon; Hartmann and terHorst suggesting caution; Buchen proposing delay; Zeoli preaching mercy. It was enough to muddle his mind. Still, Ford assumed that most reporters' questions would be about the struggling economy, the Middle East, the USSR, legislative decisions that lay ahead. He was wrong. The opening question at the press conference that afternoon came from Helen Thomas, UPI's senior White House correspondent.

"Mr. President," Ms. Thomas said, "aside from the Special Prosecutor's role, do you agree with the bar association that the law applies equally to all men, or do you agree with Governor Rockefeller that former President Nixon should have immunity from prosecution? And specifically, would you use your pardon authority, if necessary?"

"Well," President Ford replied, "let me say at the outset that I made a statement in this room a few moments after the swearing in. And on that occasion I said the following: that I had hoped that our former President, who brought peace to millions, might find it for himself. Now, the expression made by Governor Rockefeller, I think, coincides with the general view and the point of view of the American people. I subscribe to that point of view, but let me add, in the past ten days or two weeks I have asked for prayers for guidance on this very important point.

"In this situation, I am the final authority. There have been no charges made, there has been no action by the courts, there has been no action by any jury. And until any legal process has been undertaken, I think it unwise and untimely for me to make any commitment."

To Ford's relief, the next questions were about his political philosophy, a public-service program, and whether he and Vice President-designate Rockefeller planned to run in 1976. His answer for himself: probably. As for Rockefeller on the ticket, "the final judgment . . . will be that of the delegates to the national convention."

The fifth question provoked Ford's ambivalent and most troubling answer. "May I follow up on Helen's question?" a reporter asked. "Are you saying, sir, that the option of a pardon for former President Nixon is still an option that you will consider, depending on what the courts will do?"

"Of course, I make the final decision," Ford replied. "And until it gets to me, I make no commitment one way or another. But I do have the right as President of the United States to make that decision."

"And you are not ruling it out?" the reporter said.

"I am not ruling it out," Ford said. "It is an option and a proper option for any President."

Following up, the next reporter asked: "Do you feel that the Special Prosecutor can in good conscience pursue cases against former Nixon aides as long as there is the possibility that the former President may not also be pursued in the courts?"

"I think the Special Prosecutor, Mr. Jaworski, has an obligation to take whatever action he sees fit in conformity with his oath of office, and that should include any and all individuals," Ford said.

In their next questions, reporters asked about the code of ethics in Ford's White House, inflation, wage and price controls, then again returned to Nixon.

"Mr. President, to further pursue Helen's inquiry, have there been any communications between the Special Prosecutor's office and anyone on your staff regarding President Nixon?"

"Not to my knowledge," Ford said.

He then answered questions about a naval base in Diego Garcia, veterans' benefits, the Federal budget, his domestic priorities, his policy toward Israel, and toward Cuba, before still another question about Nixon: "Mr. President, you have emphasized here your option of granting a pardon to the former President."

"I intend to," Ford said.

"You intend to have that option," the reporter said. "If an indictment is brought, would you grant a pardon before any trial took place?"

"I said at the outset that until the matter reaches me, I am not going to make any comment during the process of whatever charges are made."

The last question, to Ford's gratification, was about strategic arms limitation talks. Secretary Kissinger, he replied, will soon meet with his counterparts in the USSR, "and we, of course, will then proceed on a timetable to try and negotiation SALT Two."

After twenty-nine minutes of grilling, Ford strode from the East Room back to the Oval Office an angry man, and that anger rising with every step. He was disgusted with himself and his performance, and furious at the press for asking so many questions about Nixon. He knew he had said too much. He knew he had repeatedly contradicted himself. God damn it, I am not going to put up with this, he said to himself. "It is wrong for the country. I could visualize every press conference from then on, regardless of the ground rules, degenerating into a Q&A on, 'Was I going to pardon Mr. Nixon.' It would come after he was indicted, which he was going to be. It would come after he was convicted, which he was going to be. It would come after his appeal. It was a never-ending process."

How, Ford thought to himself, can I get rid of that issue so that I can concentrate on the more important things that involve two hundred and thirty million Americans? "There must be a way to take the American people's minds off this terrible experience. There must be a way for me to get my attention to the major problems facing us."

As soon as the transcript of the press conference was ready, Buchen took it in to the Oval Office and showed it to Ford. Ford read through the text of his answers, grimacing at his mistakes. "Your answers are not all consistent," Buchen said quietly. Ford scowled, and agreed that his answers had been confused and ambiguous. In his gentle way, Buchen advised: "You will continue to get these questions until the Nixon situation is resolved." Ford looked at Buchen, compressing his lips in anger and nodding his head in agreement.

In all their thirty-five years together, Buchen had never seen Ford more exasperated. "The trouble was," Buchen said, "he had given three different answers to questions about the pardon, answers that were manifestly inconsistent. That annoyed him greatly, because he wanted to have a press conference about his Presidency. It was his first press conference as President, and so very important to him."

Ford could recall, years later, his anger at being blindsided. "I can assure you that from the moment I took the oath of office until five weeks later, after the press conference, I never *thought* of a pardon. There was no reason to do so. Nixon was gone. We were working on our problems. And the God damn press spent three quarters of a press conference raising questions and making comments about Nixon. Looking backward, not forward."

Ford's blunder at his first press marked a turning point in his Presidency. It provoked his most significant decision—the one for which most Americans will remember him and the action that will intrigue most historians.

From that mid-afternoon, Wednesday, August 28, 1974, and for the next ten days, the resolution of Nixon's status preoccupied and engaged not only President Ford, but also two other principals involved: Leon Jaworski, Watergate Special Prosecutor; and Nixon himself, secluded in his compound at San Clemente, California, waiting in fear and anguish that he would be indicted, put on trial, and sent to jail.

Of the millions of Americans who watched Ford's first press conference, none was more interested that afternoon than Jaworski, sitting in the Special Prosecutor's office at 1425 K Street, NW, four blocks north of the White House. He too was conflicted. It was his responsibility to make a momentous decision: should he indict Nixon or not? He alone held the responsibility to say yes or no. And he was undecided.

From the first day on the job Jaworski had been alone, isolated from the brilliant and dedicated prosecutors he had inherited from Archibald Cox, and demeaned by some on his staff as more Texas politician than lawyer. This close partnership of zealous Cox recruits and bloodied veterans of the Saturday Night Massacre had spent more than a year collecting evidence against President Nixon. Now that the man was out of office and thus no longer immune from prosecution, they were almost unanimous in their determination to indict him, convict him, and send him in jail. They insisted that the evidence not only justified bringing Nixon to trial, but that the legal system and the principle of equal justice for all demanded it. Their view was supported by thousands of letters to Jaworski: 3 to 1 for prosecution.

Jaworski was not convinced. He had a broader view: it was not just the man who would be tried but the Presidency. The highest office in the land would be disgraced—not only in the opinion of the American people but in the judgment of the world. Calmly, deliberately, he weighed his obligation as prosecutor and judged what would be in the country's best interest.

Jaworski had delayed and delayed his decision while Nixon was in office, assuming that if he indicted him while he was President, Nixon would not resign but fight even harder to hold on to his office and Constitutional immunity. Jaworski had hoped, and expected after his conversation with Haig, that Congress would order him to grant Nixon immunity from prosecution. When he heard Nixon put the blame on Congress in his resignation speech, Jaworski realized there was no chance of that—Haig had been misinformed.

A few days later, Jaworski was approached by two powerful and loyal Congressional supporters of Nixon. Senator James Eastland, chairman of the Senate Judiciary Committee, telephoned Jaworski and asked him to come to his Senate office. When he arrived, Jaworski found Senator Roman Hruska there as well. Eastland came to the point: Nixon had telephoned Eastland that day from San Clemente. With a sad shake of his head Eastland said, "He was crying. He said, 'Jim don't let Jaworksi put me in that trial with Haldeman and Ehrlichman. I can't take any more.'" His voice filled with pity, Eastland added: "He's in bad shape, Leon."

Jaworski asked Eastland if he and other leaders of Congress might initiate a resolution calling an abstention of prosecuting of Nixon. "We'll think about it," Eastland replied. "We'll be in touch." Eastland never called again. To Jaworski's disappointment, Congress declared the customary August recess and went home.

With no prospect of Congressional action, Jaworski continued to put off his decision. He reasoned that instructing the Watergate Grand Jury either to indict Nixon—or not to indict Nixon—could prejudice the jury in the upcoming trial of Mitchell, Haldeman, Ehrlichman, and the others charged with Watergate crimes. His assistant prosecutors, though eager to bring charges against Nixon, conceded that indictment could and should wait until after the jury in the conspirators' case had been sequestered.

Meanwhile, Jaworski pondered, reflected, weighed. For all his professional life, Jaworski had been a stickler for a fair trial. The principle applied to all. "What if this man, no longer a sitting President, were to be indicted for obstruction of justice?" Jaworski wrote. "Like any other citizen, and regardless of his resignation and the unprecedented accusations of guilt, he was presumed to be innocent until proven guilty according to judicial standards. The Grand Jury, I knew, would indict him in a minute. But could he receive a fair trial, his Constitutional right?"

To find out, Jaworski called in his two press assistants, James Doyle and John Barker. They, unlike the Cox lawyers he inherited, had become Jaworski's close friends and he confided in them. He told Doyle and Barker to prepare a complete chronology and record of every report, article, and commentary published and broadcast about Nixon and Watergate since the beginning. The summary—186 pages—concluded that 96 million persons had watched the House Judiciary Committee vote to impeach Nixon, that every network had been broadcasting nightly reports of Nixon's guilt for more than two years, and that every daily newspaper in the United States had documented Nixon's collusion in Watergate. In Jaworski's judgment, if prosecutors could find no court in America where Nixon could get a fair trial, that could be a valid legal justification for blocking a Grand Jury indictment.

To the more zealous on his staff, that would be a travesty of justice. George Frampton, a senior prosecutor who reflected the strong views of most of his fellow lawyers on the staff, put his objections in writing: " . . . Reliance on prejudicial pre-trial publicity to avoid prosecution altogether would be widely perceived (and stamped in history) as a resort to a completely novel legal theory—and thereby judged a 'cop-out . . .' The Constitution indisputably contemplates prosecution of a former President even after impeachment. There is no precedent for dismissal of an indictment on publicity grounds, much less for a decision not to indict at all."

Only one lawyer in the Special Prosecutor's office questioned his fellow prosecutors' zeal to indict Nixon: James Neal, a masterful Tennessee trial lawyer brought in by Jaworski to conduct—with outstanding success—the trials of Mitchell, Haldeman, Ehrlichman, and the other defendants in the Watergate conspiracy. "Leon took a broader view, that I'm a citizen, and a citizen with a great deal of power, and I should use that power in a way that redounds to the ultimate good of the country," Neal said.

On Jaworski's desk was a memorandum from Nixon's defense lawyer, Herbert J. Miller Jr. A legend in the profession, Jack Miller had been recruited in 1961 by Robert Kennedy to head his Justice Department Criminal Division, even though he was a Republican. In private practice, Miller had successfully defended clients who seemed doomed. One notable example: on a technicality that Miller discovered, former Attorney General Richard Kleindienst received a slap on the wrist instead of a conviction for lying to a Senate Committee while under oath.

Miller had been retained by Nixon on the recommendation of Fred Buzhardt, still serving Nixon in Ford's White House. After Buzhardt telephoned Nixon and got his assent, he and Miller flew to California to discuss his case. At San Clemente Miller was shocked by Nixon's appearance and mental state; he immediately agreed to take over Nixon's defense. Defending the ex-President, Miller said later, was an historic opportunity.

Acting swiftly, Miller submitted to Jaworski a memorandum arguing against indictment of Nixon on the grounds of pretrial publicity. Citing two years of unprecedented press coverage of the Watergate events and the televised impeachment proceedings of the House Judiciary Committee, Miller wrote, "even those most critical of Mr. Nixon [must] doubt his chances of subsequently receiving a trial free from preconceived judgments of guilt."

Jaworski listened to all arguments but withheld any decision. But to Doyle, the Pulitzer Prize-winning Boston journalist who was not only Jaworski's senior spokesman but had also become his trusted confidant, his intent was unmistakable: Jaworski opposed indicting Nixon. He was against it even though he knew that many if not most of the able prosecutors on his staff might resign in protest if he so decided. Doyle believed that Jaworski shared his conviction, "that the indictment and trial of Richard Nixon would have caused a national trauma greater than that caused by the Watergate scandal itself."

To Barker, who had also won Jaworski's confidence, there were "three Leons." First, he was a wealthy Houston lawyer who did not like Washington but came out of a sense of duty. "He lived at the Jefferson Hotel, missed his wife, and his ranch in Wimberly. If Nixon were indicted, he would have to stay with the job to the end, at least eighteen months. He told me he did not want to do that." The second Leon, Barker said, "believed morally that you don't kill the king. He did not want to be remembered as the man who put a former President in jail." The third Leon, he said, "felt deeply that Nixon could not get a fair trial. He was willing to bear the burden of taking that stand."

Barker believed that Jaworski had made up his mind: He would not indict Nixon. "Jaworski would not subvert the nation's system of justice, but at the same time he was aware of his right of prosecutorial discretion, his right not to prosecute President Nixon should he so choose."

Jaworski's memoir reflected his deep concern with ultimate justice. "With all the advice, all the suggestions, with all the study I did myself, I knew in my own mind that if an indictment were returned and the court asked me if I believed Nixon could receive a prompt, fair trial as guaranteed by the Constitution, I would have to answer, as an officer of the court, in the negative."

Back in Texas in his later years, Jaworski and his grandson, author Robert Draper, talked often about the grandfather's dilemma. Even to his grandson Jaworski never confided whether he would have indicted Nixon if Ford had not pardoned him. But he did come close. "He told me," Draper said, "that he found it would be traumatizing to the nation for a man who had been Vice President and President to be carted off to jail." In his discussions with his grandfather, Draper took the position that if pretrial publicity prevented a fair trial for Nixon, it would be the same with any future President who was impeached for having committed crimes in office. "He was not moved," Draper said.

Henry Ruth, as Deputy to Special Prosecutor Cox and then Jaworski, was the lawyer in the best position to read Jaworski's intentions. "I don't think Leon ever wanted to indict Nixon," Ruth said.

James Neal confirmed that. He and Jaworski had agreed on a plan: "Mr. Jaworski and I concluded that we could not simply ignore the wishes of the longest running Grand Jury in history," Neal wrote. "We would go before this Grand Jury, point out the problems of the indictment of Mr. Nixon, recommend that he not be indicted, but advise the Grand Jury that if it insisted on the indictment of the former President, we would prepare the indictment and prosecute the case." Given the legal standing and eloquence of the two eminent advocates, they might well have swayed the Grand Jury to accept their recommendation—had Ford not intervened.

So it was with intense interest that Jaworski listened to the live broadcast of Ford's first press conference that August afternoon. "I couldn't determine exactly what the President had meant in his replies to the reporters," he said. "I told some of the top members of the staff, however, that I certainly would not ask the Grand Jury to indict Nixon if President Ford intended to pardon him." His counsel, Philip Lacovara, suggested he go to the White House and try to find out what President Ford intended to do about a pardon. Jaworski said no, it would be better to wait and see.

Ford did not know that Jaworski might not indict Nixon. It did not occur to him, or to his best advisers, or to most in the Washington establishment, including the press, that Jaworski questioned whether Nixon should be indicted. Ford, like most, believed that once Nixon resigned, the pent-up power of the Special Prosecutor's formidable legal force would be irresistible. Ford, like most, assumed that the Watergate Grand Jury would soon indict Nixon for—at the very least—obstruction of justice. Ford never even considered permitting anyone to approach Jaworski. After Nixon was brought down by interfering with the FBI investigation of Watergate, it would have been unthinkable for the new President to intervene with the prosecution of the accused in Watergate. To him, the stark evidence on the tapes made it certain that within weeks Special Prosecutor Jaworski would initiate proceedings to bring Nixon to trial.

Buchen concurred: "I was just so sure that, one, Nixon would be indicted, and two, he would be convicted." That was Buchen's best legal judgment, and he so counseled Ford.

Since indictment was imminent, Ford knew he must act without delay. If he intended to intervene, he must do so before Jaworski took the case against Nixon to the Grand Jury. Waiting until after an indictment would, in Ford's judgment, make his intervention even more controversial—even more difficult.

For two days after he bungled his answers at the press conference, Ford pondered what he might do to rid himself and his new administration of the Nixon problem. In the moments and hours between his full schedule of appointments, he weighed the idea of a pardon carefully—

deliberating with himself, just as he had done on important decisions all his life. Ford considered the critical choices: should he act now, or should he let Jaworski indict Nixon, try him, then wait for the verdict? He calculated the risks; they were sobering either way. By Friday morning, August 30, Ford had made his decision: the pardon was the right thing to do—if he had that power.

"In the back of my mind," Ford said later, "was what Al told me in that meeting on August 1, that a president had a legal authority to grant a pardon to an ex-president. But I didn't consider that to be viable legal authority." First, Ford decided, he must get Buchen to give him a legal opinion on whether he could grant a pardon to a person who had not been convicted of a crime, or even indicted. As to whether he should do it, Ford thought it both prudent and necessary to first consult his four closest and most trusted advisers.

Before leaving to give a speech in Columbus, Ohio, on the morning of August 30, Ford summoned Haig, Hartmann, Marsh, and Buchen to the Oval Office. When Hartmann arrived he was disquieted to find Haig already there; Hartmann sensed that he had interrupted a momentous discussion. When Buchen arrived and saw Haig there, he was also worried. Haig's loyalty, he had learned, was not to Ford but to Nixon. Marsh, who had a better opinion of Haig, was less concerned.

When they were seated around the President's desk, Ford began by swearing all four to secrecy. The reason, he emphasized, was that he had not reached a final judgment about a decision he was considering.

Ford first told them how disappointed and deeply troubled he was by his first press conference, by reporters' persistence in asking about a pardon of Nixon, and by his own ineptness in responding. He paused, and as he often did when he needed time to put his thoughts into the right words, he methodically filled and lit his pipe. After a long moment, Ford said: "I am very much inclined to grant Nixon immunity from further prosecution."

The Oval Office became so quiet, Hartmann remembered, that the ticking of the antique clock on the wall sounded like gunfire.

Ford broke the silence. "Phil," he said to Buchen, "you tell me whether I can do it and how I can do it. Research it thoroughly and as fast as you can, but be discreet. I want no leaks."

The expression on Ford's face and the tone of his voice left Buchen in no doubt about his old friend's resolve. "I knew Jerry Ford, and I knew he had already made up his mind. In his book Jerry wrote that he was undecided about the pardon when he first talked to us. I didn't agree with him on that point. What I remember so distinctly is that he had his mind made up. And he told us so. When he said to me, 'Buchen, you tell me whether I can do it and how I can do it,' I thought, my God, I know Ford. I better not even think of the merits of the case, whether he should do it or not. For two reasons: One, if I come to the opinion that he shouldn't do it, then I'll feel duty bound to tell him so. That won't change his mind. I know him. Secondly, I'm afraid it might prejudice my research. He was not asking for my judgment as to *whether* he should pardon Nixon, but *how* he could do it. It was my job to find out. So I just shut up about whether it should be done or not, and knew I had to work like hell."

At that point in the meeting, Haig rose from his chair, suggesting that his close association with Nixon made it improper for him to be present. Ford motioned for him to resume his seat. He then stated his reasoning to the four: "The degrading spectacle of a former President in the prisoner's dock . . . the difficulty of finding any place where he would get a fair trial . . . the press stories about every step in the legal process that would revive the whole rotten mess of Watergate . . ." Indictment, trial, and appeal could take years, Ford said, and if eventually Nixon were to be found guilty, the American people might conclude he had suffered enough and insist that the President, whomever he might be at that time, should pardon him.

Ford looked in turn at each of the four men and said: "If eventually, why not now? Why not get it over with and get on with the urgent business of the nation?"

After a paused he added: "My mind is ninety-nine percent made up, but if anyone in this room has another view, I will welcome it."

Marsh spoke first: "I can't argue with what you feel is right, but is this the right time?"

"Will there ever be a right time?" Ford said.

After another long silence, Buchen suggested: "We ought to get Mr. Nixon to settle his papers at the same time, because you're giving this guy a great thing, you ought at least to make him give his papers to the United States. As you know, we have physical custody of them, but the Attorney General's opinion is that these papers are his, by right of history. So let's get that settled at the same time. We also ought to get a real statement of contrition when he accepts the pardon."

"Phil, do what you can to get both those things," Ford said. "But for God's sake don't let either one stand in the way of my granting the pardon. I also want you to get from Jaworski two things; One, the list of offenses for which Nixon is the target. Two, how long after indictment might it be before he could be fairly tried?"

Buchen quickly grasped that part of his mission. "In his own mind Jerry wanted to know how bad were the crimes for which the Special Prosecutor was preparing charges. Was there something so bad that Nixon shouldn't be pardoned for it? Second, Jerry knew—we all knew—that a long trial would not help the country, or his Presidency."

Hartmann, worried that Ford's pardon of Nixon would be political suicide, suggested the President wait to see what action the Special Prosecutor might take. "You are going to have a firestorm of angry protest," he said.

"Sure, there will be criticism," Ford said. "If I wait six months, or a year, there will still be a firestorm."

At least, Hartmann said, wait for the public to become more sympathetic to Nixon. "A *Newsweek* poll says fifty-five percent of the people think further prosecution should be dropped."

"I don't need a poll to tell me the right thing to do," Ford said.

Marsh advised that there would be a strong negative reaction on Capitol Hill. Members of the House and Senate, he suggested, will be privately relieved that they are spared from having to vote on a resolution prohibiting criminal prosecution, but publicly they are more likely to denounce a pardon for Nixon. Ford said he expected the more vocal in Congress would criticize him on the floor, and in the press.

To keep to his schedule for his trip to Columbus, Ford closed the discussion, firmly reminding the four that his secret must be kept among them until his final decision was made.

Immediately after the meeting, Hartmann went back in to see President Ford alone. "Don't do it now," he pleaded, "These first weeks of your Presidency have gone so well."

Ford shook his head. "Bob, I thought that over. I decided that since it has to be done, it should be done as soon as possible."

After Ford's return from Columbus, Buchen also went in to see President Ford. To research the legal issues as thoroughly as necessary was more than he could accomplish alone, he said. He would work over the Labor Day weekend, but he needed Ford's permission to enlist Benton Becker as his assistant. Ford agreed, with a condition: Becker must be sworn to secrecy.

Marsh left the morning meeting deeply concerned. The question on his mind had been too sensitive to bring up with Haig present, but he had to find out: could there be some connection between Haig's August 1 proposal—Nixon to resign for a Ford pardon—and Ford's decision, a month later, to grant that pardon? "I wanted the President to see the linkage," Marsh said. "I know that Jerry Ford has a naïve streak, and it is there because he trusts people and doesn't see motives that people have. So I felt the obligation to myself to know that the pardon would raise questions of linkage to the meeting in August when Al Haig raised the option of a pardon for Nixon."

So concerned was Marsh that he went in alone late in the day to see Ford. Quietly, carefully, he raised the touchy subject. "Now, I don't want to make you mad, Mr. President, but I feel an obligation to know myself that you have thought through all aspects of this, including the events of August, and the possibility that at some time the press or someone may learn about those August events and suggest there was some kind of a deal."

Ford was not surprised that Marsh—the man he called "the conscience of my Administration"—was reminding him of a potentially dangerous misconception. He looked Marsh in the eye and said firmly: "Jack, I know exactly what you mean, and what you are talking about. I have thought it through. I have no problem in that regard. I know what people are going to say. But this is the right thing to do."

To Marsh that was assurance enough, assurance that this was not part of a secret bargain. "I knew in my own heart, in my soul, that Jerry Ford had not made a deal. I could see that Ford had decided that pardoning Nixon was in the national interest, and that he was going to do what was in the national interest whatever the cost to himself."

Ford had indeed calculated the cost. He told Buchen: "Phil, I think this will end my political career."

CHAPTER 14

The Pardon

The secret sworn to in the Oval Office was not kept. The next day, Saturday, August 31, 1974, Haig informed Nixon that a pardon was forthcoming—not directly, but through Ron Ziegler, Nixon's chief of staff in California. From Haig, Ziegler learned not only that Ford would grant the pardon, but also that Nixon, in accepting the pardon, would not need to accept blame for Watergate or make any statement of contrition. "I was on the phone with Al every day, sometimes more than once every day," Ziegler said. As Haig informed Ziegler of Ford's daily progress toward the decision, Ziegler reported each development to Nixon. "We knew what was coming," Ziegler said.

So did Jack Miller, Nixon's new defense attorney, who had learned from Haig that a pardon was likely. On Tuesday morning, four days after the secret meeting, Miller asked for a private meeting with Jaworski. A wary Jaworski agreed to meet in the Jefferson Hotel's restaurant. When they were seated, Miller asked: would the Special Prosecutor challenge a Presidential pardon or attack it in the press? No, Jaworski replied. He told Miller that a pardon, if it should be granted was, constitutionally, the prerogative of the President. Miller reported that good news to Nixon.

Returning to his hotel room, Jaworski felt an enormous sense of relief. He surmised that Miller would not have asked that question without knowing that President Ford was at least considering a pardon for Nixon. Possibly, Jaworski thought, he would never have to decide whether to indict Nixon.

Back in his office, Jaworski informed Ruth and others of the Miller meeting and asked for their counsel. The question was what action, if any, the Special Prosecutor should take in anticipation of a Presidential pardon. Ruth, in his memo, sympathized with Jaworski's reluctance to indict Nixon. "I know of few decisions as difficult as this one must be personally," he wrote to Jaworski. "Indictment of an ex-President seems so easy to many of the commentators and politicians. But in a deep sense that involves tradition, travail, and submerged disgust . . . One can make a strong argument for leniency, and if President Ford is so inclined, I think he ought to do it early rather than late."

On that same Tuesday, Buchen went in to see President Ford alone. Over Labor Day weekend, far into the night, he and Becker had pored over the statutes and precedents relating to pardons. Now he was ready to report what he and Becker had found.

"Phil came in alone, leaning on his cane as he always did from his infantile paralysis, and took a chair to my left," Ford said. "Very deliberate. Very precise." With a document in his hand, he gave Ford his report. First and most important was Article II, Section 2, of the Constitution: "The President . . . shall have the Power to grant Reprieves and Pardons for Offenses against the United States, except in Cases of Impeachment." That means, Buchen advised, that Ford had singular and absolute power to pardon Nixon of Watergate crimes, but could not expunge his impeachment. Second, Buchen said, Ford could pardon Nixon of crimes he may have committed even though he had not yet been indicted.

The precedent, Buchen said, was a pardon by President Wilson in 1914. In that case, George Burdick, city editor of the *New York Tribune*, refused a court order to reveal the source of articles about customs fraud in the city. Before Burdick was indicted for contempt of court, President Wilson pardoned him "for all offenses [he] has committed or may have committed." The pardon was challenged and reached the Supreme Court. After arguments in the case, *Burdick v. United States*, the court held unanimously on January 25, 1915, that "the President has power to pardon for a crime of which the individual has not been convicted and which he does not admit." However, the Court added, a pardon "carries an imputation of guilt; acceptance a confession of it."

Ford did not ask Buchen for a written opinion. "I had great reliability in Phil's legal expertise and judgment. He was a very precise lawyer with an excellent legal mind, and I knew from thirty years experience with him that if he made a categorical statement as to what the law was, it would be an accurate representation. He was my counsel. I felt his word was sufficient." Ford did not feel it was necessary, or even appropriate, to go to Attorney General Saxbe. "Had I done so," Ford said, "the Attorney General's legal responsibility for the Special Prosecutor might be affected, in my judgment."

Ford did ask Buchen: If the decision is made to pardon, would that clear the decks from that point on, whatever the status of Nixon in the legal processes? Yes, Buchen replied.

With that response, and assured by Buchen's legal judgment and citations, Ford then knew with certainty that he could act on solid Constitutional ground. Methodically, he thought through the probable sequence of events: By using his undoubted authority to grant a pardon, he would stop the Special Prosecutor from indicting Nixon. In effect and in legal fact he would close the Nixon case. If Nixon accepted a pardon, he would be admitting his guilt.

Yet Ford was still uncertain. "I began thinking, worrying, cogitating about whether I should or should not," he said. He talked again and individually to Haig, Hartmann, and Marsh. "Haig tilted for a pardon," Ford said. "Hartmann analyzed the political pros and cons, and I think was for it. Marsh analyzed the pros and cons and tilted against it." Ford also mentioned it to Kissinger. "I wanted to probe for his judgment, and I said, 'Henry, you've got to keep this on a most confidential basis.'"

Kissinger did not hesitate. "If you make that decision, Mr. President, it will be the right decision," he told Ford. "From a foreign policy point of view, the rest of the world will not understand a former President being a prisoner in the dock. A trial, and all the publicity would harm the image of the United States, focus world attention on the former President being criminally charged. It would be far better to clear the slate and get the issue off the front pages."

Ford also talked to his wife, when they were alone in the private sitting room where they relaxed after dinner, he with his coat off and tie loosened, Betty in her favorite pink robe. "I said to her, 'I'm considering issuing a pardon to President Nixon, and the reasons are, number one, I want to get the matter off the front pages of the newspapers so it won't be aggravating the American people for whatever time that will be. Number two, I am fed with up people raising legal questions involving Nixon's documents, his future. It is time consuming and I don't want to be hamstrung with those questions when we have the problems of the economy.' She didn't go into the technicalities of it, she wasn't qualified.

But she had seen the trauma Dick and Pat went through that last day, so she was favorable to it." He cautioned her then, and later, "under any and all circumstances to keep it most confidential."

Once he had consulted the people he trusted most, Ford's decision was all but final. But he knew that Nixon was unpredictable, and so Ford took the next precaution. He assumed that Nixon would accept a pardon, but he needed to make certain. To find out, Ford instructed Buchen to inform Miller, Nixon's lawyer, that a pardon was being considered, but not certain. In response, Buchen suggested that he also discuss with Miller a statement of contrition and an agreement on the Nixon tapes and documents. Ford, out of long experience with Nixon, knew his insecurities, his inability to admit a mistake. So he told Buchen: "If you can, fine; but I don't want to condition the pardon on his making an agreement on the papers and tapes. And I don't want you to insist on any particular terms."

Within the hour Buchen and Becker met with Miller, who made no mention of the fact that he had already knew, from Haig and Nixon, that the pardon was coming. As instructed, Buchen said that Ford was considering a pardon but it was not definite. "If it is granted," Buchen said, "a statement of contrition by President Nixon would be appropriate." Miller, who had already discussed with Haig and Nixon a possible Nixon statement, advised Buchen that he would do his best but doubted that Nixon would admit any guilt in Watergate.

Working together, the three negotiated a plan for the Nixon tapes and papers. Nixon would deed them to the United States if they could be stored in a vault in a Federal warehouse near San Clemente with only two keys—Nixon to have one, the General Services Administration the other. If President Ford and former President Nixon approved the plan, the tapes and documents would be moved to California.

The next day, Wednesday, September 4, Buchen asked for a private meeting with Jaworski, as Ford had directed. Both lived at the Jefferson Hotel, so they could meet upstairs without attracting the attention of the press. "Buchen said Ford wanted my opinion on how long it would be before Nixon could be given a fair trial if he were indicted," Jaworski said. "And the president wanted to know the areas of investigation involving Nixon's activities."

Jaworski responded that same day, in writing to Buchen: "The factual situation regarding a trial of Richard M. Nixon within Constitutional bounds is unprecedented," he wrote. Citing Nixon's impeachment, the evidence on the tapes, the shifts by prominent Republicans from insistence on Nixon's innocence to public declarations of his guilt, the nationwide coverage by the media of his involvement in Watergate—Jaworski submitted that all compounded into unprecedented pretrial publicity. These factors, Jaworski said, "require a delay, before selection of a jury is begun, of a period from nine months to a year, and perhaps even longer." As to even beginning a trial, because of "the complexities involved in the process of selecting a jury and the time it will take to complete the process, I find difficult to estimate at this time."

In sum, a year to find a place for Nixon to get a fair trial, and then, no one could calculate how much longer it would take to select an impartial jury and conduct the trial.

With his letter, Jaworski sent Buchen a memorandum from his deputy, Henry Ruth, listing ten areas under investigation beyond Watergate, including using the IRS to punish political enemies, tapping the telephones of White House aides, and obstructing justice in the Pentagon Papers trial. That memo included Ruth's comment suggesting leniency for Nixon.

For Jaworski, Buchen's inquiry confirmed his sense of deliverance. He had not mentioned his visit from Miller, but he was confident that Buchen spoke for the President. And Buchen had not come unless a pardon of Nixon was imminent. If and when the pardon was granted, Jaworski would be free to return to Texas. His responsibility to make that critical decision—to indict a former President or not—would end.

For Ford, Buchen's report and Jaworski's letter affirmed his own judgment: the indictment and trial of Nixon would go on for years. "The Jaworski report was the deciding factor," Ford said later. It had confirmed his expectation that the nightmare of Watergate would not, in fact, have ended; probably, it would dominate the headlines and plague his Administration for as long as he would be in office.

Ford also read Henry Ruth's words: "One can make a strong argument for leniency, and if President Ford is so inclined, I think he ought to do it early rather than late." This was the sober and considered judgment of a prosecutor. "It was written by a person who probably knew the facts about Watergate as well as anybody, and from a lawyer who, I'm sure, had no sympathy for Nixon," Ford said. "It was a strong statement, and it did have an impact on the timing of the action I took."

After the prosecutors' opinions, Ford moved forward. He had had enough of Watergate, and it was his judgment that the American people had also had enough. Painful it was going to be. He recognized that permitting Nixon to escape punishment for crimes that would imprison his Watergate coconspirators suggested a dual system of justice. "But the others had not been elected President and forced to resign," he said. "I equated the resignation of the President to a prison sentence."

After weighing all factors, all questions, Ford concluded it had to be done. "It was the most difficult decision of my life, by far," he said, "but in my mind and in my judgment, I knew it was not just right, but best for the country."

More than once Ford considered consulting with friends in Congress, but rejected the idea. "Obviously I thought of it," he said, "but I had three reservations: One, any such discussion with anybody, virtually anybody on the Hill, would have inevitably leaked. Number two, I thought this was such a personal judgment, that my judgment on this was better than anybody on the Hill because nobody on the Hill was going through the agony in the Oval Office of what to do about Nixon. I was the only one experiencing that. Nobody on Capitol Hill could transpose themselves down to where I was. Thirdly, I thought my overall judgment on this matter was as good, if not better, than any of theirs."

Not from staff advice, but on his own, Ford wondered about sending up a trial balloon to test public reaction. "I thought it would have been a terrible idea," he said. "When I granted the pardon, I saw what the reaction was. If I had floated it as a possibility, everybody—well, not everybody but a hell of a lot of people—would have jumped all over me. And it would have been much harder to do."

At some point in his deliberations Ford remembered that in his confirmation hearings for Vice President he had been asked by Senator Howard Cannon if he thought Nixon might escape prosecution if he resigned, and then-Congressman Ford had replied, "I do not think the public would stand for it." His opinion had changed. "That was a hypothetical question," he said. "A year later I was dealing with reality."

On Thursday, September 5, 1974, Ford told Buchen to arrange for his assistant counsel, Becker, and Nixon's lawyer, Jack Miller, to fly immediately to California to inform Nixon of his decision.

Late that afternoon, with Buchen and Haig in the Oval Office, Ford delivered his instructions to Becker: First, inform Nixon that he is considering a pardon. Second, negotiate an agreement with Nixon on his tapes and documents if you can. Third, make certain that Nixon will accept the pardon if offered, for the acceptance of a pardon is an admission of guilt. Fourth, get a statement of contrition if possible. Finally, he said to Becker: "It's not final; but in all probability a pardon will be forthcoming. Be very firm out there and tell me what you see."

When Becker and Miller arrived at the Nixon compound in San Clemente shortly after midnight, they were met by a defiant Ziegler. "Let's get one thing straight immediately," Ziegler said. "President Nixon is not issuing any statement whatsoever regarding Watergate, whether Jerry Ford pardons him or not."

Becker found Ziegler's words and manner so offensive that he called the Air Force pilots and told them to get ready to fly him back to Washington immediately. Miller intervened, and persuaded Becker that their mission was too important to walk out without an effort. After Becker calmed down, the three agreed to meet the next morning to negotiate what to do about Nixon's tapes and documents.

On Friday morning they reached a tentative agreement on Nixon's tapes and papers, and Becker telephoned Buchen to go over the details. In guarded words, Buchen also told Becker to expedite a Nixon statement, as Ford wanted to announce the pardon on Saturday. Despite the urgency, Becker rejected Ziegler's first draft of a Nixon acceptance statement: it placed all the blame on the White House staff. Miller offered a draft. Ziegler took it to Nixon, made changes, and presented it to Becker. Unacceptable, Becker said. Ziegler brought out a new version. Becker suggested changes. Ziegler took it back to Nixon, who made more changes.

Becker, on the telephone to Buchen and Ford, kept them advised, emphasizing that Nixon was reluctant, unwilling to make any statement of acceptance. Although Ford knew that Nixon had never admitted any guilt for Watergate, he still hoped that the offer of a pardon would change his mind. "I was surprised, disappointed," Ford said. "I had expected him to be forthcoming. But I could not permit his nit-picking over words to alter my decision."

Becker did his best to be firm, as Ford had directed, but late on Friday, Becker realized that trying for a statement of contrition was futile. He had been negotiating from a disadvantage: he did not know that Nixon and Ziegler had been informed by Haig that Ford would grant the pardon even if Nixon confessed to nothing. Finally, Miller persuaded Nixon to accept the deal. Becker concluded that Nixon would make no apology, admit no guilt, so he must return to Washington with the best statement he could get from Nixon.

> In accepting this pardon, I hope that [President Ford's] compassionate act will contribute to lifting the burden of Watergate from our country . . . Looking back on what is still in my mind a complex and confusing maze of events, decisions, pressures, and personalities, one thing I can see clearly now is that I was wrong in not acting more decisively and more forthrightly in dealing with Watergate . . . No words can describe the depth of my regret and pain at the anguish my mistakes over Watergate have caused the Nation and the Presidency . . .

To the end, and even with the great gift of a pardon, Nixon would admit to no crime and accept no blame for Watergate.

Long after, Ziegler said, "In private, he took full blame for what he had done. I don't know how many times he said to me in one way or another—It's not Mitchell's fault, or Haldeman's, or Ehlichman's. It's my fault. I don't blame anyone else.'" Why then would he not say so in public, especially in accepting the pardon? "I don't know," Ziegler said. "I have often wondered, and I think it was just his personality, his nature. That's who he was. There was just something about him that would not let him say in public what he often told me in private, that Watergate was his fault."

With assurance that Nixon would accept a pardon and thereby the implication of guilt, but lacking any word of contrition, Becker and Miller flew back to Washington. On Saturday morning Becker reported to Ford on Nixon's appearance: He was thin and frail, his skin wrinkled and his hair disheveled. He looked at least twenty years older than his sixty-one years, Becker said, and his mind "was at times alert, at times seemed to drift." So gaunt was his appearance and so listless his manner that Becker thought Nixon was nearing death. After that meeting, Buchen and Becker secluded themselves to draft the formal legal wording of the pardon.

For diversion, at midday Ford played a round of golf at Burning Tree with his close friend Mel Laird, but he told Laird nothing of his plan to pardon Nixon. In the afternoon he returned to the White House to meet with USSR Ambassador Dobrynin and Russian cosmonauts.

Back in the Oval Office, Ford sat alone, reflecting on his decision. Not for a moment did he consider changing his mind. "I just knew it was the right thing to do, for the country, and for my ability to get on with the job," he said. He remembered from a college history lesson that President Lincoln, in considering the Emancipation Proclamation, had asked each Cabinet Member for his opinion and all had been opposed. But Lincoln had the only vote that counted. "That was how I felt about the pardon," Ford said. "My name was going to be the only one that went on that piece of paper."

Ford was deeply disappointed in the statement Nixon would make in accepting the pardon. "I had thought he would be very receptive to the idea of clearing the decks, but he had not been as forthcoming as I had hoped. He didn't admit guilt. I was taking one hell of a risk, and he didn't seem to be responsive at all."

Late that Saturday afternoon Ford summoned the pardon team to go over his plan to announce the pardon on live television on Sunday morning. This time he brought in his press secretary, Jerry terHorst. Until then, Ford had deliberately kept the secret from terHorst. "We didn't tell Jerry," Ford said, "because I knew that if a reporter asked him a question about whether I was considering a pardon, Jerry couldn't tell a lie. By not telling him, I thought I was protecting him and his relations with the press."

TerHorst was stunned. He knew at once that the pardon would be an unprecedented public relations problem for the President and for himself. He was offended that he had not been consulted on such a dramatic and unprecedented news story, and thought it improper that Ford had not consulted the Attorney General. Ford told terHorst he had deliberately not asked for Saxbe's advice, and had made his decision on his own. To terHorst would fall the responsibility for arranging the television broadcast and alerting White House reporters to a major Sunday story.

After making the arrangements, terHorst went home and thought over his situation. Even before this extraordinary news development, he had recognized that his month-old job of press secretary was more demanding that he had expected. He had confided to Milton Pitts, the White House barber, that he planned to resign, for "the hours are too long, the work too hard, and the stress too much." Late that Saturday evening, terHorst wrote a letter of resignation to President Ford: "It is with great regret, after long soul searching, that I must inform you that I cannot in good conscience support your decision to pardon former President Nixon."

He realized that his resignation would provoke the White House press to be even more critical of the pardon and the President, but he decided he must quit his job as spokesman for the President. "I couldn't defend a double standard of justice," he said, "and I didn't intend to spend the rest of my career trying to explain it."

Ford rose early on Sunday morning and walked across Lafayette Square to attend 8:00 a.m. communion service at St. John's Episcopal Church. His decision to announce the pardon on Sunday was deliberate; he never considered announcing the pardon on prime-time television. "Because of the solemnness of the decision, I thought Sunday morning after church was the appropriate time," Ford said. "From the time I made the final decision, I prayed every night for guidance. I felt it would be helpful for me to go to St. John's Church that Sunday, pray that what I was doing was not only right for the country but right for all parties involved." Sitting in the President's pew, and taking communion was comforting, reassuring. He strode across Lafayette Square to the White House with confidence. "It just seemed to me that having gone to church, and having convinced myself without any reservation that it was the right thing, that the Lord himself was giving me the guidance, I wanted to do it then."

When he returned to his office about 9:00 a.m., Hartmann was waiting with the draft of his statement. They made a few changes, and Ford inserted, with a pen, a line about Nixon's health. With Hartmann as his audience, Ford read the statement aloud, then again.

Comfortable with the text and his delivery, Ford moved into his small office and telephoned Speaker Albert, Senate Majority Leader Mansfield, House Minority Leader Rhodes, Senate Minority Leader Scott, and other Congressional leaders to tell them what he was about to do. Senator Goldwater objected and angrily told Ford: Nixon did not deserve a pardon. He was a liar, Goldwater said, and he had deceived Congress and the American people.

To his close friend House Majority Leader Tip O'Neill, Ford confided: "Tip, I've made up my mind to pardon Nixon. I'm doing it because I think it's right for the country, and because it feels right in my heart. The man is so depressed, and I don't want to see a former President go to jail."

O'Neill was stunned. "You're crazy," he told Ford. "I'm telling you right now, this will cost you the election. I hope it's not part of any deal."

"No, there's no deal," Ford said.

"Then why the hell are you doing it?" O'Neill asked.

"Tip, Nixon is a sick man," Ford said. "And Julie keeps calling me because her father is so depressed."

"I know you're not calling for my advice," O'Neill said, "but I think it's too soon."

Ford said that for the good of the country, he would not wait. "Tip, I can't run this office while this [Nixon] business drags on day after day. There are a lot more important things to be spending my time on."

His calls finished, Ford sat alone in the Oval Office, practicing the delivery of the statement Hartmann had prepared. Thirty minutes before he was to go on the air, terHorst walked in and interrupted him. "Mr. President, here's my letter of resignation."

Ford stood up in surprise. "Jerry, I think you've made a mistake," he said. "I respect your views, and I hope you'll reconsider."

TerHorst shook his head. "My decision is firm, Mr. President." His reasoning, he said, was in the letter. Ford walked around his desk, shook terHorst's hand, and put his arm around terHorst's shoulder. "I am very sorry for this development, Jerry. I hope our friendship will continue."

As soon as terHorst left, Ford summoned Marsh and handed him terHorst's letter. Marsh immediately rushed to terHorst's office, closed the door, and pleaded with him to delay announcing his resignation at least until the next day. At first ter Horst agreed. Then he changed his mind. He said he had already told one reporter he was resigning, and so he must go ahead with his plan and leave that day.

At 11:05 a.m., Sunday, September 8, 1974, on live television and radio, Ford began reading his prepared statement. It was not Hartmann's best work. It lacked a memorable sentence or phrase that evoked the gravity of the situation; neither did it encapsulate the reason for such an unexpected and unpopular action. "Bob's heart was not in it," Buchen said. Nor was it Ford's best performance. When a President must deliver bad news, the best of them open with words of grim reality, then call for national resolution and promise better times to come. Ford's statement lacked conviction. In manner he was serious and resolute, but he muddled his message. His intent was to show that he was pardoning Nixon for one reason: the national interest. His central and convincing argument to his four closest aides had been that he must rid the country of its preoccupation with Nixon's fate so that he could get on with the more important business of governing. But much of his public statement on that Sunday morning dealt with untimely and misplaced sympathy for Nixon.

In the opening paragraph of his speech, Ford expressed the essence of his decision: "In my own mind and in my own conscience (the pardon) is the right thing to do." He then meandered, citing his oath to uphold the Constitution, and mentioning that he has "sworn to uphold our laws with the help of God"—from Whom he had sought guidance "to determine the right thing for me to do with respect to my predecessor in this place, Richard Nixon and his loyal wife and family. Theirs is an American tragedy in which we have all played a part." The latter sentence was a curious insert contrary to fact: Nixon initiated, and with his coconspiring senior staff, provoked that American tragedy.

Further sympathizing with Nixon, Ford observed that "it is common knowledge that serious allegations and accusations hang like a sword over our former President's head . . ." Mindful of what Becker had told him about Nixon's deathly pallor, Ford had added at the last minute in his own handwriting, "<u>threatening his health</u> as he tries to reshape his life, a great part of which was spent in the service of his country and by the mandate of its people." Advised, Ford stated, that months and years might pass before Nixon could get a fair trial, Nixon "would be cruelly and excessively penalized either in preserving the presumption of his innocence or in obtaining a speedy determination of his guilt . . ."

Near the end of his statement Ford reached his best argument for the pardon: During the inevitable and years-long public commotion of a Nixon trial, he said, "our people would be polarized in their opinions. And the credibility of our free institutions of government would again be challenged at home and abroad . . . It is my duty, not merely to proclaim domestic tranquility but to use every measure that I have to ensure it . . ."

"Finally," Ford said, "I feel that Richard Nixon and his loved ones have suffered enough and will continue to suffer, no matter what I do, no matter what we, as a great and good nation, can do together to make his goal of peace come true." With that, Ford read the proclamation granting the pardon.

> Now, therefore, I, Gerald R. Ford, President of the United States, pursuant to the pardon power conferred upon me by Article II, Section 2, of the Constitution, have granted and by these presents do grant a full, free, and absolute pardon unto Richard Nixon for all offenses against the United States which he, Richard Nixon, has committed or may have committed or taken part in during the period from January 20, 1969, through August 9, 1974.

When he finished reading, Ford signed the pardon, witnessed his signature, and ended the broadcast.

As the red light on the television camera blinked off, Ford rose from the chair. "I felt the unbelievable lifting of a burden," he said. "I knew I could proceed without being harassed by the Nixon problems. A heavy, heavy load was off my back, and I felt free to work on those things that were so necessary for the welfare of the country."

But it was not over.

In an instant, Americans were outraged. Angry callers immediately overwhelmed the White House switchboard, their protests running 8 to 1 against the pardon. In the White House press room Ford's intended message became even more confused. TerHorst, walking out of the White House, told reporter friends that Ford's pardon of Nixon was "an act of mercy." With no press secretary, Buchen—although totally inexperienced in dealing with reporters—was dispatched to the press room to explain Ford's action and respond to press questions. Asked why Nixon had not been required to make a statement of contrition, answered: "You do not put conditions on an act of mercy."

Ford blamed himself for botching his message. "I didn't explain my reasons well enough," he said. "Compassion for Nixon as an individual had not prompted my decision at all. I have to confess that my televised talk failed to emphasize adequately that I wanted to give my full attention to grave economic and foreign policy matters. Nor did I explain as fully as I should have the strong judicial underpinnings, in particular, the Supreme Court's ruling that acceptance of a pardon means admission of guilt."

Worse was to come. Two days later, acting press secretary Jack

Hushen, when asked if Ford intended to pardon other Watergate defendants, replied that it was "under study." The words had been given him by Buchen, who made the legal point that Haldeman, Ehrlichman, or any other Watergate defendant could apply for a pardon, and every application would have to be studied on its merits. Ford was furious at the mistake. "I immediately shot that down," he said, "There was not a scintilla of truth in it. It aggravated an already difficult situation." Congress, however, was not satisfied. To make sure there would be no more Watergate pardons, the Senate passed a resolution 55-24 that Ford should grant no more Watergate pardons.

Day by day, opposition mounted. Significantly, the most severe criticism of the pardon came from those who knew most about Nixon's crimes. Senator Sam Ervin, Chairman of the Senate Watergate Committee, spoke for many in Congress. "President Ford ought to have allowed the legal processes to take their course, and not issued any pardon to former President Nixon until he had been indicted, tried, and convicted," Ervin said. "President Ford did infinite injury to the indispensable principle of good government embodied in the phrase 'Equal Justice Under Law.'" Judge John Sirica, who had broken the Watergate case, said the pardon was wrong, that justice had not been served. "Nixon should have been indicted," Sirica wrote. "And then, no matter how long it took, he should have stood trial. It would have been better for the country if the legal process had been allowed to run its course, either to acquit the former President or find him guilty."

The pardon made Sirica's judicial responsibility even more difficult: he must preside over the trial of Nixon underlings—Mitchell, Haldeman, Ehlrichman—while the former President, who contrived the obstruction of justice and abetted the perjury for which they were being tried, would never even have to appear in court.

At the office of the Special Prosecutor, the more zealous members of the staff insisted that Jaworski challenge the pardon on the grounds that it interfered with the independence of action guaranteed to Jaworski when he accepted the appointment. Under that guarantee, made by Nixon and endorsed by the bipartisan leaders of Congress, Jaworski alone could decide whom to prosecute. "Bring on a court test of the legality of the pardon," some Members of Congress and others urged Jaworski. He and his fellow prosecutors did research the possibility, but "I came to the conclusion that a President had a Constitutional right to grant a pardon, regardless of his motives," Jaworski wrote.

In the press the hue and cry against Ford mounted. The *New York Times* thundered: "This blundering intervention is a body blow to the President's own credibility and to the public's reviving confidence in the integrity of its Government." To the *Washington Post,* the pardon was "nothing less than the continuation of a cover-up." Because of the pardon, Ford's approval rating in the Gallup Poll plummeted, from 71 percent to 49 percent.

Ford, never adept at anticipating press or popular reaction to events, was shocked at the anger and resentment he had provoked. "What I had failed to anticipate was the vehemence of the hostile reaction to my decision," Ford said. "I thought perhaps the public would consider the resignation of a President as sufficient punishment, shame and disgrace. I thought there would be greater understanding and perhaps forgiveness. I began to wonder whether instead of healing the wounds of Watergate, I had rubbed salt in them."

To the principals who would contend in court against and for Nixon, the pardon was a Presidential action to be commended. An hour before the pardon was announced, Buchen telephoned Jaworski and informed him that President Ford was going to pardon Nixon. Jaworski immediately telephoned Doyle so that he could handle press questions and added, "Jim, I am very relieved."

Jack Miller was also relieved. "I'm biased of course, but it was the best thing for my client," Miller said. "It was also right for the country." To defend Nixon, his lawyer had planned a long legal siege. He would first argue that there was no place where Nixon could get a fair trial. If a judge were assigned, he would argue that no impartial jury could be found in that city. Step by step, Miller would challenge prospective jurors, attack witnesses, question evidence, undermine testimony, argue for a mistrial. If a jury found his client guilty, Miller would initiate a series of appeals, take his case to the Supreme Court. How long would a Nixon trial and subsequent appeals have taken? "Years. Years!" Miller said. "In long-range litigation, there is a strong advantage to the defendant. I was certain that in the end, I could win the case."

Nine days after the pardon, with popular resentment against the pardon unabated, Nixon telephoned Ford. Warily, Ford made careful notes of the conversation: *9/17/74—about 10:30 PM. President Nixon called me. Said at outset he would reject pardon if that would help. Sorry he caused me so much trouble. Also discussed foreign policy and the im-*

portance of Henry Kissinger. Seemed in reasonably good spirits, but not as strong as usual in his conversation.

As he listened, Ford decided he should consider Nixon's offer as nothing more than a gesture. Furthermore, if in fact Nixon did say anything in public, Ford was sure it would only create a new controversy that would make the situation even worse. So, on the phone he told Nixon no, that the matter was done and finished.

To Ford, he had done his best to resolve the Nixon issue and to end Watergate once and for all. Now he could devote all his time and energy to dealing with the more important and more immediate problems confronting the country. Or so he thought.

CHAPTER 15

Testifying

From the first moment of Ford's pardon of Nixon, the question was bound to be asked: had there been a deal? The precipitousness of Ford's action, one month after Nixon's resignation; the timing, on a Sunday morning; the secretiveness, after Ford had promised an open Administration; the muddled explanations from the White House, the deep-rooted suspicion of government after years of Presidential duplicity during Vietnam and Watergate—all these elements combined to suggest there could have been a deal.

Ford confronted that suspicion from the first day. His best Democratic friend, Tip O'Neill, raised the question. Mel Laird, Ford's close Republican friend, was too dismayed to discuss it at golf that Sunday afternoon. On his first trip after the pardon, to Pittsburgh on Monday, a blue-collar worker told White house reporters at the airport: "It was all fixed. Ford said to Nixon: 'You give me the job. I'll give you the pardon.'"

An official bargain in the public interest—Nixon to resign in exchange for a Congressional grant of immunity from prosecution—had been responsibly proposed. Five days before Nixon's resignation a distinguished Constitutional lawyer, William T. Coleman Jr., advocated immunity for resignation on the editorial pages of the *New York Times*. Three Senators—John Tower, Robert Griffin, and Edward Brooke—had suggested that the Senate pass a resolution to exempt Nixon from prosecution if he should resign. Special Prosecutor Jaworski supported the proposed resolution, hoped it would happen, and had been told that Congress would pass it.

There was a precedent. Only eight months earlier, official Washington had approved—in fact, welcomed—the plea bargain granted Vice President Agnew: he resigned in exchange for the government promise that he would not be prosecuted for accepting bribes in office. That deal had been negotiated by the impeccably upright Elliott Richardson, then Attorney General, to prevent the possibility of a felon succeeding to the Presidency.

But this was different. Agnew had taken bribes for his personal use. Nixon, to further his reelection, had corrupted the Constitution. He had obstructed justice, suborned perjury, bribed witnesses. He had lied—consciously, deliberately and repeatedly—to Congress, to Federal judges, and to the American people. To most Americans, Nixon's serial crimes warranted punishment. Yet Ford had set him free.

To at least one Member of the House of Representatives, the pardon was suspect. She was Bella Abzug of New York, a brilliant lawyer, as widely respected by her peers for her legal ability as she was disliked for her overbearing cantankerousness. Four days after the pardon, Abzug initiated a formal House inquiry to Ford: had he or his representative discussed a pardon with Nixon or his representative before Nixon resigned? The question was one of twelve she asked in a Privileged Resolution of Inquiry.

Since President James Monroe—possibly earlier, the records are incomplete—the House of Representatives has used this little-known legal instrument to "exercise the right to call on the President and heads of departments for information." Though not mentioned in the Constitution, the precedents of 200 years require a prompt and full response from the President or his Cabinet Members to this polite but imperative inquiry.

Abzug's resolution, cosponsored by ten other House Members, was referred to the Judiciary Committee, then to Chairman William Hungate's Subcommittee on Criminal Justice. He considered it a valid inquiry. "I viewed as vital the need to receive answers to the questions" Abzug raised, Hungate said. "The pardon not only clouded the issue of whether the full story of Watergate would ever be known, but it also raised serious doubts as to the sincerity of the new President in declaring that his would be an open Administration."

When Abzug's privileged inquiry reached the White House, it was routed for action to the new Counsel, Philip Buchen. Unaware of the importance of the House resolution, Buchen drafted a brief letter for the President's signature. It did not respond to Abzug's questions at all; he sent copies of Ford's proclamation of the pardon and a transcript of the White House press conference that day.

To Chairman Hungate and the sponsors of the Resolution, Ford's letter was an insult. We were being told, Hungate said, to go look for the answers somewhere in the Ford statement and press reports. Hungate and other Members were surprised that Ford, who knew the importance of a House Resolution of Inquiry, "had not extended to the subcommittee the courtesy of a more appropriate response." Unsurprisingly, the lack of specific answers from Ford prompted Abzug and other Members to become even more suspicious: there must have been a deal.

White House Counselor Jack Marsh, always alert to anything of consequence occurring on Capitol Hill, heard about the blunder and talked to Hungate. The chairman agreed to send Ford a new inquiry. His committee put the blunt question: had Ford discussed a pardon with Nixon or his representative before he resigned?

Again Buchen drafted the reply, and to that question he answered no. Marsh, monitoring the response this time, went in alone to see the President, showed him the draft, and said: "Look, you can't send the letter up to the Hill this way because the answer is wrong."

Ford looked at the letter and told Marsh: "Go talk to Phil."

Marsh, well aware that Buchen had never been told of Haig's proposal to Ford on August 1, walked upstairs to Buchen's office and closed the door. "Phil," he said, "there's something I have to tell you." Then he told him the whole story of how Haig had met alone with Vice President Ford eight days before Nixon resigned, and proposed to Ford that Nixon would resign if Ford would agree to pardon him after he became President.

Buchen was shocked; his immediate reaction was that there may have been a deal. "Jack," he said sadly, "I guess I ought to resign. All I have is my integrity. That's all I brought to Washington."

Marsh persuaded him to stay. There was no deal, he assured Buchen, and told him the whole story: how Haig had initiated the proposal, how Ford considered it his duty to evaluate whether the best interest of the country would have been to expedite Nixon's resignation, how he and Hartmann had opposed the idea and brought in Harlow to reinforce their judgment. Ford, Marsh said, had listened to Harlow's reasoning, agreed with him, and telephoned Haig to reject the deal.

There was no reason for Buchen to resign, Marsh said, because there had been no deal. Moreover, Marsh pointed out, if Buchen should quit, it would provoke new suspicion and irreparably damage the President, personally, publicly, and permanently.

When Marsh reported back to Ford on his talk with Buchen, Ford said: "Jack, the best thing for me to do is just go up to Capitol Hill, testify, and spell it out."

Hartmann, told of Ford's plan, objected. The risk of answering hostile questions on so sensitive a subject in a public forum was too great, Hartmann argued. He advised Ford to ignore the House resolution. Haig also objected; his reputation and future in the military service might be compromised. Buchen also objected, arguing that there was no precedent for a President testifying before Congress.

Ford disagreed. "I could see the storm gathering," he said. "This thing would boil and boil and boil with all kinds of innuendoes. The only way to stop it was for me to go up there." He knew there was a risk in being interrogated, but the greater risk was to say nothing. Stonewalling, as Nixon had done, would only encourage suspicion. "The news stories and speeches in the House will go on and on," he told the four. "The only way I can clear the air and put the issue behind me is to go up and testify. I can answer their questions face to face, far better than I could in any letter."

Nevertheless, Hartmann, Haig, and Buchen still argued against it. "They were all scared to death," Ford said.

Ford shut off the discussion. "Look," he said, "I've got nothing to hide. I am going up there."

To make certain that Congress' leaders did not object, Ford directed Marsh to clear the appearance with Speaker Albert and Senate Majority Leader Mansfield. Albert immediately agreed. "There is everything to be gained by his coming, nothing to be lost," he said. Mansfield listened to Marsh, puffed on his pipe, and finally gave a laconic answer: "All right, Jack. But tell the President not to make a habit of it."

Rodino, Chairman of Judiciary Committee, welcomed the plan. He told Marsh that he believed that Nixon had tried to manipulate Ford, "but Jerry Ford is not the man who would ever make a deal like that."

The three—Rodino, Hungate, and Marsh—settled on the rules for Ford's testimony. In respect to his position, the President would not be sworn in. Ford would read a prepared statement and take questions only from members of Hungate's subcommittee. Each would have two five-minute periods to ask questions. The hearing would be one session, in the morning, to end by noon. Ford's appearance would be televised, live.

At 10:12 a.m. on October 17, 1974, in room 2141 of the Rayburn House Office Building that Ford knew so well, Chairman Hungate called his committee to order. Ford, in the witness chair, faced twenty-three of his former colleagues. In its way, it was a historic meeting. President Washington, Hungate wrote later, had twice gone before the full Senate to lend a hand with advise and consent proceedings on a treaty with the Creek Indians, but found it such a disagreeable experience that he never went back. "Lincoln was said to have appeared before Congressional committees on at least ten occasions," Hungate said, "but painstaking research has revealed no substantiation through primary sources, such as diaries, letters, memoirs or the unpublished records at the National Archives." After all the Committee's research, Hungate concluded of Ford's appearance: "This was the first documented appearance of a President of the United States before a committee or subcommittee of the United States Congress."

Ford opened his testimony by welcoming the opportunity to set the record straight about his pardon of Nixon. "I want very much to have those facts and circumstances known" to Congress and to the American people, he said. "That is why I have volunteered to appear before you this morning."

His purpose in granting the pardon, Ford testified, "was to change our national focus. I wanted to do all I could to shift our attentions from the pursuit of a fallen President to the pursuit of the urgent needs of a rising nation," specifically, a struggling economy and a dangerous world. Directly addressing the question of whether he had discussed a pardon with Nixon before or after the resignation, Ford said no. However, he volunteered the information—new to the committee and to the public—that Haig had mentioned to him the possibility of a pardon eight days before Nixon resigned. Crafting the details of that meeting for his testimony, Ford had relied not just on his memory, but also on Haig's and Buzhardt's notes.

About 3:30 p.m. on August 1, 1974, he said, Haig had come to the Vice President's office in the Executive Office Building with the understanding that they must meet alone. Haig began by saying that he had just learned that a Nixon tape in Oval Office on June 23, 1972 contained evidence so damaging that Nixon would be forced to resign or be impeached. Consequently, Haig asked, was the Vice President ready to assume the Presidency within a very short time?

"I cannot really express in words how shocked and how stunned I was by this unbelievable revelation," Ford said to the committee. The impact was twofold: He had always believed and said publicly that he believed Nixon was innocent; Haig was telling him Nixon was guilty. Second, he was struck by the fact that he would become President of the United States.

Preoccupied by such new and hard-to-grasp realities, Ford neverthe-less listened as Haig discussed the means of an orderly transition. He did not know, Haig said, whether Nixon would resign or fight impeach-ment, but he outlined "courses of action" being considered by "White House staff." Some suggested the President "ride it out" by letting the impeachment take its course through the House and Senate trial, with Nixon fighting all the way against conviction, Haig said. Others urged resignation.

"On the resignation issue," Ford testified, "there were put forth a number of options which General Haig reviewed with me."

1. The President temporarily step aside under the 25th Amendment.

2. Delaying resignation until further along the impeachment process.

3. Trying first to settle for a censure vote as a means of avoiding either impeachment or a need to resign.

4. The question of whether the President should pardon himself.

5. Pardoning various Watergate defendants, then himself, followed by resignation.

6. A pardon to the President himself, should he resign.

Ford's description of the sixth option had carefully avoided the word "deal," but the implication was unmistakable: Nixon would resign with the understanding that Ford would pardon him.

Haig, Ford said, then asked for his views on the options. "I inquired as to what was the President's pardon power, and he answered that it was his understanding from a White House lawyer that a President did have the authority to grant a pardon even before any criminal action had been taken against an individual. As I saw it, at this point the question clearly was, . . . what course of action should I recommend that would be in the best interest of the country?

"I told General Haig I had to have some time to think. Further, that I wanted to talk to James St. Clair. I also said I wanted to talk to my wife before giving any response." The next morning, he said, St. Clair told him the evidence in the June 23 tape was "so damaging that impeachment in the House was a certainty and conviction in the Senate a high probability." When Ford asked St. Clair about the six options, "he told me he had not been the source of any opinion about Presidential pardon power."

During that day, Ford said, he thought carefully about what how he should respond and decided to make no recommendations on any of the points Haig had raised. "For that reason, Mr. Chairman, I decided I should call General Haig the afternoon of August 2. I told him I wanted him to understand that I had no intention of recommending what President Nixon should do about resigning or not resigning, and that nothing we had talked about the previous afternoon should be given any consideration in whatever decision the President might make. General Haig told me he was in full agreement with this position."

Point by point, Ford answered each of the ten questions raised in the Resolutions of Inquiry, and other questions the Committee had posed. In his responses he was firm and consistent about why he granted the pardon: "My prime reason was for the benefit of the country, not for any benefits that might be for Mr. Nixon."

It was Representative Elizabeth Holtzman of New York City who asked bluntly whether or not, in fact, there was a deal.

"There was no deal, period, under no circumstances," Ford answered.

Unconvinced, Holtzman said she suspected that tapes might show Ford and Nixon had discussed the pardon, and suggested that in his care they might be destroyed. Ford kept his temper, replied that they were intact, locked up in a secure place, and available in full to the Special Prosecutor. "I see no way whatsoever that they can be destroyed," he told Holtzman.

With her final question, Holtzman asked, "whether anybody brought to your attention the fact that the Constitution specifically states that though somebody is impeached, that person shall nonetheless be liable to punishment according to law?"

"Ms. Holtzman, I was fully cognizant of the fact that the President on resignation was accountable for any criminal charges," Ford replied, "but I would like to say that the reason I gave the pardon was not as to Mr. Nixon himself. I repeat, and I repeat with emphasis, the purpose of the pardon was to try and get the United States, the Congress, the President, and the American people, to focus in on the serious problems we have both at home and abroad. And I was absolutely convinced then as I am now that if we had had an indictment, a trial, the conviction, and anything else that transpired after that, the attention of the President, the Congress, and the American people would have been diverted from the problems that we have to solve. That was the principal reason for my granting the pardon."

Riding from Capitol Hill back to the White House, Ford told Marsh that he was gratified that the House of Representatives, so great a part of his life, had given him such an extraordinary opportunity to confirm, in a public forum, the truth about the pardon. He was certain he was right in insisting on testifying, despite staff objections. "Thank God I did," he said. "It had to be done. If I had hidden behind the façade of being President and not going up to testify, that controversy would have gone on and on and on. And the truth was that I looked forward to it, and enjoyed it, even when Liz's turn to interrogate came up—because I had no guilty conscience, period. And I didn't give a damn what she asked me. What I told her was the truth, and there was no evidence to the contrary."

He had performed well, in his judgment; now Ford could go back to solving the country's most compelling problem: the worst economic recession since the Great Depression of the 1930s.

The facts were grim. Prices were rising. People were losing their jobs. Inflation was increasing by more than 12 percent annually. Wholesale prices had risen by more than 20 percent in less than a year. Unemployment was more than 5 percent and rising; more than 5 million Americans were already looking for work. Housing starts were down. Interest rates were rising. The U.S. trade deficit reached a record $1.1 billion. Wall Street traded stocks in fear. Pessimism ruled. For the first time since President Hoover, a Gallup poll of the American people revealed that the majority were bracing for worse to come.

The causes of the recession were manifold—the 1973 Arab oil embargo, the slow erosion of confidence in Washington brought about by the decline and fall of Nixon, and a long train of excesses in the U.S.

government itself. Federal spending on the Vietnam War and President Johnson's entitlement initiatives had plunged the country deeply into debt. Not since 1969 had a Federal budget been balanced.

Ford, up to that time, was one of the few Presidents who understood economics. He actually liked the dismal science, having elected to study it in college. His favorite reading, next to biography, was economic theory. In his dozen years on the House Appropriations Committee, Ford had learned the economic realities of Federal budgets, spending, and the consequences. There he had seen at close hand how every President governs through the budget.

Philosophically, Ford was close to the "Chicago school's" Milton Friedman, and sometimes he quoted the Nobel Prize-winner's prescription for a healthy U.S. economy: "First, a steady course on the part of government which can be known in advance by the people in the marketplace, and second, a course that is directed toward reducing the role the government plays in controlling our affairs." Not by accident, Ford's philosophy also reflected the Grand Rapids way during his growing up: self-reliance, thrift, prudence, initiative, avoiding debt.

So it was that Ford began to deal with the recession with some knowledge of finance and economics. By habit he turned to Congress. As it happened, Senate Majority Leader Mike Mansfield had proposed a summit conference of the most respected economists, leaders in industry and labor, and the powers in the House and Senate. Out of these sessions came a consensus. To a man, the nation's best economists from John Kenneth Galbraith to Alan Greenspan, Ford's principal economic adviser, declared the problem to be inflation.

The solution, Ford determined, would require joint action by himself, Congress, and the public. So he asked for their help. In a formal address to a joint session of Congress, Ford proposed a multiple effort: Congress to pass legislation to increase energy supplies, cut Federal spending, and raise taxes by 5 percent on incomes over $15,000. Farmers to grow more food; contractors to build more houses; drillers to produce more oil and gas. All Americans to conserve, hold down wages and prices, and join him in a volunteer effort to Whip Inflation Now. Standing on the rostrum of the House, on live television, Ford proudly gestured toward the oversize WIN button on his lapel.

The proposals were sound. However, reflecting Ford's legislative disposition, they lacked any provision for execution. In particular, WIN was based more on Ford's ingrained optimism than reality. Hartmann had suggested the idea; Ford accepted it. The objective was valid, the cost minimal. It also appealed to Ford's sanguine belief in the American character—his sunny view that he could count on their innate goodwill; that they would respond to his appeal.

Out of inexperience, Ford had adopted WIN without asking other Presidential advisers to examine the proposal for merit or practicality. "If both the government and the people tightened their belts voluntarily and spent less than they had before, that would reduce demand, and the inflation rate would start going down," Ford said. A week later, still appealing to Americans' best nature, in Kansas City, Ford admonished the Future Farmers of America: "Clean up your plate before you get up from the table." That homely advice from a President, like the WIN program, was ridiculed by the press and brought little response from citizens. After a few weeks, WIN buttons disappeared, along with Ford's hopeful initiative.

More embarrassment was to come. Some six weeks after the economic summit had proclaimed that America's problem was inflation, the same expert economists—notably including Greenspan—reversed themselves. Instead of inflation, the problem was unemployment and a looming recession, the economists said, and Ford's proposal to raise taxes had been exactly the wrong remedy. Though it was the economists who had blundered in their opinions, it was the President who was embarrassed and diminished by bad advice and the capricious WIN initiative.

Ford learned from his mistakes; at that, he was much better than most Presidents. Never again would he make a major decision—on any issue—before organized discussion and careful deliberation.

From this experience he saw that the White House he inherited needed a strong, Cabinet-level, well-organized entity that focused entirely on economic problems and issues. The National Security Council had been set up by statute under Truman; the Domestic Policy Council by executive order under Nixon. To Ford, the third essential of Administration policy—economics—was missing. After discussions with Haig and others closer to him, Ford created, by executive order, the Economic Policy Board (EPB) to advise him on national and international economic policy, and to coordinate and put into effect his economic decisions.

It would not be just another time-wasting committee. Ford gave it prestige and authority by appointing EPB members solely on merit and experience, and by giving them power and easy access to the Oval Office. To chair the board, Ford named Treasury Secretary William Simon, who in his fifteen months in office had earned the respect of both Houses of Congress for his mastery of the intricacies of government finance. A Wall Streeter by experience, always well-informed, plain speaking by nature, Simon was designated by Ford to be his principal spokesman on economic affairs.

To serve with Simon on the EPB, Ford included his Chairman of the Council of Economic Advisers, Alan Greenspan. Despite his mixed signals on the recession, Greenspan combined a breadth of statistical information with a talent for low-key persuasiveness that enabled him to ingratiate himself with Ford. Another key EPB member was Ford's new OMB Director, James Lynn, whose diligence and analytical ability matched his volubility, making him one of the best budget directors in history. The upper tier of the Cabinet was included. Federal Reserve Chairman Arthur Burns, a longtime friend and counselor to Ford, could not be an EPB member because of his statutory independence, but was invited to attend principal sessions.

To serve as Executive Director of EPB and manage its day-to-day operations, Ford appointed William Seidman, a Grand Rapids lawyer and business executive with a firm grasp of economic theory, a savvy political mind, and a proven record of getting things done. With the new title and additional status of Assistant to the President for Economic Affairs, Seidman regularly briefed President Ford on economic issues and problems, initiated programs, pacified the egos of EPB members, and saw to it that Presidential decisions were carried out. As Hartmann described the EPB, "Bill Simon was its mouth and Bill Seidman its muscle."

Seidman was most ably assisted by an unusually talented young man, Roger Porter, then a 28-year-old White House Fellow and student of government who coordinated meetings and the constant flow of materials to EPB members. Porter, by Greenspan's appraisal, was "bright, very effective, an excellent administrator, essential to the effective operation of the Seidman team."

As it turned out, the EPB was not only a most effective new Cabinet-level operating team for the duration of the Ford Administration; it succeeded so well that Ford's Economic Policy Board was continued in some form by the next six presidents.

The EPB was more. In office two months, Ford had initiated and completed his first significant move toward better management of his

White House, a first step toward transforming himself from a legislator to an executive. His initiative showed that his new Administration was evolving, slowly, leaving behind the debris of Nixon's folly, finding its way toward order and competence.

Better organization was necessary, and quite overdue. In its first six weeks, Ford's Presidency had come across to official Washington as disorderly, an operation of amateurs. In fact it had been poorly managed. Ford's clemency program, timely and compassionate, had foundered from little planning and incompetent administration. The pardon, necessary though it was, had been ineptly presented to the public, to the press, and to Ford's friends on Capitol Hill. Haig and the other Nixon holdover staff members were denigrating, out-maneuvering, and battling with the far smaller cadre Ford had brought over from his Vice President's office. Consequently, the new Administration was a house divided.

Ford saw that he must make changes. For one thing, he realized that his notion of a spokes-of-the-wheel system was not working. "I was trying to do too many things," Ford said. "I was trying to see too many people. And too many people that I saw were oblivious as to time." He recognized the reality: he needed professional help in managing the policies and actions of his Presidency. Moreover, Ford had no doubt about the best man to bring in to do the job. In fact, on the morning of his inauguration, Ford had written his choice: Donald Rumsfeld. At that time, he had summoned Rumsfeld from Brussels, where he was Ambassador to NATO, and put him in charge of the transition.

Some ten days into the August transition, Rumsfeld went in to see the new President and said: "This is not a workable situation. The transition team has met, Scranton, Morton, Marsh, and a few others, and we've concluded that it's not healthy for you or the government to have two apparatuses that are functioning in competition. People are coming to me if they don't like the decision by Al Haig. If you ask the transition group to do something, and the people don't like it, they go to Haig."

"So I think we should wrap up the transition. We'll give you a report, provide you a way to stay in touch with your friends in Congress and have sounding boards that are different from the White House apparatus, and disband. And I'll go back to NATO." Reluctantly, Ford had agreed. He had wanted Rumsfeld to stay.

From their first meeting twelve years earlier, Ford had been impressed by Rumsfeld. "He was an excellent Member of the House, and over time we developed good rapport. Rummy has impeccable personal integrity. He is a very hard driving guy, very deliberate, and a very good organizer. He can irritate some people with his demands, but he knows how to get things done."

On a Saturday in September, Ford telephoned Rumsfeld in Chicago, where Rumsfeld was attending his father's funeral. After expressing his sympathy, Ford said. "I have to see you, Rummy. Can you be here tomorrow?"

"I can't do it," Rumsfeld said. "I'll be back in Brussels on Sunday."

"Look, you've got to come," Ford said. "I've got to see you. There is no choice. I've got to change Haig. It just isn't working. There's a lot of hostility between my staff and Haig's people. Someone's got to come in and put some order in this place."

Ford had already made up his mind: Rumsfeld must come back and manage his White House. "The only person I really considered for that responsibility was Don Rumsfeld," Ford said. "He was an absolute demon when it came to working long hours and organizing himself and everybody else. He knew the ball game. He was extremely loyal to me. I knew he would do a good job."

The next day, Rumsfeld flew to Washington and met Ford in the Oval Office that afternoon. Ford told Rumsfeld that he could no longer tolerate the conflict and turmoil in his White House. He was ready to move Haig out. He wanted Rumsfeld to come in, organize the staff, stop the petty infighting, get everyone working together, recruit fresh talent, and manage White House operations.

Rumsfeld resisted. "I didn't want to do it," he said. "I had been in the White House from '69 to '72. I had no desire to go back there. I had told my wife and family that I wouldn't think of doing it. I liked being at NATO. I had a lot of respect for the NATO people and felt that the United States was not treating that institution with the seriousness it merits. I told the President I would help him figure out someone else to come in and replace Haig."

Ford did not want someone else. "Rummy gave me a hard time," he said. "He told me, 'I'm happy in Brussels. I'm doing something I like.'" But Ford was adamant. "Rummy, I need you," he said. "The country needs you. You have got to come."

Rumsfeld insisted that he would not come in as long as the President stuck to the spokes-of-the-wheel concept. "Ford was running his White House the way he had managed his position as House Minority

Leader," Rumsfeld said. "He was a very successful legislative leader. He was comfortable with that way of working. He had never been an executive, never run a large staff."

Rumsfeld had been an executive. He had managed the Office of Economic Opportunity and the economic stabilization program for President Nixon. As a counselor to Nixon and quick-to-learn student of the ways of governing, Rumsfeld had observed from within how the Nixon White House operated. "I knew that the spokes-of-the-wheel concept from a legislative viewpoint was rational. And surely it was optically attractive to President Ford because it was in contrast to the Nixon-Haldeman-Ehrlichman operation. But it just wouldn't work in the Ford White House." He said so to President Ford. "You cannot run the Presidency that way," Rumsfeld said. "It is just not going to work. You will be consumed and destroyed." But Ford, remembering Haldeman's autocratic rule, told Rumsfeld that he had said publicly that he would have no titular Chief of Staff, and he meant it.

In the end, Ford persuaded Rumsfeld with a compromise: Rumsfeld would leave Brussels, reluctantly, and return to Washington to manage the White House. "I promise you that you will be Chief of Staff in fact," Ford said. "We aren't going to call you that for a while." Ford, in turn, accepted Rumsfeld's firm condition: that Rumsfeld would replace the spokes-of-the-wheel fiasco with a pyramidal staff structure that was, in effect, a modified Nixonian hierarchy. Changes he would make, Rumsfeld emphasized, but they would be gradual. "We can't go from where we are to where we need to be in five minutes," Rumsfeld said to the President. "We're going to have to migrate over there, have a decent interval, and I will work with you on this."

"Fine," Ford said.

At that point Rumsfeld brought in Richard Cheney, then 33, to meet President Ford. "Look, you don't want an imperial White House," Rumsfeld said. "And if we keep getting consumed, and everyone here works fifteen hours a day, we're going to begin to think we are indispensable. And we're not. It's not healthy for you. It's not healthy for us and our families. So I am going to require that everyone have a deputy. Dick will be my deputy. You're going to have to get comfortable with him."

With great relief, Ford agreed to Rumsfeld's conditions. "I knew Rummy was the man I needed," Ford said. "He came in because I really put the screws to him. I put it on a patriotic basis. I didn't give him any choice. When you put it on the basis of what's good for the country, I've never known Rummy not to respond."

With Rumsfeld committed, Ford moved to relieve Haig. Ford had mixed feelings about Haig. He had needed him to stay only during the first weeks of transition, but found him more of a divider than an asset. In particular, Ford disliked Haig's egocentricity and effrontery. Yet Ford respected Haig for his valiant service. "I thought Al deserved a hell of a medal for keeping the country going during that last year of Nixon," Ford said. Certainly, in his judgment, Haig had earned and deserved a proper assignment, so Ford asked him what he would like to do next. Haig's first choice was to achieve his career ambition and become Chief of Staff of the U.S. Army. The post was vacant; General Creighton Abrams had died in office.

Since that assignment required Senate confirmation, Ford asked Marsh to raise the possibility with Senator John Stennis, Chairman of the Senate Armed Services Committee. In his courtly way, Stennis responded with a firm answer: No. Absolutely not. Any Haig appearance before his committee would reopen Watergate, Stennis warned, and that was the last thing the country, or the new President, needed.

Ford respected Stennis's judgment. "I knew that all of the pain of Watergate would have been replayed, probably in even greater detail, and with more blood and gore," Ford said. But there was one high military office that did not require Senate confirmation: Supreme Allied Commander Europe. "It was a unilateral decision by me with the approval of our Allies," Ford said. So he called Haig in. "Al, forget Chief of Staff for the Army, but if you want to go to NATO, I'll send you there."

Haig accepted, and began packing his papers to leave for Europe. Looking back on his White House years and forward to rejoining the Army, Haig confided to his assistant, Jerry Jones: "You know, Jerry, it's time for me to go. We got Nixon out of here. We got Nixon pardoned. That's a good day's work. I've done all I could do."

CHAPTER 16

Managing

On September 27, 1974, Rumsfeld assumed the complex and exacting responsibility of managing Ford's White House. What they found, his deputy Cheney said, was chaos: decisions were being made impromptu or not at all; lines of authority were tangled; scheduling was haphazard. "The President would be in an NSC meeting on Soviet arms control and fifty Legionnaires would show up from Grand Rapids for their appointment with him," Cheney said.

Briskly, confidently, Rumsfeld immediately took control over the President's schedule, the flow of documents going to his desk for information or decision, and personnel. For Rumsfeld, as for every White House Chief of Staff, the responsibilities are manifold: He must impose and maintain order. He must save the President's time. He must make choices—inform the President of what he needs to know, spare him from problems that do not require his immediate attention. He decides who needs to see the President, and when, and for how long. He serves as the honest broker between conflicting departments and individuals. On every major issue and initiative and problem, the Chief of Staff makes certain that all Cabinet Members and senior White House staff with a stake in that issue have an opportunity to state their views, for or against, to the President before he makes a decision. The Chief of Staff oversees press operations, speech writing, Congressional relations. He shepherds staff egos. When there is a vacancy in the Cabinet or other high office, the Chief of Staff presents the names of prospects, with carefully researched background information and qualifications, for the President's decision. He must, when he believes the President is about to make a mistake, have the self-confidence and courage to tell him so—diplomatically and constructively. He must put aside, at least while he serves, any political ambition he harbors for himself. His loyalty must be, and must appear to be, first and foremost to the President, and to his success in the office.

From his first day in the Ford White House, Rumsfeld recognized he confronted a serious situation. "Jerry Ford had begun as an instant President," Rumsfeld said. "He took over an existing organization that had suited Richard Nixon not as President of the U.S. but Nixon in the heat of Watergate, which was a vastly different organization—in arrangement, authority, and focus—than the one that normally ran a White House." Change was imperative, doubly so: change from Nixon's shaky structure for self-preservation; change from Ford's centripetal legislative habits.

As a first step in bringing order into White House operations, Rumsfeld knew he had to convince the President to turn away from his Congressional ways. Ford accepted that; from childhood, he had always responded to good coaching. He had followed the instructions of Scoutmaster Kindel, of Coach Gettings at South High, of Coach Kipke at Michigan, of Coach Pond at Yale, of Commander Atwood on the bridge of the USS *Monterey* in the Pacific. On the House floor he had been coached by a crusty but wise mentor, John Taber. In the White House, Ford's management coach would be Donald Rumsfeld.

Good coaching emphasizes basics: to the executive, it is delegating. "We tried like the dickens to get the President to delegate responsibility to the Cabinet, to his Vice President, to his senior staff, to his counsel, to his press secretary," Rumsfeld said. "He saw that he wouldn't be a good President if he didn't have strong Cabinet officers who had the authority to speak for him and to work the Hill for him and to talk to the world for him. So he would need to strengthen them by supporting them and communicating with them directly, and keep other people out of their business. And that's not easy."

"Second, he had to have priorities, decide what was important. Everybody in the world would want to see him, and he couldn't do that. There are only so many hours in the day. What he needed was a disciplined staff system, where everybody who needs to see him gets to see him, but only on a professional basis and at times that make sense. So that other people know what's going on, if the Attorney General needs to see him, his counsel Phil Buchen ought to be there. If it's legislation, Jack Marsh and the other legislative people need to be there. If the right people are cut out, they are embarrassed and weakened by not knowing what he is doing."

One immediate need was to change the White House staff. "The construct was, on the one hand you've got to reassure the American people and the world that the government has momentum and direction and is functioning," Rumsfeld said. "On the other hand, we recognized that the White House was an illegitimate institution under Nixon. The question was, how do you transform the Nixon White House into the Ford White House, an illegitimate government into a legitimate government? So President Ford was facing that dilemma, feeling the tension between the two."

"His bias, his personal view, partly because he was such a decent, kind human being, partly because he knew the people in that Administration were not evil people and had come there to serve the public and had done nothing wrong, he did not want to see them harmed because of misdeeds by others. Also, the President was a cautious person and favored continuity over change. What he needed was to change enough of the Nixon people, fast enough, so that by altering the critical mass of what he inherited he would be seen as transforming an illegitimate government into a legitimate government."

As Cheney, the student of political science, observed on the question of continuity versus change, Ford's situation was unique. "Before, every Vice President who became President by accession buried his predecessor," Cheney said. "The key to both providing stability in the institutions of government and in the political success of the new man, in virtually every case, has been to wrap himself in this mantle—to embrace his programs wholeheartedly and to pursue them and to do everything you can to use the mantle of your predecessor to establish your own right to rule. We couldn't do that. We were under two conflicting pressures that didn't exist for any other President. In this case, President Ford felt that he must send out a signal of stability and continuity in foreign policy and national security. So Don and I focused on the non-national security area, on the relationships between the White House and the Secretaries, OMB, the agencies, on how the White House was organized internally. That was our way to make certain that as far as the American people were concerned, a new crowd was in power in Washington."

"Change and continuity—it was something we wrestled with all the way through our time in office. We never did have the luxury of being able to wrap the mantle of our predecessor around us—the guy who won the last election. And it makes a hell of a big difference whether you bury your predecessor or you pardon him."

Moving to show the public that this was indeed a new White House and a new and different Presidency under Ford, Rumsfeld sat down with him and laid out a schedule for personnel changes, for the resignation of the Nixon holdovers who should go. "Don gave me a precise day-by-day, month-by month, schedule for the changes," Ford said. "We agreed that by December 31, 1974, all the ones we wanted to go should go. Then Don talked with each of them and laid out a schedule that was acceptable to each one and fitted in with our own requirements."

To Rumsfeld, it was not easy. He had the unpleasant task of talking to each Nixon appointee and, as he put it, "figuring out where possible a gentle way to move them out and move other people in—so that the Administration would be a Ford Administration. What amazed me was how little had been done, how little change there had been from the Nixon White House." The reason was obvious: Haig had done nothing to remove the Nixon staff. As they had proved their loyalty to him, Haig would in turn prove to be loyal to the Nixon staff.

In another action to show the Ford Administration was different, Rumsfeld suggested to Ford that he create and impose a code of ethics for everyone serving in the Executive Department. Ford agreed. "I told him, 'You are right and I've been thinking about it. Will you take the lead and get it done.' He did," Ford said.

Rumsfeld recruited two outside lawyers, Don Murdock and Don Willets, who reviewed codes of ethics reaching back to Eisenhower and delivered to Rumsfeld a comprehensive report and recommendation. As a result, White House Counsel Philip Buchen issued these strict standards for everyone serving in the Ford Executive Offices: no political campaign activity in the White House, no gifts to be accepted by White House staff, no being involved in a decision in which the staff member or any member of his family has a financial interest, no using information gained by official duty to invest in stocks or bonds, no disclosing classified information, no associating with outside persons having important stakes in government actions.

Some of these restrictions had been in force for decades; but, they had not been observed by every White House—notably not in Nixon's. Rumsfeld considered it necessary that they be restated, and met. "We not only should see that we had and were following a new code of ethics," Rumsfeld said, "but we should also see that it was *known* that we had a new code of ethics and would enforce it. It worked. It kept us out of trouble."

Ford, in his first days as President, intended to look to his Cabinet to carry out his policies and decisions. To Rumsfeld, the notion of "Cabinet government" is misleading. "It leaves people with the impression that it's possible to allow cabinet officers to proceed semi-independently in their respective areas of jurisdiction," he said. "The way our world works, it's rare when you find an issue that is the jurisdiction of only one cabinet officer."

Making his point, Rumsfeld said: "Take a grain embargo with Poland, for example. Imposing an embargo or terminating one obviously is a foreign policy issue as well as an agriculture issue. It may very well be a Defense Department issue. It's clearly a Treasury issue on the balance of payments. It may be a Department of Labor issue because in some cases, the unions have refused to load. It's obviously a Congressional issue. It's certainly going to be a press issue. It may be a legal issue. You have all these threads, and the White House staff's function is to see that those threads go through the needle's eye in a reasonably coherent way. The staff's job is not to make the decisions, but by the same token, the staff has to avoid letting the President be blind-sided by allowing a single Cabinet officer to go out and make a decision like that. Because he can't."

To keep President Ford informed day-to-day, Rumsfeld adopted a pattern: after his own meeting with senior White House staff in the Roosevelt Room every morning, Rumsfeld would see Ford and bring him up to date on what happened during the night, and what he learned of consequence from the principal Presidential assistants. Together they would walk through the scheduled events of the day. In the late afternoon Rumsfeld would see Ford again and bring him up to date on what had happened during the day. "He would hand me the volumes of work he had done since I had last seen him. He was a work horse. He would plow through papers and briefs and information and make notes in that left-handed scrawl of his, checking boxes, approving, disapproving, writing comments: 'Go ahead.' 'Check with Jack Marsh.' 'Material for a speech?' 'Let's meet on this.'"

After each session Rumsfeld would come out with notes on a yellow pad, sit down with Cheney, and spell out instructions for what the President wanted to have done, decide who would be best to do it, and relay the assignment. Usually it was Cheney's job to follow up and make sure it was being done.

By design, Rumsfeld and his deputy, Cheney, opted—whenever in doubt—to present an issue to Ford, or send him a document. "He never complained," Rumsfeld said. "He read everything. He came to rely more and more on written options. He would use the one dimensional paper always, but on anything of great significance, he also wanted the three dimensional human reaction. He would have a meeting with the key people so he got the intensity and feeling, the human part which is important to a decision as well."

Often, in their sessions, Ford would overrule Rumsfeld, especially on scheduling. With Cheney and others, Rumsfeld would screen the invitations and proposals for meetings, events coming up two to six months ahead, and the staff recommendations. "I would go in and say, here are the requests we believe you should do," Rumsfeld said, "and here are the others, which we think you ought not to do." Ford would look over the rejects and say, "Oh, come on, Rummy, we've got time. We'll do one more, maybe two more. It's just a speech, maybe forty minutes."

"Just forty minutes for the speech," Rumsfeld would respond, "but three hours to prepare the speech, and an hour getting there and an hour back, and you'll want to do something else because you don't want to do just one thing, and you'll meet with the press, and you've blown a whole day. But the President would laugh and go right on doing it his way."

Long after, reflecting on the attributes of an effective White House Chief of Staff, Rumsfeld said: "The first is loyalty to the President. There is no question—that person has to put his own interests aside. You need, obviously, intelligence and organizing ability. You need a sense of the President, his character, his temperament, his aspirations. You need a sufficient knowledge of how the government is arranged with the society. You need to have a sense of Congress. You need to have a sense of the press. You need to have some substantive background in economics and domestic policy, defense and foreign policy, so that you know what the issues are and who the key people are. You need to be able to communicate one-on-one with individuals. You have to have energy, and patience, because it takes time to deal with human beings. A sense of humor helps. Now, nobody's going to have all that, and know all of that. So what you look for is significant chunks of that."

It took some months, but Ford did learn to be an executive. "The longer he was there, the better executive he became," Rumsfeld said. "He learned management, understood it, and became damned good at it."

Cheney, who succeeded Rumsfeld as Chief of Staff a year later, testified to Ford's growth in the office. Ford, from his House career, had "practices and values in mind when he became President," Cheney said, yet the office "changed him in fairly fundamental ways—especially in terms of his style of operation. He became a much tougher critic in the quality of his staff work, a much better judge of people, tougher on himself in terms of what he thought was acceptable. He also became much more confident of his own judgments. He watched bright and able and talented people work for him and sometimes make mistakes, and I think he quickly developed a recognition that his judgment was as good or better than theirs."

Ford was a man of deep and profound emotions, but he rarely displayed his feelings in public, or in private. As President, the closest he came to breaking down in front of anyone occurred when he learned, six weeks into his presidency, that Betty had breast cancer.

The new First Lady had accompanied her secretary, Nancy Howe, to the U.S. Navy Medical Center in Bethesda, Maryland, for what both considered a routine check-up. There, the doctors found a marble-size lump in Mrs. Ford's right breast and recommended immediate surgery to determine if it was malignant. Ford got the news from Rear Admiral William Lukash, the White House physician.

"I left Lukash's office and took the elevator up to the second floor, and immediately went to our bedroom where she was resting," Ford said. "She had had a pretty tough day. I put my arm around her and kissed her and I said, 'I am sure that things are going to turn out all right. I was just thinking how lucky we are that this examination was held. And I know you will have the best of care.'

"I sat on the bed beside her and we talked about how good life was, and the fine kids we had, and our plans for the next day." They had agreed to take part in the groundbreaking for the LBJ Memorial Grove on the Virginia bank of the Potomac River, and Mrs. Ford was to host a tea for Lady Bird Johnson and her daughters after the event. "We decided to proceed with the event, and Betty would enter the hospital that evening," Ford said. "We had dinner alone, and talked about it more. I was deeply concerned, and I am sure Betty was too. But we didn't break down. We didn't get hysterical. We knew we had to deal with the reality. Neither one of us becomes overly emotional when a crisis arrives. If anything, we act the opposite. We tend to tighten up and put up a strong front to one another as well as outside." As they turned in for the night, as always, they held hands and prayed together.

After the LBJ Memorial dedication events on Friday, Mrs. Ford entered the hospital. The President and their daughter Susan went out later. "We skirted talk about the operation and the possible diagnosis," Ford said. "I didn't want to upset her more, and she was concerned about me." After he returned to the White House he sat alone for a long time in the family quarters. "That night was the loneliest of my life," Ford said. "The thought that the woman I loved might be taken away from me was almost too much to endure."

The surgery was scheduled for Saturday morning, and Dr. Lukash suggested that President Ford not be at the hospital. Ford was in the Oval Office going over a speech with Hartmann when Dr. Lukash called to say the lump was malignant and the surgeons would proceed with a mastectomy. It would take the lab several days to determine whether the cancer had spread.

Ford rose abruptly and walked into an adjacent private office. "When he returned, his eyes were red and he was noisily blowing his nose," Hartmann wrote. "He picked up the speech text, cleared his throat and tried to say something—but words wouldn't come."

"Go ahead and cry," Hartmann said. "Only strong men are not ashamed to cry." Both men wept, and Ford said, "Bob, I don't know what I'd do without her. I just don't know what I'd do . . ."

With her indomitable spirit and excellent medical care, Mrs. Ford fully recovered within weeks. Her well-publicized ordeal with cancer, and her openness about the impromptu examination and necessary mastectomy prompted many women to learn from her experience. Hospitals and clinics all over the United States reported that an unprecedented number of women were following the First Lady's example and lining up for a breast examination. No statistics exist, but doctors estimate that thousands of lives may have been saved because of Betty Ford's open and candid discussions about her experience with breast cancer.

Even though he was President, Ford never really left the House; so, he would always honor what he felt was his responsibility to help his fellow Republicans in their campaigns. For the ten years he had been their Leader, he had diligently crisscrossed the continent, appealing for support for incumbents and challengers, raising money, enduring bad dinners and late nights, risking his neck in single-engine airplanes and on icy roads. So many had counted on Ford for so long that he could not say no when his former colleagues, unfairly damaged by Watergate, pleaded for help. Against Rumsfeld's advice, Ford committed to three weeks of almost constant campaigning, traveling to eighteen states to speak for forty-seven Republican candidates.

"I was terribly disappointed when he agreed to campaign all over the country during his first three months in office," Rumsfeld said, "I felt it was harmful to him, that he would lose a lot of the luster that he personified in declaring the national nightmare over. Moreover, we had to work with a Democratic House and a Democratic Senate."

Ford may have saved some of his friends, but in November 1974, his party lost forty seats in the House and four in the Senate. As a result, for two years he had to cope with an unusually hostile 94th Congress—61 Democrats in the Senate, 292 in the House. In sheer numbers, Ford faced more partisan opposition on Capitol Hill than any other President before him.

While President Ford was campaigning in Des Moines, Iowa, in Melvin, Illinois and in Chicago, Secretary of State Kissinger was in Moscow laying the groundwork for Ford's first Presidential visit abroad. This meeting would demonstrate both Ford's mastery of a complex subject and his instinct for negotiating. The trip was to Vladivostok, Siberia, to meet with Soviet Premier Leonid Brezhnev. It was a journey of consequence, for this, the first Ford-Brezhnev meeting, held the promise of being a turning point in the thirty-year-long Cold War.

Earlier, in September, Soviet Foreign Minister Andrei Gromyko had come to Washington to meet President Ford, discuss U.S.-USSR relations and Soviet interests in the Middle East, and propose the Vladivostok summit. Significantly, Gromyko hinted that the USSR might now be willing to make some concessions to the new President that would lead to an agreement for sensible and practical limitations on nuclear arms. Ford, always a close observer of foreign leaders, found Gromyko dour, dogmatic, lacking in humor, showing none of the agreeable nature of a good diplomat. "He was stone faced, spoke in a harsh voice, all business, and very tough in laying out his position," Ford said. "He comes in with an agenda and goes through it item by item. He is dull in discussion and a nitpicker for details."

In their two days of talks, Gromyko kept bringing up the Middle East, as Kissinger had briefed him to expect. Repeatedly, Gromyko complained that the USSR was not permitted to participate in U.S. efforts to bring peace in the Middle East. Realistically, Ford said later, "We didn't want the Soviet Union injecting themselves into the Middle East. Theirs was a spoiler's role. I did not believe they wanted a *bona fide* settlement in the Middle East. The Soviet partners were Iraq, Libya; neither sought stability in the Middle East. With their relationships, they were trying to keep the pot boiling in that part of the world." Gromyko persisted, Ford said, "but we were vague in our response. We would not make a fully frank statement, but tell him, 'We will keep you informed.'"

In planning the Vladivostok trip, Ford agreed to stop in Japan and South Korea on the way. The visit to Japan was primarily ceremonial; Ford was keeping a commitment by his predecessor. In his formal call on Emperor Hirohito, Ford said he could not help being conscious that Hirohito had been the enemy in World War II. "I just had to put that out of my mind," Ford said. When he met with Prime Minister Kakuei Tanaka, he found him aggressive and presumptuous. But Ford listened, and assured Tanaka that as President, he remained committed to free trade and would resist efforts in Congress to restrict imports from Japan.

In South Korea the talks were more substantive. President Park Chung Hee asked about Nixon's promise to keep the 38,000 U.S. force in South Korea as a military and psychological guard against another North Korea invasion, and to provide $1.5 billion in aid to modernize South Korea's army. Ford reassured Park on both issues, on one condition; confronting Park with no one else present, Ford told him that he must restore human rights in his country. He pointed out to Park, who had set aside the Korean constitution and disbanded the National Assembly, that Park could not expect U.S. support if he continued to rule as a dictator.

From his first hour in Vladivostok, Ford knew he was going to get along with Brezhnev. Air Force One landed in bitter cold at a Russian combat air base fifty miles from Vladivostok. As Ford walked down the ramp of his plane, he saw Brezhnev on the tarmac, jovial, joking with the American press, obviously in a good mood, admiring the beautiful wolfskin coat Ford had been given when his plane stopped in Alaska to refuel. Ford appraised the Russian leader: "He was a big man, six feet or taller, with a heavy muscular frame. He moved with ease, like an athlete. He would have made a good offensive tackle. He had a strong rectangular face, broad forehead with a heavy head of black hair which was graying. Heavy, heavy black eyebrows. He had a very prominent nose, long ears flat against his head, and a heavy pouch of flesh under his chin. Very interesting eyes, behind wire-rim glasses, eyes that reflected his mood, jovial or disturbed or angry. He laughed easily, had a good sense of humor. He enjoyed kidding Henry about his weight, and being kidded by Henry about his cigarette smoking. He was a charming host, very gregarious."

As they shook hands for the first time, Ford said, "I understand you are quite an expert on soccer."

"Yes, I play the left side, but I haven't played in a long time." Brezhnev said.

"I haven't played football for a long time either," Ford said. "I wasn't very fast, but I could hold the line."

The Russian and American parties boarded a train for the ninety-minute ride to Okeanskaya, the small resort city where they would hold their formal meetings. En route they gathered in the railroad dining car, sitting across a linen tablecloth with plates of Soviet cookies and candies. Brezhnev, jovial and ebullient, kidded Kissinger about his appetite for the delicacies. Ford, observing the bleak Siberian snowscape that late November, asked what crops the land produced in this maritime province. Brezhnev turned to aides for the answer.

Ford, earnest to get serious talks started, asked Brezhnev how they should proceed with the working agenda.

"Let us not speak as diplomats but as human beings," Brezhnev began. "Both you and I fought in World War II. That was child's play as compared to nuclear war."

Ford concurred that nuclear war was unthinkable, and he had come to this far place to amend and improve their 1972 agreement on nuclear-arms limitations. Brezhnev responded with a philosophical discourse on the consequences of both sides being committed to creating ever more sophisticated and more terrible weapons, with attendant risks and costs that might better be spent on the needs of the Russian and American peoples.

Ford, more interested in specifics than generalities, replied: "I am interested, Mr. General Secretary, in your statesmanlike approach, . . . but

I believe it important at this meeting to discuss these issues in specific terms and step by step."

For their first formal session, which began about 6:15 that evening, they met in the winter garden of a large and aging stone building that had been freshly painted for the occasion. Ford thought it looked like an ill-kept YMCA gymnasium.

Well briefed on Brezhnev's manner of negotiating, Ford had also studied the secret documents detailing specifics and numbers of missiles at the ready on both sides. Theoretically, they were equal in might, if not in numbers. The United States had 1,710 missiles in land silos and on submarines; the USSR, 2,360. But the United States had fleets of long-range bombers, and almost half of its missiles had multiple warheads (MIRVs). Counterbalancing, Soviet missiles had bigger warheads loaded with magnified explosive power that could create greater devastation. Each country had enough nuclear bombs to destroy the populous centers of the other at least fifteen times over; indeed, either could destroy civilization.

Ford's goal was to get an agreement on "equal aggregates," a technical term meaning that each would have the same numbers—2,400 launchers and 1,320 multiple warheads. "We had hammered out our strategy in several NSC meetings where Jim Schlesinger and Bill Clements were present, and we had reached an agreed position," Ford said. "Both doubted the Soviet would agree, but I felt we had a strong case."

For hours the two sides debated, over technicalities, new refinements in weapons, and side issues. Ford, the better briefed of the two leaders, could also draw on his ten years' experience on the House Appropriations Committee—evaluating and financing weapons systems, understanding the mentality of men who advocated and created those systems. He could handle technical details. Breshnev pursued concepts and turned to technicians for details. At one point, after talking with aides, he proposed a higher number of missiles, but Ford insisted the limit should be 2,400. Brezhnev insisted that the count include British and French nuclear weapons, and U.S. nuclear weapons deployed in Europe: Ford stood firmly against that. Brezhnev proposed that the United States halt production of the Trident submarine and the B-1 bomber. Not possible, Ford responded. "Mr. General Secretary, our national security requires that we move ahead with both," Ford said. "I didn't say so there, but I remembered that all those gung-ho Air Force pilots who had been flying B-52s for twenty years were looking toward the opportunity to fly a high performance aircraft. I believed the morale, the esprit de corps, of the Air Force would plummet and the whole character of the Air Force would change dramatically if we did not go ahead with the B-1."

Ford said later that he fully enjoyed the contest. "My briefing book was well done. And Henry had given me a personal fill-in. He said that in almost every instance, and it was verified by my experience, Brezhnev would start with something that gave him an opportunity to make points with his hierarchy. It is a technique that Soviet leaders have. They have to show strength. They have to bluster. They have to show disappointment, anger. They are testing you. They want to see you if you bend or fight back. We knew not to back off but speak right up. Which is what I did.

"Henry also told me that Brezhnev would dominate the discussion, but on crucial points he would indicate that he wanted to check with his technical people. He had this group of people that he could not ignore. It's not just a one-man rule. And Brezhnev recognized that in Congress, I had a group of people I could not ignore."

Ford, in that first session in Vladivostok, concluded that Brezhnev was a man of vigor and action. "I also thought he had an intuitive mind and a tremendous native shrewdness. I did not know how well educated he was, or how well read he was, but he was very shrewd. Not as suave as other leaders but every bit as shrewd. He would pick up on a comment or question by Kissinger or myself, and he would catch the point instantly."

The debate, vigorous but civil, continued through the evening, with three breaks: Brezhnev wanted to consult with his technicians. Once, he telephoned Moscow to talk with his defense minister, Andrei Grechko. During the time-outs, Ford, with Kissinger and his other advisers, walked outside so they could talk without being bugged. In the biting cold, they appraised their progress and plotted their next moves.

Finally, after the last break near midnight, Brezhnev said to Ford: "Well, Mr. President, . . . let's do it this way. What we should do . . . is attempt to agree in principle to the following: 2,400 launchers for you and 2,400 for us, 1320 MIRVd missiles for you and 1,320 MIRVd missiles for us." Ford repeated the numbers and asked Brezhnev to confirm that this was the essence of the agreement, with no unspoken qualifications. No, Brezhnev replied. "You can return and report to your people that you have reached agreement on the basis of full equality."

Ford was elated. The agreement meant that the USSR had to cut back about 200 launchers, and the United States could add about 150. As the U.S. team expected, there had been no dramatic reduction of arms: that would be a goal for a later date. But for the first time, the two great nuclear powers would become equal in overall numbers and agree to limits—a condition firmly supported by Defense Secretary Schlesinger and the Joint Chiefs of Staff.

Back in his Spartan dacha that night, Ford was hungry. "We had missed dinner, and we were sitting in the kitchen of our quarters, and the Soviet chefs were making us some wonderful Russian food," Ford said. As he waited, he remembered it was Saturday back home—no ordinary Saturday, but the day of the Michigan-Ohio State football game. "Bob," he said to his brisk, efficient, and waggish military aide, Army Major Robert Barrett, "wake me at six tomorrow with the score of the game."

At exactly 6:00 the next morning, Barrett came into his room. "Mr. President, time to wake up."

"How did the game turn out, Bob? What was the score?"

"Twelve to ten," Barrett said, and turned to leave the room.

"Wait a minute, Bob. Who had the twelve and who had the ten?"

"Mr. President, I was afraid you would ask me that."

From the look on Barrett's face, Ford knew the answer. Barrett commiserated: "The same poor kid who missed the Michigan field goal last year missed another one seconds before the end of the game."

Ford, who had known defeat too often when he played at Michigan, sat back. "I knew how heartbroken that Michigan player must have been," Ford thought. "I found myself wishing I could pick up a telephone and try to brighten his day."

Ford's sessions with Brezhnev resumed at 10:00 the next morning. Encouraged by the Soviet leader's concessions the previous evening, Ford proposed that Brezhnev agree to reduce the number of multiple warheads they could place on their heavy missiles. Gromyko, not Brezhnev, countered with a proposal that the United States put off building more launchers. The dialogue, Kissinger wrote, had by that time become "essentially theological." Both sides were talking about armament the other had no intention of building. After brief and routine discussions of other issues—Soviet participation in Middle East peace negotiations, trade, Jewish emigration from Russia—the two sides adjourned for lunch and toasts. Ford felt a great sense of accomplishment. "Our meeting the night before had far exceeded my expectations," he said. "I was euphoric." The terms of the agreement would be carried out after a treaty had been drafted by professionals representing both sides, then signed.

After lunch, Brezhnev invited Ford to join him in a drive into Vladivostok, some thirteen miles away. Brezhnev had been there only once before, so they climbed into a long black limousine, Ford on the right in the back seat, Brezhnev on the left. A big man in a heavy coat, a stranger to Ford, sat on the jump seat in front of Ford, and the Russian interpreter, Victor Sukhodrev, sat on the jump seat in front of Brezhnev.

"We started out with chitchat," Ford said. "I asked who this gentlemen was in front of me, and Brezhnev said he was the local commissar, and spoke some English." Ford asked the commissar about Vladivostok, how many people lived there, what was the main industry, how the people earned a living. "As we drove down into the city, you come off a high plateau, and weave down into the city, and come down into a square area right on the harbor," Ford said. The commissar identified the monuments on the square and told him how each was historically significant. "It's a gorgeous city, old Russian, the architecture more European than Soviet," Ford said. "It reminded me of San Francisco, with hills that fall right down to the naval base. I purposely did not ask what kind of Soviet ships were based in the navy yard there." As their limousine drove slowly around the square, the Siberians, gathered in small groups, applauded as they passed.

As the car moved out of the center of town, the light in the sky began to fade into dusk, and Ford started talking directly to Brezhnev. "Mr. General Secretary, I believe we made very significant progress, and I hope the momentum of our Vladivostok meeting will continue and we can finalize what we have done at this important meeting," Ford said. "This is a step forward to prevent a nuclear holocaust."

Brezhnev replied, as Ford recalled: "I agree with you. We have made significant headway." Brezhnev then, with his right hand, grasped Ford's left hand. Ford was startled, and felt slightly uncomfortable to be holding hands with a man, but he thought it was too dark in the back seat for either the commissar or the interpreter to witness the gesture. "We have accomplished something significant," Brezhnev continued, "and it's our responsibility, yours and mine, on behalf of our countries, to achieve the finalization of this document."

As they rode into darkness, Brezhnev continued to hold Ford's hand, "trying to convey his sincerity, the need for good Soviet-U.S. relations," Ford said, "and with each point he would squeeze my hand." The conversation got more vigorous about the need for an agreement and the responsibilities of the USSR and the United States to take leadership through Salt II, and other matters involving detente. "We both believed that we had a great opportunity, that we had the capacity to bring peace in the world, that we shared responsibilities for our countries and to mankind," Ford said. He felt that Brezhnev was continuing to press his hand to communicate his emotional feeling about their success in negotiations and the promise of the future. Brezhnev held on to Ford's hand until the car pulled up in front of the dacha assigned to Ford at Okeanskaya. "Then he was all business again," Ford said.

Reflecting on the episode later, Ford said: "It was startling and unusual, a fascinating experience. I really believed that within the constraints on him by the hierarchy of the Soviet Union, the Communist party, Brezhnev did honestly want to find peace. He was a tough negotiator and he did not confuse the interests of the USSR with those of the U.S., but I thought he realized the potential danger of an all-out nuclear arms race."

So much had been accomplished, so full had been their discussion, that the train ride back to the Soviet air base was "anticlimactic," Ford said. As Brezhnev walked with him to the ramp standing beside Air Force One, Ford noticed that Brezhnev "was eyeing my wolfcoat enviously. It had served me well in Siberia. So just before I mounted the steps, I took off the coat and gave it to him. He took off his dark greatcoat, put on the wolfcoat, and seemed truly overwhelmed." After a warm handshake, the two leaders parted, and Ford waved goodbye from the door of his plane.

Taxiing down the runway for the takeoff, Ford reflected on their agreement. "One launcher for us. One launcher for them. One MIRV capability for us; one MIRV capability for them. Our Joint Chiefs, and Schlesinger, did not think we could get that because it forced the Soviets to cut back 200 launchers and gave us the opportunity to add 150 launchers. From our point of view, the Joint Chiefs and Schlesinger considered it an excellent agreement. We came out of Vladivostok in great shape."

As it turned out, however, influential voices back in the United States did not agree. On the Left, critics argued that the limits were unacceptably high. An unnamed and unrealistic editorial page writer in the *New York Times* proposed that Ford go back to "the conference table to seek more meaningful arms control." An editorial writer for the *Washington Post*, also unnamed, equally distant from reality, wrote that somehow the Vladivostok agreement "threatened" U.S. security. In the Senate, conservatives and liberals alike began denouncing the agreement. Senator Henry Jackson, ambitious to be President and strongly influenced by two anti-Soviet aides, Richard Perle and Dorothy Fosdick, rejected any understanding with the USSR. Once potential allies became critics, Kissinger wrote, "Ford and I watched with dismay as the Vladivostok agreement dissolved before our eyes."

In the Soviet Union, it was later learned, Brezhnev had suffered a stroke in Mongolia, on the way back to Moscow. Consequently, from that point on, he never regained the authority over his peers that he had displayed in negotiating with Ford in Vladivostok.

The Vladivostok agreement was never signed.

CHAPTER 17

Progress

December 1974 marked the crossing of a great divide in Ford's Presidency. He had climbed out of the debris left by Nixon and was looking ahead. His Presidency was going well. He was gaining confidence every day. He invested more time on foreign affairs, meeting in Washington with Canada's Prime Minister Pierre Trudeau and Germany's Chancellor Helmut Schmidt, and in Martinique with France's President Valéry Giscard d'Estaing. All three meetings went well. In his White House, Rumsfeld had imposed order and efficiency. On schedule, the Nixon loyalists were leaving: three cabinet and six senior holdover White House staff resigned that month, opening the way for more of Ford's new team. In the nation's consciousness, the trauma of Watergate was fading.

Ford held his best press conference that month, answering with ease and precision reporters' questions about setting limits on nuclear weapons in Vladivostok and defining the continuing economic problem—inflation, recession, and energy. Could he promise that the price of gasoline would not go up to $1 a gallon, one reporter asked. Ford knew the current price—45 to 50 cents a gallon—and responded: "I don't foresee gasoline going to a dollar a gallon." To Ford's relief, at that press conference, not one reporter mentioned Nixon.

In a session with the editors of *Newsweek*, Ford again displayed his competence. Editor Osborn Elliott and Managing Editor Edward Kosner flew down from New York City for the interview. "We assumed that this guy was the stupidest person ever to become President," Elliott said. "So Kosner and Mel Elfin [*Newsweek*'s Washington Bureau Chief] and I spent the evening before thinking up the most difficult questions we could possibly ask him. We were loaded to prove how dumb he was."

"We showed up at the White House the next day, the grounds beautiful after a snowfall, and he greeted us warmly in the Oval Office and made us welcome. So we sat down and started firing our questions, and he answered every one—quickly, knowledgeably, no hesitation, no ducking, no waffling. He knew every subject, every issue, talked with candor and directness. So we came away astonished, thinking hey, this guy is pretty smart after all. He knew more than we did."

Most of those December days, Ford concentrated on preparing for his first State of the Union Address and assembling the 1976 budget, the first he must send to Congress. One would verbally set his priorities and agenda; the other would ratify words with specifics and dollars. Both required extensive discussions and deliberations, and crucial decisions.

So Ford placed a priority on budget talks with Roy Ash, the holdover OMB Director, and Paul O'Neill, Ford's choice to continue as Deputy at OMB. Ash had told Ford he wanted to leave, but agreed to stay on through preparations of the new budget.

To Ford, O'Neill was the model of a career public servant. The son of a career Army First Sergeant, O'Neill grew up on military bases in Missouri, Hawaii, Alaska, and California. As a graduate student in economics at Claremont, he scored so well on a civil-service exam in 1961 that he was given a choice for advanced placement in the Federal government. He chose the Veterans Bureau because it offered an opportunity in a technology then in its infancy, but promising: computers. Unlike most in government at that time, O'Neill—something of a visionary in that then arcane science—foresaw and later demonstrated the computer's usefulness in collecting, processing, and storing numbers and information. He rose quickly. Brought into the Budget Bureau during the Johnson Administration, he continued throughout the Nixon Presidency, taking an active role in the reorganization of the Budget Bureau into the Office of Management and Budget. Ash, Nixon's third budget director, promoted O'Neill to Deputy Director of OMB. There he continued to flourish, impressing, among others, Congressman Jerry Ford with his encyclopedic knowledge of government operations and finance. "Paul was one of the most outstanding career people in government that I ever met," Ford said. "He literally worked his way up to the top by his brilliance and dedication. He was thin, neat in appearance, and behind those owlish spectacles was the mind of a computer." Though only 38 when appointed OMB Deputy Director, Ford called on him often. "He spoke, one-on-one or in a group, with a tremendous background of knowledge, experience, logic, persuasion," Ford said. "A demon for work. A catalog of a mind. Had a knack of correcting people if they were wrong without offending them."

The two were a good match. "We both had an interest in programs and how they worked, in who was best at running them and why," O'Neill said. "It was really great, great fun to interact with him on program and budget and allocations and people because he and I thought a lot alike." Over time, O'Neill observed that Ford had a much deeper grasp of fiscal policy than of monetary policy. "He understood, relatively better, how Federal spending and tax policy affected the direction of the economy better than he understood money supply, how Federal Reserve actions affected the drift of the economy," O'Neill said.

Ford had a habit of sending O'Neill clips from the Grand Rapids newspapers about how Federal programs worked at the local level. "From the Grand Rapids newspapers he understood how the abstract of a piece of legislation really operated at the home level." O'Neill said. "He would constantly send me clippings, 'Did you see that?,' 'Did you think about that?,' and he would call later to see if I had followed up."

The Federal Budget: of all the documents published in Washington every year, the Budget of the United States government is the most important by far. This all-encompassing five-book set opens the whole of the Federal government to the American people—its bank account, where the money comes from, where it goes, how much we all owe. The budget books show Washington's concern for the newborn child, the aged, the worker, the farmer. The dollar amounts provide for the soldier in combat, the student in elementary school, the motorist on the highway, the passenger in the air, the investor in Wall Street, the patient in the hospital. By detailing all Federal programs, their purpose, their reach, and their cost, the budget tells how Washington affects every man, woman, and child not only in the United States but in much of the rest of the world. It records America's past; it charts its future.

Written by hundreds of authors, the annual budget is read by few. One was Jerry Ford. As a Congressman, as Vice President, and as President, Ford not only read the budget books, but he knew what was in them. He could tell you what any department or agency of government was doing, why, and how much each program would cost.

Composing the Federal budget is a rite of creation that begins every spring. OMB initiates the process in late April when the OMB Director and his Deputy sit down with the President and his economic advisers for a first assessment. They show the President where a continuation of present policies and programs would take the government without changes, and recommend how, if at all, the trends should be changed. The President makes a set of decisions that are guidelines for Cabinet Secretaries and agency heads in planning for the next year. OMB then sends the numbers to the departments and agencies. During the summer, the OMB staff, each a career professional, work with the budgeteers in departments and agencies so that OMB will know in advance the changes and money requests to be expected. After counterproposals come in to OMB in September, the Director and Deputy meet alone with every head of a department or agency so that each understands the other's point of view.

October brings the Director's review sessions, where the Director, Deputy, or both, sit down with the professional staff and go through every program, past, present, and proposed future. From these sessions the Director compiles his recommendations into a thick notebook and sends it to the President. After the President studies the book, he meets with the Director and Deputy to go through their recommendations, department by department, issue by issue. The Director then relays the President's first-round decisions back to the departments and agencies. A Cabinet Secretary or department head who believes there is a sound basis for an appeal may do so, in which case he or she will meet with the President, with OMB present, and argue the merits of that appeal. The President will then make a final decision.

Since the budget process was at the halfway point when Ford came into office, he had to catch up. In his first week as President, Ford met with Ash to accelerate the schedule. Through the fall he met weekly, often several times, listening to OMB's presentations. He tracked their income and spending estimates with Alan Greenspan's economic and fiscal projections, and reviewed the responses of the departments to OMB's allotments. "Their reactions are always, 'You don't give us enough,'" Ford said. By December, OMB had renegotiated its numbers with each department. Where OMB and a Secretary differed, Ford granted a hearing. One who asked was Secretary Schlesinger at Defense. "Jim came in, made his pitch with Ash, O'Neill, and Don Ogilvie [OMB's senior expert in defense] present," Ford said. "I listened, asked questions, and made notes. When I had heard enough I thanked them, went back to the office, went over my notes for a couple of hours and made my decisions." OMB kept count: in November and December 1974, Ford spent 150 hours listening to Cabinet Secretaries and department heads appeal the amounts allocated by OMB.

All, Ford insisted, must trim operations and costs. In his time he had seen Presidents and Congresses create worthy benefits without regard for future costs: Medicare and Medicaid were prime examples. In Ford's judgment, Congress had instituted many more programs than the bureaucracy could properly manage. Looking at the burgeoning programs and costs since the end of World War II, he was deeply concerned about a fiscally ominous trend—Federal spending was growing faster than the gross national product. So Ford made the decision that would set the fiscal course—and public image—of his Presidency. For the 1976 fiscal year he would cut Congressional spending by $17 billion and limit the Federal budget to $349.4 billion. To stay within that budget, Ford would initiate no new spending programs except for energy, which had become such an immediate and dangerous problem that it required a bold initiative. Moreover, he would not hesitate to use his singular authority—the veto—against any new spending programs initiated by Congress.

"Money is policy," Ford said. "A President controls his Administration through the budget." Proving his determination to curb spending, not only in the Executive branch but also in Congress, Ford had, in his first five months, vetoed twenty-eight spending bills. Of those, twenty-five had been sustained by the Congress, in part by his own interventions with Members, in part by the proficiency of his new legislative team.

Ford had appointed Marsh to oversee all Congressional liaison, and 45-year-old Max Friedersdorf to "head the legmen," as Ford put it. A natural in the political game, Friedersdorf had been Indiana Representative Richard Roudebush's right hand in the House. There Republican Leader Ford observed Friedersdorf's easy affability and effectiveness, noting that he was respected by Democrats as well as Republicans. So highly regarded was Friedersdorf on Capitol Hill and in the White House that in 1971 he was invited to join President Nixon's staff as Special Assistant for Legislative Affairs. As the evidence of Nixon's crimes unfolded during his final year in office, it fell to Friedersdorf to carry out an historic assignment: counting House votes for and against impeachment. With the change of Administrations, Friedersdorf expected to be relieved until, passing through the receiving line after Ford's oath-taking, he heard the brand new President say, "Max, I want you to stay on. I'm going to need you."

As Assistant to President Ford for Legislative Affairs, Friedersdorf and his partners—William Kendall covered the Senate; Charles Leppert, the House—virtually camped on Capitol Hill. They roamed the offices and corridors, talking and listening to leaders and committee chairmen and Members, gauging support, counting votes. Ford trusted and relied on Friedersdorf. In the late afternoons the two met, with Friedersdorf reviewing House and Senate actions of the day, discussing Congress' schedules for the next day, relaying Members' concerns and requests, plotting legislative strategy. "Max had excellent judgment on how to handle people on the Hill, and he had a storehouse of information on where legislation stood and how you could maybe get a vote or win an amendment," Ford said. "He was sort of a redhead, had a Hoosier twang, tall, well-kept physique. Damn good man." Friedersdorf was in the favored position of being the messenger who regularly brought the President the latest news about the people and happenings in what had been Ford's hometown for twenty-five years. Reflecting long after, Ford said: "Every day I looked forward to seeing Max."

To Ford, the number-one problem that he and the country faced that December was the continuing—and by some measures—worsening, recession. Industrial production had declined more in the last quarter than at any time since 1958. Unemployment had reached 7.1 percent, necessitating another extension of unemployment benefits. Auto sales had plummeted; plants were closing.

The causes of America's economic plight were complex, Ford recognized, but he was certain that one major element was the rising and unpredictable costs of imported oil. In 1973, the Organization of Petroleum Exporting Countries (OPEC) had embargoed crude-oil shipments to the United States in retaliation for President Nixon's decision to send military arms and supplies to Israel in the Yom Kippur War. Although the embargo had eased slightly, Ford had seen the cost of imported oil quadruple to $12 a barrel. In four years, imports had almost doubled, and the annual cost to America for OPEC oil had soared from $3 billion to $25 billion. In 1974 consumer prices had gone up by 10 percent, with higher oil prices the biggest single reason for that inflation.

OPEC, by shutting off supply, had distorted the free market. Uncertainty led to speculation. Speculation inflated prices far beyond crude oil's intrinsic value. Demand, growing at 5 percent annually in the United States, also boosted the price of gasoline and fuel oil.

At the same time, America's oil wells were drying up. Imported oil had been so cheap that domestic production of oil and natural gas had dwindled. The risk of drilling a dry hole outweighed the chance of a profit. Natural-gas production had dropped because of price controls. Coal, which once produced 80 percent of U.S. energy, was generating less than 20 percent by 1973. Nuclear plants supplied only 9 percent of electric power; complex government regulations and legal challenges put the cost of building more nuclear power plants out of reach. Yet, Ford said, "Congress refused to believe that a crisis was at hand."

To meet this crisis Ford brought together in a series of meetings his top economic and energy advisers: Secretary Rogers Morton from Interior, Secretary William Simon from Treasury, Arthur Burns from the Federal Reserve, William Seidman from the Economic Policy Board, Alan Greenspan from the Council of Economic Advisers, and Frank Zarb, the newly appointed administrator of the Federal Energy Administration.

Zarb was another Ford favorite. A whiz kid of a manager in Wall Street in his twenties, Zarb had been recruited in 1971 by President Nixon's OMB deputy, Fred Malek, to serve as Assistant Secretary for Management in the Labor Department. There, Zarb performed so well that he was promoted to OMB, first as Assistant Director for Management, then Associate Director for Natural Resources, Energy, and Sciences. Ford, when Vice President, spent a lot of time with Zarb. Their discussions ranged from national parks to nuclear power to the price of oil. "He was gutsy, had command of the facts, and had infinite patience," Ford said.

John Sawhill, Nixon's last FEA administrator, had persisted in being at odds with the new President. Sawhill, presuming independence, insisted on his "obvious solution" to the energy problem—a twenty-cent increase in the Federal gasoline tax, advocating it publicly and persistently. Ford thought it inequitable because it would put the burden on motorists. Moreover, he was sure that Congress would not pass such a tax. It did not take Ford long to realize he could not work with Sawhill, so he let him go, knowing he had a better candidate to manage energy. "We had a real gem in Frank Zarb," Ford said. "Frank was knowledgeable and open-minded. Though small in stature, he was strong in appearance, compact, well built, wiry, neat, immaculate, Wall Street conservative in dress. Talked in a very low, soft, persuasive voice. Excellent negotiator. I liked the fact that he was competent, loyal, had a good sense of humor and a nice little chuckle."

Zarb was 37 years old when Ford offered him the appointment. "I took it right away," he said. "I knew the territory. I knew there was a vacuum in leadership. Nixon had talked about 'Energy Independence' but it was a set of words, no substance. I knew there was a job to do."

In the Cabinet Room Ford told his energy team what he wanted. The immediate objective was to lessen the impact of the oil crisis, to manage the onerous price controls left over from Nixon, and to avoid shortages. But Ford's greater emphasis was long term. "He wanted to reduce the nation's independence on sources of energy that were not reliable," Zarb said. "He saw the economic dynamics of the world. And our vulnerability. The country was exposed: A group of Arab countries could turn off our supply. There could be terrorist activity in the Straits of Hormuz. And he knew it was up to the government, up to him, to act in the face of that. He told us to come up with a comprehensive energy plan that would be effective for a ten-to-fifteen year period, long after he left office."

So, in the Cabinet room, in the Roosevelt Room, and at Camp David, the energy team worked through the month. "We examined the problem," Zarb said. "We did the analysis. We identified the options."

The possible solutions ranged from boosting domestic production, to developing alternative fuels, to raising prices at the pump, to rationing, to eliminating controls over prices, to taxing excess profits. At one point in the discussions Zarb said: "Mr. President, Republicans as well as Democrats are going to oppose parts of this plan." Ford's response was: "You tell me what we need to do to get results, and I'll worry about the politics."

Over the weeks, the energy team assembled a 135-page briefing book that Zarb, in a cover memo, described as "the culmination of the most extensive analysis of our energy problems ever undertaken by the Federal government." The next day, December 20, 1974, Zarb and his energy team met with President Ford, narrowed the range of options, and asked for Ford's instructions in initiating discussions with the incoming Congress. When Ford and his family left on Sunday, December 22, for their Christmas holiday in Vail, he took the energy brief with him. There he studied it, making marginal notes, "Meeting [Hébert] early Jan," "$12 price floor," "Decontrol," circling and initialing his preferences among scores of options. Two days after Christmas, Ford brought his energy team to Vail for further discussion. He then made his final decisions.

The Ford solution would rely on basic economics: increase the domestic supply of energy in all forms—petroleum, coal, nuclear, geothermal, solar—and reduce demand. Let the price of crude oil reach a market level. It would be higher, he foresaw, but a market price would simultaneously have a double-edged impact. Supplies would go up; consumption would go down.

As a first action, by Presidential executive orders, Ford would decontrol the price of domestic crude oil and impose an import fee of $3 a barrel on imported oil. Raising the price on a barrel of foreign crude pumped into an American refinery would simultaneously encourage domestic oil extraction and reduce consumption of gasoline, heating oil, and industrial uses. Motorists and homeowners would object, but better that import fees benefit the U. S. treasury than that OPEC's politically motivated price hikes continue to benefit foreign producers.

To expand U.S. production in the long term, Ford proposed to proceed with exploration, leasing, and production on the Outer Continental Shelf, and to allow commercial production from Naval Petroleum Reserves in California and Alaska. Ford would also provide money for research and development in synthetic fuels and shale oil with the goal of adding another million barrels a day. As a safeguard against any future disruption of foreign supplies, he would create a strategic petroleum reserve by storing underground 300 million barrels of oil for national defense, and a billion barrels for domestic needs.

The Ford energy plan was broad and ambitious but practical. In addition to dealing with the oil crisis, Ford proposed to revise rules that would enable companies to mine more coal. He would give utilities a 12 percent tax credit as an incentive to build more electric plants that burned clean coal. He advocated new laws to expedite the siting and construction of nuclear power plants. To conserve energy, Ford would set thermal efficiency standards for all new buildings in the United States, and give taxpayers $150 credits for insulating their homes. He would ask Congress to direct the auto industry to improve gas mileage by 40 percent within five years.

Ford first announced his bold plan in a speech to the nation, then in his 1975 State of the Union address to Congress. "Americans are no longer in full control of their own national destiny when that destiny depends on uncertain foreign oil at high prices fixed by others," Ford said. It was imperative, Ford told Congress and the American people, that together they set and meet ten-year energy goals: 200 major nuclear power plants, 250 new coal mines, 150 new coal-fired electric power plants, 30 new oil refineries, 20 new synthetic-fuel plants. He envisioned drilling thousands of new oil wells and insulating 18 million American homes. "We can do it," Ford said. He reminded Congress that to win World War II, aircraft workers had produced 125,00 planes each year. "They did it then," he said. "We can do it now."

In the hope that Congress would act promptly on his proposals, Ford asked Speaker Albert and Senate Majority Leader Mansfield to create special ad hoc committees to consider and pass legislation to meet the energy crisis—as President Eisenhower had done to create NASA after Sputnik: both declined. Their members would not give up the power assigned their standing committees.

As it turned out, the response by the 94th Congress to the energy crisis was minimal, pusillanimous. Members expanded the strategic petroleum reserve, mandated auto efficiency standards, ordered the labeling of household appliances for efficiency, and phased an end to price controls of domestic oil and natural gas. Otherwise, both the Senate and House rejected Ford's plan and proposals. "It was a combination," Zarb said. "A lack of understanding the energy problem, and sheer dedication to politics. Short term political thinking. Don't do anything to raise the price of gasoline and hurt the consumer; that would cost us at the next election. Don't mine more coal; the environmentalists oppose that. Don't do anything to increase nuclear power; the anti-nukes oppose that. Here we were, the only country in the world that knew the problem and could do something about it; but we didn't."

Economically, Ford's proposals made sense; politically, they were unacceptable. Looking back thirty-five years later, Zarb said: "President Ford's program was the first and last time a truly comprehensive energy plan was formulated and sent to Congress. Had we implemented the Ford plan, we would not have an energy crisis today. We would not be dependent on unfriendly sources of foreign oil. We would be self-sufficient in energy. We would not have the economic dislocations that we have today. Probably we would not have needed to go into Iraq."

Ford was far ahead of Congress in understanding and addressing the energy crisis. His responsibility, he believed, was to provide the leadership lacking in Congress on energy. "President Ford's thinking in 1975 was that we should get done as much as we could with the first push, and after his election we would go back with the same menu," Zarb said. "It was his view that we would get a lot more from the Congress in 1977 because the dynamics were moving in our favor with the voters not happy with Congressional foot dragging, and as an elected President he would have more strength. He was well aware of the limited success we would have with his initial energy effort."

In late December, Ford's choice for Vice President finally joined him as his partner in governing. The confirmation of Nelson Rockefeller by the two Houses of Congress, required by the Twenty-Fifth Amendment, had taken 121 days—more than twice as long as Ford's. It had been delayed by Members' repeated probings into the size and reach of Rockefeller's wealth—reflecting their own and populist curiosity about the fortune of a nominee whose last name was an everyday byword for riches beyond the dreams of the common man. It was delayed by Democratic Congressional staffers contriving dirty tricks hoping to find a scandal that would bring Rockefeller down and diminish President Ford. It was delayed by Democratic leaders blocking the nominee from campaigning in off-year Congressional elections. It was delayed by sequential and irrelevant intrusions into the private affairs of the extensive Rockefeller families.

For the then 64-year-old candidate, the experience was arduous and combative, controversial and revealing, and at the end, a Pyrrhic victory—a microcosm of Rockefeller's thirty-four years in politics and public life. On Capitol Hill, as before and after, liberals opposed him as obscenely rich, a military hawk, and tool of Big Business. There, as before and after, conservatives condemned Rockefeller by reflex, suspecting him of being a closet liberal, damning him as an advocate of bigger government, a habitual big spender, a One Worlder who secretly conspired with the illogically feared Trilateral Commission. Yet the majority in the political mainstream of that 93rd Congress, as in New York State and much of America, respected Rockefeller's undoubted competence. They liked his engaging gregariousness. They commended his record as a practitioner of government responding to the needs and aspirations of the many. Through it all, Rockefeller relished the challenge; he was always a fighter.

From the hour of his nomination, the Rockefeller money was an issue of interest. After President Ford announced his choice on live television, Rockefeller strode from the Oval Office across the corridor into the Roosevelt Room to chat with White House aides. Tom Korologos, White House emissary to the Senate and adviser-in-chief for confirmations, introduced himself and suggested they find an office to talk.

"Governor, I am going to say to you what I say to every Cabinet officer and judicial nominee up for Senate confirmation. Is there anything in your background, or record, or personal life, that could embarrass you and the President during confirmation hearings? I don't need to know what it is, but just to advise that you and your lawyers must find a good explanation for it, because the FBI and the IRS and other investigators, and the press, will find it out."

"Yes, Tom, there is one thing that bothers me," Rockefeller said. "When I disclose my financial situation, my friends and Congress and the public will find out that I am not nearly as rich as people think I am."

He was right. Pressed to provide the Senate Rules Committee with an immediate statement of net worth, the Rockefeller family business managers put together a preliminary and conservative estimate of $33 million. Assured that this quick evaluation would be kept secret, Rockefeller turned it over to the Senate Rules Committee designated to hold hearings on his qualifications.

But as so often happens in Washington, within hours the number was leaked to newspapers. To the press, $33 million was instantly suspect: Rockefeller must be hiding his fortune.

The figure was in fact low. Preparing their report in haste, the Rockefeller brothers' business staff had calculated most of the nominee's assets at cost and omitted works of art in his possession, but pledged to museums. Revised, Rockefeller's net worth rose to $62,581,225. For a further revision, the committee insisted he include two trusts set up by his grandfather and father for his benefit, which technically he did not own or control. This added another $116,503,758. Again the estimate was revised to include trusts the nominee had established for his children and his wife; the final number was $216,810,138.

In response to a Committee request, Rockefeller reported that for the five years before his nomination, his income had ranged from $2.5 million to $5 million annually, on which he paid about half in Federal, state, and city taxes.

To Rockefeller's surprise, the Senate Committee members were intrigued not only by how much money he had, but also by how much he had given away. "I had been brought up as a Baptist that it was more blessed to give than to receive," he said, "and being very fortunate in financial resources, I had tried to share. Why, if you help a friend, is there something suspicious about it?"

But the Committee was suspicious. Why, Rules Chairman Howard Cannon asked, had he given $550,000 to William Ronan? The nominee's answer: Ronan was a close friend, partner in public service, and had performed well. Ronan had headed the brain trust that strategized Rockefeller's first election as governor. As the Governor's first chief of staff, Ronan created bold initiatives, carried them out, and thereby earned Rockefeller's respect as a strong, get-it-done executive. After Ronan left state office, Rockefeller made the gift to assist Ronan's transition to private life. To Ronan's successor as chief of staff, Alton Marshall, Rockefeller gave $306,867 when Marshall entered private life and took over as president of Rockefeller Center. To his press chief, Hugh Morrow, Rockefeller gave $165,000, partly to assist with the medical expenses of a terminally ill teenage child. To his political adviser and chief speechwriter for his 1968 Presidential campaign, Emmet John Hughes, he gave $155,000. To Henry Kissinger, his foreign-policy adviser for that campaign, he gave $50,000. To twenty other aides, secretaries, and friends, he made gifts ranging from $20,000 to $100,000—in appreciation for their loyal service and friendship.

For some on the committee, such gratuities were puzzling, if not suspect. Again and again they questioned Rockefeller's motives, looking for bought favors or conflicts of interest. In the end they found none. One bemused observer, Rockefeller's speech writer Joe Persico, commented: "Many politicians are found to be on the take; Rockefeller is first to be accused of being on the give."

Exploring his seven political campaigns—three for president and four for governor—the committee found that Rockefeller had spent some $20,000,000. Of that, about $6,000,000 was his own money, $2,850,000 came as gifts from his three brothers and one sister, and $11,000,000 from his stepmother.

Rules Committee Chairman Cannon, reflecting a popular myth about the hidden omnipotence of the "House of Rockefeller," repeatedly showed his concern. Citing "the economic power which you and your family exert directly and indirectly upon the domestic and international economy in oil, real estate, banks, insurance," Cannon asked Rockefeller: "How can you . . . avoid even the appearance of conflict of interest in decisions you may make?"

"This myth about the power which my family exercises . . . just does not exist," Rockefeller said. Unconvinced, the Committee continued to question the specifics of family investments and influence.

Since it was generally known that Rockefeller had often disdained the office of Vice President as "standby equipment," and had turned down the opportunity to be nominated in 1960 and 1968, Senator Pell asked: "What caused the change of heart?"

"I have reached a different point in my life," Rockefeller testified. "This country has reached a point where we are in very critical circumstances . . . If I can be of any use to the President, for whatever assistance I might give him should I be confirmed, I would be honored."

Given the opportunity to make his case for confirmation, Rockefeller recounted in detail his family history and his experience in business and public life. He told of his mother's descent from Pilgrims on the *Mayflower*, and his father's forebears who were French Huguenots driven into Germany. There they changed their name from Roquefeuille to Rockefeller. From Germany they emigrated to America in 1723. Rockefeller described an exceptional heritage: His maternal grandfather, Nelson Aldrich, a U.S. Senator representing Rhode Island from 1881–1911, had earned and used enormous political power in national affairs at the turn of the century. His paternal grandfather, John D. Rockefeller, became the most successful entrepreneur of his day in transporting and marketing oil. A deeply religious man, the first John D. Rockefeller concluded that "Providence had made him a trustee of his fortune for the benefit of man," so he devoted his later life to philanthropy.

His parents, Rockefeller pointed out, had instilled in their children a comparable obligation. He told of his own education, Phi Beta Kappa at Dartmouth, of his early business training in banking and real estate, of working with his father in building and managing Rockefeller Center during the Great Depression. "In the national field, I had the privilege of working for or with six of the last seven Presidents"—Roosevelt, Truman, Eisenhower, Johnson, Nixon, and Ford. As Governor of New York for fifteen years, he said, "I had the opportunity to devote my concerns and responsibility to the total range of human affairs and social and economic problems."

By November the hearings were mired in minutiae and ignored by the press. At one point the Committee, looking for scandal, resurrected an incident that discredited Rockefeller's veracity. John Wells, a shrewd

New York City lawyer and Republican political sage, came to see Rockefeller in 1970 with a proposition: since his Democratic opponent for Governor that year, Arthur Goldberg, was not well known in New York State, Wells proposed that he commission a book about Goldberg. The voters in the state, he said, "are entitled to a factual report of Mr. Goldberg's record from a critical, but fair and responsible point of view." The premise was sound. No New Yorker, Goldberg was a Chicago labor lawyer, former Secretary of Labor in the Kennedy Administration, former Supreme Court Justice, and former U.S. Ambassador to the United Nations. "He had never run for public office," Wells said, so "had not been subjected to examination of his history and record in an adversary political proceeding." A book about Goldberg could serve that purpose, Wells suggested to Rockefeller.

Initially, Rockefeller testified, he had dismissed the proposal. When evidence turned up that in fact he had been involved, he clarified his testimony. His revised account stated that he had relayed the proposal to a family attorney for action; the lawyer in turn involved Laurance Rockefeller, who invested $60,000 in the venture. Family lawyers then set up a dummy corporation to publish the Goldberg book.

Wells then commissioned Victor Lasky, a political author, to write the book. By the time it was published, Goldberg had turned out to be an unusually inept candidate; the more he appeared in public, the more votes he lost. Nobody bought the book, blandly titled *Arthur J. Goldberg: The Old and the New*. Nobody read it. When a box of books was delivered to Buffalo Republican headquarters for campaign use, a clerk, thinking it misaddressed, sent it over to Democratic headquarters, which promptly handed it out to their campaign workers. Goldberg, told of the book, complained to Rockefeller—even though he confessed he had not read it. Rockefeller accepted responsibility and apologized.

Wells, testifying before the Senate Committee, was as fearless on the stand as he was in a courtroom. Refusing to show any remorse about his enterprise, Wells disdained the Senators' questions and defended his action on what he believed were unassailable grounds: "The people's right to know."

After months of hearings and deliberations, the Senate Rules Committee voted unanimously to confirm Rockefeller, and on December 10, 1974, the full Senate confirmed him as Vice President by a vote of 90-7. Three Republicans, including Barry Goldwater, voted against his confirmation.

Confronting the House Judiciary Committee was the more difficult ordeal for Rockefeller. Two-thirds of the twenty-one Democratic Members of the Committee were Far Left liberals by philosophy and open antagonists to the rich. Led by Don Edwards of California, Robert Kastenmeier of Wisconsin, John Conyers of Michigan, and Robert Drinan of Massachusetts, this faction set out to harass the nominee, brand him a sinister force of power and influence, and if possible, prevent his confirmation.

When President Ford learned of a committee move to postpone action on his nominee's confirmation until after the new Congress met in January, he intervened. Recognizing that an electorate weary of the Vietnam War and unforgiving of Watergate and the pardon of Nixon had elected an antagonistic and possibly irresponsible House, Ford was concerned that new Members would not confirm his choice for Vice President. He assigned Jack Marsh, his counselor and overseer of Congressional relations, to track developments daily and accord first priority to advancing Rockefeller's confirmation. Ford also intervened personally. "I called the Speaker," Ford said, and urged Albert to permit no further delays. "I called Tip and said you can't do this to the country," Ford said. Pressed by Speaker Albert and Majority Leader O'Neill, Rodino informed his committee members that they must act promptly.

But the committee faction opposing Rockefeller continued to delay a vote. They tried everything: They cited and repeated the danger of joining "enormous fortune with high political office," questioned whether Rockefeller "could distinguish between the private interest and the public good." They attacked his support of the Vietnam War. They accused him of murder at Attica prison. They charged that he wasted New York taxpayers' money. They condemned the Rockefeller drug laws, charging that New York State judges were forced to impose long jail sentences for minor offenses. A group of Jewish members demanded that Rockefeller commit under oath that, if he should ever become President, he would never negotiate with the Palestine Liberation Organization: he refused. He testified that he never expected to be President but that no responsible official should bar in advance any prudent action that might bring peace.

Convinced that his family secretly manipulated decisions and profits of oil, banking, real estate, and other industries, the Far Left faction on the committee demanded that Rockefeller provide Members with a detailed account of every asset held, individually, and in trust, by the four

Rockefeller brothers, their children, grandchildren, and great grandchildren: in all, eighty-four descendants of John D. Rockefeller.

Rockefeller found this unacceptable. It would be an intolerable invasion of family privacy, he told his staff. Furthermore, it would destroy the family, he revealed to one aide, for he and his brothers had not always given their children equivalent assets. Disclosure would provoke resentment, bitterness, and lasting discord among siblings.

With negotiations at an impasse, Robert Douglass, a wise counselor and longtime confidant of Rockefeller, suggested to him that if the time had come to withdraw his nomination, this excessive invasion of an extensive family's privacy would be valid justification as the reason. Certainly, Douglass suggested, it would be understood by President Ford and the public. Rockefeller thought it over for a few minutes and said, "No, Bob, I'm going to fight this through."

Douglass, a virtuoso at negotiation, asked for a private meeting with Chairman Rodino. Armed with a significant piece of information, Douglass executed an artful stratagem of political chess. He told Rodino that Rockefeller could not accept the committee's demand for such detailed family information, and if the committee persisted, he would be forced to withdraw his nomination. In that event, Douglass said, the Chairman should know that he had been advised that a Democratic Member of the Judiciary Committee—one of the most vocal opponents of Rockefeller—had at the same time been soliciting campaign contributions from Boston members of the Rockefeller family. If the nominee withdrew, Douglass said, there could be no guarantee that an inquisitive press might not learn of the Judiciary Committee Member's conflict of interest and make it public—thereby embarrassing not only the Member and the Chairman, but raising questions about the integrity of the committee's proceedings. Douglass suggested a compromise: Rockefeller would make available to the committee the senior overseer of the extensive family investments, Richardson Dilworth, with a detailed listing in the aggregate of all the stocks, bonds, real estate, and other investments held by the eighty-four family members. Dilworth would appear before the committee, Douglass said, with the understanding that he would testify on total investments, but not be charged with contempt of Congress if he refused to answer questions about any individual Rockefeller investment.

Rodino agreed to propose the Douglass compromise to his committee. The next day, he informed Douglass that the offer and terms were acceptable. So Dilworth testified at length before the committee, bringing an array of charts and graphs that revealed the totals of diverse family investments—in Exxon, Mobil, Standard Oil of California, General Electric, Caterpillar Tractor, Sears Roebuck, IBM, Dow Chemical, Weyerhaeuser, Eastern Airlines, Norfolk and Western Railroad, American Express, General Motors Acceptance Corporation, Wells Fargo, the Chase Manhattan Bank, among many others. In all entities save one, the total of aggregate holdings of the four brothers and their descendants in any public or private corporation was less than 1 percent. The exception: 1.34 percent in Chase Bank.

As part of his testimony, Dilworth revealed the entire family worth: the family members' investments outright and in trust came to $295 million, and the aggregate of investments in trust for their benefit was $738 million. The total: more than $1 billion.

With all committee questions answered and 1,450 pages of testimony recorded, with Marsh pressing individual Democratic committeemen to demand a decision, and the 93rd Congress nearing its end, Rodino brought the question of the Rockefeller confirmation to a committee vote. With the support of seventeen Republicans and nine Democrats, primarily from the South, the committee voted 26-12 to confirm Rockefeller.

Still the contest was not over. Majority Leader O'Neill warned that a collective of passionate liberals, rabid conservatives, blacks, and Jews would oppose him. In speech after speech, they did so. As the floor debate continued, one New Yorker, Representative Shirley Chisholm of Brooklyn, asked for recognition and delivered the most spirited and memorable defense heard in either House of Congress. She had crossed swords with Rockefeller many times, she emphasized, but fairness demanded that her colleagues consider the record of the man and his family. The drumbeat of negatives before the Judiciary Committee and in the press had been unwarranted and excessive, she said. "I could not be silent."

Turning to face her black colleagues, she reminded them that the Rockefellers had a century before established the first black college, Spelman, and had in modern times been the most dependable contributors to the United Negro College Fund, the NAACP Legal Defense Fund, and the Urban League. Confronting Jewish Members, she reminded them that Nelson Rockefeller had persuaded the Defense Department to send fighter planes to Prime Minister Golda Meir in an hour of Israel's peril.

In the way of God remonstrating Job, Chisholm rebuked labor Members: "Where are the voices of labor today? Why have not they and the American people been made aware of the fact that it was . . . Nelson Rockefeller who in New York set up the first statewide minimum wage law and extended the right of collective bargaining to public employees . . . ?" Confronting women opponents, she asked: "Where are the wonderful women who have spent endless hours in New York working toward an equitable and intelligent abortion law? . . . It was Nelson Rockefeller who stood in the eye of the storm and in the face of heated controversy pushed through New York's abortion law." To a liberal faction she said: "Where are those social workers and community organizers who called on Governor Rockefeller to initiate and organize the largest state Medicaid program as he did?" To another group, she asked: "Where are those environmentalists who should come forward and tell us it was Governor Rockefeller who created the state's pure waters program, the largest in the nation, and a department of environmental conservation?"

Chisholm may not have changed a single vote, but her trenchant questioning brought a fresh voice of balance to the constant criticism that Rockefeller had endured on Capitol Hill. When the roll was called in the House, 129 Members voted to reject Rockefeller, and 287 voted to confirm him. At 10:30 p.m., on December 19, 1974, Rockefeller was sworn in on the floor of the Senate as the 41st Vice President of the United States.

For Rockefeller, the responsibility he had accepted out of a sense of duty to a new President Ford and to the country had come at a high cost. For more than half a century, the Rockefeller family had zealously guarded its privacy; now, few secrets remained. In one four-month span Rockefeller had defended against more attacks on his character, his principles, and his record than in all previous years of his political campaigns and public life. In legal fees, accounting bills, research expenses, travel for himself and staff who had committed full time to dealing with Congressional Members and staff, the total bill had come to $1 million, an amount the IRS ruled was not deductible.

All this, Rockefeller accepted with grace. In his brief remarks after taking the oath of office, he emphasized his gratitude to President Ford and to Congress "for the privilege of serving the country I love."

With particular pride, he said he looked forward to presiding over the Senate where his mother's father, Senator Nelson Aldrich, had represented Rhode Island "in this very chamber for 31 years." Alluding to the unprecedented problems President Ford had inherited, he affirmed his deep-seated optimism: "There is nothing wrong with America that Americans cannot right."

On a rainy Saturday afternoon two days later, Rockefeller flew to Washington to hear President Ford define his job. With Rumsfeld, Marsh, and Scowcroft flanking his desk in the Oval Office, Ford gave Rockefeller specific assignments: He would participate in all discussions and decisions relating to national security and foreign policy. He would assist Ford in recruiting quality staff and Cabinet members. He would undertake some travel to campaign for the party and represent the President internationally, but this would be a lesser part of his job. He would assume responsibility for a commission on privacy that Ford had been forced to relinquish when he became President. More significantly, as Ford had promised in August when he asked Rockefeller to consider the job, the Vice President would be in charge of domestic policy.

The prospect of creating and advancing domestic policy transported Rockefeller. For his meeting with the President, he had brought along Ann Whitman, who was to be his chief of staff; Bob Douglass, a particularly close friend and counsel; Hugh Morrow, his amanuensis and press secretary; and me, his assistant for working with Congress and the White House. On our flight back to New York City, Rockefeller began to talk about how he would operate in the Ford White House. President Ford had handed him power in their seventy-minute meeting, and so he was certain that his Vice Presidency would be different.

The White House entity through which Rockefeller expected to manage his broad assignment was the Domestic Council, created by President Nixon in 1970 to parallel the National Security Council. Nixon had been impressed by Kissinger's facility for presenting a national-security issue or foreign-policy initiative in a single, compressed, but comprehensive document, with historical perspective, brief arguments for and against, and options for Presidential decision. This appealed to Nixon; he much preferred to read opinion rather than listen to oral arguments. In Kissinger's National Security Decision Memoranda, Nixon could pore over the judgments from State, Defense, Treasury, NSC, CIA, NSA, and choose the option that would be conveyed back to Kissinger and the departments as his decision.

Domestic issues, by contrast, reached Nixon's desk in fragments: one Cabinet officer proposing aid to cities; a White House aide advocating welfare reform. So Nixon, by Executive Order 11541, created the Domestic Council to match the orderly process of the NSC. He appointed John Ehrlichman, a rising power in the White House, as Executive Director; Ehrlichman in turn recruited a wide-ranging staff of experts in government action—education, energy, housing, transportation, the environment. Within a year, the Domestic Council had become a center of power and influence second only to the NSC. By design, Nixon had taken policy-making power away from Cabinet members and concentrated that authority and responsibility in the White House.

As governor, Rockefeller had observed that concentration of power in the Domestic Council. He had personally negotiated with Ehrlichman to the benefit of New York State. Hugh Morrow, who for ten years had written for Rockefeller, knew his proclivities. On the day after Rockefeller had met with Ford, Morrow said: "Never underestimate the arrogance of Nelson Rockefeller. He calculated that he would be in charge of everything that wasn't Kissinger's."

CHAPTER 18

Challenges

In the first hour of his Presidency, Gerald Ford had promised the American people straight talk and candor. Five months later, in his first State of the Union address, he kept that promise. "I've got bad news," he said, his voice solemn but firm. "I must say to you that the State of the Union is not good. Millions of Americans are out of work. Recession and inflation are eroding the money of millions more. Prices are too high, and sales too low. This year's Federal deficit will be about $30 billion; next year's probably $45 billion. The national debt will rise to over $500 billion. Our plant capacity and production are not increasing fast enough. We depend on others for essential energy."

These were the facts, sobering and critical, Ford said, but it was a time for resolution, not despair. It was time, he said, for immediate action. For himself and for Congress the first priority: "Let us mobilize . . . to put all our people to work." To spur industry and create jobs, Ford proposed to cut taxes for one year: For individuals, a cash rebate of 12 percent of 1974 payments; for business, large and small, a 12 percent investment tax credit.

"Cutting taxes now is essential if we are to turn the economy around," he said. "Unfortunately it will increase the size of the budget deficit." That too must be addressed, he said. Confronting Congress head on, Ford told Members they must stop uncontrolled spending, stop enacting programs when "no one knows what they will cost." As one strong move to curb the growth of Federal spending, he proposed to limit Social Security and Federal pension increases to 5 percent. Affirming his sweeping budget decisions of December, Ford told Congress his Administration would lead the way. For the Executive departments,

"No new spending programs can be initiated this year, except for energy. Further, I will not hesitate to veto any new spending programs adopted by Congress."

Ford's immediate audience—Members of the House and Senate—sat on its collective hands as they listened to his grim appraisal of the economic crisis facing the country. Ford had expected little applause, but he was sure he had been right to deliver the bad news. In his judgment, it was his obligation to speak plainly about "what the facts are as to the economy and our situation." It was Ford's hope that Congress would share his concern and respond.

He was mistaken. Ford's call to action was disdained or ignored. House Ways and Means Committee Chairman Al Ullman responded that his Members would not even hold hearings on a corporate tax cut, or even consider a limit on Social Security and Federal pension increases. Economizing was not on the 94th Congress' agenda. Liberal in philosophy, this Congress was even more liberal with public money. From freshman to veteran, Members were committed to creating new programs without regard to cost; to spending and more spending. Ford was learning, seeing the House and Senate from a new perspective, recognizing that he would have to defend the U.S. Treasury from the profligacy of his former colleagues.

In the White House Ford was also learning to be an executive, and one measure of his progress was the quality of the new Cabinet he formed. Six months earlier he had insisted on keeping the Nixon Cabinet; now Ford realized that Rumsfeld was right. He must make changes, for the country would not fully recognize that this was a Ford Presidency until he formed a Ford Cabinet.

Ford knew what he wanted. "I like to work with people who have a high degree of intellectual capacity and capability, and who are independent individuals in their own right," he said. "I don't pretend to be an intellectual. But in fact, I get strength from having those kinds of people around." Since he had not campaigned for the office, he had no political obligation in appointing his Cabinet. Nevertheless, he respected political experience. "If I had two people of equal ability available for an important job, I would favor the one who had the experience of being elected to office."

Ford's way of choosing his Cabinet exemplified his methodical approach to decisions: Evaluate each department's need. Get the facts about possible choices, pro and con. Talk, face to face, to the most promising candidate. Decide. Move on.

In appointing his Cabinet, Ford relied on an orderly, businesslike process that Rumsfeld had put in place. When either learned of an upcoming vacancy, Rumsfeld would ask Bill Walker, Ford's first Director of Personnel, to come up with four or five names to stimulate Ford's thinking. The three would then discuss what President Ford wanted in that position, and how he wanted to create a balance in his Cabinet and in his Administration. After Walker proposed more names, Ford would select one or two and ask for information about background and possible availability. Ford would then make a tentative choice, and ask Walker to conduct a more detailed check of the prime prospect's background. If that more rigorous scrutiny was positive, then Ford would ask Rumsfeld to bring the candidate in for a meeting. Face to face, Ford would decide.

When he began changing the Cabinet, Ford's first priority was the Department of Justice. Long before he became President, Ford had been particularly concerned about this department. Under Eisenhower and every President since, Ford said, "the Justice Department had been overly politicized. I wanted to go in the opposite direction."

Ford had also observed the erratic course of Justice's leadership. In two years, the direction of the Justice Department had veered from John Mitchell to Richard Kliendienst, both indicted; to Elliott Richardson, who resigned as a matter of principle; to Robert Bork, acting as senior officer present; to William Saxbe, a stop-gap. Some in Congress—particularly, Senator Ted Kennedy—proposed taking the Justice Department out of the Executive branch and making it totally independent. Ford opposed that notion, believing it would be unwise, perhaps dangerous, for Justice or any other government department to be accountable to no one.

As candidates for a new Attorney General, Rumsfeld brought in five names; at the top of the list he had placed his fellow Chicagoan, Edward Levi. As Dean of the University of Chicago Law School and later President of the University of Chicago, "Ed Levi was known as having towering integrity," Rumsfeld said. "The President wanted to bring in someone from the outside. I said I thought it ought to be someone who was known for integrity. We would get him confirmed and the President would be seen as turning over a new leaf in the Department of Justice."

Ford looked over the documents Rumsfeld and Walker had written summarizing Levi's background. "I saw that he had an impeccable record as a lawyer and an administrator," Ford said. Reading that in 1950 Levi had served a special assignment as chief counsel to a House Judiciary Subcommittee on antitrust, Ford telephoned former Representative Emanuel Celler, in Brooklyn. Before he retired in 1973, Celler had chaired the Judiciary Committee. He told Ford that Levi had performed well. Committee Members and staff had been impressed by young Levi's sound judgment and they liked working with him.

The son and grandson of rabbis, Levi was a scholar in the law—Phi Beta Kappa as an undergraduate at the University of Chicago; top of his class in law school there; a Sterling Fellow at Yale where, in 1938, he earned his doctorate in law. After serving for five years as an assistant to Attorney General Francis Biddle during World War II, he returned to the University of Chicago to teach law. Appointed dean of the law school in 1950, Levi was elevated to provost of the University in 1962, and in 1968 to president of the university.

Looking beyond Levi's academic record, Ford was also impressed by his cool courage and practical leadership. At a time when college students were protesting the Vietnam War, hundreds of students at the University of Chicago occupied the administration building for an eighteen-day sit-in. Instead of confronting them, or calling the police to eject them, Levi informed the protesting students that he would not attempt to go into his office in the building while they occupied it. However, if the protesting students wanted to come outside and discuss their issues with him, he would do so—but he would not consider amnesty for their conduct. President Levi did meet the students and listen. That ended the sit-in. Then, carrying out his responsibility as president, Levi expelled thirty-four of the protest ringleaders from the University, and suspended sixty more.

"Everything I read about him convinced me that he was firm but fair, an excellent administrator and unflappable," Ford said. He asked Rumsfeld to invite him in for a discussion. Rumsfeld telephoned Levi: "Could you come in to the White House next week and give me a considerable amount of time for a discussion in depth, say two hours?"

Levi assumed that he and Rumsfeld would discuss aid to education, so he asked his staff for a quick study on Federal grants the university was then receiving. Well prepared, he arrived in the White House and was ushered into the office of the Chief of Staff. After thanking Levi for coming, Rumsfeld bluntly asked: "What kind of person should be Attorney General?" After a ten-minute discussion Rumsfeld said: "I think we should talk to the President."

"Sure," Levi said.

Rumsfeld rose. "Come along."

"What? Now?"

"Yes, let's go see the President."

As they were sitting down in the Oval Office, Ford took out his pipe and began filling it with his favorite Field and Stream tobacco as he studied his visitor. "I would like to get my pipe too," Levi said. "Fine," Ford said.

With both wreathed in pipe smoke, Ford mentioned the names of Yale law faculty members both must have known (Levi graduated in 1938; Ford, in 1940). Then, Ford asked: "What do you think the Department of Justice needs?"

"Justice needs a non-political administration," Levi replied. "Nothing is more important to the country, Mr. President, than restoring confidence in the administration of justice."

This was exactly what Ford wanted to hear. "Something has to be done about the Justice Department," he said, "and we have decided that we must start at the top." It took less than ten minutes of discussion for Ford to decide that Levi was his choice. "He was the right man to come in and change the office for the better, change it to what it ought to be," Ford said.

In that brief encounter Levi found himself impressed by Ford's directness and his manifest concern for the urgent need at the Justice Department. "I had no doubt about it," Levi said. "What the President wanted was an Attorney General who would bring about a straightforward, non-partisan administration."

Then, to Levi's astonishment, Ford said: "Mr. Levi, would you be willing to take the job of Attorney General?"

"I was appalled," Levi said later. "I thought, 'I need this like a hole in the head.'" What he said was: "Mr. President, I have an enormous obligation to the University of Chicago, and we are in the middle of a major fund drive."

Ford looked Levi in the eye: "With the administration of justice in such difficulty, how can you possibly turn your back on it?"

Levi was taken aback. After a few moments he said he would consider the offer, but must first talk to his trustees at the University. Walking out, Levi said to Rumsfeld, "Isn't that a little sudden?"

"No," Rumsfeld said, "and the President would like your answer tomorrow."

"Impossible," Levi said, but he confirmed what he had told the President: he would think it over. For ten days he debated with himself, consulted with his trustees, and reflected on his obligation to the university and to President Ford. "I was enormously taken with him," Levi said of Ford. "I was not thirsting for the position. But his asking, 'How can you turn your back on the administration of justice?' stuck in my throat. I decided I should not turn it down." He telephoned Rumsfeld to say he would accept.

On Jan 14, 1975, President Ford announced the appointment of Edward Levi as Attorney General, and another of equal merit: William Coleman was to be Secretary of Transportation.

Coleman was no stranger to Ford. They had met during the Warren Commission's investigation of the Kennedy assassination; Chief Justice Warren had chosen Coleman to be chief counsel for the investigation. Born in the Germantown section of Philadelphia, Coleman graduated summa cum laude from the University of Pennsylvania, and magna cum laude from Harvard Law School. First in his class at Harvard, Coleman clerked for Supreme Court Justice Felix Frankfurter—the first person of color to serve as a law clerk to the Supreme Court. Later, with Thurgood Marshall, Coleman coauthored the brief for *Brown v. Board of Education*—the historic case that ended with the Supreme Court ruling in 1954 that racial segregation in public schools violated the Constitution. Coleman moved on to be President of the NAACP Legal Defense and Educational fund. Versatile and sound of judgment, Coleman had also served President Eisenhower on labor policy, President Johnson as a consultant on arms control, and President Nixon on the U.S. delegation to the United Nations General Assembly.

Coleman, Ford concluded, belonged in his Cabinet. During their service together on the Warren Commission, Ford said, "I saw Bill on many occasions interrogate witnesses and present staff recommendations to the Commission, and I was tremendously impressed with him as a lawyer and a gentleman. So I invited him to come in for a discussion." After reviewing several possible posts, Ford—who had been briefed that in private practice Coleman had become an expert on transportation law—said: "Would you consider Transportation?"

"Yes, but I need to think about it," Coleman said. At home that evening, a Friday, he mentioned it to his daughter, Lovida, a Yale law student home for the weekend. "You must take it," she told her dad, and offered good reasons. On Monday, Coleman called Ford and said he would be honored to serve as Transportation Secretary. Ford was delighted. "I told him about the responsibilities that I wanted him to undertake at Transportation," Ford said. "He came on board, and—as I expected—did a great job."

Four days later Ford announced that William Simon would continue at Treasury and Earl Butz at Agriculture. While still in Congress, Ford had been impressed by Simon's effectiveness as head of the Federal Energy Administration. As Vice President, Ford commended Nixon's decision to appoint Simon to Treasury and observed that Simon was not only well regarded by the financial community, but had been straightforward and effective in his relations with Congress. "I liked Bill's drive, his intelligence," Ford said. During the first months of the new Administration, Simon indicated he would like to return to Wall Street. Ford talked him into staying. "Bill was more conservative, more fiscally responsible than anybody else in the Cabinet," Ford said. "He represented the viewpoint that I felt was necessary in my Administration. He was articulate and he was dedicated. We needed his voice. We needed his views."

Butz, after four arduous years as Agriculture Secretary in the Nixon Administration, also wanted to leave Washington. He told Ford he was tired and had accomplished what he had set out to do at Agriculture. Moreover, he said he had just been offered a lucrative opportunity back home in Indiana, and he intended to accept it. At 65, he argued, he had reached an age when job offers were scarce. But Ford would not let him go. "Earl had turned farmers around, from depending on government price supports to relying on better farming practices, more businesslike operations, and market prices," Ford said. "I twisted his arm to stay. I told him, 'The country needs you, Earl. I need you. Agriculture needs you. You just can't leave.' He responded as a good American, as a patriot."

On one other Nixon Cabinet holdover, James Schlesinger at Defense, Ford was ambivalent. Personal relationships counted with Ford; he found Schlesinger "aloof, austere, disdainful of people he doesn't think are as intellectually smart as he is." Yet, Ford judged, Defense was too important to change just because he did not particularly like the man in charge. In his mind, he placed Schlesinger on probation.

To head his Department of Labor, Ford looked over the five prospects Rumsfeld and Walker had collected. His first choice was John T.

Dunlop, a master of negotiations between labor and management, an eminent theorist and professor of labor policy and an author of standard works on industrial relations. As Vice President, Ford had listened to Dunlop's practical observations and quiet wisdom in White House sessions on cost-of-living and labor-management issues. "I had seen him at work, and I knew he had the respect of George Meany and the labor unions," Ford said. Looking over a summary of Dunlop's background, Ford saw that he had an extraordinary record: The son of missionaries, Dunlop had grown up in the Philippines, earned his PhD at the University of California, and studied under John Maynard Keynes at Cambridge (where his roommate was John Kenneth Galbraith). As a professor, Dunlop chaired the Economics Department at Harvard. Gruff, outspoken, he was said to be "more at home at a plumbers' convention than with the Harvard faculty." Of Dunlop, Harvard President Derek Bok said: "John Dunlop saved the university after the student riots of l968 and 1969."

His mind made up, Ford said to Rumsfeld: "If we can get John Dunlop, that would be ideal." In the Oval Office, Ford promised Dunlop that if he took the job, he would not only serve as Secretary of Labor, but would also be a key member of the Economic Policy Board, which guided all of Ford's economic decisions.

To Ford, of all the departments and agencies reporting directly to him, the Office of Management and Budget was second to none. For his budget chief, Ford decided early on the man he wanted: James Lynn, then Secretary of Housing and Urban Development. The two had once had an uncharacteristic public fight. Ford, then still House Republican Leader, had recommended a highly qualified Michigan constituent for a job at HUD. After a long bureaucratic delay, HUD gave the job to a Wisconsin man. At a crowded Washington social gathering, Ford upbraided Lynn not just for turning down his recommendation, but for taking so long to do it. "It made me mad as hell," Ford said. "I'd had a few drinks, and Jim and I got into a shouting match against each other." The incident did not deter Ford. "I liked Jim's aggressiveness, his feisty spirit," Ford said. "He was a total extrovert, an outstanding lawyer, articulate, a superior public official, with a mind both detailed and all encompassing." For Ford, Lynn also had an incomparable asset for his Budget Director: a record of success in persuading Congress to pass his department's programs.

One potential problem was that Lynn had often and seriously battled with OMB's senior staff over money for HUD. "Rumors came to me that many people in OMB would resign if Lynn was appointed Director," Ford said. Always sensitive to egos and pride of position, Ford moved with caution. "There was one person at OMB that I knew we had to retain—Paul O'Neill," Ford said. "And Lynn couldn't afford to lose him because Paul O'Neill knew more about the Federal government than anyone else in Washington." To reassure O'Neill, Ford talked to him. "I need you both," he said.

For O'Neill, serving with Lynn was not a problem. As Deputy Director, O'Neill held enormous responsibility and power. Uncommon in his dedication to public service, O'Neill was fully committed to serving Ford and the country. Moreover, he felt totally secure in his personal and professional relationship with the President whose views matched so closely his own.

In forming his budget team, Ford calculated that the two personalities would be complementary. "Jim would be the hard-liner who would bluntly say no, usually making the person angry, and Paul the moderator who could smooth things over. It ended up that Lynn and O'Neill made the best one and two combination at OMB ever," Ford said. Moreover, he had exactly what he had planned: "Lynn the outside man to deal with Congress; O'Neill the inside man to run the place."

From their first months in the White House, Betty Ford had been, as Ford put it, "prodding me to find somebody among qualified women for a position in the Administration or appointment to the Supreme Court." When Rumsfeld brought in a list of highly qualified women in and out of government, "One really stood out," Ford said. She was Carla Anderson Hills, Assistant Attorney General in charge of the Civil Division in the Department of Justice. Appointed by Attorney General Elliott Richardson days before his resignation, she had been appointed again by his successor, Attorney General Saxbe. At the Justice Department, Hills had administered the complex division with skill and verve, keeping the caseload flowing and raising the division's morale and prestige. A Californian, Hills had graduated cum laude from Stanford, attended Oxford, and graduated twentieth in her class (of 177) from Yale Law School. After three years as an Assistant U.S. Attorney in Los Angeles, she became, in private practice, a highly accomplished litigator.

After discussing her merit with Elliott Richardson, Ford instructed Rumsfeld to invite her in for a talk. "I got a call on a Saturday morning from a staff person in Rumsfeld's office saying, 'The President would like to see you on Monday.'" Hills said. She was impressed: It was her first call ever from the White House. "I guessed the President must be interested in the Nixon tapes case, or complex litigation involving HEW."

On Monday she was escorted in to see Rumsfeld. "The President wants to talk to you about going over to HUD," Rumsfeld said.

"I really think he needs me at Justice," Hills said. "I'm a litigator, and we have a heavy backlog of litigation that is complex and politically sensitive."

"You'll have to talk to him about that," Rumsfeld said, as he rose to take her to the Oval Office.

Seated to Ford's right, Hills said: "Mr. President, I'm not an urbanologist. I'm not a housing expert. I am honored, but I probably should stay at Justice."

"I don't need an urbanologist," Ford said. "I don't need a housing expert. I need a manager for that Department. You come recommended as a manager, and I want you to do it."

Hills asked questions: What needs to be done at HUD? What does the job involve? "Good questions," Ford said. "She was immediately very impressive. Extremely bright. She confirmed my decision that it was better to get somebody from the outside who could assimilate all the information and make good judgments."

On the spot, Hills made a quick calculation. With Ford contending with double-digit inflation, double-digit unemployment, turmoil in the markets, and a housing crisis, she felt she had only one choice. She answered: "Mr. President, I am happy to do what you like."

Ford was relieved. Home builders in Grand Rapids had complained to him about the red tape and bureaucratic delays that impeded HUD's mandated grants for housing and community development. He knew the statistics: normally the housing industry produced 1.8 to 2.2 million units a year; in 1974, it had fallen below 1 million units. At this one meeting, Ford was certain he had made the right choice. He was confident that Hills would impose order on HUD's operations and, he hoped, "give the housing industry a shot in the arm."

Up for confirmation in the Senate, Hills found herself a witness on trial, accused of the very inexperience she had mentioned to President Ford. Opening her hearing before the Banking Committee, Chairman William Proxmire immediately put her on the defensive: "Mrs. Hills, you do not have a winning record in housing or in other urban problems. You have no record: winning or losing . . . You have been a competent lawyer [administering] a division of the Justice Department whose responsibilities with respect to housing and urban development have been the Government lawyer in bringing suit against the transgressors. In my view that experience tells us nothing about your capacity to reverse a disastrous housing program within this mammoth department . . ."

Furthermore, Proxmire continued, your predecessor James Lynn was, "like you, a highly intelligent, personable, successful lawyer . . . and a full-fledged total disaster for housing."

Unfazed, Hills was forthright in acknowledging her inexperience in housing. Calmly, circumspectly, she avoided specifics "before I have even stepped my foot inside the building," but answered all questions and proposed her approach to the job. If confirmed, she testified, she would begin by examining the fundamental needs of the housing industry. She would consult with all concerned, "the builders, the lenders, the labor unions, the environmentalists, the consumers, public officials, those concerned with civil rights, and all the others who have an interest." Then she would set high but realistic goals, and use the HUD instrument "most clearly appropriate to the particular problem."

Even though Hills was strongly opposed by the principal and powerful lobbyists contriving to win public money for their trade—the National Association of Home Builders, the National Rural Housing Coalition, the Mortgage Bankers Association—Hills was confirmed 11-2 by the committee. Only Proxmire and Biden voted against her, and she was confirmed 85-5 by the Senate. Hills was sworn in on March 10, 1975.

One refreshingly candid commentary about the way of Congress was recorded during Hills's hearings. A freshman senator, Jake Garn, in office less than two months, observed: "Congress . . . always seems to want to find scapegoats for its own failures, to blame everybody but themselves for their own acts." To his fellow committee members, Garn pointed out that HUD's problem was not its secretary, former or future, but Congress itself. As a former Mayor of Salt Lake City, Garn had dealt with HUD's tangle of programs and restrictions. Quoting from an earlier survey that Chairman Proxmire himself had contracted for the committee, Garn read: "At no time . . . has Congress or the Executive developed clear goals of what it wanted to do through housing subsidies and how to do it. Instead, legislation has been proposed, debated, amended, enacted, piece by piece, with political situations dominating economic and managerial aspects of the problems. The result has been the creation of a crazy quilt system of too many subsidies, many of which are hidden from budget review, some that provided excessive rates of return to investors, staggering subsidy and housing cost increases, a deficient housing product in far too many cases, and numerous other deficiencies."

Garn's criticism spoke to one committee's manner of writing laws, but it reflected not merely the actions of that one Senate Committee, but the way of Congress—then and thereafter. With little regard for how a new program is to be managed, and even less for economic or fiscal consequences, Congress legislates piecemeal. Rarely does any House or Senate committee present to the public a clear and succinct definition of a problem, propose logical options for solving the problem, and reach a workable decision. Instead, with rare exceptions, the bill that Congress passes is a conglomeration of lofty and unrealistic objectives and responses to pressures from disparate special interests.

Before he appointed a new Secretary of Commerce, Ford concluded he should rejuvenate the Department. After being neglected by Nixon, Commerce needed a lift; of that he was certain. In Ford's mind, he imposed three requirements for the appointee: By character and temperament he must become the Ford Administration's chief salesman for America's free-enterprise system. Second, he must inspire the Commerce staff. Third, he must command the respect of Congress. To Ford, the person who best met all three requirements was his wise and amiable colleague from the House, Rogers Morton.

Before he served in Congress, Morton was a businessman. After graduating from Yale and commanding a Field Artillery battery in Europe during World War II, he served as president of the family's prosperous flour business, Ballard and Ballard, in Louisville, before his company merged with Pillsbury. In the 1950s Morton laid the foundation for public life. He bought a 1,400-acre farm on the Eastern Shore of Maryland, where he raised cattle, corn and soybeans, made money, and made Talbot County his legal residence. Continuing a strong family interest in public service—his older brother Thruston Morton represented Kentucky in both the House and Senate—Rogers Morton ran for Congress in 1962, won, and represented Maryland's First District for five terms.

In the House, Ford and Morton bonded. "We had the same philosophy and the same beliefs." Ford said. "He had a good mind, politically and otherwise, and he was very successful in the House. A forceful speaker, Rog's presence and drive and enthusiasm made people listen to him," Robust in size—6 feet 7 inches, with a frame to match—Morton was just as imposing in integrity and affability. "Nobody ever got mad at Rog Morton," Ford said. "He had a happy, gregarious personality. You could look at him and say, 'Gee, there's a big teddy bear fellow,' but he could be damn serious."

Ford respected Morton's judgment in all things. "He would come in and say, 'Mr. President, this isn't going right. I think you've got to do this.'" Ford said. "He could be kind of a 'Dutch uncle' to me. We had the kind of rapport that permitted him to come in and tell me I was wrong, and he knew I wouldn't throw him out of the office, but I would listen. And more often than not, he was right." In appointing Morton to Commerce, Ford was certain that "one of my closest and best friends" could restore the confidence of the business community in government, and the confidence of the public in the business world.

For his Secretary of the Interior, Ford turned, as Presidents do, to the West. Rumsfeld's list included Stan Hathaway, Governor of Wyoming, who had just finished his second term. Ford liked his record. "Wyoming's economy depended on the proper development of its resources and the preservation of its beautiful environment," Ford said. "Stan, as governor, tread that narrow path of responsible development and proper conservation." To Ford, Hathaway had another asset: He had balanced the state budget, bringing Wyoming out of the red with a mineral severance tax that earned the state a $2 billion surplus.

Hathaway was a son of the West in every sense. Born in Nebraska, he was orphaned at age 2, and taken by a first cousin and her husband into their homestead outside Torrington, in eastern Wyoming. For a time the family lived in a tent, then in a hay barn built by his stepfather, then in a one-room house without plumbing. At 18, after Pearl Harbor, Hathaway left college to volunteer for the U.S. Army Air Corps. After his training, Hathaway flew as a radio operator and gunner in a squadron of the Eighth Air Force that took very high casualties. On one of his thirty-five missions, his B-17 was hit by antiaircraft fire, lost three engines, and crash-landed in France. He and his crew were rescued by the French Resistance, hidden, and smuggled back to England. On another mission a bomb got stuck in the B-17's bomb bay, making it impossible for the pilot to risk a landing. Hathaway volunteered to stand on a ledge in the open bomb bay and kick the bomb loose into the English Channel. For that and other deeds he was awarded five Air Medals. Hathaway never considered himself a hero. Back home after World War II he said: "We simply did what we had to do at the time." For years he had nightmares about American bombers going down in flames around him.

Aided by the GI Bill, Hathaway earned his bachelor's degree and his law degree at the University of Nebraska. To begin his practice, Hathaway returned to Wyoming. "Because he survived the war, he felt he had a duty to repay through public service," his law partner said. Hathaway committed to public life. He began as a prosecuting attorney, and moved up through the ranks to governor.

Hathaway's nomination immediately provoked an organized campaign by environmentalists to block his confirmation by the Senate. The Sierra Club and other groups of ardent conservationists charged that Hathaway supported cheap leasing of Federal lands for mining and timber cutting, selling public lands for private commercial development, building a jetport in Grand Teton national Park, killing golden eagles, and using strychnine and sodium cyanide to poison coyotes. "Mr. Ford . . . has picked the all-out promoter of exploitation," the *Baltimore Sun* editorialized. "Mr. Hathaway is unqualified to be trusted with America's woodlands and waterways." Colorado Senator Gary Hart charged that Hathaway would pursue "a policy of profligacy, of development at any cost." Representative Morris Udall condemned Hathaway's public record, contending "that as far as natural resources are concerned, he suffers tunnel vision and can only see dollar signs."

The Wyoming Congressional delegation came to Hathaway's defense, and he was confirmed, 60-34, by the Senate. But his time at Department of the Interior was brief. He could not endure the continuing vituperation heaped on him by hostile environmentalists and an antipathetic press. Even his routine decisions were suspect. After four months in office, Hathaway sent word to President Ford that he needed to see him to resign because he was near a mental breakdown. "I couldn't believe that," Ford said. "Here was this rugged strong man I had known for years. Stan came in and he was literally in tears."

"Mr. President," Hathaway said, "I just can't carry on."

"Stan, before you make that decision, I want you to go over and see Dr. Lukash," Ford told him. "If he thinks it is wise, I hope you will go out to Bethesda and get a rest."

Hathaway's doctor flew in from Wyoming to consult with Dr. Lukash at Bethesda Naval Hospital. At first Hathaway seemed to be recovering, but then the two doctors agreed he should resign. Hathaway returned to Wyoming and, away from the warfare of words he had experienced in Washington, he had a full recovery and practiced law for another twenty years. Back in Cheyenne, he wrote to Ford: "I would have been able to dismiss the editorials that labeled me the worst appointment that you made to your Cabinet, but I could not dismiss the apprehension I felt when they continued to write about me as being the most controversial member of your Cabinet. I became convinced that I would not have done an effective job for you because of all the adverse publicity." He thanked Ford for his warmth and friendship, and for intervening to get him medical assistance. "Since I had never had a depression before, I really didn't know what was happening to me," Hathaway said in his letter. "No one could have done more to ease my pain than you did, even to having me flown from Washington to Denver in your personal plane."

To replace Hathaway, Ford turned to another Westerner, Tom Kleppe of North Dakota, a man he had come to know well in the House. Also a son of homesteaders, Kleppe grew up on his family farm, quit college to perform in rodeos, and served as a warrant officer during World War II. In Bismarck he used a knack for figures to succeed in banking and business, and put aside a modest fortune. Going into politics, at age 30 he was elected Mayor of Bismarck. He served as the state's only Representative in Congress for two terms. He left in 1970 to run for the Senate, and lost.

Ford assessed his qualifications. "I knew that Tom knew the problems of the Department of the Interior," Ford said. "Under Democrats and Republicans, Interior had usually suffered from inertia and was bogged down in red tape. Tom was a decision maker, and that Department needed one: off-shore oil development, negotiations with the states on surface mining, managing Federal land. He would go in and get things moving. He knew how to deal with Congress. He was very bright, very articulate. A good analytical mind. I was confident that Tom would do a good job."

To lead the Department of Health, Education, and Welfare, Ford turned again to an academic. "The job of Secretary of HEW is most demanding in the need for strong administration," Ford said. "It spends more money, has such a wide variety of programs—welfare, Social Security, education, health, research—it covers the waterfront. It may well have outgrown the capability for any one person to be Secretary. It may because of its size now have to be broken up.[1] How one person can oversee all the problems in that department is almost an insurmountable task. So I was looking for a person who had a record of administering substantial organizations. I was looking for a person who would be a moderate in the political sense. I was looking for a younger person. Also, frankly, I wanted a Southerner. We did not have any person in the Cabinet who represented that geographical area."

Ford thought of David Mathews, President of the University of Alabama. Ford had met Mathews on several occasions as the two took part in preliminary planning for the Bicentennial. As President, Ford had given an award to Mathews for the University of Alabama becoming the first Bicentennial campus. "I think I had an eye and ear to pick people out, to discern people of quality," Ford said, "and I was attracted to Mathews almost immediately. When Cap Weinberger told me he must leave HEW I said to Rumsfeld: 'Don, I've always been impressed with David Mathews. Let's find out about him.' Don did, and every inquiry verified my intuition that here was a first-class person. In almost every way you looked at it, David Mathews fitted precisely with what we wanted."

When Mathews first received a call from the White House—"The President would like to see you about a possible Cabinet position"—he thought a close friend was playing a joke on him. Then he realized it really was a call from the White House.

In the Oval Office, Ford looked Mathews over and liked what he saw: "A tall, lean, boyish looking person with a professorial manner." The two discussed health insurance, the problems of integrating public schools—Mathews had peacefully integrated the University of Alabama—and the more serious administrative problems in HEW. Ford found Mathews intelligent, personable, and confident. "He had a strong voice, but his statements were a giveaway of his academic background, sort of a soft-sell appraisal, pro and con. You could almost feel that was the way that he ran the University; that's the way he handled his classes. He was young [39], and obviously he had come up on the basis of ability."

After half an hour of discussion, Ford asked him to accept the appointment to HEW. "I was astounded," Mathews said. "I had never

1. It was broken up in 1979 and The Department of Education was created as a separate entity.

even thought about something like that. But I accepted without hesitation. From my undistinguished career as a second lieutenant in the Army, I knew it was my duty. I had no qualms. I was confident that I could handle the job."

Ford was gratified. "David was, I would say, startled with the opportunity. He had no forewarning. But I convinced him that he was the right man, that we wanted him. So he worked out his situation with the university trustees, came on board, and I think he did one fine job. He could act decisively and quickly. He was very shrewd politically. He was a fine representative of my Administration."

In sheer intellectual firepower, the Ford Cabinet deserves to be ranked first among all Cabinets of the twentieth century. Four members graduated from Harvard; three from Yale; one from Penn; one from Columbia; one from Stanford; one from California, Berkeley. Eight were cum laude—magna or summa. Six were PhDs; all six taught at colleges. Two were former university presidents. Versatility and achievement were common to all. Five were eminently successful lawyers. Three were businessmen who had prospered, one a Wall Street financier and entrepreneur. One had been a governor, and one a mayor; but no Member of Ford's Cabinet was there through political influence. In brains and breadth of experience, no Cabinet since comes even close.

Without warning, at the outset of his first full year as President, Ford was confronted with a critical situation that imperiled national security and his responsibilities as Commander in Chief. The Central Intelligence Agency—every President's prime source of foreign intelligence to safeguard America—was attacked on three fronts. Within weeks, the CIA was battling for survival as an effective agency.

The assault began on December 22, 1974, when the *New York Times* published an article charging that the CIA had illegally spied on American citizens in the United States. The nine-column *New York Times* story written by Seymour Hersh was short on specifics, but long on anonymous sources. Nevertheless, the essence was valid. One example cited in the article was that the CIA had been indirectly involved in President Nixon's order to break into the office of Daniel Ellsberg's former psychiatrist. Another was that President Johnson had ordered the CIA to conduct surveillance and tap the telephones of some Americans protesting the Vietnam War. The charges were serious, possibly criminal, because the National Security Act of 1947, which created the CIA, prohibited the agency from collecting intelligence on Americans within the United States.

With President Ford on Christmas holiday in Colorado, National Security Council Director Kissinger, on duty in the White House, immediately grilled CIA Director William Colby to find out what had happened. Kissinger's report revealed that in May 1973, when investigators probing the break-in at Watergate revealed possible links with the CIA, James Schlesinger, then Director, ordered all CIA departments to report to him any involvement by the agency in Watergate. Suspecting other CIA misdeeds, Schlesinger ordered every agency officer to report anything and everything the agency had done beyond its legal charter. Two months later, when Colby succeeded Schlesinger as CIA Director, he continued the internal investigation. Completed, the CIA's self-examination covered twenty-seven years. Condensed, it ran to seventy pages of questionable activities and outright violations of American law.

This Pandora's box of improper and illegal activities was characterized as "the family jewels" inside the CIA and locked in a safe. Inexplicably, Colby took this package of evidence of CIA wrongdoing out of the safe and handed it over to the Senate and House committees overseeing intelligence. Inevitably, in time, someone in Congress, a Member or a staffer, leaked part of Colby's report—to Hersh, as it happened. Hersh talked with Colby and confirmed that CIA had in fact spied on Americans. The *New York Times* printed Hersh's story.

Colby's aberrant action in giving CIA secrets to Congress without a President's approval was at best an incomprehensible lapse of judgment by so high and trusted an official; at worst, perfidious. By law, the CIA is an executive agency, directly responsible to the President's National Security Council. Colby had disclosed top-secret information not merely without authority, but also without even informing NSC Director Kissinger that he had done so.

In Colby's mind, he was not bound by the National Security Act of 1947. In his memoirs Colby wrote: "In 1975 the center of power had moved to Congress." He was, he said, "guided by the Constitution [to] educate the Congress, press, and public." His premise was unfounded: the Constitution does not mention the CIA.

Ford was surprised at Colby's effrontery; he had come to respect the CIA Director. "He was a good briefer," Ford said. "Very factual. NSC meetings would usually begin with Colby giving a CIA report on what the facts were. An analysis of where we stood. What the latest information was."

After he found out the degree to which Colby had endangered the CIA, Ford would have been fully justified in dismissing him. But that would have inflamed the attacks by the CIA's enemies. Instead, Ford decided the immediate and more important responsibility was to defend the CIA as an agency essential to national security. "CIA abuses were being brought forth in the press and in Congress," Ford said, "I could not leave sole jurisdiction up to Congress. I felt that we had to take the initiative to first, get the facts about how the CIA might have violated its charter and second, make certain it did not happen again."

After discussion with Rumsfeld, Marsh, Kissinger, and Scowcroft, Ford decided to appoint a blue-ribbon, bipartisan commission with unprecedented power to investigate the CIA. Ford's charge to the commission: Probe the CIA's most secret actions. Find out and report what the agency had done that was wrong. Recommend changes that would keep the CIA within the bounds of U.S. law.

This Presidential commission, appointed on January 4, 1975, was experienced, diverse, and distinguished. Ford designated Vice President Rockefeller—a factor in intelligence before World War II, and after—as Chairman.[2] Serving with him were General Lyman Lemnitzer, former Chairman of the Joint Chiefs of Staff; Erwin Griswold, former Dean of the Harvard Law School and President Johnson's former Solicitor General; Douglas Dillon, President Kennedy's Secretary of the Treasury; Ronald Reagan, former Governor of California; John T. Connor, President Johnson's Secretary of Commerce; Lane Kirkland, President of the AFL-CIO; and Edgar Shannon, President of the University of Virginia. The collective probity of this group guaranteed that the investigation would be no whitewash.

No sooner had Ford acted to defend the CIA than both Houses of Congress opened attacks on the agency. The Senate voted 82-4 to create a Select Committee to expose wrongdoing by intelligence operatives. Senator Frank Church sought and won the chairmanship; he saw exposing the CIA as a way to advance his Presidential ambition. He announced his committee's conclusion even before his investigation be-

---

2. Before and during World War II, Rockefeller provided office space in Rockefeller Center, and clandestine assistance, to William Stephenson, code-named Intrepid, master spymaster for the British.

gan: the CIA was, he said, "a rogue elephant out of control." His fellow Senator, Walter Mondale, referred to the agency as "those bastards."

Not to be outdone with so promising an opportunity for press and public attention, the House created its Select Committee on Intelligence. The Chairman, Representative Otis Pike, was directed to inquire "into the organization, operations, and oversight of the intelligence community of the United States Government." By definition, "the intelligence community" includes all U.S. agencies that pursue and collect information related to national security—the CIA, the Defense Department and each of the military services, the FBI, the State Department, the Secret Service, the National Security Agency, the satellite photograph and mapping agency, among others.

The two committees differed in focus: The Church Committee targeted individuals in the CIA—Who were the bad guys? Who broke the law? Pike concentrated on organization, issues, and policy. "Why," he asked repeatedly, "do we need a CIA and a DIA? Why do we have two agencies that have duplicate responsibilities?"

Although focused on intelligence, these Congressional inquiries also reflected the changing balance of power in Washington. During World War II and the derivative wars in Korea and Vietnam, the President had outpowered Congress. The Vietnam experience prompted the beginning of an emerging assertion of Congress' authority over the Federal system. For example, Congress passed the Freedom of Information Act to reduce executive departments' power to hide information; and the War Powers Act, enacted in 1973, limited a President's authority to send American troops into combat without Congressional approval.

President Johnson's failed leadership in war and Nixon's criminal cover-up of Watergate had further diminished the Presidency. Then, in 1974, Democrats swept the off-year elections, sending a record forty-nine new Members to the House of Representatives. Well organized, intent on avenging the political crime of Watergate, committed to imposing a liberal agenda, this freshman class shifted the balance of power within the House and beyond.

With both the Church and Pike committees competing for public attention, the risk mounted that one or both would expose vital information. Counting members and staff of the two committees, some 200 persons on Capitol Hill had keys to the CIA's "family jewels." All, moreover, had full access to CIA's current and recent activities, for Colby had been collaborating with Congress' probes of the CIA, and had told Church and Pike that he would continue to do so. And Colby ordered senior CIA officers to suspend their oaths to keep CIA secrets and testify freely before the Congressional committees.

Opening the CIA's brimming file cabinets to public view in Congressional hearings could disable or destroy the effectiveness of the early warning system that informs the President and protects the nation. In intelligence, secrecy is essential. All governments spy. Some, like the United States, admit it. CIA officers live in shadows and work in peril. The vital information that they collect—by spying, eavesdropping, tapping telephones, penetrating e-mails, bribing foreign officials, coercing sources—is necessarily hidden from public view. The intelligence they collect could become useless if exposed. Moreover, what a spy learns may show how he contrived to get the information, and that could put the CIA officer and his or her source at risk of being exposed—or killed.

To Ford and to his national-security staff in the White House, the danger was clear. "The President was determined to protect the CIA from potential destruction by the Congressional inquiries," Michael Duval, a special assistant to the President for intelligence wrote in his assessment at the time. "He felt that abuses had occurred and should be identified, corrected, and steps taken to prevent their reoccurrence. He believed that the 'lynch mob' mood in Congress could result in the virtual destruction of our intelligence community and he was determined to prevent this."

Colby's collaboration with the Congressional enemies of the CIA magnified the danger. Until Colby, Kissinger wrote, "no CIA Director had ever advanced the proposition that he had the unilateral right to determine what intelligence information could be made public, even less that he had a responsibility to interpret Constitutional principles on his own."

Ford warned Congress to be careful. Speaking to a joint session he said: "In a world where information is power, a vital element of our national security lies in our intelligence services. They are essential to our Nation's security in peace as in war . . . It is entirely proper that this system be subject to Congressional review. But a sensationalized public debate over legitimate intelligence activities is a disservice to the Nation and a threat to our intelligence system. It ties our hand while our potential enemies operate with secrecy, with skill, and with vast resources." Avoid, he concluded, "crippling a vital national institution."

His appeal made little difference. The two committees disclosed some abuses. They found evidence that President Kennedy and Attorney General Robert Kennedy had authorized plots to assassinate Castro in Cuba, Lumumba in Congo/Zaire, Trujillo in the Dominican Republic, and Ngo Dinh Diem in Vietnam. One committee also implied, without evidence, that the CIA had been involved in the killing of an army general in Chile. But both the Pike and Church committees unaccountably and unwisely revealed far more U.S. intelligence successes. Among them was information that U.S. submarines had tapped Soviet undersea cables and learned the results of their long-range missile tests. Intercepts made it possible to record Soviet leaders' telephone conversations. The *Glomar Explorer* had raised parts of a sunken Soviet submarine from the deep Pacific. One leak was fatal: a committee staffer gave the names of CIA officers to publications that printed the list, exposing the CIA station chief in Greece; as a result, he was assassinated.

"Frank Church and Otis Pike, with their headline seeking committees, were just running wild up there," Ford said later. "The Church investigation, particularly, was having a devastating impact on the morale of the CIA." Department heads feared losing their cover. Good men were resigning. The British and West German intelligence agencies were becoming alarmed that their cooperative exchanges of information with the CIA would be exposed. "I was on more than one occasion warned that a continuation of the activities of the Congressional investigating committees would dry up our sources abroad," Ford said.

In contrast to Congress' playing to the press, the Rockefeller Commission worked behind closed doors, meeting regularly in the Vice President's Conference Room in the Executive Office Building. Commissioners interrogated Colby; former Directors John McCone, Richard Helms, and James Schlesinger; counterintelligence legend James Angleton, and other CIA officials, past and present. They examined agency files, probing, evaluating, and negotiating the language of their findings. Governor Reagan, commission counsel Peter Wallison recounted, turned out to be most adept at fashioning language that all commissioners could accept. "How did you learn how to write so well?" Rockefeller asked him one day. "Labor negotiations," Reagan replied.

After five months of intensive investigation and deliberation by staff and members, the Rockefeller Commission published its 299-page report. Their document disclosed to the public only a part of what Members found, but enough to show that the CIA had repeatedly broken laws.

In the 1950s the CIA had opened mail in New York City, Miami, San Francisco, and Hawaii. Attorney General Robert Kennedy had ordered the CIA to tap the telephone lines of three newsmen to learn their sources. In the 1960s, by President Johnson's order, the CIA infiltrated peace groups opposing the Vietnam War and tapped the telephones of left-wing radicals. At the direction of President Nixon, CIA agents infiltrated the Black Power Movement, and investigated radical student groups and draft evasion movements.

Probing the Watergate break-in, the Rockefeller Commission confirmed that no one at the CIA knew in advance about the planned burglary. While it was well-known that former CIA employees—Howard Hunt and others—had been involved, no one working for the CIA at that time had taken part in the crime. Nixon's counsel, John Dean, had asked the agency to pay the salaries and bail for the jailed Watergate burglars, but CIA Deputy Director Vernon Walters turned him down. In the end the commission completely cleared the CIA on Watergate: "There was no evidence that officers of the Agency joined in the cover-up conspiracy of the White House staff, or in any way impeded the FBI investigation of Watergate."

As part of its responsibility, the Rockefeller Commission also investigated the recurrent rumors, persistent for a decade, that the CIA had in some way been involved in President Kennedy's assassination. Random skeptics advanced two theories: one, that Howard Hunt and Frank Sturgis had personally taken part in the crime; two, that Lee Harvey Oswald and Jack Ruby had CIA connections. The commission questioned both Hunt and Sturgis at length. Hunt presented evidence that he had been working with the CIA in Washington on November 22, 1963, the day of the assassination. Sturgis brought forward witnesses who confirmed he had been in Miami on that day. Members accepted the testimony that neither had been in Dallas at that infamous hour.

Although no responsible entity had ever found evidence of a CIA connection to Oswald or Ruby, commission lawyers interrogated witnesses who professed to believe that there had been such a connection. No witness came forward with evidence. The commission concluded that the accusations of a CIA connection to Oswald or Ruby were "far fetched speculation . . . a strained effort to draw inferences of conspiracy from facts which not would not fairly support the inferences."

With the Rockefeller Commission report confirming CIA abuses and recommending changes, and the continuing Congressional focus on intelligence, Ford saw that the situation presented a rare, if not unique, opportunity. It would not be enough to correct mistakes; this, he believed, would be the time to examine the operations and methods of the entire intelligence community. This was the time to reorganize, define responsibilities, eliminate duplication, improve management, strengthen the effectiveness of all the intelligence agencies. For twenty years, Ford had seen these agencies innovate and proliferate. As a Congressman and thereafter, he had been informed of technological breakthroughs in signals intelligence, in electronic surveillance, and in communications. Yet at no point had anyone in government taken an inventory of all the multifarious intelligence activities and assessed the logic and mission of their operations. With an Executive Order, Ford could impose order, set borders. In doing so, he hoped to preempt impulsive action and unwise restrictions by the House and Senate.

Ford was looking ahead. He felt it was his responsibility to ensure the capability of the CIA and the other intelligence agencies as essential to national security, not only to inform him during his Presidency, but also to be there for future Presidents. "We had to get rid of some of the organizations in the intelligence community and make necessary reforms," Ford said. To get it done, he put his trusted get-it-done counselor, Jack Marsh, in charge.

It was a formidable assignment. Marsh would have to open up the deepest secrets of agencies sworn never to reveal or discuss secrets. He must invade the closed dominions of four Cabinet officers—Defense, State, Treasury, Energy—and the directors of CIA, NSC, NSA, and OMB. He must placate and negotiate with the Church and Pike committees in Congress. He must propose changes in agencies' responsibilities; take power and money from some, transfer it to others. Not least, he must make certain that all U.S. intelligence collection be accomplished in accord with Constitutional process and U.S. laws.

To President Ford, Marsh had the professional qualifications and the judicious temperament for the task. A veteran of World War II, Marsh had dealt with national-security issues during his four terms as a Democratic Congressman from Virginia, and had served two years as an Assistant Secretary of Defense. In the House he had earned the respect of the leaders of both parties, not only for his record in national security affairs, but also for his knowledge of the Constitution and his courage in standing up for its principles. Skilled in negotiation, resolute by nature, indefatigable in carrying out a mission, Marsh had often demonstrated to Ford that he could handle the most sensitive and demanding of Presidential assignments.

Not everyone in the White House agreed with Ford's choice. Kissinger argued that his National Security Council was the most logical entity to reform the intelligence agencies. Vice President Rockefeller went in to the Oval Office to support Kissinger's claim on the assignment. Ford turned both down. He was well aware that Kissinger had enemies on Capitol Hill; Marsh had none.

To manage the operation, Ford created the Intelligence Coordinating Group (ICG), chaired by Marsh and including the Secretaries of Defense and State, the CIA Director, Attorney General Levi, and White House Counsel Phil Buchen. Tackling his assignment, Marsh said: "The first problem we ran into was cultural. We were dealing with highly competent, well trained professionals who had spent their lives protecting the secrets of their activities, their methods, and their results, as they had sworn to do." Even in the secure and well-guarded Situation Room in the West Wing, even though all attendees were under Presidential orders to disclose everything about what their departments and agencies were doing, their responses were often hesitant, reluctant.

Meeting three times weekly, sometimes more often, the Marsh team probed, interrogated, and searched for answers. They found differences at the highest level of Cabinet officers and agency directors over jurisdiction, territory, and authority. "Discussions were never acrimonious but civil and respectful, often clinical in arguing a case," Marsh said. At Marsh's direction, his deputy, Michael Duval, conferred with Robert McNamara, McGeorge Bundy, Theodore Sorensen, and other former national-security veterans, looking for suggestions on improving the collection, presentation, control, and use of intelligence.

The ICG's task was complex and unprecedented. To compound their difficulties, the Church, Pike and other Congressional committees constantly intruded. "They were hitting NSC and State with subpoenas for information," Marsh said. "We were fighting for our lives not only to protect against disclosure of secret information, but also to protect Kissinger from being found in contempt of Congress. We had Congress making inroads into intelligence community information and then leaking it to the press." Members based their claims on a House rule that authorized any Member to demand any information from any Executive Department and, if he or she chose to do so, make it public. To Ford, this defied common sense and infringed on the independence of executive operations, so Marsh and Levi devised arguments to defend Ford's position.

The internecine struggle for primacy between the President and Congress on intelligence lasted for months. "It was one of the toughest jobs I ever had," Marsh said later. "We had to protect the intelligence agencies and the people who ran them. We had to coordinate all the responses of the intelligence community to the demands of the Hill and negotiate what information to give the Hill." They had to deal with Constitutional issues, such as the 1967 Supreme Court decision that defended an individual's right to hold a telephone conversation unless a court had authorized a wiretap. At the same time, they had to proceed with a very substantial reorganization of the intelligence community. "It was," Marsh said, "like teaching Sunday school in Hell."

Attorney General Levi played an essential role both in defending the Executive branch and in reorganizing the intelligence community. Softspoken, a good listener, Levi made the final judgments on what could be done legally, and what could not be done. "His intellect, combined with his grasp of the practical and his knowledge of the law, were such that no one could contest his judgment," Marsh said.

Together, Marsh and Levi put together for President Ford a series of options for reorganizing the entire intelligence community, with pro and con arguments for each change. Objective and precise, it ran to more than 200 pages. Ford studied this options notebook, discussed it at length with Marsh, Levi, Kissinger, Rumsfeld, Cheney, Scowcroft, and others, and made his decision: The changes that were imperative, he would make by executive order. The changes that were peripheral, he would ask Congress to legislate.

In Executive Order No. 11905, Ford first clarified the charter of the CIA. The purpose of the agency he made clear and far-reaching: collect and provide to the President and the NSC all foreign intelligence, throughout the world, relating to national security—political, economic, scientific, technical, military, geographic, and sociological—plus terrorist activities and narcotics traffic. He put a strict limit on covert operations: the CIA could conduct them only if authorized by the NSC and the President. Forbidden were assassination plots anywhere in the world, and spying or conducting electronic surveillance on Americans within the United States.

The Director of the CIA would continue to be the President's "primary adviser on foreign intelligence." He would be the CIA's spokesman to Congress; however, lest any future CIA Director be in doubt about allegiance, he or she would report to and be accountable to the President and the NSC—not to Congress.

The National Security Agency, by far the largest and most costly division of the broad intelligence community, was directed to continue to be responsible for signals intelligence. "Sigint" encompasses a vast and esoteric field: constellations of orbiting satellites and other visionary devices that listen to and record—everywhere in the world—transmissions by radio, television, radar, computers, e-mail, telemetry, and lesser known forms of communication. NSA's mission would remain global reconnaissance—on land, at sea, and in the air, twenty-four hours a day, every day of the year.

The Defense Intelligence Agency would collect military intelligence, through Defense attachés in embassies and by other means, for the Secretary of Defense, the Joint Chiefs of Staff, the Army, Navy, Marines, and Air Force. Not least among DIA responsibilities was to know the location and security of nuclear weapons in foreign countries.

In the intelligence field, the Federal Bureau of Investigation would be responsible for counterintelligence within the United States, with the specific charge to "detect and prevent espionage, sabotage, subversion, and other unlawful activities by or on behalf of foreign powers." A limit was placed on FBI wiretaps; they could be done only if authorized by the President and approved by the Attorney General.

The State Department, through its embassies, would openly collect political, economic, social, technical, and biographical information relating to U.S. foreign policy. The Department of the Treasury, also working in the open, would collect financial and monetary information. The Secret Service, part of Treasury, would continue its dual mission: safeguard U.S. currency, and guard, in person, the President, Vice President, and other U.S. officials, plus leaders of other countries visiting the United States. The Department of Energy would collect intelligence related to nuclear power plants and other installations related to nuclear and atomic energy.

To Ford, it was essential that he reaffirm the authority and responsibility of the National Security Council. The statutory members—himself, the Vice President, the Secretaries of State and Defense—would continue to guide and direct foreign intelligence, as well as serve as his closest advisers in all matters relating to military engagements and threats to national security. Ford's Executive Order made it clear: the director and staff of the NSC would be accountable to the President, and the President would be accountable to the country.

By using his Executive authority, Ford had accomplished the greater part of reforming all U.S. intelligence actions and enterprise. But some changes required new law. His first priority was to stop the Pike and Church committees' irrational leaks of vital intelligence secrets. In a written message to the House and Senate, Ford proposed a new law that would make it a crime for anyone in the government with access to intelligence secrets to "willfully and wrongfully reveal this information." Well aware that the press always claimed a First Amendment right to print any and all secrets, Ford emphasized that the law he proposed would not affect a reporter publishing a leak, but only the person who disclosed a secret. As a corollary, Ford proposed that Congress replace the separate House and Senate oversight committees and staff with a Joint Foreign Intelligence Oversight Committee. Fewer members and smaller staffs would lessen the risk of leaks, he said. Ford also asked Congress to ratify with a new law his prohibition against assassinating a foreign official in peacetime.

As it turned out, the 94th Congress passed none of the laws that Ford recommended.

From the perspective of history, it can be argued that Ford saved the CIA. Not from extinction, and not from being battered. As Kissinger wrote, "The cumulative damage to the intelligence community lasted a long time. Having been so thoroughly dissected and occasionally ridiculed in the full glare of publicity, the CIA was stripped of its mystique of competence, reliability, and self-assurance so important to its mission." Some members of the Church and Pike committees had set out to expose and destroy the CIA. By acting promptly and responsibly, Ford had countered the two committees and deflected Congress from ravaging the agency. Had Ford not intervened when he did, and as he did, the CIA would have been so stripped of merit and credibility that it might have ceased to be the prime asset to the nation's security that it had been, and would still prove to be.

Ford's action was an example of leadership, of statecraft. He had turned a crisis into an accomplishment that has stood the test of time. The intelligence reforms and reorganization that he imposed have, with minor exceptions, been followed by every President since.

CHAPTER 19

Ford's Way

When President Ford appointed me to be Assistant to the President for Domestic Affairs and Executive Director of the Domestic Council, I did not know him well. That changed. I never met anyone so easy to like, or so comfortable with who he was. He was a man contented. He envied no one, wanted for no attribute or asset he did not have. Self-esteem was part of his character, yet matched by a deep and genuine humility. He was driven by principle, not ego. He knew his reach and he knew his limits. He liked being Jerry Ford. He was at peace with himself.

Ford's temperament was remarkably well suited to the office. He was cheerful, good humored, open, mentally alert, physically strong. In crisis he was calm, resolute. With his easy grin and ingrained optimism he radiated self-assurance. He was invariably curious—about people, problems, situations, issues, crises. He listened. He read, purposefully and prodigiously. He studied. He asked the right question. His inquiry was pragmatic: How does this affect the guy in a hardware store in Grand Rapids? He welcomed advocates with strong views, always making sure he heard from those who differed with him. He respected every opinion. He learned. He remembered.

Visitors, whether staff or outsiders, he quickly put at ease. He rarely kept anyone waiting. Quintessentially punctual, Ford believed a visitor's most precious asset, and his own, was time. After a warm handshake, Ford would get down to business. He was easy to talk to. He welcomed facts, statistics, reason, logic, good arguments. He expected brevity, conciseness. He would ponder for a moment, give his answer, and the visit was over. He allowed no one to waste his time in idle talk.

Equanimity ruled in President Ford's office. I never saw him anxious or rattled. Vexed he could become, particularly when, right in front of him, his staff engaged in petty squabbling. Ford rarely lost his temper, but when he did, it was unforgettable. Once, in the Cabinet Room, when rival factions of speechwriters were haggling over inconsequential speech points, Ford slammed that big left fist down so hard that the top of the Cabinet table seemed to bounce six inches off its base.

At least half of a President's job is office work, and at that, Ford excelled. Every major problem in the world that cannot be solved elsewhere lands in the Oval Office in-box. As President, Ford spent most of his time at his desk, and there he was at his best, studying position papers, discussing a problem with advisers, weighing alternatives, meeting Congressmen. My favorite portrait of President Ford shows him at that desk, head down, glasses glinting in the sun coming through the bulletproof window behind him. He is reading.

Ford's ability to concentrate was extraordinary. Observing him at work or on the tennis court, you saw that he had an innate ability to focus on the subject at hand and block out all distractions. His attention in a meeting never lagged. Marsh once remarked on how one morning Ford immersed himself in a national-security crisis for one hour, engaged in a critical economic discussion in the Roosevelt Room for the next hour, then chaired a complex legislative discussion with House leaders in the Cabinet Room the next hour—and never lost concentration on the problem at hand.

I once asked the President how he managed to compartment his mind. "I always had that capability to a degree," he said. "In high school I had to learn to concentrate on my academics and play three sports—football, basketball, and track. I never fretted on the football field about my academics, and vice versa. So I learned that particular discipline back then, and it became better tuned as I went along in life. At Michigan I had classes, football, managing the fraternity house. If you don't separate things, you screw up everything. At law school I scheduled classes in the early morning, met with the Yale football squad from 10 to 12, attended class from 1 to 3, coached on the football field from 3:30 to 6, and then I had to study at night. In addition I was courting Phyllis against heavy competition. With that kind of schedule, I couldn't get behind. Even more so when I went on the Warren Commission, and still had all those House committees."

In the White House, Ford filled every day, rising early, sometimes having a swim, usually arriving in the Oval Office before 8:00. After a full schedule, he would normally leave his desk at 7:30 or so in the evening for dinner in the residence with Betty. After dinner he sat in their living room for hours with his homework, reading and marking briefing papers. "He was a workhorse," Rumsfeld said. "He never complained about the stacks and stacks of material we gave him to read."

Working hard was Ford's way. He had always done so. His parents expected that; his teachers and coaches expected that. He grew up expecting it of himself. Boy and man, Ford epitomized the Grand Rapids virtues—hard work, honesty, trustworthiness, enterprise, self-reliance. The habits he learned early in life he never lost.

In making judgments Ford was careful, thorough, and deliberate—never impulsive. If, on reading a decision paper, no option satisfied him, he would call in the responsible staff and work out a better recommendation. Always, he looked for the practical answer, knowing from long experience in democratic government that all decisions are compromises, that no solution is perfect. Once he heard the pros and cons from those most knowledgeable and responsible, Ford made his decision, snd stuck with it. He never second-guessed himself.

Ford was at his worst before a television camera—his plain, midwestern voice coming across as stolid, often dull; he lacked flair, charisma. With Ford, the smaller his audience, the more impressive he was—an uncommon trait in public life. Over time his public speaking and his responses at press conferences improved, but he never mastered the all-seeing media.

Ford lacked showmanship, and in this age of imagery, showmanship is the other half of the Presidency. The White House is a stage, the main attraction in the best-attended theater in the United States; indeed, the world. Since every President is expected to perform, and perform well, that part of the job calls for an actor. Presidents Roosevelt, Kennedy, and Reagan—they knew how to act. Truman, Johnson, and Ford could only play themselves, roles not always to their benefit.

In surroundings that invite arrogance, Ford never lost his down-to-earthiness. He stopped military bands from introducing him with the traditional and vainglorious "Hail to the Chief." He considered the customary ruffles and flourishes pretentious. As his signature music, Ford preferred the Michigan football team's spirited fight song. He asked for no historic desk in his Oval Office. Ford simply sat down at the desk that was already there. He did change the official designation of the house where he lived: to him, it was no longer "the mansion," just "the residence." He vetoed a bill Congress sent him that would have named the Federal Office Building in Grand Rapids for him; he told Congress that naming a building for a President in office would set a bad precedent.

Ford's shipmates in World War II told of his self-discipline and courage under fire. In Sacramento, when Secret Service Agent Larry Buendorf grabbed the Colt .45 automatic pistol and stopped Lynette Fromme from assassinating Ford, I observed his steadiness and calm from ten feet away. Other agents tried to hustle the President to safety, but he told them, "Slow down. Everything is all right." He proceeded with dignity to his scheduled meeting with Governor Jerry Brown and got right down to business, discussing California issues—offshore oil drilling, welfare, a crime bill Ford was proposing. At one point the President looked around at Hartmann and me to make sure someone was taking notes. After thirty minutes of a lively policy interchange, Rumsfeld came in and interrupted to deliver a brief report on the incident. Governor Brown seemed puzzled and asked what had happened. "Oh," Ford said, "someone had a gun in the park as I walked over here." Ford then spent half an hour greeting Brown's sister and staff, and—sticking to his schedule—addressed the California legislature. Not until Marine Helicopter One delivered us to the White House South Lawn that night did we find out how near Fromme had come to succeeding.

Working for President Ford, it did not take me long to see not only what a great man he was, but also how well he met his responsibility to lead the United States at that moment in history. The circumstances he inherited would have daunted a person less sturdy, less confident, less interested in the mundane, but vital, day-to-day business of governing. Ford knew from long experience how and why the Federal government operated as it did; how public need and Congressional politics and unfettered bureaucracies had combined to create an incomprehensible tangle of complex programs. In the House, Ford had excelled in his knowledge of how Americans were taxed and how their money was spent—wisely or otherwise. As President, he put this information to good use. No President, before or since, matched his knowledge of the Federal government, the Federal budget, and how Washington affected the American family. He knew what parts of the Federal system worked, and what parts did not, and why. He routinely applied this knowledge, and his understanding of the parts brought him more readily to see and manage the whole. This made Ford a far better President than most Americans realized at the time.

My appointment as Executive Director of the Domestic Council was both firmly supported and strongly opposed. In the week after his confirmation as Vice President in December, Rockefeller began pressing the President to name me to the post. Five months before, when Ford asked him to accept the Vice Presidency, Rockefeller had been ambivalent, but agreed in part because of a sense of duty, and in part because Ford promised him meaningful assignments—specifically that, in Ford's words, he would be "in charge of domestic policy." Remembering that assurance, Rockefeller presumed that his choice would head the Domestic Council.

Chief of Staff Rumsfeld opposed my appointment; he had his own candidate for the job. Moreover, in the intervening months between Rockefeller's nomination and confirmation, Rumsfeld had—at Ford's direction—put in place an increasingly effective White House staff organization and operation. Separating domestic policy, making it a separate division of White House operations, would be a serious mistake, Rumsfeld contended.

Making his case, Rumsfeld told Ford: "First, when you went out on the front lawn the night before you became President and announced that Kissinger would be your Secretary of State, in the minds of the American people you gave foreign policy to Kissinger. You gave away half of your Presidency. If you make Nelson Rockefeller your czar for domestic policy, you've given away the Presidency. Second, it would be a mistake politically. You are more conservative than Vice President Rockefeller. My impression of the Republican Party is that it would not be enamored if you turned over domestic policy to Vice President Rockefeller. Third, having worked in a White House, it is clear to me that there is no way in the world that any Vice President is going to be present sufficiently to serve as a staff coordinator," Rumsfeld said.

"I respect that the Vice President is enthusiastic and wants to be involved. But he has such a multiplicity of tasks—presiding over the Senate, advising on foreign policy, investigating the CIA, traveling in the U.S. and abroad—that he can't deal with the day-to-day work of the Domestic Council. He will not have time to sit in on staff meetings, to consult with Congressional relations or the legal shop or the press office." Relying on his White House experience and his best judgment, Rumsfeld told the President: "It won't work. It. Will. Not. Work."

Rumsfeld's argument was hard to refute. Domestic policy is a President's job. As he cannot delegate national security, he also cannot hand off the substantive and political decisions that affect Americans' everyday lives, fortunes, and well-being.

What had happened in August? Ford, new to the job by a week and a day, had erred in promising domestic policy to Rockefeller if he accepted the Vice Presidency. Rockefeller had erred in dismissing the prescient advice that Bill Ronan, his oldest and best adviser, had given when Ford asked Rockefeller to consider the appointment: Ronan had warned Rockefeller that Cabinet members, OMB, and White House staff had their own responsibilities, their own power, and could use that power to contest any Rockefeller domestic initiative. "The President cannot give you a free hand in domestic policy," Ronan told Rockefeller. Relying on Ford's assurance, Rockefeller rejected Ronan's advice.

Confirmed as Vice President in December, Rockefeller expected that Ford would immediately assign him responsibility for domestic affairs, but Ford demurred. He had come to realize that Rumsfeld was right, that making the decisions in domestic policy was central to his responsibility. The decision was Ford's; Rockefeller blamed Rumsfeld.

At one point Rockefeller read what he believed to be a Rumsfeld draft demeaning his responsibilities, and Rockefeller erupted in anger. "I've been around government a long time," he said. "I know when I'm undercut by an underling. I'm going to see the President!" The differences between Rockefeller and Rumsfeld began over White House staff organization but withered into persistent and open conflict. As Jerry Jones observed, "The two were heavyweights, going fifteen rounds."

Finally, on February 13, 1975, Ford made a split decision. At a political dinner in New York City honoring Rockefeller, Ford announced that Rockefeller would "oversee" the work of the Domestic Council and "assist me in carrying out my responsibilities for . . . domestic policy." On that point, Rumsfeld won; Rockefeller would not be in charge of domestic policy.

In that same speech President Ford announced that he would appoint me as Executive Director of the Domestic Council; on that point, Rockefeller won.

The next round went to Rumsfeld: for day-to-day activities, the Domestic Council and I would report to Chief of Staff Rumsfeld and continue to be an integral part of Rumsfeld's organization and staff.

Defining its role, Ford assigned the Domestic Council four responsibilities: "First, assessing national needs and identifying alternative ways of meeting them; second, providing rapid response to Presidential needs for policy advice; third, coordinating the establishment of national priorities for the allocation of available resources; fourth, maintaining a continuous policy of review of our ongoing programs and, as we look down the road, proposing reforms as we need them."

Flying back to Washington, Rockefeller was exuberant. He had his choice as Director of the Domestic Council, and he was excited about Ford's assignment of responsibilities to the Council—"assessing national needs . . . policy advice . . . coordinating priorities . . . proposing reforms . . ." To Rockefeller, Ford's speech constituted a mandate for him to pursue what he liked most and did best in government: identify public needs and initiate programs to meet those needs.

For thirty-five years, Rockefeller had started any new assignment by recruiting able people, and so it was with the Domestic Council. "Our first priority," Rockefeller told me that night, "will be to put together the best staff in the White House, better even than Henry's. So we'll start by getting rid of everyone now on the staff, and by my assigning you three people: Dick Dunham, Dick Parsons, and Art Quern."

No gift in all of Rockefeller's extensive holdings could have exceeded that one. All three were experienced craftsmen of government. All three were incomparably able and dependable. Dunham, then 46, my first deputy, was both a scholar and practitioner of government. He had an outstanding record at the University of Rochester, then earned his master's in government at the University of Michigan's School of Public Service. After a two-year assignment by the U.S. State Department to serve as fiscal and economic adviser to the government of Cambodia, Dunham joined New York State's Budget Division. There he rose steadily on his performance, moving up through the ranks to become Budget Director, the state's most powerful civil servant. As chief financial officer of the multi-billion-dollar operations of New York State, Dunham dealt daily with the Washington bureaucracy that ran the myriad Federal programs that both benefited and burdened the state. Going into the White House, Dunham's assets matched his responsibilities: he knew economics, finance, and government operations.

Parsons, then 27 years old, was in the first stage of a meteoric career in law and business. A Brooklynite by birth, he grew up in Queens. "Wanderlust"—his word—took him to the University of Hawaii where he enjoyed the sun, played basketball, and excelled in the classroom. For his legal education Parsons moved on to the little-known but rigorous Albany Law School, a training academy for public life. There again he excelled, and later had the highest score of all the thousands who took the New York State bar exam. Recruited as a junior counsel to Governor Rockefeller, Parsons demonstrated his formidable talents—intellect and self-confidence, precision in reasoning, and an unerring sense of judgment.

The anchorman of this trio was Arthur Quern. Brooklyn-born, "and proud of it," Quern had in his youth considered becoming a Catholic missionary, but decided instead to study history at St. John's University. Working his way through college, he sorted punch cards for Rheingold's brewery and rode shotgun on beer trucks. During the Vietnam War he enlisted in the Army and was assigned to intelligence schools. There he learned to assess information, evaluate sources, and compose a succinct report. After the Army, Quern enrolled in graduate school at the State University of New York, Albany. A chance acquaintance, a senior adviser to Governor Rockefeller, was so impressed by Quern that he persuaded him to apply for a job on the Governor's staff. Alton Marshall, Rockefeller's always decisive chief of staff, took one look at Quern and said, "Welcome aboard!" Rockefeller, impressed by Quern's skill in analyzing complex education and environmental issues, promoted him to manage New York State's Washington office.

In the Ford White House, Quern, then 33 years old, demonstrated the mind of a scholar, the patience of a priest, and the get-it-done qualities of a rising corporate executive. Versatile, self-effacing, imperturbable, he could crisply clarify an issue, moderate among advocates, inspire subordinates, and write a one-page analysis that required no editing. By sheer merit and temperament—wisdom matched his affable nature—Quern became counselor and mentor of the Domestic Council staff.

From the beginning, the four of us knew we must rise from the level of our New York State experiences to a new dimension of responsibility. Reflecting, years later, Quern said, "The turmoil of the times, the uncertainties following Nixon, the Ford succession, the economic recession, the public disillusion about the Federal government, and the disillusion *within* the Federal bureaucracy—we knew we were getting into big challenges. But we did not realize the variety and the depth of the issues we would have to deal with."

My initiation as a Presidential assistant began on my first appearance in the White House. On the morning after my appointment, I was summoned by Rumsfeld to his 8:00 a.m. senior staff meeting, but I had no idea what to expect. Entering the Roosevelt Room, I found a vacant chair halfway down the long table. Rumsfeld, at the head of the table, began calling on each staff member for a report. In turn, Hartmann, Marsh, Scowcroft, Lynn, and Friedersdorf described briefly the issues and problems that he and his department would deal with that day. With each report my anxiety mounted. I knew nothing about what the Domestic Council would do that day. When it came my turn, I hesitated and stammered for a few moments until Rumsfeld interrupted. "You are obviously not prepared. This Vice President was said to have good staff people. Where are they?" His voice was curt, disdainful. "Don't you know what your job is? Get up to speed before you come in here. Next!"

Four or five other senior staff reported and the meeting ended. Dazed and humiliated, I sat for a moment while the others left. Budget Director Jim Lynn walked around the table, leaned over beside my chair, and said quietly, "Welcome to the NFL."

It was a memorable lesson: never again did I go into any White House meeting unprepared.

After that encounter I walked upstairs to my new office. This large, walnut-paneled room on the southeast corner of the second floor of the West Wing was then reserved for the Domestic Council Executive Director. Looking around at the tasteful, ready-for-business furnishings, I noticed by the couch a polished mahogany box, about one cubic foot in size, resting on slender, finely turned legs. Was this, I wondered, where they kept the tapes? Gingerly I lifted the lid. Inside was a bottle of liqueur, with the label "Bottled especially for John Ehrlichman." Holding the bottle in my hand, I said to myself: John began in this office as an honest man. Don't make the mistake that he did.

Replacing the liqueur bottle as a reminder, I telephoned Parsons and asked him to come over from his new office in the Executive Office Building. "Would you open that box, Dick?" I asked. He picked up the bottle and read the label.

"Dick," I said, "your first responsibility is to keep me out of jail."

"I can do that," Parsons said. "But I will need to have access to every meeting you have, every telephone call you make, and every document you sign."

"You have it, Dick. Everything that I do, say, or write is open to you. Your second responsibility is to be the chief counsel for everyone on the Domestic Council, to make sure that no one of us breaks a law. Or does anything that will bring discredit on the President or ourselves."

"I can do that," Parsons said. He did.

Parsons and I were still talking when Christy Valentine, an extraordinarily able young woman assistant I had inherited, brought in my first assignment. It was an eighteen-page document with a cover note from Rumsfeld: "Staff this out."

I knew what the phrase meant; Staff Secretary Jerry Jones had briefed me on the term. Jones was an engaging and briskly efficient young Texan, a Harvard MBA who managed the collection and flow of documents to President Ford's in-box. "The objective," Jones said, "is to subject every problem, issue, and initiative to a rigorous evaluation by every Cabinet officer, department head, and senior staff member with an interest in the issue. In particular the idea must be pitted against its natural enemies. Great ideas often turn out to be not such great ideas. The purpose is to make certain the President knows not only the merits in the subject at hand but also the flaws, and that he has the best judgment of each of his advisers before he makes his decision."

One glance at the document from Rumsfeld and I was startled. It was no routine proposal, but a high-level recommendation from the Vice President to the President. This put me on the spot; Rumsfeld was directing me to critique the work of my mentor and patron.

The subject was familiar: should Ford create a science adviser to the President? Some weeks before, Rockefeller had mentioned to me that President Ford had asked him to study the issue and make a recommendation. As was his way, Rockefeller had convened a group of distinguished scientists, such as Edward Teller, William O. Baker, and Hans Mark, to join him in developing a proposal. They had deliberated for weeks, completed their report, and sent it to Ford. Now Rumsfeld had turned over their considered recommendation to me for evaluation by at least three Cabinet officers and eight or so senior staff.

Rockefeller, I knew, would not like this. I also knew that I must inform him of the situation before someone else did, so I picked up the document, walked at once to the Executive Office Building and into his office where he was meeting with his staff. After they left I said, "Governor, as my first assignment I was given your recommendation to the President for a Science Adviser, and I have been instructed to staff it out."

As I expected, his pride was hurt. After a long silence, Rockefeller said: "If the President didn't want to follow my recommendation, why did he ask me to do it?"

Staffing out proposals to the President, I explained, would be part of the Domestic Council's responsibility. He shook his head, and suggested the process was—at least in this case—unnecessary, a waste of time. I promised that his proposal would be treated expeditiously and with respect. "This is Rumsfeld's doing," he said with a grim look. "He is trying to block the recommendation that the President asked me for." Suppressing his anger, he said: "Well, do your job."

Since this would be my first memorandum to the President, my next step was to go to the Oval Office for instructions. "Mr. President, how do you like your memoranda written?"

"You're the writer," he told me. "That's up to you. Nothing fancy, just good plain English. I like brevity, but at the same time I want to know all the facts. And everyone's opinion. So tell me where each person stands, and why he is for or against it. Include your own recommendation as well." After a pause he added, "Now, in this case, a group of scientists and several Members of the House are pushing me to create this office in the White House. Before I decide, I would like to know this: what did each previous Science Adviser to a President believe he accomplished? Find out and include that in your report."

Impressed by the clarity and common sense of Ford's instructions, I went to work. One unique advantage of working in the White House is that everyone accepts your telephone call. Dr. George Killian, President Eisenhower's first science adviser, told me that after Sputnik shattered Americans overconfidence in their missile and space program, he believed he helped reassure the American public. He and his successor, Dr. George Kistiakovsky, also proposed the creation of NASA, provided a sound scientific basis for the 1963 nuclear test ban treaty, and advanced the technique of photo reconnaissance by satellite. Dr. Jerome Wiesner, Kennedy's science adviser, advised on advanced weapons and used his influence to ban DDT around the world. "Improbably," Dr. Wiesner told me, "every time President Kennedy and I talked, we ended up with him asking me to explain how radio works. He would say, 'Jerry, how does my voice get from a microphone in this office to someone sitting by a radio in Boston?'"

President Johnson's science adviser, Dr. Donald Hornig, said he initiated studies of the environment and world hunger, but his opposition to the Vietnam War provoked such a stormy relationship with Johnson that he had little influence on policy. President Nixon clashed with his appointee, Dr. Edward David, also over Vietnam policy, dismissed him, and abolished the office.

In my action memo to President Ford, I summarized that the fifteen-year record indicated that "when a Presidential science adviser had a clear and specific objective within the President's broader goals, provided a wider range of solutions for the President, and kept his own ambitions and ego in check, he made great contributions to government and was a major political asset."

As options for President Ford, we proposed a one-person liaison with the scientific community, a single director of a scientific office with assistants, or a three-person council of scientific advisers with staff. President Ford read our report and decided to meet with the Congressional cadre of advocates before he made his decision. There he listened to all views, left the Cabinet room and called me into his office. "Jim, I am going to take the middle option, with this addition. I want the Congress to create this office by legislation. They will respect the office more if it is their initiative than if I create it by Executive Order. So call all the parties involved and tell them of my decision. Then, confirm it in writing. I learned a long time ago that when people meet with a President, they tend to hear what they want to hear."

Staffing out—this two-stage process of evaluating domestic issues—constituted a major share of our Domestic Council operations. We were the honest broker, defining the issue, stating the relevant facts, assembling opinions, and delivering a comprehensive and fair report to President Ford for his decision. We were, in addition, outposts for an early warning system. Since our staff exchanged information every day with Cabinet and sub-Cabinet members, we could anticipate problems developing in the domestic departments and agencies—and sometimes resolve them before they became problems. We were also an information bank for the President; we kept this storehouse current with daily updates to the President's 450-page, tabbed briefing book on domestic issues—complete with questions he might be asked, and suggested answers. Our Domestic Council staff met with constituents whose requests for a White House meeting did not warrant time with the President. We were responsible for liaison with governors, mayors, county executives, and state legislators. Consequently we were the point of White House contact for any governor or mayor caught in a hurricane or fiscal crisis. From time to time we rode up to Capitol Hill to meet with members of the House and Senate to advocate the President's programs.

To meet these and other impromptu assignments, we were budgeted for a staff of forty-five. For one half, the professional staff, we needed MBAs, lawyers, political operatives, educators, and generalists. Quern best described our goal: "Our experience in New York led us to look for a certain character, a profile, people who were going to work quietly, professionally, skillfully, knowledgeably. And be circumspect. We were not big ego people. None of us cared if anyone in the Washington press knew we were there."

The other half of the Domestic Council staff was already in place—highly qualified researchers and secretaries. They had served the country and were untainted by Watergate; we kept them. I also asked Dr. James Cavanaugh and Warren Hendriks to remain. I knew that we would need a couple of experienced hands who knew the players, process, and pitfalls of White House operations. A health-care economist, Dr. Cavanaugh's counsel was also invaluable in dealing with the early stages of an intractable domestic problem—the escalating costs of health coverage to Federal and state governments, and to an aging population. Hendriks, a former political advance man, proved to be an accomplished administrative assistant, his capabilities diverse and manifold.

The responsibility to dismiss the other Nixon holdover professional staff fell to me; recruiting of new Ford staff I assigned to Dunham. But first, I took the precaution of asking the President if we should clear proposed new hires with him or the White House personnel office. "No," he said. "You'll be working with them. You choose them."

Dunham set a high standard with his first recruits. Stephen McConahey, then 32 years old, was an honors graduate of the University of Wisconsin and the Harvard Business School. He had taken leave from a promising career at McKinsey and Company to serve a year as a White House Fellow, and another year to help set up the Urban Mass Transit

Agency in the Department of Transportation. We brought McConahey in at once and assigned him to work with Secretary Coleman and the Department of Transportation.

Cheney sent Dunham an excellent prospect. Paul Leach, then 29 years old, a Dartmouth graduate, with an MBA and a law degree from Stanford, was working in a venture capital firm in Chicago when a college fraternity brother, Henry Paulson, recounted how much he had enjoyed working in the early Nixon White House. Leach contrived with a Chicago friend of Rumsfeld to arrange a White House interview. Rumsfeld handed Leach off to Cheney, who sent him to Dunham. "Dunham and I hit it off right away," Leach said. Dunham made Leach his macroeconomic expert, and assigned him to cover Treasury, Commerce, and Agriculture.

Elliott Richardson recommended another promising young man, David Lissy. Phi Beta Kappa at Penn, honors graduate of Penn's law school, Lissy had—at 32 years old—served twice as a Cabinet Member's executive assistant, first at State, then at HEW. We brought Lissy in with dual responsibilities—to advise on education and to be the liaison with the Jewish community. To assist him, Lissy recruited another young man of great capability, William Diefenderfer, also a Penn Law graduate with experience on a House committee education staff.

From Rockefeller's New York State staff, we drafted George Humphreys and Kathleen Ryan. Humphreys, who starred as a fullback at George Tech and graduated with a degree in industrial management, turned out to be a natural as a political manager and government executive. From his job as Director of the New York City Office of Environmental Conservation, we hired him to be our expert on environmental issues and as liaison with the Department of the Interior. Ryan, a graduate of Georgetown's school of foreign service, had served as an assistant to Kissinger and as a policy adviser to Rockefeller. She was our expert on cultural affairs, and brought us her insightful wit and incomparable enthusiasm.

One day I had a call from Doug Bennett, the White House personnel chief. "There's a young woman in my office who graduated from Harvard Law and wants to work in the White House. Would you have any interest?" We did.

Judy Hope was personable and articulate, her credentials impeccable. One of 15 women who had graduated in a law class of 550 at Harvard in 1964, she had invested eleven years in both private law practice and public service. She told us: "I want to help President Ford. After the meltdown in government, I think anyone who has the ability to help should do so."

Dunham and I decided Hope was a person of talent and promise, though we had no immediate opening. So we retained her as a consultant and assigned her to research and writing.

Among the Nixon holdovers whom I had advised to look for other jobs, two—Glen Schleede and Tod Hullin—performed in limbo with such pluck and fidelity that I considered keeping them on the Ford staff. What do you think? I asked Dunham. "Well," he said, "Both were told they had lost their jobs, then worked even harder and very effectively for us. If you have no problem reversing yourself, let's keep them." We did, and both excelled—Hullin diligent and intuitive at HUD; Schleede indispensable as we dealt with energy and scientific issues.

One morning the President called me to his office and said: "I am making you responsible for renewing Revenue Sharing." I was surprised but complimented. Revenue Sharing had been one of Ford's proudest accomplishments as House Leader. A Republican initiative in 1972, Ford had mobilized a bipartisan coalition to pass a five-year program to distribute more than $26 billion in Federal money to states, cities, counties, and local governments, with no strings attached; they could use the Federal aid as they best saw fit. It was immensely popular at the grassroots level; 38,000 communities used the money to hire an extra policeman, renovate a children's park, buy a new fire truck, and improve the quality of community life. It was due to end on December 31, 1976.

President Ford remembered, he told me, that then Governor Rockefeller and I had worked closely with him in persuading thirty-four of the thirty-five Members of the New York State Congressional delegation to support the legislation. "It's time to renew Revenue Sharing, so let's get it done," the President said.

To accomplish this, I knew, would require a major campaign in Congress. We could count on the Republican minorities in the House and Senate. But this was a Democratic Congress that routinely scorned Ford's legislative proposals. The problem would be to persuade enough Democrats to win Revenue Sharing a second time.

By good fortune, I knew where to go for the right Democratic ally. I went back to my office and put in a call to Paul Myer.

A 31-year-old liberal Democrat, Myer had been a Congressional staffer and unusually effective lobbyist for the American Federation of State, County, and Municipal Employees Union. In 1972 he and I had spent months working together to pass Revenue Sharing, so I knew him to be a young master of legislative strategy. Moreover, Myer could count votes. And he could get votes. To make sure the Ford legislative staff could work with Myer, I checked him out with Max Friedersdorf. He knew Myer, respected him, and was confident that this likable Democrat could work side by side with the Ford legislative staff—Bill Kendall in the Senate; Charlie Leppert and Tom Loeffler in the House. This was important, since Myer would have to keep them informed of his actions. So I brought Myer in to the Domestic Council with the sole responsibility to extend Revenue Sharing.

Opposing us was one of the craftiest and most powerful Members of the House, Jack Brooks of Texas. As Chairman of the House Government Operations Committee, Brooks was the gatekeeper to the House legislative process. And he despised Revenue Sharing. The day we introduced a bill to extend the program, Brooks told the press: "We are going to do to Revenue Sharing what we do to rattlesnakes in Texas—kill 'em while they're young."

Undaunted, Myer systematically worked Capitol Hill, lining up Democratic votes one by one, moving steadily toward the numbers we needed. When he was certain we had the votes, Myer and I, with Friedersdorf to back us up, showed our House count to Ford. He accepted it as solid, so we asked him to invite Brooks to the White House and persuade him to open the legislative gates and let the House decide. After a histrionic performance by Brooks in the Oval Office, "It's lonely here at the foot of the cross, Mr. President," and a round of laughter, Ford recounted the merits of the program. For an hour the two bantered, with Ford emphasizing how communities across the land had benefited. Finally, Brooks agreed to permit Revenue Sharing to be brought to a vote. In the House Ford's bill passed on a key procedural vote by 233-172, and in the Senate by 77-4. For the second time, Ford delivered in Congress on Revenue Sharing. For Middle America, it was an even greater victory.

On February 6, 1976, an Army recruit stationed at Fort Dix, New Jersey, reported that he felt tired and weak; he died the next day. Within a week, twelve of his fellow soldiers reported the same symptoms and were sent to the hospital. Studying the cases, Army doctors found that the soldiers had been stricken by swine flu. Laboratory tests showed that the soldiers' strain of flu was similar to the Spanish flu that caused a pandemic in 1918. Then, one-fifth of the world's population was infected with the disease, and 675,000 Americans died, ten times the battle losses the United States suffered during World War I.

The ominous news from Fort Dix swiftly reached HEW Secretary Mathews, and he promptly informed Ford. The choices for Federal action, Mathews said, were both bad: we could expect the worst, anticipate a pandemic and act immediately to develop and manufacture a flu vaccine and inoculate millions of Americans; or we could wait and see if an outbreak occurred in autumn and act then. Either way, Mathews told Ford, "The Administration will be criticized. If there is no outbreak, we will be painted as alarmists who exaggerated the threat. If it does occur, there will inevitably be some glitches, and we will be charged with mismanagement." Mathews offered to take the responsibility, and the heat, for the decision.

"No," Ford said. "This is my responsibility. But before I make the decision, I want all the evidence available in the scientific community, pro and con. I want to hear from the leading health professionals."

In March, he did so. Some thirty public-health experts and scientists—including polio conquerors Jonas Salk and Albert Sabin—gathered in the Cabinet Room. One by one, Ford asked each for his judgment: what action should the Federal government take? The verdict was unanimous: the Administration should act immediately to develop a flu vaccine and inoculate millions of Americans. At the end of the meeting Ford made an unusual request. Aware that one or more of the experts might have hesitated to disagree in public with his peers, Ford said: "I will be in my office for thirty minutes. If any one of you has an opinion he wants to express privately, just tell the secretary outside my door that you want to see me." He waited, but no one came. So Ford immediately announced his decision and directed HEW to institute a nationwide immunization program.

The Domestic Council was handed the responsibility to work with Mathews and others at HEW, so we assigned Quern, Dr. Cavanaugh, and Sarah Massengale to the task. A graduate of Goucher with a master's in Urban Planning from the University of Virginia, Massengale had specialized in health-care policy at McKinsey and Company. On swine flu and other health issues, Massengale's performance was exemplary.

At best, it would take six months to develop and manufacture a flu vaccine. One immediate consideration was fertilized chicken eggs. Nobody knew whether there were enough roosters in the United States to fertilize the millions of eggs manufacturers would need as hosts for cultivating the vaccine. Quern called Secretary Butz and asked him for a rooster census. After a few days Butz called back and reported: "Yes, there are just enough loyal American roosters. They will meet the challenge."

At another point, the drug makers notified the White House that they must have indemnification from lawsuits in case some who were inoculated fell ill from the vaccine. We had sent a bill to Congress to do that, but no action had been taken. Cavanaugh went to Ford, and he immediately telephoned Tip O'Neill, the House Majority Leader.

"Tip, we need this bill. Can you move the House to act on it?"

"Let me see what I can do," O'Neill replied. He moved the bill through the House that afternoon, and the Senate promptly followed.

By August 100 million doses of vaccine were in production and 40 million Americans were vaccinated. One of the first was President Ford.

By good fortune, there was no flu pandemic in the fall of 1976. Looking back twenty years later, Ford said. "I had people urging me to take action and people urging me not to take action. I finally decided that the risk was the lesser on the positive side. It was a gamble, but it required action. I had no hesitancy. It was the right thing to do."

We were challenged by all our Domestic Council assignments—the diverse, the unexpected, the mundane, and the consequential. Andre Buckles, a special assistant in his twenties, stopped me in the Executive Office Building corridor one afternoon to suggest that we schedule a meeting with Ford to get his approval for the regulations for electronic transfers. What, I asked is an electronic transfer. "It's how banks will move money by computer," Buckles said.

Having never seen, much less operated, a computer, I said: "Andre, no bank is going to give someone money without a signed piece of paper. We can't take up the President's time with something that's not going to happen." Buckles persisted, pointing out that a Scotsman had invented an electronic machine to dispense money, so we set up the meeting with the President.

In the meantime my misgiving increased. I learned that Ford, in his early years as a lawyer, had represented a Grand Rapids bank. When we brought up electronic transfers, I expected we would be ridiculed. Neverthless, Buckles and the OMB regulations expert made their presentations. President Ford listened; he asked questions about the process, the provisions for passwords, and the reliability of the electronics and machinery. After forty-five minutes of discussion he said, "With the double coding you describe, and reliable machines, and careful supervision, it will work. Let's go ahead." The result was that Ford's action brought the United States the Automatic Teller Machine (ATM)—and the ATM became the most ubiquitous and efficient dispenser of cash in the country.

George Humphreys, our environmentalist, telephoned me one night to inform me that two New York congressman and the Environmental Protection Agency (EPA) had reported that Long Island's beaches were polluted by unsanitary trash washed up by wind and sea. Humphreys flew to the scene, arranged for a volunteer association of unemployed New York City teenagers to clean up the beaches, and—speaking for President Ford—stood by the Atlantic Ocean with the Congressmen to declare the beaches of Nassau and Suffolk counties clean and safe. Humphreys also persuaded Ford to commit, if elected, to doubling the number of national parks.

We defended sheep herders against coyotes. A bipartisan delegation of western Senators and Representatives, mostly enraged, met with Ford in the Cabinet Room to complain vociferously about EPA restrictions against poisoning coyotes. For a western shepherd, many of them Native Americans, a flock of sheep was his most precious asset. Sheepmen wanted to poison coyote pups in their dens, but EPA said no; the golden eagle would feed on the poisoned carcass and die. One solution, as Russ Peterson, chairman of the Council on Environmental Quality, suggested, was to buckle a protective girdle on the hindquarters of each lamb and ewe. To this, one irate western Congressman burst out: "Goddammit! The coyotes are not trying to screw the sheep; they're trying to eat them."

In an effort to reduce the noise of jet aircraft, we worked with Secretary Coleman to craft a Presidential Executive Order directing the industry to retrofit all old aircraft with new engines that used less fuel and made less noise. We negotiated with Congress to set standards for reducing auto emissions. We worked with Secretary Butz to carry out a Ford concept: food stamps should go to those who needed them, not to college students with well-to-do parents.

When Cheney told me one day that the Administration should define its policy on the status of Puerto Rico, I decided to dispense with staffing it out and just ask the President. "Well," he said, "I've always thought Puerto Rico should be given the opportunity to become a state. It's their choice. They should vote—to keep their present status as a territory, or become a separate nation, or apply for statehood. Check with State and Interior. If they have no problem, that's our policy." A prime example of Ford philosophy: let local governments decide.

My greatest disappointment came over the lost opportunity to lead the world in supplying fuel for nuclear power plants. At that time the United States was so far ahead in nuclear research and production that we had initially become the world's most reliable supplier of nuclear fuel. But we had closed the order books in 1974 because plant capacity was fully committed to supply more than a hundred new nuclear power plants scheduled to begin operation in the United States by the early 1980s. As Kissinger wrote at the time, "Not only are we losing significant nuclear trade, but the leverage that our nuclear position afforded us . . . in guiding non-proliferation efforts, has been weakened." With fuel available from the United States, small nations would have no reason to build their own plants, ostensibly to enrich uranium for electric power but possibly to convert some material for nuclear weapons.

The immediate issue for President Ford was how to expand a nuclear enrichment plant in Portsmouth, Ohio, to supply fuel for nuclear power plants. The Portsmouth plant, left over from World War II, was no longer needed for weapons, but with added capacity, this plant was ideally suited to produce enriched uranium fuel rods used in nuclear power plants. Ford decided to expand Portsmouth, not as a government plant, but to turn it over to private industry for development. This required Congressional action, so he sent up the Nuclear Fuel Assurance Act of 1975. In the House we won by one vote; in the Senate we lost by two votes. As a result, France and Russia became the world's chief suppliers of nuclear fuel. Looking back at the lost opportunity, Ford said: "The U.S. could have become to nuclear fuel what the Middle East was to oil."

CHAPTER 20

Initiatives

As the 41st Vice President of the United States, Nelson Rockefeller's prime ambition was to rise above the first Vice President's description of the job. It was, John Adams wrote, "the most insignificant office that ever the Invention of Man or his Imagination conceived." Rockefeller's experience in government, his energy, his upbringing, his pride, his temperament—not one of these would permit him to accept insignificance.

His accomplishments have been little recognized but one is historic: as President of the Senate, Rockefeller made rulings that resulted in changes to cloture, the process through which filibusters are halted. Instead of requiring two-thirds of Senators present to vote to close debate, sixty votes would be necessary. In a Senate that practices and reveres unlimited debate—and the more important the issue, the longer they talk—reducing potential roadblocks to the nation's business is significant.

Rockefeller did not act alone in making this change. In January 1975 a bipartisan coalition led by Senators Mondale and Pearson mobilized the votes to break from the past. What Rockefeller did as presiding officer was to clear the legislative path so that a well-organized Senate majority could make the change. In any history of meaningful advances in Senate procedure, changing Rule 22, the Senate rule governing cloture, will stand as one that made a difference.

Until 1917, the Senate had no way to limit debate. By filibustering—talking without stopping—one Senator could block a majority of the other ninety-five Senators from passing a bill or confirming a nomination, and often did. At the urging of President Wilson, the Senate adopted Rule 22, which provided that debate could be ended by a vote of two-thirds of Senators present and voting. Cloture was imposed for the first time in 1919, to end a filibuster against ratification of the Treaty of Versailles. Thereafter, for more than half a century, a faction of senators, primarily from the former Confederate states, needed no more than thirty-four votes to block civil-rights legislation.

In 1963, and again in 1971, a bipartisan majority of Senators organized to amend Rule 22, but both Vice President Lyndon Johnson and Vice President Spiro Agnew refused to make the parliamentary rulings necessary to change. At the opening of the 94th Congress in 1975, Senators Javits, Pearson, and other moderate Republicans convinced Rockefeller of the need to reform Senate rules, and he enthusiastically accepted the opportunity to be the instrument of change. He assigned his counsel, Richard Parsons, to plot his course through the maze of parliamentary rules he must follow as the Senate's presiding officer. Parsons created an ingenious chart—it resembled a railroad switching yard—that Rockefeller could follow and keep on track.

Out of courtesy, Rockefeller informed President Ford of his plan to initiate the reform in the Senate rules, but he deliberately did not ask for approval. Ford did not object; this, Ford told Rockefeller, is a decision to be made by the President of the Senate and Members. When Senator Tower and other conservative senators threatened retaliation against Ford and Rockefeller, that only fortified Rockefeller's determination; he had never yielded to his party's conservatives. As for Tower, the Vice President said: "Nobody threatens Nelson Rockefeller."

For nine weeks the Senate haggled over the issue, with Senator Allen of Alabama using the arcane rules of the Senate to filibuster the effort to change the filibuster. At one point, Rockefeller, fed up with Allen's repeated interruptions and delaying tactics, refused to recognize him—a gross violation of Senatorial courtesy for which Rockefeller later offered a superficial apology.

Initially the Senate Democratic leaders, Mike Mansfield and Robert Byrd, used their authority to preserve Rule 22, but their parliamentary maneuvers in defense of the rule were repeatedly defeated. Convinced that change was the will of the Senate, Mansfield and Byrd turned around and supported it. With their backing, it was done.

Rockefeller never considered his role in amending the Senate rules to be one of his notable accomplishments. When anyone complimented him for improving Senate procedure, his response was a shrug of dismissal. One reason was that he had mixed feelings about the Senate. He was proud that his maternal grandfather, Nelson Aldrich, had dominated the Senate at the turn of the twentieth century, but Rockefeller himself never wanted to be a Senator. In the service of five Presidents, Rockefeller had come to know the institution well; to him, the Senate was the most ineffective and inefficient arm of the Federal government.

To his credit, however, Rockefeller never neglected his duty to preside over the Senate. When called to break a tie, or chair a special event, he was always there; nor did he neglect his responsibilities as surrogate for President Ford. He journeyed abroad to attend the state funerals of King Faisal in Saudi Arabia, Chiang Kai-shek in Taiwan, and Francisco Franco in Spain. When the President or major party leaders asked, he delivered political speeches for Republicans across the United States. But his chief objective was to aid President Ford in the business of governing and to advance Ford's chances for election. To accomplish that, Rockefeller's instinctive way was to come into the Oval Office with ideas, to identify the problems confronting the nation and propose solutions, to initiate, to recommend.

Vice President Rockefeller had formed and advanced his career on collecting the best minds, thinking anew, creating, initiating, and building. The grander the project, the better he liked it.

His first job out of Dartmouth College was assisting his father in creating Rockefeller Center in midtown Manhattan. For President Roosevelt he brought together a World War II alliance of Latin America nations in the cause of freedom. For President Eisenhower he organized the Department of Health, Education, and Welfare, and initiated open skies for international peace. As Governor of New York, he built highways and airports to advance the commercial interests of the state. He amassed the largest comprehensive set of educational institutions in the world—sixty-four universities, colleges, and community colleges that make up the State University of New York. He built and built in New York City, leaving an indelible mark on the metropolis.

One Friday afternoon in the summer of 1975, Rockefeller, Hugh Morrow, and I were aboard Air Force Two en route to Westchester Airport when our flight path took us directly over Manhattan at an altitude of about 3,000 feet. The air was unusually clear, the view spectacular. As the plane crossed the island northbound, Rockefeller looked out the window and, as we passed some of his edifices, he called them off: "Battery Park City. World Trade Center. United Nations. Rockefeller Center. Museum of Modern Art. Lincoln Center. New York State Office Building in Harlem. UDC housing." Musing, Rockefeller said, "Except for a certain governor, some of those buildings might never have been built."

"Yes," Morrow waggishly observed. "I think his name was Cheops." The Vice President gravely nodded his head in appreciation.

In every office where he had served before, Rockefeller had made a difference. Appointed to the second office in the land, he could not stop being who he was and what he had been. He disdained my briefings about the Domestic Council's day-to-day operations. Routine did not interest him; initiatives did. As Vice President he saw a unique opportunity to move the President and the country forward, so he appointed himself to be the Ford Administration's idea man, the initiator-in-chief.

In his weekly one-on-one lunches with Ford, he would have a list—talking points of sweeping innovations that Ford might propose. Ford listened, but made no commitment. Their goals diverged. Ford saw a Federal government too big, too costly, too great a burden on the individual. In his first weeks as President, Ford had taken a firm stand: "We already have too many Federal programs; let's try to do a better job of managing the ones we have." In contrast, Rockefeller saw social and economic problems to be solved, and he envisioned doing so through bold new programs, most of which cost money.

Their differences—management versus innovation—were never personal. In fact, Ford and Rockefeller became close friends and strong political allies, their relationship cemented by near-identical views on national security and strong defense. Although they differed on domestic policy, Ford never attempted to curb Rockefeller's bold proposals. The White House staff did.

One Sunday night Jim Lynn called me at home to relay an important message: the Administration's budget and economic advisers had just met with Ford and he had made a major decision—he would offer no new initiatives throughout the balance of his term. "I was instructed to let you know," Lynn said.

Since this sweeping verdict clearly limited domestic policy, I wondered why neither the Vice President nor I had been included in this meeting. If, as I assumed, Rockefeller did not know about it, I must inform him. Rather than telephone him at home in Pocantico, I called the

White House military office and arranged to be on Air Force Two when the Vice President's plane picked him up at New York's Westchester airport the next morning.

Boarding his plane, Rockefeller said: "Well, Jim's come to meet me. This must be important."

"It is, Governor. I received a telephone call at home last night from Jim Lynn, telling me that the President had met with his advisers Sunday night and decided he would propose no new initiatives for the rest of his term."

The Vice President's face fell and he shook his head. "How does he expect to get elected if he offers nothing new?" he said. After a pause he asked: "Were you not included in the meeting?"

"No, I knew nothing until Lynn called."

"Since this involved domestic policy, why weren't you there?" Rockefeller said. "You told me that in Rumsfeld's system, every White House staff person with an interest in an issue would have a fair chance to be heard before the President makes a decision."

"So I was told, Governor. Last night's action is a sweeping domestic policy decision. It restrains us from any domestic initiative we might propose, yet I was not included."

"This is Rumsfeld again," Rockefeller said.

"Governor," I said, "Leaving us out of this decision on domestic policy is so serious that I am prepared to resign in protest if you believe that would be appropriate."

He looked away as the plane rolled down the runway. "No," he finally said. "I think it would be better for you to stay there so we will know what's going on."

Not long after, we learned that the Sunday-night meeting had been organized by Cheney and Greenspan to curb Rockefeller's habit of handing Ford a fresh menu of political initiatives at their weekly luncheons.

Undaunted, restless, simmering with barely concealed frustration, Rockefeller would not yield in his determination to make his Vice Presidency meaningful. Early in the summer of 1975 he persuaded Ford to commission him to initiate, organize, and conduct across the United States a series of public policy forums focused on domestic policy problems and issues of public concern. As governor of New York, he had chaired comparable Town Hall meetings, county-by-county, from Long Island to

Buffalo. These sessions of participatory democracy had made the difference in Rockefeller's come-from-behind reelection in 1966. That experience convinced him that nationalizing his Town Hall meetings would bring out ideas and issues that would boost Ford's chances of election.

So he assigned his most experienced political counselor, Jack Veneman, to oversee his initiative—The Domestic Council Forums. Veneman, a former California assemblyman, former undersecretary at HEW, and savvy public-relations operative, assembled a diverse and able staff and laid out the plan: six one-day public policy forums—in Denver, Tampa, Philadelphia, Indianapolis, Los Angeles, and Austin. The Vice President would chair each. With him on the platform would be the domestic Cabinet secretaries—Agriculture, Commerce, HEW, HUD, Interior, Labor, Transportation—the directors of OMB and the Environmental Protection Agency (EPA), and Paul MacAvoy, a member of the President's Council of Economic Advisers.

For the morning sessions Veneman arranged that the governor of the state, the mayor of the city, and other city and county officials, would make presentations; Cabinet secretaries would respond. In the afternoons, private citizens would speak at smaller concurrent topical sessions. The six conferences ranged over successive weeks, involved hundreds of witnesses, and recorded some 12,000 pages of testimony. This was condensed into an 800-page report—findings and recommendations—that Rockefeller delivered to Ford and encouraged him to rely on for his 1976 State of the Union address.

The Town Hall enterprise, unique to that time and eminently successful, showed Rockefeller at his best. He had directed a serious examination of public policy, responding to Ford's charge to the Domestic Council to "assess national needs and identify alternative ways of meeting them." In the process, he and the Cabinet secretaries had stated and explained Ford's position on current domestic issues. This was important because Ford, having never campaigned for President, had never articulated his views and political philosophy to the American public. At the same time, Rockefeller found a way to show that the Domestic Council could initiate policy as well as handle the day-to-day responsibilities of attending White House meetings and staffing out issue papers.

Thanks to Veneman, the Domestic Council also struck gold in talent. From the Forum staff, Quern recruited Janet Brown as his versatile utility assistant. A Washingtonian, then only 24 years old, and a graduate of Williams College, Brown learned fast and carried out her responsibilities with panache and infectious enthusiasm. In her assignment, Brown was invaluable—tracking paperwork, assuaging egos, and saving Quern's time.

Allen Moore, the forums' issues director, performed so well that Quern recruited him to be the Domestic Council's Associate Director of Policy and Planning. Moore, a Californian, then 31 years old, had served in the Peace Corps in the Bolivian Andes after graduating from Pomona College, then returned for an MBA at Stanford and a stint at HEW. Brainy and meticulous, Moore proved to be adept at writing, editing, and managing the flow of documents that filled our days.

Complex issues were Moore's specialty. His experience in working with Federal income support programs at HEW made him the right choice to take on decoupling Social Security. Before 1972, increases in Social Security benefits required an act of Congress. Politicians liked getting credit, but they were less fond of the growing pressure from outside interests, particularly the elderly, to be more generous. It was very tempting to grant a politically charged increase that was larger than cost-of-living increases. At the same time, during periods of high inflation, beneficiaries had no assurance of an increase to offset the higher cost of living. Over time, experts in and out of the government called for automatic increases based not on political advantage, but on increases in the cost of living as measured by the Consumer Price Index.

In the election year of 1972, President Nixon requested both—a 20 percent across-the-board increase and a new automatic cost-of-living-adjustment (COLA) thereafter.

These increases would benefit those already in the system and new applicants. Unfortunately, by linking or "coupling" the treatment of current and future beneficiaries, policy makers inadvertently created a system that gave a financial windfall to new applicants by effectively double-counting inflation.

By 1975 the problem became increasingly clear. The 1972 law would have to be modified by decoupling the treatment of current and future Social Security recipients. The goal was that current beneficiaries would receive a straight COLA; new Social Security recipients would receive an initial benefit based on an entirely new formula.

The question for policy makers was how best to get the Social Security system back on a more affordable spending path without breaking promises, and without political damage. The financial implications were enormous—potentially more than one trillion dollars over time. A contentious debate followed within the Ford Administration about how to decouple the system. A wage-based formula for determining a person's initial benefits was truer to the intent in the 1972 law and consistent with previous statements by President Ford. But it would be far more expensive over the long term than a CPI-based approach because wages historically increase faster than prices.

Moore had outlined the problem and possible solutions in a nineteen-page decision memorandum—long by White House standards—that reflected adamantly opposing positions. Treasury and OMB favored a CPI-based approach; HEW and Labor pushed for a wage-based formula.

For the decision meeting, the Cabinet Room was jammed, since so many Cabinet departments had a stake in the issue. Settling in his chair and opening his folder to Moore's memorandum, Ford said with a smile: "I finally understand what decoupling means."

After an hour-long discussion during which all sides were heard, Ford thanked all participants and left the room. Shortly thereafter, he decided to endorse the more generous wage-based formula for determining initial benefits. In 1977, Congress enacted amendments to do precisely that. Ford's judgment was affirmed.

The forums also brought us Dean Overman, an extraordinarily versatile young lawyer of aplomb and intellect. Rockefeller had chosen Overman as his White House Fellow; he was one of 14 selected that year out of 3,000 applicants. Overman had grown up in Congressman Ford's Congressional District, graduated from Hope College in Holland, Michigan, spent a year at Princeton Theological Seminary, learned law at the University of California in Berkeley, and business at the University of Chicago's Graduate School of Business.

We entrusted Overman with an array of assignments. With Paul MacEvoy, he staffed the regulatory reform task force that we set up at the President's direction to cut red tape and eliminate unnecessary government regulations restricting truckers, railroads, and airlines. During the New York City financial crisis, Overman was a vital source and transmitter of information. He met regularly with Dr. Norman Hurd, who, as New York State's former Budget Director, knew the true state of New York City's financial peril and its cause. With facts and figures,

Hurd detailed the specifics underlying the city's financial morass, relayed them to Overman, who briefed Rockefeller, and he in turn kept
Ford updated and informed.

Of all the problems that President Ford inherited and confronted
during his 895 days in office—domestic, economic, and international—
none tested his convictions, his resolve, and his negotiating skills so well
as the New York City financial crisis of 1975. By his persistence, Ford
accomplished his purpose, but he paid a high price. Portrayed as a cur-
mudgeon, Ford suffered irreparable political damage.

For Vice President Rockefeller, New York City's plight was his as
well. He had been powerless to prevent the city's prodigality when he
was governor; as Vice President, he was powerless to provide the swift
aid that he believed the people of the city desperately needed and deserved. "Hardliners blocked my way to the President," he told his political supporters in the state. "I can't get past them." Believing Ford to be
misguided by Right Wing conservatives bent on punishing New York
City and demeaning him in the process, Rockefeller publicly broke with
Ford at one point.

For six months, New York City drifted close to bankruptcy and the
peril of civic disorder. The crisis was an early and stark example of what
can happen when any government pays current operating expenses with
loans, when political leaders borrow beyond their prospects of paying
off the debts they have imposed on taxpayers. In 1975 this greatest of
American cities came dangerously close to a catastrophe.

Long before he became President, Ford had observed New York
City's fiscally irresponsible habits. He had admired John Lindsay's charisma and political savvy in the House of Representatives and thought
him a leader with a future, but he deplored Lindsay's managerial record
as Mayor. "John's salesmanship was better than his performance," he
once said.

Ford knew the numbers that caused the city's plight: spending up 12
percent yearly versus income up only 5 percent; the city budget tripling
in ten years. So on May 13, 1975, when Governor Hugh Carey and
Mayor Abraham Beame came in to the Oval Office to ask for a Federal
loan of $1 billion for ninety days to prevent bankruptcy, Ford was pre-
pared with blunt questions. "What are you going to do about your deficit?" he asked Beame. "Are you going to put some limitations on pay increases for city employees? On increases in retirement benefits? Are you

going to cut down your overhead in the number of city employees? Are you going to stop giving free tuition to the city's university students?"

Face to face, Ford did not reject their appeal, but promised to answer in twenty-four hours. Dunham and I were commissioned to draft a briefing paper providing more specifics about the reasons for the city's financial plight. In it we suggested three options for President Ford: (1) support Federal aid, (2) reject the request, and (3) deny the request but leave open the possibility of assistance on certain conditions.

Ford chose the second option and wrote Beame: "A ninety day Federal guarantee by itself would provide no real solution but would merely postpone, for that period, coming to grips with the problem. For a sound judgment to be made on this problem by all concerned, there must be presented a plan on how the City would balance its budget." The next sentence reflected what was, for Ford, an article of faith: "We must stop promising more and more services without knowing how we will cover their costs."

On the recommendation of Rockefeller, Ford proposed to Mayor Beame that he ask New York State, not the Federal government, for a bridge loan.

In the first weeks of the city's financial crisis, Ford did not believe bond-holders' warnings that a default by New York City on its obligations would jeopardize the nation's banking system. Federal Reserve Chairman Arthur Burns had advised him, "Don't let them sell you that bill of goods." Nevertheless, Ford instructed Burns and Treasury Secretary Simon to monitor the situation closely.

Turned down in Washington, Governor Carey turned to Albany. He created the Municipal Assistance Corporation (MAC)—a state finance agency authorized to borrow up to $3 billion to rescue the city. With help from MAC, the city struggled on through June, escaping default, the *New York Times* reported, "by a hair's breadth."

In midsummer MAC officials came to Washington twice to appeal to Secretary Simon for a Treasury loan. Simon told them that he would not even discuss Federal aid "until there is a viable, concrete program of self-help." After the meeting, Simon gave Ford his ominous opinion that New York City was headed for default.

As the city's peril mounted, Ford became concerned that his adamant stand against bailing out the city would hurt its citizens. He loved New York City, its vigor, and its people; he had never forgotten all the good times he had in the city during his Yale years. "I'm not a Scrooge by nature," he said, but he thought he might be coming across as Scrooge. He began to ask himself: If the city trims its budget, will there be enough police and fire protection? Will schools have to close? Can hospitals continue to care for the sick?

On September 2 Governor Carey again met with Ford, who was sympathetic but firm. Ford recognized that New York City needed help. Money, or credit, was necessary; political backbone was even more necessary. Ford restated his position that the Federal government would do nothing unless and until the city, with the legal backing of the state, brought out a plan to solve its underlying fiscal problem—cutting costs to meet income. Back in Albany, Carey persuaded a special session of the New York Legislature to take away Mayor Beame's authority over the New York City budget and give that power to a new Emergency Financial Control Board. A strong move, but it would take months for the board to work out a plan to raise taxes and cut labor costs.

Meanwhile, the city treasurer had no money to pay bills and bonds. To Rockefeller, torn between loyalty to President Ford and fealty to his beloved New York City, a limit had been breached. Breaking with Ford, Rockefeller proposed in a Columbus Day public address that Congress vote to aid the city. After reading a news account of Rockefeller's speech, Ford telephoned him: "Nelson, we should not make things more confusing."

October marked a turning point in the deliberations; Federal Reserve Chairman Burns softened his stand. He told Congress that if the city came up with a balanced budget backed by the state, and brought forth a long-term fiscal policy to maintain that balance, then he would recommend Federal aid. In a private meeting with Ford, Burns amended his earlier opinion. He advised Ford that "a New York City default could trigger a recession."

Ford made one concession. Concerned that the spending cuts he demanded might affect public order in the city, he informed Governor Carey and Mayor Beame that, if necessary, he would provide emergency funds from the U. S. Treasury to pay police and firemen, and to maintain other essential public services.

Still, Ford had not yielded on his insistence that the city balance its budget. To reaffirm his stand to the city and Congress, he took a hard line in a speech to the National Press Club on October 29. "I am prepared to veto any bill that has as its purpose a Federal bailout of New

York City to prevent a default," he said. "If the city is unable to act to provide a means of meeting its obligations," he said, let it go into bankruptcy. Then, he said, a Federal court would devise a plan to pay the city's creditors and order a long-term plan for solvency.

Ford concluded his stern message with a warning: what has happened to New York City could happen to the country. His coda reflected a deeply held conviction: "If we go on spending more than we have, providing more benefits and more services than we can pay for, then a day of reckoning will come to Washington and the whole country, just as it has in New York City . . . When that day of reckoning comes, who will bail out the United States of America?"

The response was not what Ford wanted, or expected. Instead, by seeming to advocate bankruptcy for the city, he came across as intransigent, unfeeling. The *New York Daily News* responded with a devastating headline: "Ford to City: Drop Dead."

By speaking as he did, Ford also hoped to mobilize public opinion and win support in Congress: it did not happen. The next day, the Senate Banking Committee reported a bill that would guarantee $4 billion for the city to avoid default. Four days later the House Banking Committee reported a near-identical bill, and Chairman Thomas Ashley dispatched a messenger to the White House with a personal letter to Ford. In a warm and friendly way, Ashley encouraged Ford to consider his committee's bill as a basis for negotiation, and advised his good friend and former colleague: "You have far more to lose (certainly than the Congress) if your assessments of a New York City–State default prove to have been underestimated, which many of your best supporters fear will be the case." To Ford, it was sobering advice; he had always respected Ashley's judgment.

That same day, Senate Majority Leader Mike Mansfield brought in to Ford a small bipartisan group of senators to review the near-disastrous situation in New York City and consider what might best be done. Later that week, John Rhodes, the Arizona Congressman who had succeeded Ford as House Minority Leader, came to see President Ford. "I just found out that the biggest savings and loan bank in my district has about 60 percent of its money in New York City paper," Rhodes told Ford. "So, I guess we have to do something."

Ford was moved but stood firm. Ten days later Governor Carey and the leaders of the New York State legislature brought to Ford a plan of budget cuts and new taxes that would balance the city's budget—the whole of it depending on a loan from the U.S. Treasury to meet immediate obligations. The action by the state government, and the leadership of Governor Carey was convincing. Ford accepted Carey's commitment and pushed a bill through the House and Senate to authorize the loans. With Seidman setting the conditions, the Treasury made the bridge loans the city needed to avoid bankruptcy.

Ford's forceful action saved New York City, Governor Carey said later. Before one New York audience, Carey paid Ford a high compliment: "President Ford acted in the best traditions of leadership in this country, helping New York City lift itself up by its own bootstraps."

Over the next three years the city borrowed a total of $3.6 billion from the Federal government, and paid it all back, plus interest.

Thirty years later, Ford was still dismayed that it took six months for New York's political leaders to understand his position. "I was sympathetic to New York City and its problems," he said. "I wanted to be helpful. I did not tell them to drop dead. I told them, 'We will cooperate if you straighten out your finances.' That's all they had to do."

The rift between Ford and Rockefeller over aid to New York City marked a critical turn in their relations. Personally they continued to be close. Every week they met and talked, just the two of them. But the experience diminished Rockefeller, and he felt it. Yet he was not defeated; he believed he could still make a difference as Vice President and he resolved to do so. Not in words, but by his actions, Rockefeller disregarded Ford's statements barring new initiatives. As Vice President, Rockefeller continued to press on with proposals that he believed would be good for the country and politically beneficial to President Ford. He would do all he could to make it a positive, aggressive Administration.

One of Rockefeller's successful initiatives was a comprehensive look at drug abuse. As governor of New York he had observed its cost to individuals, families, and society. To him, drugs were "one of the most serious and most tragic problems this country faces." He commissioned Richard Parsons to undertake a review of what the Federal government was doing about the problem, evaluate its effectiveness, and recommend what more should be done.

Parsons set up the Domestic Council Drug Abuse Task Force to carry out his mission. Starting up, he brought together senior officials of the twelve Federal departments and agencies that bore some legal responsibility for dealing with the drug problem. This being the government, these Federal officials had never worked together, or even met before. After a month of meetings and discussions, Parsons's task force completed a comprehensive White Paper on Drug Abuse. Among the recommendations: reducing drug demand through education, treatment, and rehabilitation; cutting supplies by better enforcement of the laws against trafficking in drugs, especially from Mexico; closer coordination among the Federal agencies responsible for enforcing the laws against trafficking in drugs. The team's investigations turned up a striking example of the economics of importing drugs. A dentist in Florida invested $1,000 in one drug buy, and received $10,000 in return. He left his gain in for a second buy and received $100,000.

With his report complete, Parsons and his team briefed Ford in the Cabinet Room on the drug-abuse problem and their recommendations. Ford acted. In a message to Congress he proposed mandatory minimum prison sentences of three years for a first conviction of selling heroin or similar narcotics, and six years for a second offense. Since almost half of all drug dealers arrested were out on bail for a previous offense, Ford proposed that bail be denied to previous offenders.

Most Rockefeller ideas were sound; some were quixotic. At noon one day he called and asked me to come over to his Executive Office Building office at once. With his face mirroring a secret, he closed the door, sat me down, leaned over, and said, "Greenland."

Puzzled, I must have frowned. This time he said it with more emphasis: "Yes, Greenland. We are going to buy Greenland." He had read in the *New York Times* that morning that Denmark was finding Greenland more of a financial burden than an asset, so he decided that the United States should buy it. Denmark, we learned later, had no interest in selling Greenland.

On another occasion Rockefeller dictated to his chief speechwriter, Joseph Persico, a plan to create a vast new fleet of warships to guarantee the freedom of the world's seas. Rockefeller had read intelligence reports suggesting that the USSR was building naval forces equal to those of the United States. In that case, Rockefeller concluded, Russia might impede the movement of oil tankers that fueled the free world's economies. His solution: a $200 billion Freedom of the Seas Bond Issue. This would finance new fleets of warships so the U.S. Navy could maintain the free movement of all international shipping. Persico drafted the plan; the Vice President never mentioned it again.

Impulsive Rockefeller could be at times; more often he was fore-sighted. At grand designs and far-reaching ideas he was at his best. One day, Ford asked him to bring him an idea for creating jobs, and this gave Rockefeller the opening for the most ambitious proposal of his time in office.

Long before he became Vice President, Rockefeller had been deeply concerned about America's growing dependence on foreign supplies of oil. "Abundant, locally available, cheap energy has been a major element contributing to America's high standard of living and a major bulwark for national security," he had written in the first of four-teen volumes published by his Commission on Critical Choices for Americans; this from the man whose grandfather had virtually in-vented cheap and abundant fuel oil for the masses. Now, Rockefeller the grandson warned, "The United States [is] in a new and precarious energy position."

Rockefeller's analysis—valid then, still valid more than three de-cades later—deserves mention: "First, the era of cheap and abundant energy is gone. Second, domestic supplies of energy are not adequate to meet the United States' needs. Third, the dependence of the United States on foreign oil has reached the point where at times more than 50 percent of the total consumed has been imported. Fourth, environmen-tal restrictions have hampered the development of nuclear and coal-powered electric generating facilities and the exploration and develop-ment of new oil, gas and coal deposits. Fifth, the rising costs due to inflation, plus the difficulties of raising capital, are deterrents to new energy source developments. Sixth, energy conservation remains more a verbal policy than a practical reality despite all the public attention de-voted to it. Seventh, with over half of the supply of petroleum necessary for daily life in America dependent on foreign countries, OPEC nations could cut off supplies to the United States at any time and the supply could be interrupted by hostile military action. Eighth, new forms of energy—solar, geothermal, wind, urban waste, tidal, nuclear fission, or-ganic from various crops, are still in the experimental stage and far from economic practical application on a large enough scale to substitute for present day coal, oil, gas, nuclear, and hydroelectric power."

Moved by this peril to the nation, Rockefeller proposed his solution: that Congress create the Energy Independence Authority of 1975, a $100 billion government corporation that would finance the expansion of proved domestic sources of energy and the creation and development of new sources of energy. There were solid precedents for the Federal government initiating projects in the national interest, he pointed out. As examples he cited Tennessee Valley Authority (TVA), the space program, and uranium enrichment.

The backbone of his proposal was abundant capital available at low interest. With $100 billion available, the Energy Independence Authority (EIA) would finance entrepreneurs to produce synthetic fuel, crude oil from coal, synthetic gas from solid waste. EIA capital would develop geothermal energy, expand solar energy, build clean-burning coal plants and nuclear power plants, produce nuclear fuel, create energy parks, buy machinery, lay pipelines, expand refineries, stimulate research and development, and promote conservation. In a score of ways, EIA would produce jobs—good jobs for Americans.

Taking care to defend and advance his idea, Rockefeller avoided the White House staffing process. Instead he staffed it out himself— discussing it personally with Secretary of State Kissinger, Treasury Secretary Simon, Commerce Secretary Morton, Labor Secretary Dunlop, OMB Director Lynn, Energy czar Zarb, economic adviser Greenspan, business adviser Seidman, and Federal Reserve Chairman Burns. He also invited Members of the House and Senate to his Capitol office to discuss his plan and ask for their support. He consulted with David Packard, Chairman of the Business Council, and with George Meany. The AFL/CIO endorsed the plan. Rockefeller then directed his counsel, Peter Wallison, to write the legislation to create the authority, and Wallison brought in lawyers from all the related departments and agencies to work on the draft. Some passages were borrowed from FDR's New Deal statutes.

With a comprehensive bill and what he believed was backing throughout the Administration, Rockefeller went to see Ford. "Here's my energy proposal," he said. "You asked me to do it. I've talked to these people. They support it and here it is."

An hour later Ford handed the proposal to Rumsfeld. "Did you approve it?" Rumsfeld asked

"No, I just listened," Ford said.

"Do you want me to staff it out?" Rumsfeld asked.

"Yes, you must staff it out. Simon and Zarb, and Kissinger. Energy is international," Ford said.

"So I staff it out. The Vice President finds out and goes ballistic. He thinks I am sandbagging his energy proposal that the President asked him to do. So I go back to the President, and he says, 'What do people think of it?' So I start telling him what Zarb thought of it, and what Greenspan thought . . ."

"Well, that's different from what Nelson said," Ford responded.

"You shouldn't be surprised at that," Rumsfeld said. "People are not going to argue with Nelson Rockefeller, the Vice President of the United States. If they're going to have any differences, they're going to be muted, in a quiet voice, and they're going to be expressed quite differently than if I ask them what they think of it."

"Well I got the impression from the Vice President that it was pretty well approved," Ford said.

"I'm sure he believes that," Rumsfeld said, "but the fact is that you get these guys off to the side and ask them if they agree with it, they say, no, it's too costly, or the government doesn't belong in the financing business, or for some other reason you can't do this."

Ford summoned the principals to the Cabinet Room to hear firsthand their endorsements or objections. "Bill Simon was against it," he said. "Alan Greenspan was against it. Jim Lynn was against it." Frank Zarb opposed it as "bad economics. It was throwing money at unproved technology that could not compete in the marketplace."

Nevertheless, Ford felt a certain obligation to Rockefeller. He had asked his Vice President to propose a way to create jobs, and Rockefeller had done that. So Ford decided to overrule his staff and support Rockefeller. On September 27, 1975, he sent Rockefeller's forty-nine-page bill to Congress to establish the Energy Impendence Authority and commit $100 billion to make it work—well aware that the 94th Congress was unlikely to pass a plan so enormous in cost and so bold in concept.

Ford was right. At first, House committees showed some interest in EIA, but the House never brought any part of Rockefeller's concept to a vote; neither did the Senate.

The 94th Congress also failed to act on the comprehensive but attainable energy proposals in Ford's 1975 State of the Union message. To members, it was an endemic disease: they were afflicted with the fear of voting for—or even proposing—a long-term solution that might cause their constituents the short term pain of paying another 50 cents at the gas pump. Consequently, Americans continued their addiction to cheap gasoline and their growing dependence on imported oil.

CHAPTER 21

Vietnam

The Vietnam War had already been lost when Ford became President and inherited that tragic conflict begotten by his predecessors' serial misjudgments.

Truman made the first mistake. After U.S. and Allied forces liberated Southeast Asia from Japanese occupation at the end of World War II, Truman reinstated France as the colonial master of Indochina, which included Vietnam, Cambodia, and Laos. When the French were losing their colony to nationalist Vietnamese forces led by Communists, Eisenhower rejected proposals that U.S forces come to France's aid and get entangled in a land war in Asia. He considered it wrong military strategy, and doubted that the American people would support such a venture. Nevertheless, he committed $100 million in aid to South Vietnam and sent 200 Army mechanics as technical advisers to help the French hold on to their Asian colony. Kennedy, determined to show Khrushchev that America had the will, and would use its power to oppose Communism, sent more than 15,000 military advisers, helicopter teams, and Green Berets to lead and instruct South Vietnamese troops in defending their land. Johnson, after declaring in the 1964 Presidential campaign that he sought no wider war, fabricated a *casus belli* in the Tonkin Gulf to make Vietnam an American war, and dispatched some 540,000 U.S. troops to Vietnam. Nixon bombed North Vietnam to the negotiating table. At Nixon's direction, Kissinger negotiated a peace treaty in Paris with North Vietnam's chief negotiator, Le Duc Tho, but the Communists had no intention of honoring that treaty. And they did not. Under the terms, Nixon withdrew the last U.S. combat troops from Vietnam and won release of American prisoners in Hanoi. By the time

Nixon left office, Vietnam had cost the United States more than $150 billion and more than 55,000 young lives. No greater, but no less, was the wound to the national spirit: the United States had become a house divided on Vietnam, and for the first time in modern history the United States had been defeated in war.

Long before he became President, Ford had made up his mind about Vietnam. In his early years in the House he had become convinced that American intervention in Vietnam was not merely justified, but imperative. "I always believed we were right to go into Vietnam originally," he said. "In the immediate post-World War II period, the United States committed to a monumental worldwide foreign aid program to rebuild Western Europe, to make their economies viable and strengthen them to be reliable and effective allies. Through our global economic and military aid programs we helped scores of other nations. These massive programs were an integral part of American foreign policy and national defense strategy. The basic thrust was anti-Communism and containment of aggression by Communist forces. Our initial commitments to Vietnam were economic aid, military advisers, and war materiel. At the outset, our programs in Vietnam were not different from U.S. programs in other nations. After World War II, U.S. policy was containment, exemplified by the Korean War. It was right to follow the same pattern in Vietnam."

Moreover, Ford believed that the United States—once American troops were engaged—could have won in Vietnam with an all-out effort. As Republican Leader in the House, he had gone to the Oval Office in a spirit of bipartisanship to urge President Johnson to commit the overwhelming forces—ground, sea, and air—that would bring victory. "You cannot fight the war piecemeal," Ford told Johnson. "You have to use whatever weapons you have, short of nuclear weapons. Senator Dick Russell was there and he agreed with me."

Ten years later, by the time Ford became President, his optimism had faded. "When I came in I knew the situation was lousy," he said. "The North Vietnamese had violated the accords they had signed in Paris in January of 1973. I knew those agreements; I had flown over with a bunch of Congressmen and Senators. The Communists had committed to withdraw their regular forces from South Vietnam, about 150,000 as I recall. They did not. They promised to give us full information on prisoners of war and MIA's. They gave us none. They did not live up to a single thing they had agreed to."

During Ford's first months as President, open warfare in Vietnam diminished. This truce was deceptive; North Vietnam, taking advantage of the cease-fire negotiated by Kissinger, was mobilizing for the final drive to invade and conquer the South. "They never considered the Paris Accords the end of the conflict," Ford said.

South Vietnam, not yet defeated in Asia, was nevertheless losing support in Washington. Congress, as weary of Vietnam as the majority of Americans, slashed he money the United States had promised the South Vietnamese for military equipment, fuel, and ammunition they needed to defend themselves. This action, fatal to Saigon, was observed for what it was not only in Hanoi, but also in Moscow and Beijing. "Largely because of our neglect and indifference," Kissinger wrote, "the time for new Communist offensive operations had arrived."

So it had. Freshly provisioned by Russia and China, the North Vietnamese Army moved south in full force. On January 7, 1975, with tanks, artillery, and well-led troops, the Communists struck from their bases in Cambodia and overran the capital of South Vietnam's Phuong Long Province, some sixty miles north of Saigon. Short of ammunition and resolve, South Vietnam armies retreated and were sometimes routed. On January 25, 1975, Ford appealed to Congress for $300 million in emergency military aid to South Vietnam and $22 million in military and economic assistance to Cambodia. He reminded Congress that under the terms of the Paris Agreement to end the fighting and bring home American prisoners, the United States promised South Vietnam "the means to defend themselves." Now, he said, "we [must keep] our end of the bargain."

The response from Senate Majority Leader Mike Mansfield was no. Speaker Carl Albert said, "I'm not sure I can get the House to go along." And he could not.

Week after week, the Communist armies attacked and the South Vietnamese retreated, abandoning their northern provinces, and often their guns. Pressing on, the Communists captured Hue and Danang and advanced toward Saigon.

Ford was not ready to accept defeat. On the recommendation of Jack Marsh, he brought the Army Chief of Staff, General Frederick Weyand, to the Oval Office on March 25, 1975, and handed him a mission. With

Kissinger and Scowcroft present, Ford told Weyand: "I want you to make an immediate and on the ground assessment of the situation in Vietnam. Come back and tell me what the hell is going on, and what needs to be done to save the situation, enough so that we can insist that the North Vietnamese live up to their agreement."

After the meeting ended, David Kennerly, who had been taking photographs during the discussion, asked to accompany General Weyand on the trip. For a moment Ford was hesitant. Then he realized that Kennerly would give him a boots-on-the-ground perspective that would complement Weyand's high-level briefings and inquiries. "Do it," Ford said to Kennerly. "Tell Scowcroft to take care of the arrangements."

As General Weyand and Kennerly took off from Washington the next day, the State Department announced it would begin evacuations of those imperiled in Saigon—6,000 U.S. citizens aiding the Vietnamese, and far more thousands of Vietnamese who had worked for and been loyal to U.S. forces in Vietnam.

In Saigon, as General Weyand began his meetings with President Nguyen Van Thieu, Vietnamese officers, and U.S. military advisers, Kennerly set out for points of action. He hitched a ride to Nha Trang on the coast, arriving the day before it was abandoned by South Vietnamese troops, then on to Cam Ranh Bay, where ships were arriving with refugees. He photographed the panic and chaos of retreat—lost orphans, civilian refugees, deserting soldiers. The next day he flew to Phnom Penh, photographed the wounded in a makeshift hospital, watched a grieving Cambodian man cling to his wounded and dying wife, and returned to Saigon to talk with veteran correspondents about the hopeless situation, and with Ambassador Graham Martin about evacuation plans.

Returning after a fortnight in the war zone, General Weyand delivered his report in Palm Springs, where Ford had gone for the Easter weekend. In brief, Weyand told Ford, "The situation is dire but salvageable." He said that South Vietnam could not survive unless the country immediately received $722 million for military equipment, ammunition and supplies, and another $300 million in economic aid. For his separate report, Kennerly showed Ford his photographs of fleeing civilians, defeated soldiers, and weeping orphans. "This is what's going on," Kennerly told Ford as they studied the grim pictures. At the end, Kennerly said: "Mr. President, Vietnam has no more than a month left, and anyone who tells you different is bullshitting."

Back in Washington, Ford resolved to make one more effort to rescue South Vietnam. He appealed to Congress in what he considered as serious a speech as he would ever make. "I had always had strong convictions about what we should do in Vietnam. I saw the situation crumbling, and I felt that if Congress let us down, there would be serious repercussions worldwide. Our enemies might be tempted. Our allies would lose respect for the United States." So, on April 10, 1975, before a joint session of Congress, Ford delivered a comprehensive and sometimes eloquent account of America's obligation to the free world, including the United States' commitment to the South Vietnamese. To defend their country, Ford said, they urgently need $722 million in military assistance and $250 million for economic and humanitarian aid.

Four days later, the members of the Senate Foreign Relations committee asked to meet with Ford. Their response to Ford's appeal, delivered by Senator Javits, was blunt: "We will give you large sums for evacuation, but not one nickel for military aid."

Ford was disappointed but not surprised; Javits reflected the will of Congress—not only the great majority of Members but also the leaders. "Mike Mansfield was never strong for supporting Vietnam," Ford said. "Carl Albert stuck with me as long as he could, but Tip O'Neill never did. So Congress ended the Vietnam War. They refused to give what was necessary to salvage the accord of January 1973.

"But I knew I had to keep the situation in Saigon from disintegrating. Schlesinger wanted to pull out two or three weeks earlier, but I told him we must hold out in Saigon as long as possible to get all our Americans out and as many of the loyal Vietnamese as we could. I ordered Schlesinger to fly planes in empty and bring out everyone possible, Americans and Vietnamese. Schlesinger disregarded my orders, flew some planes out empty. He wanted to cut and run. That experience with Schlesinger was one of the reasons that I later asked him to leave Defense.

"Well, we were getting the hell kicked out of us. I did not trust the Defense Department, so I gave a direct order to the carriers to fly in their helicopters to bring people out, repeating and repeating their flights. They were under fire. The Saigon airport was under fire. Marines were shot boarding helicopters. But those pilots kept going in, kept going in." The evacuation succeeded. Seventy American helicopters brought out more than 1,000 Americans and some 6,000 Vietnamese in a span of eighteen hours. In addition, 120,000 Vietnamese escaped by boat. Most emigrated to the U.S. Half were children.

The week before, Ford had accepted the reality of a disastrous end in Vietnam. "I saw the doom," he said. "The war was over." He told Hartmann, his chief speechwriter: "Let's put Vietnam behind us. It's time for unity, for healing." In a speech at Tulane University in New Orleans, Ford declared that Vietnam was "a war that is finished as far as America is concerned . . . The time has come to look forward to an agenda for the future, to unify, to bind up the Nation's wounds, and to restore its health and its optimistic self-confidence."

Fifteen years later, the memory of the day that Saigon fell, April 28, 1975, was still vivid to Ford. "I can still recall sitting in the Oval Office at my desk, watching those helicopters come and go, live on TV. I saw the war right in front of me. I saw the fear, the hell of war. I saw our country defeated. It was one of the saddest days of my life. Someone told me later that it was the first time since the Civil War that an American President could see the immediate consequences of war."

Ford was never in doubt about why America lost in Vietnam. "One, U.S. military capabilities were not fully utilized. We limited our air power. Under Johnson we had plenty of manpower—five hundred thousand or so. If Johnson or Nixon had gone all out with the bombing of Hanoi and it got results, the American people would have supported it. Let me give you this analogy. The American people supported dropping the atomic bombs on Japan because it ended Word War II. Yes, the bombs did terrible things to the Japanese people. But by not having to invade Japan, we saved lives on both sides.

"Two, the South Vietnamese government never achieved the strength that I envisioned. Three, the people of South Vietnam never supported their government and their army never met the challenge of the North Vietnam forces. Four, Congressional support of the U.S. effort waned as public backing of the war waned among the American people."

Looking back, Ford deplored Vietnam's cost to America. "The greatest loss was the irreparable loss of life—fifty five thousand lives and countless thousands who were wounded. The loss of U.S. prestige around the world. The division that Vietnam created in this country among good people."

Bitter though the end in Vietnam was for Ford, he learned from the experience, and hoped future presidents would also learn. "If you commit to war," he said, "commit to win. Don't let any war drag on. Go in with the will and manpower and weapons to succeed. Reach your objective. Declare victory, Pull out." Moreover, he considered that if war was just and necessary, the American people should be asked to sacrifice—at the least by paying a tax to finance that war. "There was a terrible disruption in our economy by President Johnson's effort to have guns and butter without a tax increase," he said. "That policy planted the seeds for subsequent inflation and economic distress."

Saigon was lost, Vietnam gone, and Ford assumed the United States was free of involvement in Indochina. Two weeks later, at 7:30 on a Monday morning, Scowcroft came in to the Oval Office to deliver an alarming report. An American merchant ship, the *Mayaguez,* had been boarded and seized by Cambodian troops on gunboats in open waters in the Gulf of Thailand.

The report had been relayed from the American Embassy in Jakarta, Indonesia. An oil-company executive in Jakarta, John Neal, had picked up on his radio a distress call from the radio operator of the *Mayaguez:* "Have been fired upon and boarded by Cambodian armed forces at 9 degrees 94 minutes N., and 102 degrees 52 minutes E. Ship is being towed to an unknown Cambodian port." Neal responded to the *Mayaguez* radio operator, but lost contact, then notified the Embassy. Watch officers there immediately sent urgent messages to the White House Situation Room, to the Pentagon, and to U.S. commanders in the Pacific.

"Given the murderous nature of the Khmer Rouge government of Cambodia," Ford said, "my first concern was the safety of the crew and getting the ship back." The radioed coordinates placed the *Mayaguez* near the island of Poulo Wai, some sixty miles southwest of the Cambodian port of Kompong Som. Somehow, Ford calculated, he must prevent the Cambodian gunboats from taking the men and the *Mayaguez* to any Cambodian port. "I knew we must preclude, if we could, another *Pueblo* incident," Ford said. In January 1968, North Korean Communists seized the *Pueblo,* a U.S. Navy electronic surveillance ship, in international waters off the North Korean coast, took the ship into the port of Wonsan, imprisoned the eighty-one-man crew, and kept the ship. Unable to prevent the piracy, and unwilling to retaliate against North Korea, President Johnson had been humiliated—and so had the United States.

With the *Mayaguez,* Ford recognized immediately that an uncontested seizure of a U.S. ship by Communist Cambodia had enormous foreign policy implications. The U.S. must, in his judgment, show allies and adversaries that the Vietnam debacle had neither shaken America's will nor diminished its military might. "Rhetoric alone, I knew, would not persuade anyone that America would stand firm," Ford said. "They would have to see proof of our resolve."

The immediate need was information. The nearest U.S. aircraft was three hours away, on the ground at U-Tapao base in Thailand. The closest U.S. Navy ship was more than a day distant, nearer Australia. With no way to observe ship or crew in such a remote place, Ford must act on scant intelligence. "I knew from my own experience in the Navy in World War II that specific information is hard to come by—on the *Monterey* we would get conflicting reports about where the enemy ships were, where the enemy aircraft were, and how many—the uncertainty that always exists in wartime. Here, we had no intelligence about how many Cambodian forces were in the area."

Ford called for the National Security Council (NSC) to meet at noon, to include Rockefeller, Kissinger, Schlesinger, Clements, Colby, Scowcroft, General David Jones, the acting Chairman of the Joint Chiefs of Staff, and area experts. Inform NSC members, he told Scowcroft, that he would personally take charge of the crisis. This, he said, is what "the American people expect."

By the time NSC members gathered for the meeting, a Navy P-3 reconnaissance plane had reached the area and reported that in the darkness the plane's radar detected vessels below, one large—probably the *Mayaguez*—and several smaller vessels; but deep night prevented positive identification.

To open the NSC meeting Ford asked for the facts: Where was the ship most likely located? Was it moving or anchored? Had the crew been observed? What U.S. forces could get there fastest? What were the options for rescuing the crew? Since Navy reconnaissance planes placed the *Mayaguez* 1,500 yards off Koh Tang Island, they assumed the crew was being held on the island. But with so little solid intelligence, General Jones said that no realistic plan for a rescue operation was possible. For the several next hours, Ford decided, they must rely on diplomatic initiatives. He asked China to relay a strong protest to the government of Cambodia and demand the immediate release of the crew and ship. Ford filed another protest through the United Nations and issued a statement designed to reach the Cambodian capital with the same message. Assuming the worst—that Cambodia intended to hold ship and crew—Ford issued orders to prepare for a combined operation: Navy destroyers and the carrier *Coral Sea* were to proceed, at full speed, to the area. An amphibious task force was to be assembled in the Philippines. Navy patrol planes were to maintain continuous air reconnaissance over the area.

In this and subsequent NSC meetings, Ford "was very calm and deliberate," according to an unnamed NSC member quoted in the *Washington Post*'s account of the events. "For some reason he gave me the impression of being a general himself. The impression I got was of a man who had been in the military . . . He was the one who pressed all the questions. He wasn't going to be rushed. . . ."

Some 8,000 miles away aboard the *Mayaguez*, Captain Charles Miller had been ordered by his Khmer Rouge captors to sail some thirty miles toward the Cambodian island of Koh Tang. There the ship anchored a mile off the northern shore. After daybreak the forty members of the crew were ordered off the ship by teenage black-clad soldiers armed with AK-47s. They scrambled aboard onto a small fishing boat and were taken first to Kompong Som, a deep-water Cambodian port. As the fishing boat moved toward the mainland, Air Force jets based in Thailand fired warning shots trying to stop the boat, but did not succeed. The crew spent one night on the fishing boat, were given rice for breakfast, then taken to another island, Koh Rong Sam Lem. There they were held overnight in the bamboo warehouse of a military compound. Throughout, some of the crew, aware of Cambodia's reputation for torturing and beheading prisoners, expected to be killed. Captain Miller wondered to himself if he would ever see Annie, his wife, again; but outwardly he remained optimistic and counseled patience to his despairing crew members. On the fourth day the one Cambodian officer who spoke English told Miller that military officials in Phnom Penh had given permission for the crew to be released and returned to the ship; the crew suspected this was a ruse to take them out to sea and kill them.

At daybreak on the fourth day the combined U.S. forces attacked. A wave of aircraft from the *Coral Sea* struck mainland targets—the Ream airfield, fuel-storage tanks, warehouses, Kompong Son naval installations, and railroad yards. "The air strikes had two objectives," Ford said. "We did not want the Cambodians to reinforce whatever forces they had on Koh Tang Island. We also wanted to impress on them that we meant business."

Simultaneously, an amphibious force of 175 Marines landed on Koh Tang, where they assumed the crew was being held; they were met by fierce resistance from some 200 Khmer Rouge soldiers armed with rifles, AK-47s, and mortars. Two helicopters were shot down in the landings. At the same time, the destroyer *Holt*, with a second Marine assault force of forty-eight, moved alongside the *Mayaguez*, still riding at anchor off Koh Tang. Quickly the Marines boarded the cargo ship and found it empty.

As guns blazed on Koh Tang and bombs exploded on the mainland, Captain Miller was being told by the English-speaking Cambodian that he and his crew were free to go. They boarded the fishing boat and headed for the *Mayaguez*. Seeing the Navy jets thundering overhead, they waved white flags. A Navy patrol plane spotted them and radioed the destroyers that the passengers appeared to be Americans. One destroyer, the *Wilson*, trained its guns on the fishing boat until it came within hailing distance. "Are you the crew of the *Mayaguez*?" the loudspeaker on the *Wilson* boomed. Miller shouted back: "Yes. Permission to come alongside?" The little boat eased up to the *Wilson*, and a pilot's ladder was dropped. Captain Miller was first up the ladder.

"Are all your men here?" the *Wilson's* Captain Michael Rodgers asked. "Yes sir," said Miller. "They're all safe."

Immediately Captain Rodgers reported to the Navy command, and President Ford was informed: "The crew has been recovered."

In the Oval Office, shouts of elation—with Ford, Rockefeller, Kissinger, Rumsfeld, and Scowcroft, joining in relief and celebration. Ford immediately ordered all offensive operations to stop, and the Marines to withdraw from Koh Tang. But fire from Khmer Rouge automatic weapons and mortars was so intense that it took helicopters more than five hours to bring out the Marines. The operation was costly: fifteen Marines were killed, three were missing, fifty were wounded, and ten helicopters were damaged. In addition, a troop plane moving soldiers in preparation for the operation had crashed in Thailand, killing all twenty-three aboard.

Fifteen years later, Ford's face and manner were somber in recalling the incident. "The loss of one Marine would have been too many," he said, "but *Mayaguez* resurrected America's morale. It got us out of the depths of defeat in Vietnam." Recovering crew and ship, he told Roy Rowan for his book, *The Four Days of Mayaguez*, "gave me a great sense of confidence. It did not only ignite confidence in the White

House, it had an electrifying reaction as far as the American people were concerned . . . We had all gone through a very, very difficult eight months. This sort of turned the corner and changed the course."

Ford's give and take with NSC members during the Vietnam and *Mayaguez* crises prompted him to dwell on the merits of some and the failings of others. Rockefeller had performed well, demonstrating stout support, clarity of thinking. Kissinger had spoken with his usual forcefulness and logic. Rumsfeld had offered sage advice. Scowcroft had been indefatigable. Ford had been disappointed in Colby, who had not once but repeatedly reported that the *Mayaguez* was being towed into a Cambodian port. That misinformation could have been critical; recovering the ship in port would have been far more difficult than boarding it at sea. Better, Ford thought, if Colby had just said, "We don't know." To Ford, Colby seemed exhausted. "I liked and respected Colby," Ford said, 'but this did not alter my conviction that the agency needed a change at the top."

As for Schlesinger, Ford found him irresolute in discussion and insubordinate in action. He thought Schlesinger a dove preening about in hawk's feathers. Ford was furious when he found out after the fact that Schlesinger had, at the beginning of the assault to free the *Mayaguez* crew, scaled back specific Presidential orders for Navy air strikes from the *Coral Sea*. As time went on, Ford's resentment grew; he counted the occasions when Schlesinger had been insubordinate.

For months Ford deliberated with himself over what he should do. "It came to me one day," he said. "I had gotten fed up with the conflict between Schlesinger and Kissinger. Their continuous bickering and disagreement disrupted the way I thought defense and foreign policy ought to operate together."

So Ford made up his mind: Schlesinger had to go. And since he was changing his national-security team, he would bring in a new CIA director as well. Both had proved their ineptness in dealing with Congress. To Ford, any member of his Administration who failed to show proper respect for Congress and maintain good relations with his committee chairmen had an insurmountable defect. Colby, out of poor judgment and fear of House and Senate Committees, had imprudently and without authority disclosed vital secret intelligence that cost careers and lives. Just as important, he was not fully trusted by Members of the House and Senate.

Schlesinger disdained Congress, boasting to Ford: "I know how to deal with those people." On one occasion he gratuitously offended Representative George Mahon, the chairman of the Appropriations defense subcommittee. It was a rash mistake. Mahon not only controlled Schlesinger's budget; he was also a close personal friend of Ford. "There are few people I can't get along with," Ford once said. "Schlesinger was one of them."

So without saying anything to anyone, including his closest advisers, Ford decided to change the Department of Defense and the CIA, and put in place his best choices for his national-security team. Replacing Schlesinger was easy: Ford's first and only choice was Donald Rumsfeld. To Ford, Rumsfeld was a leader, an executive, a planner, a motivator, a tireless worker, and a pro at dealing with Congress. "Rummy wanted to be in the Cabinet at Commerce," Ford said. "He had dropped a hint to me a month or so before that at some point he would like Commerce. But I felt that Rummy, with his past experience and management capabilities, his ability to deal with Congress, that Defense was the place he ought to go."

Moreover, Ford had a highly qualified replacement as White House Chief of Staff—Rumsfeld's deputy, Richard Cheney. When Rumsfeld was out of his White House office, Cheney would substitute, coming in at the end of Ford's day with documents to sign and decisions to be made. "He would have the list of things we had to talk about and do, or the schedule for the future." Ford said.

Over time, Ford observed Cheney closely. "Dick was young, only about 35 as I recall, solid build, kept himself in good shape, brownish kind of scraggly hair. He was a little old shoe-ish. A soft voice. Had a confidential tone. He could be very objective. He would disassociate his own feelings. Had a keen mind to analyze a political situation or a problem, as well as anybody I knew. Dick was a softer sell person than Don was. Don could be abrupt, ruffle feathers from time to time. Dick tried to avoid confrontation, persuade. Dick, more so than Don, tried to stay in the background, not get publicity on the outside. He was strictly an inside man, all business. Very unselfish. He was particularly good on speeches—very specific comments if he didn't think phrases or tone or a part of a speech was up to standard. Made his criticism; never backed off. For his age Dick was a really competent man. There wasn't that intimate relationship that I had with Don Rumsfeld and Joyce. I didn't have that with Dick and Lynn Cheney. I liked them, but we were brought together under different circumstances."

To replace Colby at CIA, Ford's first choice was Edward Bennett Williams, Washington's peerless defense lawyer. "He was a Democrat, highly respected on Capitol Hill, and I knew he was interested in intelligence," Ford said. Williams turned the offer down. He told Ford that his business interests—which included his thriving law firm, and ownership of the Baltimore Orioles baseball team and the Jefferson Hotel in Washington—made it impossible.

"Then I thought of George Bush," Ford said. George H. W. Bush had an impressive resume: he was the youngest pilot in the Navy during World War II; had spent one term in the House of Representatives; had one try for the Senate, defeated by Lloyd Bentsen; was appointed Ambassador to the United Nations by Nixon; appointed Chairman of the Republican National Committee by Nixon; and appointed de facto Ambassador to Red China by Ford. In the House, Ford had observed Bush's promise and became something of a mentor to him. "He was outgoing and generous, laughs easily but can be very serious," Ford said. "A very effective speaker, especially off the cuff. He had written me that he wanted to return to the U.S., and I thought George was the right person to restore the morale and reputation of the Agency." So Ford asked Kissinger to explore with Bush the idea of taking over the CIA.

In his cabled reply, Bush expressed both his reluctance and his acceptance. "I do not have politics out of my system entirely, and I see this as the total end of any political future . . . I would not have selected this controversial position if the decision had been mine . . . [But] one should serve his country and his President. And so if this is what the President wants me to do, the answer is a firm 'yes.'"

With the CIA part of his plan resolved, Ford turned next to a change he had been contemplating in his National Security Council. Having inherited the oddity of Kissinger's dual role as Secretary of State and Assistant to the President for National Security Affairs, he continued it out of his high regard for Kissinger. But over time he found it unwise. The two jobs were different—one an advocate of foreign policy, the other the honest broker of competing interests, including foreign policy. "I thought it was not good organization to have the Secretary of State also be the head of the NSC," Ford said. "Because the law passed in 1947 established the idea that the President ought to have an independent group of counselors who could analyze what Defense, State, or Treasury suggested to me. But hell, if the Secretary of State and the head of the NSC are one and the same, how could we get an independent evaluation?"

"I wanted Henry to run the State Department, to be concerned with foreign policy and not with the mechanics of the NSC. I wanted Brent to run the National Security Council."

Ford was Vice President when he first got to know Lieutenant General Brent Scowcroft. He had found him to be an outstanding adviser on all aspects of national security—military, diplomacy, intelligence, and history. His briefings were instructive, his judgment impeccable. He liked the clarity of Scowcroft's thinking, the brevity of his speech. Ford once said, "Brent can say in a sentence what Henry says in a paragraph."

Modest by nature, Scowcroft was that rarity—a military intellectual. A West Point graduate, he had earned a fighter pilot's wings, a master's and a PhD in international relations at Columbia University. He spoke Russian and had taught Russian history at West Point. A Mormon, Scowcroft was driven by a deeply ingrained sense of mission. Ford's appraisal of him was: "Scowcroft hardly fit the Hollywood stereotype of a fighting man. He was thin, short, and balding. Unfailingly polite, he never raised his voice. His strongest expletive was 'Gosh.'"

Every morning, Ford looked forward to his 7:30 meeting with Scowcroft, who would brief him up to the hour on crises and significant happenings around the world. "He was business-like, came with a list of things we should talk about and wasted no time," Ford said, "He had a fantastic memory of military and diplomatic history. In NSC meetings he was deliberate, always well-informed. If he differed with anybody, including Kissinger, he would speak his mind. But he was never contentious." Ford came to rely more and more on Scowcroft's wisdom and candor. "I used to call Brent in and talk to him about a lot of things that weren't related to his specific job because he had such a high moral viewpoint about any circumstance," Ford said. "You just knew that what he told you represented integrity."

As the first step toward reorganizing his national security advisers, Ford decided to talk to Kissinger and Rumsfeld together. On a Saturday afternoon, October 25, 1975, he brought them in to the Oval Office. "I told them what I had decided to do," Ford said, "that I was uncomfortable with some of my national security team, and that I will make these changes: I plan to fire Schlesinger, ask Colby to resign, bring Bush back to head the CIA, send Rumsfeld to Defense, take away Kissinger's NSC hat, and promote Cheney and Scowcroft."

Both were stunned, Ford said. "I had a heck of a time convincing Henry that this was not a demotion. He was crestfallen, just crestfallen.

He was concerned that depriving him of the second hat would be misunderstood in the diplomatic world, jeopardize his influence and his responsibilities as Secretary of State. I assured him that separating the two big jobs was just good organization, good administration."

Rumsfeld opposed the moves with vehemence, insisting first that it was bad public relations. "You've told everyone the Cabinet is set," he said to Ford. "It's your credibility." Changes of this dimension will raise questions about the Administration's stability, Rumsfeld said. Furthermore, he added, "The biggest challenge is the '76 election, and it seems to me that to take Bush and me, the only two people who have been active politically, and stick us in jobs where we are prohibited from being involved in the campaign is not a good move." From a personal viewpoint, Rumsfeld said, "whoever succeeds at Defense will have a difficult time because his predecessor was abruptly fired, and for me to go from the White House carries the implication that I was involved in some way in firing Schlesinger."

Ford understood his objections. "Don was afraid that it would appear that he manipulated this change, that it was a Rumsfeld coup. I told him, 'The truth is, and I'm the only one who knows the truth, is that this is totally my plan.'"

Rumsfeld suggested that since Secretary Morton must leave Commerce for health reasons, either he or Bush could be more helpful at that department. Ford told them that he planned to bring Elliott Richardson back from London to head Commerce.

As Rumsfeld continued to make the case against such sweeping Cabinet changes, Ford ended the discussion. "I have made my decision," he said.

Rumsfeld asked for a day to think over going to Defense, and Ford agreed. Kissinger accepted the change, reluctantly. He considered resigning from State; the next day he brought in to Ford a pro forma letter of resignation. Ford refused to accept it. "I need you, Henry," he said.

Ford had planned to announce the changes in mid-November, but one week after he had talked with Kissinger and Rumsfeld, the news leaked. Bruce Van Voorst, a reporter for *Newsweek*, telephoned Kissinger and asked him to confirm a tip that Kissinger was about to be relieved of his NSC position. Kissinger denied it, but immediately informed Ford that there had been a leak, and that *Newsweek* would publish the story on Monday. Concerned that *Newsweek* might also know about his plan to oust Schlesinger and Colby, Ford decided he must talk with both the next day. He assigned Marsh the responsibility to bring them in and be present for his dismissals.

Colby arrived first, at 8:00 a.m. "We are reorganizing the national security structure," Ford said. "I appreciate the job you have done at the CIA, but I ask that you resign as I am going to appoint a new director. I offer you your choice, ambassador to NATO or to Norway." Colby said he would resign as asked, but declined the offer to be an ambassador. "Their conversation was low key, no animosity," Marsh said.

Schlesinger arrived ten minutes later. "I told him we were making some personnel changes in national security, at Defense, among others," Ford said. "I need my own team, so I would like to have your resignation."

Schlesinger interrupted: "You're firing me."

"Well, Jim, you could put it that way, but that's not the way I'd like to have it understood. I think a change is necessary. That is my prerogative. And I'd like your resignation. However, I believe we can find an important place for you in the Administration." He suggested that he could be appointed director of the Export-Import Bank.

His face tense, his words bitter, Schlesinger scorned the offer. Vigorously and for almost an hour he argued that he should not be dismissed. At times arrogant, Schlesinger cited occasions where he believed he had performed better than Ford had performed. "The conversation was one of the most disagreeable I ever had," Ford said. "The more he talked, the angrier I got, and the surer I was that my decision had been right."

Witnessing the encounter, Marsh thought it unique. "This meeting was such a departure from the way Ford normally operates," he said later. "He doesn't like to sever relationships. But he was very firm in his discussions with Schlesinger, and he didn't pull any punches or retreat from his position. He kept saying, 'This is what I have decided to do.' 'I think this will be best for all concerned.' It got awful quiet in there at times. Where I was sitting I could look out on the south lawn. I saw Liberty playing with her pups, and I thought this is the one bright moment in the whole day."

Ford announced the changes in an East Room press conference on Monday, November 3, 1975, prompting newspapers to describe his action as the "Halloween Massacre." As Rumsfeld had foreseen, the press was critical. The *Washington Post* called the changes "abrupt and clumsy." Conservative columnist George Will wrote that Schlesinger's dismissal was "foolish." Liberal columnist Joseph Kraft said the action raised the question: Does Ford "have the brains to be President?" Ford's Gallup Poll rating dropped precipitously.

Ford, nevertheless, was convinced that he had made the right decisions; this was the team he wanted. In his mind, national security—peace in the world, accord with allies, crucial negotiations with adversaries, conserving U.S. military strength, maintaining leadership among free nations—was his first responsibility. With his unquestionably loyal, new in part, and more highly qualified national-security team guiding the nation's foreign policy and military actions, Ford could now turn to his second-most important priority: the campaign for election on his own to a full term as President.

CHAPTER 22

The Campaign Begins

For a man who had won election to the House of Representatives thirteen times, who had twice chaired the Republican National Convention that nominated a President, who had served as Vice President and then succeeded to the Presidency, Gerald Ford was remarkably innocent of the seamy and improbable process of running for President. The reason is plain: Ford had never run for President, and a campaign for a House seat is as different from a Presidential campaign as sandlot softball is from an Olympic decathlon.

The American Presidential campaign was never envisioned by the Founding Fathers, though they were remarkably foresighted. Instead, they applied common sense and created the Electoral College: those most knowledgeable about governing would select the most qualified to govern—as they did with George Washington. The Founding Fathers would certainly have voted down any plan so irrational as the present system for choosing a President. Two states that together make up less than 2 percent of the nation's population—Iowa and New Hampshire—play an outsized role in annunciating the peoples' choice. The political press dominates the process, treating the contest as a winner-loser sport, a political world series. Reporters concentrate on gaffes, peccadillos and blunders rather than the candidates' qualifications for the office.

Ford began his campaign for President as a rank amateur, steadily improved, but never mastered the process. A President usually needs two terms to make much of a difference in the life of the nation. In the first term a successful President earns the respect and confidence of the American people; he learns the art of Presidential power politics. Then in the second term he can practice statecraft, make his mark on history.

Though good at managing the government, Ford lacked—and never quite developed—the higher political skill he needed as a candidate to win a second term. His biggest mistake as President was failure to get himself elected; he was by far a better President than candidate for President.

In March 1975, when it appeared that nothing was being done in the White House to organize Ford's election, and with the New Hampshire primary less than a year away, I spoke to Rumsfeld of my concern that we had no campaign. "Well," he said, "I don't necessarily disagree with you but I am not going to be the campaign manager."

"But nobody else is organizing his campaign," I said, "and I intend to see the President to express my concern."

"You go right ahead," Rumsfeld said. "Go right ahead."

A couple of days later I found an opportunity to speak to Ford alone in the Oval Office. "Mr. President, I am concerned that we are not do-ing enough to plan and organize your campaign for the nomination and election."

"Well, Jim," he said, puffing on his pipe and leaning back in his chair, "I believe that if the party thinks I've done a good job here, they will nominate me. And if the people in the country think I've done a good job, they will elect me. That's the way I always campaigned for the House."

"But Mr. President," I responded with far more audacity than I usu-ally displayed in talking to him, "the campaign for President doesn't work that way. I've covered five Presidential elections for newspapers and magazines, and you have to go out and win those delegates. You have to run in the primaries, campaign in the convention states. Del-egates want to be asked, sought out, wooed."

He seemed amused by my vehemence and grinned. "Okay, and thanks," he said. "I'll think about what you say."

Ford took his time about deciding whether to try for a full term. His first indication came months later, unplanned and casual. He remem-bered the occasion: "One day in the spring, the kind of day when I could walk outside, I was walking from the South grounds to the Oval Office. Some newsman asked me, 'Are you going to run?' I said, 'I am thinking about it.'"

As he had with all major decisions in his life, Ford deliberated long and judiciously about running. Although Kissinger had persuaded him not to follow his initial impulse and announce he would not seek election, Ford had not abandoned the idea of serving out Nixon's term and retiring. "I had commitments to Betty and the children, and there was my own fatigue with the political situation," he said. "It was awful tough from August '74 'til May of '75. And I'd been Vice President during a very traumatic period. I was just tired. But the more I thought about it, the more I gradually became convinced that the things we were trying to do, whether it was energy, meeting economic problems, handling foreign policy, and that the views and policies I favored were the best that the country could have and badly needed. I looked at the alternatives in the Republican Party and I was convinced that I should lead the ticket. I looked at the options in the Democratic Party and was convinced that I could be a better President and had sounder policies than any of them, and that I could win the nomination and win the election. So I talked with Betty about our original plans, about my concern for the country's problems, about the domestic and foreign situation, and convinced her it was the right thing to do."

Looking at the Democratic field—Eugene McCarthy, Mo Udall, George Wallace, Frank Church, Henry Jackson, Fred Harris, and Hubert Humphrey—Ford thought Humphrey was the most likely to be the Democratic nominee because, in Ford's judgment, Humphrey was the most qualified to be President. It did not occur to him that the obscure ex-Governor of Georgia, Jimmy Carter, had any chance.

"I thought the Democrats would go through the arguing at their Convention, then turn to Humphrey," he said. It was moreover what Ford hoped for. "Hubert and myself would pose a bona fide choice for the American people," Ford said. "We had a different philosophy, especially on domestic issues. And I knew Hubert as a gentleman, that he and I would keep the contest on a high level, which I thought would be beneficial."

Not one of the Republicans being mentioned as possible candidates that year—Charles Percy, James Buckley, and Ronald Reagan—was, in Ford's appraisal, the man for the job. To Ford, "one characteristic that ruled Reagan out as a serious challenger was his penchant for offering simple solutions to hideously complex problems. Also, I had heard Reagan was a 9-to-5 governor, and anybody who has that as a work habit cannot be President of the United States."

Consequently, Ford initially dismissed Reagan as a possible opponent. "I never thought Reagan would run," he said. "I did not understand that he had people who would push him so hard to run. And I would bet money that Nancy Reagan was the one pushing him hardest to run."

Ford misread Reagan. It was not his staff, nor his wife; it was Ronald Reagan himself who would in due course decide whether to run for President—and he took his time about deciding.

One significant encounter in Reagan's long deliberations had been a prescient meeting in the spring of 1974 in Los Angeles with John Sears, a master theoretician of Republican Presidential nominations. Set up by Bob Walker, a conservative activist, the meeting included Reagan's inner circle of advisers—Edwin Meese, Mike Deaver, Peter Hannaford, Lyn Nofziger, Holmes Tuttle, and Justin Dart. "They were all assuming Nixon would survive Watergate and there would be an open race for the Presidency in 1976," Sears said later. "I told them Nixon would not survive, that Ford would be President but had not been through the process and could be beaten. I didn't push Reagan to run. I just told him what the situation was."

Three months later, when Nixon resigned and Ford became President, California's Republican conservatives assumed that Reagan would be considered for Vice President. To promote his chances, California State Chairman Gordon Luce wired the forty-nine other state chairmen asking them to support Reagan for the appointment. "Ford's selection of Rockefeller a week later was regarded in Sacramento as a slap in the face," Lou Cannon wrote in his authoritative biography, *Governor Reagan: His Rise to Power.* "To Republican conservatives who recalled the [California] primary battle of '64, the selection of their old enemy was an unbelievable insult." This, the nomination of Rockefeller to be Vice President, Cannon observed, "more than any other single act of Ford's, or indeed all of them combined, . . . fueled national interest among conservatives in a Reagan candidacy."

But Reagan himself reserved judgment on the new Ford Administration. He liked Ford personally; he waited to see what kind of President he would be. When Reagan ended his two terms as governor in January 1975, he told his inner circle that he would do nothing to preclude his running for President, but would also make no commitment. Instead, he initiated an impressive analogue campaign. With Deaver and Hannaford as his booking agents, Reagan made eight or more speeches each month, wrote a column that appeared in 174 newspapers, and taped homilies for some 200 radio stations. By publishing and broadcasting his conservative message he was not only attracting popular support, he was also making money—some $800,000 in his first year out of office.

At some point in June 1975—there was no one day, no epiphany—Ford made his decision to run. "I thought, considering the mess I inherited, that I had done a good job," Ford said. "In my judgment the way to win the election was to point that out. Straightforwardly. Factually."

He did not expect that Reagan or any other Republican would contest him for the nomination; to Ford, the challenge would be to defeat Hubert Humphrey in the general election. By his own account, he had only a vague idea of what a Presidential campaign would involve. "I had always run one-man campaigns for Congress—straightforward, limited money, almost certain victory," he said. "All of a sudden I was in a different ballpark. I must admit that at first I did not comprehend the vast difference."

To get started, Ford recognized that he would need a campaign manager; his first choice was Melvin Laird. A former House colleague and political sage who was both a close friend and frequent mentor, Laird would have been an excellent choice. He and Ford complemented each other: Laird overflowed with constructive political initiatives; Ford could make the best of them happen. Laird had the more comprehensive knowledge of national politics. He had another major asset as a potential campaign manager: he was better with the press. Reporters gravitated to Laird because he was open, loquacious, and almost always good for a story or a column. But Laird declined Ford's request. He had become deeply involved in the business affairs of *Reader's Digest* and had just agreed with DeWitt and Lila Wallace to manage their educational foundation. "I told Jerry I would help him in any way I could, but I could not break my contract with the Wallaces," Laird said.

Ford, after evaluating a short list of other candidates with Rumsfeld, decided to put his campaign in the hands of another House colleague, Howard "Bo" Callaway. His reasoning: "One, I had known him a number of years. Before he ran for Congress I met him at an Aspen Young Presidents Conference. We skied together, got well acquainted. He was a West Point graduate who had served his time in the Army and gone into the family business. He was then a Democrat disenchanted with the Democratic Party. I said, 'Why don't you become a Republican and run for Congress?' Well, he did run in '64 as a Republican and won. So I got to know Bo in the House, and even better when he became Secretary of the Army in '73. So we had this personal relationship. Excellent speaker, crisp, precise. Good administrator, fine reputation as Secretary of the Army. One of the most highly motivated persons I ever worked with. So Don and I looked over the field to find a person I could work with, somebody who could bolster my relationship in the South and with the conservatives. Bo was attractive, articulate, conservative enough but not a way out right-winger. I thought he would be the ideal individual to handle my campaign."

Talking to Callaway, Ford said: "Here are my central themes for the campaign: grant more freedom from Federal government intervention in the lives of citizens, preserve the free enterprise system, continue to emphasize Federal fiscal responsibility, maintain a strong national defense, and advance the rights and responsibilities of state and local governments."

On that premise, Ford asked Callaway to manage his campaign. Devoted to the Army, Callaway was reluctant to give up that responsibility. "He did it as a favor to me, and at a personal sacrifice," Ford said.

As a first move Callaway would line up Ford endorsements by leading Republicans across the country. "We felt that if we had lots of prestigious people from the political arena in every state supporting me, the Reagan people would perhaps get discouraged and not proceed with the candidacy," Ford said. "I thought it was a logical way to proceed."

To raise the money for his campaign, Ford appointed another friend, David Packard, a California electronics entrepreneur and corporate executive at Hewlett-Packard who had served as Deputy Secretary of Defense. Both Callaway and Packard were risky choices, a mark of Ford's inexperience. A President who had never run for the office had chosen a manager who had never run a national campaign and a fundraiser who had never raised money for a Presidential campaign.

At noon on July 8, 1975, Ford invited reporters in to the Oval Office and formally announced he was a candidate for President. The performance was typical Ford, absent of drama, his statement lacking any memorable phrase. His promise: "I expect to work hard, campaign forthrightly, and do the very best I can for America in order to finish the job I have begun." His priority: "Never to neglect my first duty as President."

One week later, on July 15, 1975, Reagan authorized a Presidential exploratory committee: Citizens for Reagan. He had given his assent, but had not yet committed to become a candidate. Nevertheless, Reagan's conservative backers began an undeclared campaign; the Citizens' expedient enabled his advocates to raise money, organize and recruit in anticipation of a campaign. Senator Paul Laxalt was named chairman, and John Sears took charge as chief strategist and organizer.

Ford read in the *Washington Post* about the formation of the Reagan exploratory committee; his evaluation was that the conservatives were pushing Reagan to run. But Ford was still not convinced that Reagan would actually oppose him for the nomination. For one thing, he thought Reagan would be in implicit violation of "The Eleventh Commandment" that Reagan had adopted in the 1960s and since followed: "Thou shalt not speak ill of any fellow Republican."

Early on, Ford made up his mind that he would not cater to the right wing of his party. "I had read repeatedly that I was the most conservative President since Herbert Hoover," Ford said. "My feeling was, if that's true, damn it, the extreme right wing ought to be satisfied. But the truth is they never are unless they lock you in to a little ideological circle that is a miniscule number of voters in the American public. Regardless of the political consequences, I knew that I had to call them as I saw them from the nation's point of view and at the same time from my own political experience. The facts of life are that satisfying the extreme right wing dooms any Republican in a Presidential election."

Ford's own campaign opened in ambiguity and controversy. "None of us, not the President nor any of his key staff had ever been through a national campaign," Callaway said. "We did not have clear and natural communication channels perfected by long periods of working together. The White House was clearly in charge of the overall effort, but in the Watergate era wanted to maintain separation from the campaign."

On the day after Ford's announcement, Callaway, intending to show how open the campaign would be, invited the press to President Ford Committee headquarters for a day of impromptu interviews. One recurring question: why did the committee name not include Vice President Rockefeller? The campaign strategy, Callaway pointed out, was to nominate Ford; the convention would choose his Vice President. "The point wasn't that Rockefeller should not be considered," Callaway said, "but I wanted to assure my conservative friends that it would not be automatic."

This was a significant political change; three months earlier, Ford had told Walter Cronkite: Vice President Rockefeller "has done a fine job. I see no reason whatsoever [that] there should be any change."

By the time he announced his candidacy in July, Ford had been persuaded that he should run alone. He was well aware that from the day he had chosen Rockefeller as Vice President, conservative Republicans had opposed the appointment. Since then, conservative hostility to Rockefeller had doubled, then tripled. By running alone, as the conservative President that he was, Ford hoped to appeal to Republican conservatives and expedite his way to the nomination.

Ford never wavered in his belief that appointing Rockefeller had been in the country's best interest. He had found in his Vice President a stout ally, especially on national security, a wise counselor and a highly effective political partner. Moreover, he considered Rockefeller the most qualified person to succeed to the Presidency if something happened. Ford's stratagem was to win the nomination so decisively that convention delegates would confirm his choice of Rockefeller to complement the ticket.

In an awkward Oval Office discussion, Ford told Rockefeller of his plan and the reasoning behind it. Rockefeller's response was, "Mr. President, nothing is more important to this country than your nomination and election. Anything you want, I'll do. I'll be on the ticket; I'll be off the ticket—whatever you want. If at any time you want me to step aside, I'll hand you a letter of withdrawal."

Their understanding was firm, politically sound, but the omission of Rockefeller's name on the campaign committee inevitably provoked the question: was Rockefeller being dumped from the ticket? Callaway's answer was: "A lot of Reagan people are not supporters of Rockefeller . . . and we want their support for Ford whether they support Rockefeller or not." Days later Callaway went further and told reporters that Rockefeller was the campaign's "Number one problem . . . You and I both know that if Rockefeller took himself out, it would help with the nomination . . . [Ford needs] a younger man."

Incensed, Rockefeller telephoned Callaway: "Bo, we had an agreement on the priority of nominating the President, but it didn't include calling me the number one problem." Rockefeller also complained to Ford, and said he suspected Rumsfeld was the instigator of Callaway's remarks. "No," Ford said. "Bo, as a southerner, is very acute to the inroads that Reagan could make in the south." Rockefeller, who had excellent political intelligence and far more experience in Presidential campaigns than Ford and Callaway, countered: "That's the wrong strategy for your nomination, Mr. President. Reagan has long been a solid favorite in the South; if he runs, he will take the Southern delegates. You will be nominated by delegates from the Northeast, the Midwest, and parts of the West."

Ford promised Rockefeller he would remonstrate with Callaway, and summoned him to the Oval Office. "Bo, the Vice President is very sensitive to the kinds of things you are saying," he said. "He is very important to us in getting the nomination. I personally have a great fondness for him and a strong allegiance to him. You just can't do this anymore."

"I'm sorry, I really am," Callaway said. "I got caught. The press was after me."

With the management of his campaign delegated to Callaway and Packard, Ford turned back to his main job—dealing with Congress, foreign policy, and national security. He proposed that Congress decontrol domestic oil prices, extend the Voting Rights Act, and provide more money for food stamps. He vetoed an education bill and a health bill as inflationary, and proposed cutting spending for duplicate programs in Interior, Agriculture, and HEW. He began the briefings for a ten-day trip to Europe—leaving on July 26, 1975, to West Germany, Poland, Romania, Yugoslavia, and Helsinki, Finland.

He immediately found out that campaign politics would intrude into and complicate his decisions and actions as President. Aleksandr Solzhenitsyn—an outspoken Soviet dissident in exile and author of *The Gulag Archipelago,* his expose of Soviet political prisons—had come to Washington to castigate his government before an AFL-CIO audience. Senator Jesse Helms asked Marsh to arrange for Ford to meet with Solzhenitsyn. Before deciding, Ford talked with Marsh and Scowcroft. Marsh pointed out that meeting Solzhenitsyn would help politically with conservative Republicans. Scowcroft said that he and Kissinger, who was traveling, considered it unwise. With Ford due to meet in weeks with Soviet Premier Brezhnev at Helsinki to discuss SALT and other sensitive issues, why—Scowcroft asked—sabotage these talks before they began? Ford declined the Solzhenitsyn meeting: "I decided to subordinate political gains to foreign policy considerations," he said.

Rising to political opportunity, Helms and other conservative Republicans blamed Kissinger, accusing him of appeasing the Soviet Union. The *Wall Street Journal* called Ford's rejecting the meeting with Solzhenitsyn "the most unworthy decision of his tenure."

The skirmish over Solzhenitsyn turned into a prelude to the political battle over the Helsinki meeting and pact. Ethnic groups representing Eastern Europe demonstrated in front of the White House; Congress dispatched a delegation to Ford to protest. Solzhenitsyn inflamed the issue by calling the pact the "betrayal of Eastern Europe."

The Conference on Security and Cooperation in Europe, initiated by the USSR, was to bring together thirty-five nations in Helsinki to reduce the size of the armies of NATO and the Warsaw Pact confronting each other across the Iron Curtain. As part of the agreement, the Soviets wanted the free nations to accept their hegemony over Eastern Europe, which did in fact exist. In return, the USSR would renounce their policy of using military force to keep their client states in line and agree that national borders would be changed only by peaceful means. Moreover, Soviet leaders agreed to accept basic principles of human rights and the free movement of information, ideas, and people.

On balance, Ford decided the free world would benefit. "Even if the agreements were not kept, Europe would be no worse off than before," Ford said, "If all made good on their promises the cause of freedom behind the Iron Curtain would advance. That was a worthwhile goal."

Conservatives, and, specifically Ronald Reagan, opposed Helsinki. "I am against it," Reagan announced, "and I think all Americans should be against it." The blatantly hawkish Democratic Senator Jackson said Helsinki would "take us backward, not forward in the search for genuine peace." The *Wall Street Journal* appealed to Ford: "Jerry, don't go."

"I was disappointed," Ford said. He doubted that Reagan, Jackson, Solzhenitsyn, or the *Wall Street Journal* writer had actually studied the proposed pact. "Nobody had sat down and laid out what the potentials were," Ford said. "They had been propagandized by people who didn't have the vision to see what it really was."

After stopping off in Germany and Poland, Ford flew on to Helsinki. For three days, in the ultramodern Finlandia Hall, Ford listened to the speeches by the heads of all thirty-four other participating states. His speech, one of the last, was one of his best.

"We are bound together by the most powerful of all ties, our fervent love for freedom and independence, which knows no homeland but the human heart," he told the assembly. The proposed Helsinki Accords "affirm the most fundamental human rights: liberty of thought, conscience, and faith; the exercise of civil and political rights, the rights of minorities. They call for a freer flow of information, ideas, and people; greater scope for the press, cultural and educational exchange, family reunification, the right to travel and to marriage between nationals of different states . . . They reaffirm the basic principles of relations between states; noninter-vention, sovereign equality, self-determination, territorial integrity, invio-lability of frontiers, and the possibility of change by peaceful means."

Between the Finlandia sessions, Ford met twice for long discussions with Brezhnev on SALT, hoping to advance beyond their promising ne-gotiations at Vladivostok some eight months before. "Brezhnev seemed thin and pale, not as hearty as he had been at Vladivostok," Ford said. "His speech was occasionally slurred; we had heard that he had suf-fered a stroke." Plunging into arms discussions, they agreed on count-ing multiple warhead missiles and limiting the range of cruise missiles. "Brezhnev was very friendly when we first met, but it was not a produc-tive meeting because we got into an acrimonious debate over the Back-fire bomber," Ford said. The U.S. Air Force and CIA had informed Ford that the Backfire had a transatlantic range and was therefore a strategic weapon. "Brezhnev took the information I gave him, checked with his military analyst, and totally disagreed with us." With diametrically op-posite views on the Backfire, "the prospects for an arms agreement were significantly degraded," Ford said. "But Brezhnev and I agreed to con-tinue affirmative negotiations, to submit new proposals, and to maintain continuous contact between Gromyko and Kissinger. We anticipated the signing of an agreement, and with the signing Brezhnev would visit the United States. He told me he was definitely looking forward to that."

In Ford's judgment, Helsinki had been a success; in the public's mind, it was a failure. "My popularity went down following Helsinki because the impression was that I was soft on Communism," Ford said. "That just burned the hell out of me, because while I was in Congress nobody was any more hardline than I was. And as President, none was firmer in dealing with the Soviet Union than I was." Reflecting on Helsinki, he said long after: "It was good in substance, good diplomacy, good in po-tential political benefit. We should have done a better job of educating the country about its importance. We just didn't do that well."

Sometime in the late summer of 1975, Ford decided he should try to preempt the possibility of a Reagan candidacy. "Reagan was making noises, but was not yet identified as a candidate," Ford said. In a futile move, Ford telephoned Reagan and offered to appoint him Ambassador to the Court of St. James or Secretary of Transportation. Reagan declined. Later, Rumsfeld called and offered Reagan Commerce. Again he declined, offended that Ford himself had not called.

To add experience to the Ford campaign team, Rumsfeld recruited Stuart Spencer, a master of political warfare. A Californian, Spencer's tactical expertise was second to none. He had been a key adviser to Reagan for his election as governor, but the two had a falling out. "I told President Ford I would come in and help him win New Hampshire and Florida, and then go home," Spencer said.

On his first trip to Washington, Spencer met with Ford, Rumsfeld, Cheney, and Callaway. "They were not taking Reagan seriously," he said. "I was shocked! 'Look,' I said, 'he's not just thinking about running. I know this man. *Ronald Reagan is running.*'"

Ford liked Spencer from their first encounter. "I found him one of the most astute political analysts and campaign planners that I ever ran into," Ford said. "Straggly hair, usually unkempt, sloppy dresser. He ambles, or waddles, into the room like a friendly bear. Sits in the background, listens, doesn't say very much, but then when he speaks he's well organized, says what he wants to say succinctly and precisely. A shrewd political operator. You know he speaks from a hell of a lot more knowledge in the back of his mind than what he's laying out in words or on paper."

Throughout his life, whether in sports, war, or politics, Ford rarely initiated anything, but he never hesitated to respond to a challenge. In a contest he was at his best—focused, resolved, indefatigable. The sheer possibility of defeat by Reagan provoked Ford to immediate action. He disdained the man, thought him just an actor, a make-believe executive mouthing a script. Consequently, denying Reagan the party's nomination became the prime challenge of Ford's long career in political life, and he set out to meet it with vigor and determination.

Boarding Air Force One, Ford campaigned in Minnesota, Illinois, Wisconsin, Maine, and Rhode Island; the next month, in Washington, Oregon, New Hampshire, Oklahoma, twice in Texas, twice in California. Moving aggressively to eliminate Reagan, with Callaway and Cheney Ford formed his plan: defeat him in the first two primaries, New Hampshire and Florida, then in Reagan's native state, Illinois. That, they believed, would force Reagan to withdraw. Ford appointed one House colleague, Louis Wyman, to manage his New Hampshire campaign, and another, Louis Frey, to manage his Florida campaign.

Expanding his political team, Ford recruited talented political architects and organizers: Clif White, who had designed and executed Goldwater's successful campaign for the Republican nomination in 1964. For the first time in his political life, Ford hired a poll-taker, Robert Teeter. "I had never paid a pollster to take a poll in my district; I thought I knew more about the people and the issues," Ford said. "But I knew Bob's work for Michigan candidates and for the Republican National Committee." Unlike some political pollsters, Teeter never permitted his own middle-of-the-road political philosophy or a candidate's hopes to shape his conclusions. "Bob's information," Ford said, "was invaluable."

To coordinate campaign and White House actions, Ford brought into the West Wing another favorite House colleague, Rogers Morton. When his campaign came up short of fundraising goals—David Packard raised only $900,000 of the $10 million in the campaign budget—Ford promptly replaced him with Robert Mosbacher. A Texas oilman with standing in the party and nationwide connections with the influential as well as the wealthy, Mosbacher rescued the Ford campaign. He met Ford's goals and more.

By late October the Ford campaign was moving, gaining support, getting organized. One obstacle stood in the way, and Ford confronted the stark and inescapable political reality: he could win the nomination only if he dropped Rockefeller from the ticket. Wherever he went— New Hampshire, Florida, California, Illinois, Texas—Ford heard from party officials and prospective delegates the ominous drumbeat: Rockefeller must go. Ford studied a nationwide poll and shook his head in dismay: one in four Republicans would not vote for him if Rockefeller remained on the ticket.

Ford asked Morton to convene a select group of White House aides to consider the problem. In that meeting, Seidman said later, "Not one person stood up for Rockefeller. I am ashamed to say that I didn't either."

Ford was stunned by Morton's report. "Not one, not one would keep Nelson on the ticket," Ford said. "If I had had my true druthers, I would have said, 'Nelson, I want you to stay on the ticket. We'll fight it out. It will be a hell of a fight, and we might lose. There's that risk.'" After deliberating alone, Ford decided not to take that risk. "It was the most unpleasant decision I had to make as President. I was faced with a practical solution. I was looking at winning. I had a sleepless night or two trying to figure out how to ask Nelson to take himself off the ticket."

On Friday, October 31, at their weekly meeting in the Oval Office, Ford and Rockefeller talked about the campaign and the increasing power of the right-wing conservatives in the party, and the challenge from Reagan. Ford braced himself. "Nelson, you've told me that you would do whatever was necessary for me to win this nomination, including giving me a letter taking yourself out of consideration in the future. With profound regret I believe it is time for that letter."

"You will have the letter on Monday," Rockefeller responded at once. "Mr. President, I am confident that you will win the nomination, but I agree that Reagan is a formidable threat. I believe you have this choice: history will treat you better if you lose the nomination to Reagan, for he will lose the election next year, rather than if you win the nomination by making compromises that will cost you the election."

On Sunday in Pocantico, New York, Rockefeller summoned his chief scribe, Hugh Morrow, to draft the letter.

On Monday morning Morrow telephoned me from the Vice President's office. "Jim, Nelson is about to sign a letter to the President taking himself out of consideration for the Vice Presidency. If you want to contest it, better get over here right away."

Minutes later, sitting beside the Vice President's desk, I pleaded: "Governor, don't do this. It's not right for you to take yourself out. It's not necessary. The President needs you now in this campaign more than ever."

With his eyes narrowed to slits, a sure sign of his rare but extreme anger, Rockefeller replied: "Jim, *I was asked for this letter.*"

On one page, Rockefeller had written: " . . . I have been honored by your nomination of me as Vice President and by the approval of the Congress. In association with you in the months since that time, I have come to have the highest regard for your dedication to the Presidency and for your courage, resolution, and forthrightness . . . Regarding next year and my own situation, I have made clear to you and to the public that I was not a candidate for the Vice Presidency, that no one realistically can be such, and that the choice of a Vice Presidential running mate is, and must be, up to the Presidential candidate to recommend to a national party convention. After much thought, I have decided further that I do not wish my name to enter into your consideration for the upcoming Republican Vice Presidential nominee . . ."

Together the Vice President and I walked over to the West Wing, and I waited outside the Oval Office while Rockefeller went in to give his letter to the President. Rockefeller took his usual chair to Ford's right. "Mr. President, I have this letter for you, and I would like for you to read it." Their discussion was brief. "It was a hard discussion for me," Ford said later. "I thought that Nelson was the best Vice President I could have, as a team player, as a representative of the Administration, as a potential successor."

When Rockefeller came out twelve minutes later he did not want to seclude himself, but strode into the busy West Wing lobby and took the chair beside a corner desk with a telephone. He called Happy and his brother Laurance, then held court. Staff members walking through the lobby were surprised to see Rockefeller sitting there, and stopped to commiserate. Scowcroft came through, saw Rockefeller and his face fell. "I'm sorry. I'm sorry, Mr. Vice President," Scowcroft's voice as mournful as if there had been a death in the family.

As it happened, the Fords had the Rockefellers to dinner in the family quarters that evening. At one point, as Rockefeller's demotion was mentioned, Betty Ford said, "Jerry, you're a damn fool to do this."

For Nelson Rockefeller, the dismissal from consideration for further political office was in fact also dismissal from further service to the nation. For this accomplished servant of the people it was deeply humiliating. The arc of his final public responsibility, the last trajectory of a long and distinguished public life, had soared to heights and fallen in ignominy. He had never wanted to be Vice President. He had accepted the offer from a beleaguered new President because of his ingrained sense of duty, and his love of America. He had paid a high price in being confirmed. He had been promised power to improve the domestic affairs of the nation, a well-meaning but impractical promise never fulfilled. He had used his thirty years' experience in national security and international affairs to support and counsel President Ford; but outside the National Security Council and the State Department, his influence and contributions had been little noticed and rarely appreciated. Moved by his own creative spirit and fixation on meeting public needs, Rockefeller had offered ideas and proposed initiatives to Ford—none of which reached fruition. Rockefeller had been constructive in his criticisms of White House operations that he found encumbering, but he was impeccably loyal to President Ford—in public and in private. He had campaigned diligently for the Republican Party and Republican candidates, demonstrating far more fidelity to his party than his party ever showed him. He had fulfilled his responsibilities, and more. He had done his best, but lost. The wound was deep. It never healed.

CHAPTER 23

Nomination

The removal of Rockefeller brought Ford no visible campaign benefit and gave conservative Republicans no evident comfort. If anything, the opposition saw it as a clear signal of Ford's vulnerability. A fortnight later Reagan telephoned Ford. "Hello, Mr. President. I am going to make an announcement, and I want to tell you about it ahead of time. I am going to run for President. I trust we can have a good contest, and I hope that it won't be divisive."

"Well, Governor, I'm very disappointed," Ford said. "I'm sorry you're getting into this. I believe I've done a good job and that I can be elected. Regardless of your good intentions, your bid is bound to be divisive. It will take a lot of money, a lot of effort, and it will leave a lot of scars. It won't be helpful, no matter which of us wins the nomination."

"I don't think it will be divisive," Reagan said. "I don't think it will harm the party."

"Well, I think it will," Ford said.

The conversation ended. Ford put down the phone, thinking: I knew he was wrong. How can you challenge an incumbent President of your own party and not be divisive?

Years after, Ford's resentment was undiminished. "I enjoyed the process of trying to execute the business of government," he said. "It just burned the hell out of me that I got the diversion from Reagan that caused me to spend an abnormal part of my time trying to round up individual delegates and to raise money." He had expected to concentrate on governing for the first half of 1976; now he would have to divert time and effort to winning his party's nomination.

On November 20, 1975, the day after his call to Ford, Reagan announced he would contest Ford for the Republican nomination. Ten months it had taken him to decide. Hannaford said, "He brought us together and told us, 'I have gradually come to the conclusion that the Ford-Kissinger foreign policy must change. We must stand up more firmly to the USSR.'"

"I don't think the Governor had a burning desire to be President," was the judgment of Edwin Meese, Reagan's chief of staff in Sacramento and most listened-to counselor in Washington. "His main reason for running was that he felt we were losing the Cold War. He felt that détente was being used against us, that the Soviets were cheating on almost everything, being increasingly ambitious around the world while we were in essence abiding by all the agreements. The Governor was somewhat reluctant to run against an incumbent President of his party, but he felt it was necessary because of the situation in the Cold War."

"He also had been concerned, with other conservatives, that neither the Nixon nor the Ford Administration had reversed the Great Society—but this was secondary, way behind the first reason." To Meese and to Hannaford, Reagan's decision to run against Ford was a decision he alone made, and based on principle: He opposed Ford's foreign policy. "None of us on his staff were urging him to run," Meese said. "The fact is that nobody could have talked Ronald Reagan into running for President if he didn't want to do it."

In essence the foreign policy difference between the two Republican candidates was in approach to the Soviet Union: Ford believed in negotiation; Reagan, in confrontation. Ford placed the highest priority on getting an agreement with the USSR to limit nuclear weapons. This, he said, "would be a crucial step in lifting from mankind the threat of nuclear war."

To Reagan, "Under Messrs. Kissinger and Ford this nation has become Number Two in military power . . . The Soviet Union will not stop taking advantage of détente until it sees that the American people have elected a new President and appointed a new Secretary of State."

To Ford, the best counter to Reagan's challenge was to show by his actions his qualities as President, to make the right decisions and carry them out. The political corollary, in his opinion was: the better he performed as President, the more he deserved to be nominated and elected, and the more likely he would be nominated and elected. So Ford buckled down to his job.

The immediate task was to appoint a Supreme Court justice, to replace Justice William O. Douglas, retiring because of illness. Over the years Ford had studied the court, and in his mind he rated its leaders. "I found Earl Warren to be a person who had deep conviction on social issues, the rights of the individual, the less affluent in our society," Ford said. "He believed the Court ought to be activist. So the Warren Court began legislating rather than just interpreting. The Burger Court was far more reluctant to move into judicial legislative action. The Burger Court sought to constrict or limit Federal Court jurisdiction. The net result was that the Warren Court moved to the left of center; the Burger Court moved more to the center." Ford resolved to find and appoint a justice of the highest merit and competence, and a centrist. "I was not interested in trying to make the Court over in my own image or legal philosophy. Quite simply, I wanted the finest legal mind I could find, someone with a judicial temperament who would add luster to the high court."

To do so, Ford called in Attorney General Levi and Counsel Buchen. With his usual thoroughness, Ford told them to consult legal scholars, the American Bar Association, and others and bring him a list of the most highly qualified judges in the country. With Levi and Buchen, he winnowed a list of fifteen possibilities to five, and then to two. Both were Circuit Court of Appeals judges—Arlin Adams in Philadelphia, and John Paul Stevens in Chicago. Ford then spent hours studying the decisions and opinions of each. "Both Adams and Stevens had fine records, and both were highly recommended by all the people we talked with," Ford said. "But when I looked at the whole spectrum, it seemed to me that Stevens was the better of the two." He deliberately did not confer with Stevens to discuss his views, but evaluated him solely on his record. His decision made, he telephoned Stevens that day, November 28, 1975, and announced the appointment.

As it happened, Ford had met Stevens briefly the week before. He and Mrs. Ford had revived an old custom of hosting a White House dinner for the Supreme Court justices, the Chief Judges of the circuits, and their wives. The Fords had greeted the Stevens in the receiving line. Stevens remembered the occasion, that it was at a time when the New York City fiscal crisis was a major public issue: "Having seen repeated cartoons and numerous references to his having stumbled when getting off an airplane and hitting tee shots into the gallery—all designed to create an impression that he was clumsy and not the brightest President we had ever had—I was surprised to recognize immediately that he was an extremely intelligent lawyer with a complete grasp of the issues and the strategies involved in the (New York City) negotiations."

With Stevens appointed, Ford took off the next day on a long-planned, ten-day journey to China, Indonesia, and the Philippines. "For me not to have gone to China at this point could have been interpreted, particularly by the Chinese, as a tilt toward the Soviet Union," Ford said. "So the trip had both substance and symbolism."

For the Asian journey, Ford took along—in addition to Mrs. Ford, daughter Susan Ford, Kissinger, Scowcroft, and State Department Far East experts—James Lynn, OMB Director. With the fiscal year 1976 budget only weeks from going to press, Ford calculated he could use the long flying hours to review with Lynn allocations to departments and budget decisions.

In Beijing, Ford visited Mao Zedong in his modest quarters; he found him frail, "his hands gnarled, his feet shuffling across the room to greet me," but wise and, through his interpreters, passionately articulate. For almost two hours they talked, with Mao reiterating his concern about Soviet intentions and capabilities. "He kept urging us to stand firm, to deny Soviet hegemony in the Pacific."

At a state banquet for the visiting Americans hosted by Vice Premier Teng Hsiao-p'ing (Premier Zhou Enlai was ill), Teng pointed out that neither the United States, nor China, sought hegemony. Sharing peaceful intentions, Teng continued, China and the United States contrasted to the USSR, which he said was "contentious to exercise hegemony . . . which could lead to a new world war." Ford, evaluating the two leaders, concluded that Mao was the poet, the philosopher, and Teng the brisk organizer, "corresponding to the manager of a large American corporation, such as General Motors."

Flying on to Djakarta, Ford talked with President Suharto about Indonesia's economic troubles, promised aid, and reassured Suharto that the United States would continue its responsibility to keep peace in the Pacific. In the Philippines Ford negotiated with President Marcos about keeping the U.S. air and naval bases on the islands. It was Ford's first trip to the Philippines. Arriving there he remembered that during World War II his carrier had traced figure eights at sea, supporting General MacArthur's return, but Ford had not gone ashore. Then and thereafter,

Ford knew the Philippines' importance. "Those bases were of utmost significance as an effective U.S. military presence in the Pacific," he said. "Without those bases, we would have to retreat to Pearl Harbor."

With a stopover in Hawaii on December 7, Ford spoke at Pearl Harbor memorial ceremonies. "We who remember Pearl Harbor will always remember," he said. "For us it is a moment etched in time, a moment of shock and mixed feelings and, particularly, disbelief, a moment of shame and a moment of sorrow, of anguish and of anger, an end to irresolution, a summons to action, the start of a total commitment that comes but rarely to men and to nations." Ford remembered also that thirty-four years before, he had volunteered the morning after Pearl Harbor for combat duty in the Navy, and thereby began a part of his life that formed who he was, and was to become.

Back in Washington, Ford caught up on a backlog of business: delivering a report to Congress on his efforts to settle the Cyprus conflict, recommending to Congress economic and military aid to Greece, vetoing a tax reduction bill and reminding Congress: "I have clearly stated ever since last October 6 that I would veto any tax cut if you failed to cut future Federal spending at the same time."

Against the advice of Labor Secretary John Dunlop and the promise of labor support in the election, Ford vetoed the Common Situs Picketing Bill that Dunlop had negotiated and Congress had passed. The bill would have authorized all construction unions to picket an entire site if one union had a dispute with the contractor. Ford had told Dunlop he would sign a bill to which both the building trade unions and the construction industry agreed. But small contractors around the country vehemently opposed the bill, and Ford concluded: "This bill could lead to greater, not lesser, conflict in the construction industry." As a consequence of Ford's veto, Dunlop told Ford that it had cost him his credibility with labor unions and at the Labor Department, so he must resign. That day, Ford said, "was one of the unhappiest moments of my Administration."

Campaigning, the challenge from Reagan, intruded in Ford's 1975 year-end press conference. What, one reporter asked, was his reaction to a Gallup Poll that showed Reagan ahead of Ford by 40-32 percent among Republicans, and by 27-25 percent among independents? Unabashed, Ford responded with his routine incantation: "The way I judge it is whether I think I am doing a good job as President. In my opinion, the American people in the final analysis will judge whether I should be nominated and/or elected on the basis of how I conduct myself in this office." Did he have the desire, drive, and determination to win? "No question in my mind," he said, citing motivation for his resolve: "I have a vision of what I want America to be . . . At peace with ourselves, peace throughout the world, better economic conditions, the strengthening of individual freedom in this country, the protection of our environment . . . These are the things I want."

Reflecting during the Christmas holiday in Vail, Ford assessed what he had accomplished in his first sixteen months in office. In contrast to his predecessor, "We had kept our pledge to open the White House," he said. "The country had come out of the recession and was on the way up. We had extricated the United States from Vietnam reasonably successfully. We had made considerable headway towards a Salt II agreement. We had strengthened NATO, and established good rapport with the heads of government of NATO. We had peace. We had tough political problems, but we had begun to heal the country." That—reuniting a nation that had been sundered during Vietnam, and restoring credibility to the Presidency after the anguish and loathing during Watergate—had been Ford's prime objective.

His disappointments remained: "The strong public reaction against the pardon of Nixon; continuing high levels of unemployment; failure to persuade Congress to pass an energy bill; the terrible licking Republican candidates took in the off-year Congressional elections; my inability to convince the Congress that fiscal responsibility was crucial to establishing a healthy economy in the country."

Looking ahead, his goals driving his actions, Ford opened his campaign year of 1976 by concentrating on his job in the Oval Office. In January he made two strong appointments: Anne Armstrong to the Court of St. James's, the first woman Ambassador to Great Britain, and William J. Usery to replace Dunlop at Labor. One was a bold action, the other natural. Both measured up to the high standards Ford had set for his Cabinet. Of Armstrong, Ford said: "She had brains, appearance, loyalty, poise, and a fine speaking voice. As counselor to Nixon she had a catch-all basket of responsibilities and handled all of them well." Usery's record for mediating and settling labor-management conflicts was second to none. "Everybody trusts him, and for good reason," Ford said. "For both sides, labor and management, he has the facts, he understands the emotions. A great asset on the Economic Policy Board—Bill was a very practical person who looked at economics as a layman, much like myself."

To demonstrate his continuing concern over intelligence gathering, Ford spoke at George H. W. Bush's swearing at the CIA, pledging to "safeguard the effectiveness of this agency, the confidentiality of its information, and the lives and honor of its agents and employees." He signed a bill to provide Federal aid to public broadcasting, and another that would set the rules for electronic fund transfers and stop banks from "redlining" poor and minority neighborhoods. In a wide-ranging interview with Tom Brokaw and John Chancellor on NBC, Ford delivered a comprehensive survey of U.S. foreign policy. He notified Congress that he intended to save some $700 million by holding back money unspent by HUD.

Contemplating his State of the Union address, Ford rejected Hartmann's first draft and, hands on, coupled parts with segments of an alternate draft initiated by Cheney and David Gergen, an accomplished writer borrowed from the Department of the Treasury. With time expiring, the competing writers stitched together a State of the Union message that stirred neither his Congressional audience nor the American people with memorable oratory. Instead Ford offered a working executive's status report of where the United States was as a nation—better than a year earlier, "but still not good enough"—and an agenda for where the country needed to go. "My first objective is to have sound economic growth without inflation," he said. To accomplish that, Ford would halve the annual growth of Federal spending, limit the fiscal year 1976 budget to $395 billion, reduce taxes, provide incentives for private business to create jobs, free industry from excessive government regulation, and advance toward energy independence. For the individual citizen, Ford proposed catastrophic health insurance, extensions of unemployment benefits, changes to guarantee future Social Security benefits, and measures to reduce crime. For national security he proposed to increase the defense budget and strengthen the intelligence community. The closest he came to peroration: "We know that if we meet the challenges of our own time with a common sense of purpose and conviction, if we remain true to our Constitution and to our ideals, then we can know the future will be better than the past."

Far more impressive as a performance and indicative of his insight into the complexities of governing was Ford's briefing, the next day, on the fiscal year 1977 budget. It was a rare event; not since Truman had a President explicated in comparable detail how Federal funds were allocated and for what purpose. "Money is policy," Ford often said. "A President controls his Administration through the budget."

With his Vice President and Cabinet on the platform with him in the State Department Auditorium, Ford mentioned that he had spent more than 100 hours making budget decisions, and added: "I decided to conduct this briefing myself in order to emphasize how important the new 1977 budget is to the future of the United States." Citing specifics, he forecast that unemployment would drop from 7.7 percent in 1976 to 6.8 percent in 1977; proposed $3.3 billion in aid to elementary education; consolidated fifteen categorical grants in child nutrition to provide more money for children under the poverty line, less for those above; consolidated seven grants for community development; proposed hospital care where the patient pays 10 percent of costs up to $5,000, nothing above; advocated an 11 percent increase for medical research and full funding of $450 million for summer youth-training programs. He pointed out that his budget included Federal assistance for 500,000 housing units, a 40 percent increase in non-nuclear energy, and a 35 percent increase in money for nuclear energy. For national defense, Ford proposed increasing its budget by 9 percent for arms and soldiers' pay; reducing civilian employees by 25,000; and instituting a balanced mix of land-based missiles, submarine-based missiles, and long-range bombers for the nation's nuclear arsenal. Considering the entirety of his recommendations, Ford said that his tax and spending changes were realistic, achievable, and if Congress accepted them the Federal government would have a balanced budget by 1980.

Ford's presentation was marked by spirited exchanges with some well-informed reporters. John Chancellor of NBC said later: "This was the first time that I understood the degree to which President Ford understood how the government works." Ford himself was pleased with his presentation: "I knew that budget better even than Jim Lynn, maybe even better than Paul O'Neill."

With his in-box clear of January's statutory reports, Ford turned to his campaign. Speaking to a Midwest Republican Conference in Dearborn, Michigan, he raised the national issue he considered the highest priority—jobs. Ford's position was that the Federal government must provide the climate and incentives that encourage private enterprise to create productive and lasting jobs versus, "the opposition proposal for government jobs." His way was better, Ford insisted, pointing out that in his time as President, private industry had already brought back to work three-fifths of the jobs lost in the recession he inherited. After Michigan, he addressed the Virginia General Assembly in Williamsburg, denouncing an oversize Federal government that employed three million people, "more than the combined population of the Thirteen Original States." Campaigning before the Northeast Republican Conference, he proposed "to continue the common sense policies of sound, responsible, self-disciplined growth that have brought America out of the worst recession since the 1930s."

Every political campaign needs a break. Reagan, inadvertently, gave Ford his first big break with a speech in Chicago that epitomized Reagan's ingrained flaw—proposing simplistic solutions to complex problems. Titled "Let the People Rule," Reagan proposed that the Federal budget for fiscal 1975 be cut by $90 billion by shifting responsibility for "welfare, education, housing, food stamps, Medicaid, community and regional development, and revenue sharing to the states." The speech had been written by Jeffrey Bell, a lobbyist for the American Conservative Union, cleared by Reagan's staff and given to him. He liked it, thinking it conveyed what he would do if he became President.

Ford's campaign team—notably, Stu Spencer and Jack Veneman—saw that Governor Reagan's ingenuous proposal could be the break that would change the game. It was just what they needed to defeat Reagan in New Hampshire. There the Presidential primary is retail; voters meet the candidates in person and get to know where each stands on the issues that favor their lives or harm their well-being. And in New Hampshire, voters prize—more or less equally—the gift of Federal benefits and the absence of state sales or income tax. Transferring the cost of welfare, Social Security and other Federal payments to the states, as Reagan suggested, would mean that New Hampshire would have to impose an income tax or a sales tax, or both. To New Hampshire voters, this was anathema.

As Spencer's workers and the throng of reporters roaming the state broadcast the potential impact of Reagan's $90 billion speech, New Hampshire responded. Until then, the polls and conventional wisdom put Reagan well ahead. Within weeks, Reagan's prospects dropped, and Ford followed with a timely visit.

Arriving in New Hampshire on February 7, 1976, Ford delivered no rousing political speech at his first stop. Instead he conducted a town meeting with local officials—mayors, selectmen, state legislators—in the cafeteria of Rundlett Junior High School. The exchanges addressed a longtime Ford concern: the vast chasm between Washington's good intentions and local officials' practical applications. Among the questions asked were: Why do Federal rules require welfare workers to spend 85 percent of their time on paperwork and 15 percent with clients? Why does Washington demand we spend $200,000 for a bridge over a rural road when a $60,000 bridge would carry any farm load? Why does the Federal government deprive us of the one railroad on which New Hampshire depends? Why does Washington allow illegal aliens "to feed at the public trough" and take our jobs? Why does New England pay more for fuel oil than other sections of the country?

Ford, always better at Q&A than in delivering a set speech, performed well, explaining and critiquing Congressional actions. Better than most in Washington, Ford understood how the nation's faraway capital affected the individual citizen in the distant community. He was particularly gratified that the one Federal program all the local officials liked was also one of his favorites—Federal Revenue Sharing.

After speeches in Nashua and Concord and a press conference with in-state reporters, Ford conducted a citizens' Q&A at the University of New Hampshire in Durham. One question asked of Ford was: What did he think of Reagan's proposed $90 billion cut in the Federal budget? "I have never indulged in personalities," Ford said, but "factual questions are legitimate." He pointed out that those most concerned were New Hampshire's state legislators. "They would either have to cut services or raise taxes."

Ford returned to Washington pleased with his two days of campaigning. His appearances had attracted standing-room-only crowds, and New Hampshire television and newspapers had covered him extensively and fairly. "I started out behind," he said, "but I felt a change was coming." To Ford, the trend was not just heartening but crucial. "Had we lost in New Hampshire," he said, "the ball game would be all but over."

At that point, Ford faced another potential game changer: Richard Nixon announced a trip to China, set for just three days before the New Hampshire primary. It would be Nixon's first public appearance since his resignation in disgrace. The startling news reminded voters in New Hampshire and across America of Ford's long political association with

Nixon, of the pardon, and of suspicions that there had been a deal. "I was astounded," Ford said. "The timing could not have been worse."

As an example of Nixon's ingratitude, it was unconscionable. "If we lose New Hampshire, it will be because of Nixon," Spencer said. The three major networks televised China's toast to Nixon in Beijing on Monday morning, the day before the primary. At best the Nixon visit at so crucial a moment for his successor and benefactor was inconsiderate; at worst, it was deliberate.

Teeter's final poll showed the race even. On the night of the primary, February 24, 1976, Ford watched the early returns and went to sleep some 1,500 votes behind. The next morning, Cheney called him at 5 a.m.: "Mr. President, I have some good news for you. You won."

The final New Hampshire primary vote was 54,824 for Ford; 53,307 for Reagan, a margin of 1,317 votes. Spencer was exuberant: "We had the better organization, the better workers, the better phone bank, the better message." Ford was also elated. "Well, they can't say I've never won any place outside Grand Rapids," he said. He celebrated by going to the Oval Office to carry out the day's schedule: discussing a national-security situation with Kissinger and Scowcroft; chairing a strategy session with a delegation from the National League of Cities on his Federal Revenue Sharing bill then before Congress; signing the Financial Assistance for Health Care Act; talking over economics and energy with Simon, Seidman, Greenspan, Zarb, and other members of his Economic Policy Board; and meeting a delegation of western Senators and members of the Mexican-American Interparliamentary Conference.

Ford won the next two primaries, Massachusetts and Vermont, by default; Reagan had not entered. But the next contest—Florida, on March 9, 1976—was a formidable challenge. Reagan was more popular in the state and Republicans were predominantly conservative. Ford's chairman for Florida, Representative Louis Frey, turned out to be ineffective. Consequently, Ford's Florida campaign started out with no bumper stickers, no posters, no telephone bank, and no lists of prospective Ford workers and supporters. Ford was learning. "In a hot contest you can't take a Member of Congress, Senate or House, and put him in charge of a big state and have him run it the way it ought to be run," he said.

Again Spencer came to the rescue. He dispatched his political partner, Bill Roberts, with a simple instruction: win Florida. Roberts, a field captain of many a victorious political campaign, made an assessment:

Nine of the state's sixty-seven counties accounted for 70 percent of the Florida Republican vote. Concentrating on those counties, Roberts set up campaign offices, hired workers, recruited volunteers, polled, identified supporters, and organized phone banks. Again Reagan blundered, suggesting to an audience in Daytona Beach that Social Security funds might better be invested in the stock market. For Florida's legions of old folks, any implied threat to their Social Security checks was unacceptable. Reagan's mistake, Ford said, "was almost too good to be true."

Ford did his part to win Florida. On a weekend before the primary he flew into West Palm Beach and, despite an all-day tropical rainstorm, he stood in an open car, leading his circus-like motorcade through fourteen stops before wet but large crowds, his thinning hair and suit soaked and disheveled. Floridians admired his good cheer, his resolute performance. "I don't look very good," he told one crowd, "but I think I'm a darned good President."

Openly displaying the power of the Presidency, Ford promised the state a new Veterans Hospital, announced a missile contract to the Martin-Marietta plant in Orlando, handed Cuban refugees a better naturalization process, and committed to finish Interstate 75 into Fort Myers. On March 9, 1976, he won Florida by 53 percent to Reagan's 47 percent, and picked up another forty-three delegates. "Now," Ford said, "Governor Reagan ought to know he can't win."

Illinois was next. Four days before that primary, Ford sacrificed his campaign chairman. On March 12, 1976, NBC and the *Denver Post* carried a story charging that Secretary of the Army Callaway, on his last day in office, had intervened with the U.S. Forest Service for approval to expand a ski resort in Crested Butte, Colorado, that he and his brother-in-law owned. The meeting with Agriculture Department officials had taken place after his resignation and as he was packing to leave the Pentagon. He had exerted no pressure; he simply pointed out that he had been waiting five years for a decision and hoped there would be a resolution of the issue as soon as possible. To Callaway's dismay, Colorado's Democratic Senator Floyd Haskell, up for reelection, made it an issue in his campaign.

Ford talked to Callaway, heard the whole story, confirmed it, and assured himself that his campaign manager had in no way misused his office. Nevertheless, with Nixon's abuses of executive power still in the public mind, Callaway recognized that negative publicity could hurt Ford's campaign, so he resigned. "The charge was pure political demagoguery," Ford said. "Bo's decision tells us that here is a real man, totally unselfish, willing to look at the broader picture, even if it hurts him personally." The Senate investigated. Callaway was cleared. Haskell was defeated.

As it happened, the incident made no difference in Illinois. With Governor Richard Ogilvie and the Illinois Republican organization delivering their best, Ford defeated Reagan in Illinois—59 percent to 40 percent. With that victory, Ford had accumulated 166 delegates of the 1,130 he needed to win the nomination. Reagan had 54 delegates; 51 were uncommitted.

After winning the first six states, the Ford campaign had proved its competence and effectiveness. Replacing Callaway was not a problem; for a new chairman, Ford turned to Rog Morton, wise counselor and close friend from the House. Day-to-day campaign operations were directed by four key players: Cheney, with control over Ford's appearances, travel, and speeches, had become in fact the campaign manager. Spencer, canny, candid, and the most experienced in winning elections, guided, planned, and executed as well. Teeter played a crucial role— identifying where and how Ford could win.

The fourth was James A. Baker III. Morton, in poor health, brought Baker over from Commerce to organize campaign headquarters. A Texas lawyer, inexperienced in politics but a fast learner, Baker immediately earned Ford's respect. "Jim," Ford said, "had an uncanny ability to soothe ruffled feathers, to get people to work together, to win the respect of the press as well as the people he was directing. Highly intelligent, spoke with assurance in a very lawyerlike manner." The campaign team, with Ford's consent, handed Baker responsibility for their ultimate objective: Courting, befriending, holding, and counting the 1,170 delegates necessary to win the nomination.

With the North Carolina primary coming up, Ford was brimming with confidence. He had every reason to believe he would win North Carolina. His campaign was led by popular Governor James Holshauser—"a very fine guy, and he and his organization went all out for me," Ford said. Victory in North Carolina, Ford believed, might prompt Reagan to leave the race. In fact, the Reagan campaign was foundering, and broke. Sears, on his own initiative, met with Morton to explore terms for Reagan's withdrawal. But Morton, and Ford, underestimated Reagan's tenacity and the political power of Holshauser's political rival in North Carolina, the archconservative Senator Jesse Helms.

Nor had Ford foreseen that Reagan would wield and strike with an improbable political weapon: the Panama Canal. Ford had inherited, from both the Johnson and Nixon administrations, the vexing problem of Panama. After some sixty-five years of U.S. dominion over the waterway, locks, and a ten-mile zone of Panamanian territory spanning the canal, Panama demanded change. Led by General Omar Torrijos, a socialist-inclined dictator, the government and people called for a new treaty; otherwise, Torrijos's followers threatened sabotage that could close the canal.

Panamanians were not alone in considering that U.S. control of the canal and zone violated their sovereignty; other Latin American nations supported Panama's position. In response, Kissinger initiated discussions to ease the tension and find a solution that would expand Panama's role and still guarantee U.S. use of the canal and zone for defense purposes.

To Republican conservatives, any notion of turning over the canal to Panama was unacceptable. Reagan stated the conservative position with his usual facility: "We bought it, we paid for it, it's ours, and we should tell Torrijos and company that we are going to keep it."

With the Panama Canal as the issue and his repeated scorn of Ford-Kissinger détente with the USSR, Reagan regained momentum in North Carolina. His staff composed a thirty-minute political documentary that showed Reagan at his most likable, and broadcast it on fifteen of the state's seventeen television stations. Helms motivated, organized, and delivered his conservative Republican faction at the polls. As a result, Reagan upset expectations and defeated Ford 52 percent to 46 percent in the North Carolina primary. "Helms campaigned hard against me, and effectively," Ford said. "He resurrected Reagan's campaign from a near termination point, and made it a tough campaign for me for the next three months."

The loss in North Carolina cost Ford, not so much in delegates; he won twenty-six to Reagan's twenty-eight. Instead, Reagan's victory injected vigor into his appearances, lifted the spirits of his campaign staff and followers, and replenished his campaign treasury.

Two weeks later Ford won the Wisconsin primary, 55 percent to 44 percent; but on May 1, he suffered the worst setback of his campaign. In Texas, Reagan made the Panama Canal the number-one issue, and he won the state in a landslide—66 percent to Ford's 33 percent, taking all 100 delegates. Two days later Reagan won Georgia, Alabama, and Indiana. With those four Reagan victories the lead in the delegate count switched; for the first time, he moved ahead.

The next morning, Morton stopped me in the corridor of the West Wing. "Jim, we're really hurting for delegates. If we don't show some strength, and quickly, we could lose this. Could you persuade Nelson to free up some of those New York delegates?"

"Rog, the only person who can make that request is the President. He and he alone can ask the Governor for delegates."

Ford, well aware that his prospects were in peril, recognized that asking would not be easy, but he had to do it. So, in a humble conversation in the Oval Office, he did. Could Rockefeller come to his aid by delivering New York's delegation? Rockefeller responded graciously and promptly, committing 133 of the state's 154 delegates to Ford. Not only did Rockefeller hand New York to Ford, but he also initiated a parallel effort with Governor Scranton and Drew Lewis to deliver 88 of 103 Pennsylvania delegates, and with Connecticut State Chairman Frederick Biebel and other party leaders to deliver all 35 of Connecticut's delegates.

Rockefeller's action was uncommon in politics, a rare example of fidelity overcoming hurt. He rescued the nomination of the man who had turned him out. To Rockefeller the motive was clear: "Nothing is more important to the country than the nomination and election of Gerald Ford."

With the eastern delegates committed, the lead in numbers changed back to Ford. In May, Ford continued to move ahead, winning primaries in West Virginia, Maryland, Michigan, Kentucky, Oregon, and Tennessee, while Reagan won Nebraska, Arkansas, Idaho, and Nevada. At the end of May, Baker's count was 732 for Ford, 530 for Reagan, 184 uncommitted. In June, Reagan defeated Ford in primaries in Montana, South Dakota, and California; Ford took Rhode Island, New Jersey, and Ohio. Reagan also won most of the delegates chosen by the state conventions in June. The contest was close, and getting closer.

In July, the Bicentennial Celebration of the Declaration of Independence gave Ford a welcome respite from courting delegates. For a year, perhaps longer, Marsh, an accomplished scholar of American history, had been urging Ford to make the 200th anniversary of the Declaration a significant and memorably patriotic occasion. To Marsh, the Bicentennial should present America at its best—a national salute to freedom that would certify the nation's unity and pay tribute to America's ideals and values.

The proposal met Ford's own deeply patriotic fervor and he assigned Hartmann to commit himself totally to writing a series of appropriate addresses. For the first, Ford stood in the National Archives building before the original document and said: "The Declaration is the Polaris of our political order—the fixed star of freedom." At Valley Forge on July 4, Ford remembered, "General Washington and his ragged Continental Army encamped here—exhausted, outnumbered, and short of everything except faith." At Philadelphia's Independence Hall, Ford said: "I feel both pride and humility, rejoicing and reverence, as I stand in the place where two centuries ago the United States of America was conceived in liberty and dedicated to the proposition that all men are created equal." Later that day, aboard the carrier USS *Forrestal* in New York Harbor, Ford watched the tall ships—"emissaries from thirty other nations"—parade majestically across the rippling waters under a brilliant summer sky. Extolling America's unity in diversity, not far from the Statue of Liberty, Ford said, "The sea has been a passageway for millions and millions of people from all over the world who have come to America to share its bounty and its opportunity and to enrich our future in return."

Flying back to Washington that night, "I realized that no one, in July a year earlier, could have forecast there would be such a 180 degree turn in the mood of the country, in the unity and hope, in the change from Vietnam and Watergate," Ford said. "Millions of Americans came out to march in the squares, dance in the streets, and pray in the churches. There had never been such a spontaneous celebration of love of country."

Three days later the Fords welcomed Great Britain's Queen Elizabeth II and Prince Philip, Duke of Edinburgh, to Washington, and to a sumptuous banquet at the White House. Recognizing our British heritage, Ford said: "Our Founding Fathers . . . learned representative self-government from British books and practices, . . . established a nation that adapted the best of British traditions to the American climate and to the American character." In a regal and gracious response, Queen Elizabeth II commended "the strength and permanence of Anglo-

American friendship." Closing her tribute, she said, "May it long continue to flourish for the sake of both our countries and for the greater good of mankind."

From the Bicentennial, Ford returned to the campaign. On July 18, four weeks before the Republican Convention was to open, Baker reported the delegate count to Ford: 1,102 for Ford, 1,063 for Reagan, and 94 uncommitted.

Ten days later, Reagan blundered again. On the advice of John Sears, he announced that if nominated he would choose Pennsylvania Senator Richard Schweiker, a liberal in practice and philosophy, as his Vice Presidential candidate. Sears's motive was to pick off Pennsylvania delegates and, more importantly, euchre Ford into announcing his prospective running mate. The ploy failed, completely. Conservatives rejected Schweiker, deeming that joining a liberal to Reagan violated the purity of their cause. John Ashbrook, a pillar of conservatives in the House, denounced the Schweiker ruse as "the dumbest thing I ever heard of."

The prospect of a two-faced ticket jolted, among others, the undecided Mississippi delegation, with its thirty votes. State chairman Clarke Reed was already ambivalent. In ideology he tilted toward Reagan; as a loyal Republican he inclined toward President Ford; as a leader, he wanted to end up on the winning side. A Cheney foray into Mississippi convinced him that Ford had a following there, and Cheney in turn convinced Ford. So, from the White House Ford telephoned Reed, assured him that he would have the delegates to win, and asked for his endorsement. "The train is pulling out of the station, Clarke, and I believe it is time for you to climb aboard," Ford said. After debating with himself for two days Reed agreed. He announced his support of Ford in a press conference, and branded Reagan's choice of Schweiker "an act of desperation."

To win the support of other Mississippians, Ford decided to fly to Jackson with Mrs. Ford and talk to the delegates. In a spirited session he answered questions, cited his record of two years in office, and promised "to help elect more Republicans from the courthouse to the statehouse to the Congress." His trip succeeded. He won sixteen of Mississippi's thirty delegates.

On arriving in Kansas City on August 15, 1976—the day before the thirty-first Republican National Convention opened—Ford was confident but taking no chances. Baker informed him that he had 1,135 votes—five more than he needed to win. However, Baker cautioned, a handful were soft commitments. Moreover, Reagan was not ready to accept defeat. His strategists contrived two procedural votes, hoping that winning a preliminary contest would change the final vote. The first would ratify Sears' stratagem. It proposed a change in party rules to require a candidate for President to announce his choice for Vice President before the vote on the nomination. The rule was unprecedented, its purpose transparent. Ford's delegates held firm; he won that vote, 1,180 to 1,069. Ford called it, "Sears' long pass that fell incomplete."

Reagan then proposed to use the party platform to impugn Ford's conduct of foreign policy. By implication the party document would rebuke Ford for reaching détente with the USSR, for signing the Helsinki Agreement, and for declining to meet with Solzhenitsyn. "Nelson and Henry were furious, and properly so," Ford said. "And I was goddam mad about it—it denounced Administration foreign policy. But I said to Henry and Nelson, 'Look here, we don't have the votes to stop it. Do you want to lose this vote and then lose the nomination?' I hated to swallow it, but I thought I understand the politics better than Nelson and Henry did. And I did."

Fifteen years later, Ford had not overcome his resentment at Reagan's effrontery in contriving to have the Republican Party denounce Republican foreign policy. To Ford, the act of a public man preaching Republican Solidarity and then openly violating it was hypocrisy. "They thought I would be sucker enough to take the bait, and we fooled them," Ford said. "I was thinking of winning the nomination. My view was, who the hell is going to worry about that platform when it's all through? I'm not going to go by it. I'm not going to be bound by it. I decided to concede that vote, not make a big fuss about it, and leave us in a better posture to win the final vote."

On the fourth session of the convention, the night of August 17, 1976, the nominations for President began. Reagan was first, his name placed before the convention by Nevada's Senator Paul Laxalt. A close friend of Reagan, next-door neighbor as Governor, and frequent companion on horseback, Laxalt commended Reagan as the outsider who could fix Washington's problems. He will "trim back that bureaucracy," Laxalt said, "and, more importantly, whip that irresponsible Congress into line."

Ford was nominated by Governor William Milliken of Michigan: "He already has reestablished our leadership, revived our economy, and restored our honor. He brought strength in time of crisis, order in a time of chaos."

After the usual seconding speeches and staged demonstrations, Permanent Chairman John Rhodes ordered the roll call for the nomination. Reagan led from the beginning, and he continued to lead. After the first ten states had voted, the count was 301 for Reagan to 141 for Ford. After 20 states, Reagan was still ahead—467 delegates to 335; after thirty states he continued to hold his lead—622 to 554. When the roll call reached New York, State Chairman Richard Rosenbaum proudly delivered 133 votes for Ford, 20 for Reagan. For the first time, Ford gained the lead in delegates—768 to Reagan's 704. Again, Rockefeller and New York had come to Ford's political rescue. From that point on, Ford continued to gain, with solid majorities in Ohio and Pennsylvania. The third state from the end, West Virginia, delivered the nomination to Ford, awarding him 20 of its 28 delegates and bringing his total to 1,135—5 more than he needed to win. With Wisconsin's 45 votes and Wyoming's 7 for Ford, the final tally was 1,187 for Ford and 1,070 for Reagan.

Watching the voting in his suite in Kansas City's Crown Center Hotel, Ford was elated. "It was," he said, "an exhilarating experience of my life because everybody, my family, myself, and thousands of others had really worked on it. That was a great moment." At the same time, Ford recognized that so close a victory was ominous; almost half his party had voted against him. He needed Reagan's people—all of them.

His next move was to meet immediately with Reagan; they had agreed beforehand that the winner would go to the loser's suite in a gesture toward party solidarity. Before the meeting, Sears had told Cheney: "Reagan will speak with Ford if he gets the nomination, but he must not ask him to be his candidate for Vice President."

Ford was considering asking Reagan to join the ticket; he remembered that in 1960 Kennedy had asked runner-up Johnson, and won. "I had mixed emotions," he said. "I thought Reagan would strengthen the ticket. On the other hand, we had had such a bitter fight, and we had such strong disagreements, we would have had a lot of trouble reconciling these differences publicly in the campaign. My guess was that Nancy didn't want him to be on the ticket; she wanted to wait for '80. And I was 30 plus points behind, so our future was far from optimistic. If he were on the ticket and we lost badly, then he would share the blame."

As he entered Reagan's suite in the Alameda Plaza Hotel, Ford shook hands with Reagan and said. "Governor, it was a great fight. I just wish I had some of your talent and your tremendous organization." When the two were alone, Ford felt uncomfortable. "The tension of our long campaign permeated that room," he said. But he had come with a mission—first, to discern Reagan's interest. "So I said: 'Ron, who do you recommend that I select for Vice President?' I said it that way because I wanted somehow to get confirmation that he didn't want to be on the ticket. Well, he did not take the bait. He said, 'You've got a number of good potentials.'"

After sparring for a few minutes, Ford then suggested six names he was considering—John Connally, Bill Simon, Bob Dole, Howard Baker, Elliott Richardson, and Bill Ruckelshaus. After a moment Reagan said, "Dole would be an excellent choice."

"We sparred there for another fifteen minutes or so," Ford said. "I asked him to campaign, and he indicated he would, but he didn't say how or where."

It was 2:00 a.m. when Ford returned to his hotel, with one vital decision yet to be made: his choice of a candidate for Vice President. At 3:15 a.m., Ford circled his advisers—Rockefeller, Senators Bob Griffin and John Tower, Laird, Harlow, Marsh, Hartmann, Cheney, Spencer, and Teeter.

In making his choice, Ford's first priority—as is usually the case with nominees for President—was political; his second, merit. And, as usual, the method of deciding the second place on the ticket was a process of elimination. So the ten-man team debated, evaluated, and dismissed: Richardson was too liberal. Simon was too fiscally conservative. Connally, Teeter's polls showed, polarized voters. Ruckelshaus had no record as an effective campaigner; he was defeated in his one race in Indiana for the Senate. At one point Ford mentioned Anne Armstrong, then withdrew the suggestion. "That would have been a big, big gamble, which I did not think the country was prepared to take," he said.

After an hour's discussion the survivors were Baker and Dole. "Howard was a moderate, an engaging and articulate Senator who was acceptable to every wing of the party," Ford said. "He had proved his integrity on Watergate. But Teeter's polls showed that we were not going to carry any Southern state."

"To offset the South we had to win every state we could west of the Mississippi and then gamble that we could carry our share of the Middle West, New England, and central Atlantic. Dole's strength was in the Western agricultural states. We couldn't lose Kansas, Nebraska, South Dakota, North Dakota, Montana, Iowa—those states just had to be won. Bob had a reliable record of winning a typical Middle Western plains state. He was the person who would be most helpful to implement that pure political strategy. The selection of Dole was purely a pragmatic political decision."

Ford's acceptance speech was one of the best of his public career—in great part because his preparation was so thorough. He read Hartmann's first draft to Betty. Too long, she said. After cuts and revisions, Ford brought in Don Penny to coach him. A young virtuoso of television and Hollywood, both an actor and director, Penny looked like a mischievous Puck, and directed like a Marine gunnery sergeant. Ford responded well to Penny's drilling. He practiced, studied videos of his rehearsals, and continued to practice. He asked Marsh and Cheney to critique his trial runs. His time and effort in preparation paid off: his delivery showed assurance, deep conviction in what he could accomplish in four more years if America granted him the opportunity.

"We will build a stronger and safer world," he told the Convention. "We will build an America where people feel rich in spirit as well as in worldly goods . . . We will build on performance, not promise, on experience, not expedience . . ."

Experience, Ford believed, would be his great advantage over Jimmy Carter, the former Georgia governor the Democratic Party had nominated four weeks before. Upon Carter's nomination, Ford had started thinking about debating him. "I remembered how important the Kennedy-Nixon debates had been in 1960." So on the afternoon before his acceptance speech, Ford inserted into his speech the challenge to Carter that he had written in longhand: " . . . to go before the American people and debate the real issues face to face with Jimmy Carter. The American people have a right to know firsthand exactly where both of us stand."

It was a good speech, practical, specific, stirring delegates to an ovation that prompted Ford to invite Ronald and Nancy Reagan to the dais to share in the enthusiasm. "I don't know what I'm going to say," Reagan told Nancy on their way from the VIP seats through the crowd. But he did. In a brief, impromptu address, Reagan met and summoned the emotion of the occasion: "We live in a world in which the great powers have poised and aimed at each other horrible missiles of destruction that can, in a matter of minutes, arrive in each other's country and destroy virtually the civilized world we live in." Looking ahead for a century, Reagan challenged the American people to preserve individual freedom and save the world from mutual nuclear destruction. The standing ovation that followed exceeded Ford's.

The 1976 Republican National Convention ended that August night with a mask of unity on that dais. By chance the scene was also an extraordinary tableau presaging the transformation of the Republican Party. At the center was President Ford with his new partner, Dole, the last of the party's moderates in philosophy and in practice. On Ford's left was Nelson Rockefeller, apotheosis of the progressive Republican Party of the past. On his right stood Ronald Reagan, exemplar of the conservative Republican Party that was to come.

CHAPTER 24

Election

On the morning after his nomination, Ford rose early and motored to the Radisson Muehlebach Hotel to breakfast with some 150 members of the Republican National Committee. Confidence and enthusiasm marked the occasion, but for Ford, the exhilaration of the night before was giving way to reality. Prospects were grim. Gallup's latest poll put Carter ahead 56-33; Harris's 61-32. Teeter's latest surveys showed that on the eve of Ford's nomination, he would lose the election by some 10 million votes. With his usual statistical practicability, Teeter advised Ford: "To win, Mr. President, you will need to change the minds of 130,000 voters every day for the next seventy-three days."

Yet, from the beginning, Ford was never discouraged.

"Inwardly I thought we had an excellent chance to win it," he said. "I was confident of our record. I thought we had good people in the campaign. I thought we made the right choice in Bob Dole. I thought I made a good speech at the Convention, and we had handled the situation with Reagan well. I consciously believed we could make it. It would be tough; I knew we had to work like hell. But somehow I had the feeling that my good luck was going to prevail."

Later that morning Ford and his family and staff were scheduled to fly to Vail, Colorado, for a brief vacation before beginning the campaign against Carter. On the way, Ford had proposed, he and Dole should stop off in Dole's hometown, Russell, Kansas, for a tribute to Dole. Cheney and Spencer opposed the idea; they said there was not enough time for advance teams to build a crowd, and a meager audience would be bad publicity. After a spirited debate, Ford told Spencer: "Damn it, I know what I'm doing. I know a little bit about politics."

Ford was right. The event turned out to be a major success for Russell, for Kansas, and beyond. The emotion, patriotism, and the show of affection for Kansas' native son played well on national television and with the traveling press. Dole, recalling how the people of Russell had collected funds for his recovery from the wounds sustained in World War II, was so moved he could hardly speak. "If I have done anything, it was because of what you did for me," he struggled to tell the crowd.

For his first three days in Vail, Ford golfed, swam, played tennis, and relaxed. At 8:00 a.m. on Tuesday, August 24, he met for the first time with his election campaign staff—Cheney, Morton, Spencer, Teeter, Baker, press secretary Ron Nessen, scheduler Jerry Jones, and two important new additions—Doug Bailey and John Deardourff, recruited to plan and handle advertising.

The prime item on the agenda was appointing a new campaign manager. Since Morton was ill, Ford had no doubt about the best person to take over—James Baker. "As our chief delegate hunter, Jim had demonstrated an outstanding ability to organize and manage at campaign headquarters," Ford said. "He had an uncanny ability to smooth ruffled feathers, to get people to work together. Very cool, a smooth, polite Texas gentleman. He won the respect of the press as well as the people he was directing. I credit a significant part of our success at the Convention to Jim Baker."

A rough, preliminary campaign plan was ready. Spencer and Michael Raoul-Duval, a campaign aide to Cheney, had put together a thick notebook of electoral projections and boilerplate advice and commentary. They assumed that Ford could count on a base of 15 New England and western states, with a total of 83 electoral votes. Carter would have 11 states, mostly in the South, with 87 electoral votes. From 25 swing states, with 368 electoral votes, one or the other candidate would need to win 270 electoral votes to win Presidency.

Ford was more optimistic. He was sure he could count on Michigan and his neighbors—Indiana, Illinois, and Ohio. If tradition held in upper New England, then Maine, Vermont, and New Hampshire would go Republican. Always ready to listen to expert advice, Ford relied heavily on Teeter. "Bob early on pointed out that our chances of winning states below the Mason-Dixon line were not good, with the possible exception of Virginia," Ford said. "The reason he gave at the outset, and it was proven, was that the Bible belt, which favored Carter, covers the deep South and pushes up through Tennessee and Kentucky. To offset the South, Teeter said we had to win most states west of the Mississippi River and six of eight big states—New York, New Jersey, Pennsylvania, Ohio, Illinois, Michigan, California, and Texas."

The draft plan discussed in Vail identified two campaign imperatives: Carter must blunder; Ford must make no mistakes. Ford must limit his campaigning; his prime asset was to be seen as Presidential. Teeter's surveys showed that Ford gained in a state where he campaigned but lost elsewhere. The corollary was: the more Ford traveled, the more voters viewed him as just another politician.

The contest would be won or lost on television. Since some 80 million Americans would probably vote in November, and only a million or so would see the candidate in person over the next ten weeks, television would be crucial. So the key to victory would be the debates and carefully crafted commercials to be broadcast in priority states and cities. Consequently, the planners pointed out, portraying Ford on television at his best, and in the most favorable circumstances, was essential. It was for this reason that Bailey and Deardourff were brought in: they had a track record of producing television ads for Republican candidates that won elections.

Ford liked both newcomers from the beginning and came to respect their skills and professionalism. "Bailey was the putterer-together of the television aspects of the campaign. I thought the ones where he got our family involved were superb. We got many compliments. His efforts got nothing but praise. In most campaigns the media effort is criticized, but I heard no criticism of Bailey's work." To Ford, "Deardourff was sort of the strategist, the concept man of the campaign. A very thoughtful guy, straightforward. He'd sit in on a meeting, never trying to dominate; but when he spoke you knew he had thought about the problem and he had a concept to meet the problem. Both were soft spoken, well-informed, candid. In a conference or when you saw what they produced, they generated confidence."

As his issues for the campaign, Ford relied not on polls but on his long experience in Congress and his two years as President. In Vail, just before beginning his campaign for the general election, he set forth for reporters his priorities: "Number one, jobs, and we mean meaningful jobs with an opportunity for advancement. Number two, an accelerated home ownership program . . . Number three, quality health care that is affordable to the American people. . . . Number four, [preventing] crime . . . Five, better recreation facilities . . . There is one other point to be made because it is all encompassing—peace throughout the world, peace at home and peace throughout the world."

To Ford, these were the issues foremost in governing; therefore, the priority issues for his campaign. To Teeter, a lifelong student of why people vote, the election would be decided less on issues than on visual impression. "The deciding factor in a voter's mind is, 'Do I like this guy or not?'" Teeter said. "Where that candidate stands on an issue may affect that attitude, but it is not determinative. The fact is that forty percent of voters decide, for no particular rational reason, 'I like this candidate better than the other one.' Another fifteen percent dislike or mistrust one candidate, and vote against him. Look at history. The winner is the one we like best." Teeter believed that Ford was inherently more likable than Carter; his goal was—through the writing press and through television—to convince voters of that. "There was another imponderable, and that was how many people would say to themselves, 'It's time for a change,'" Teeter said. "After eight years of Nixon and Ford, that was hard to counter."

Bailey envisioned a parallel objective. Since Ford had never campaigned for national office, millions of voters knew little about him. So Bailey knew he must use the media to introduce Ford to the greater part of the electorate where he was unknown. He proposed to "have people see Ford on the tube and feel comfortable, to believe that's the real guy. He is what he seems to be. Nothing contrived about him."

For five days the campaign staff met with Ford each morning, and once, at a long dinner meeting, to plan a Ford victory. They identified the priority states, the visits Ford would make to each, and rationed time for key smaller states. They worked out a budget, allocating the most money for television, the second most for travel. They worked out the role of surrogates, Cabinet members, governors, senators. They brought in Vice President Rockefeller to advise on New York, and John Connally to advise on Texas. They discussed, without resolving, the states where Reagan could help. Ford, still vexed that Reagan had not only opposed him, but had also publicly and repeatedly scorned the Administration's handling of foreign policy, put off the possibility of Reagan's help for later discussion. Ford's reluctance to ask for Reagan's support, as James Baker wrote, "had nothing to do with [Reagan's] personality and everything to do with the fact that he had challenged and almost beaten a sitting president from his own party."

Ford left Vail on Sunday, August 29, 1976, stopped off in Rapid City, South Dakota, to meet with Republican leaders from the Dakotas, Montana, and Wyoming, and returned to Washington and his brimming in-box in the Oval Office. For a fortnight he concentrated on governing, meeting with his Cabinet, with Kissinger and Scowcroft on national security, with Congressional leaders, with Lynn on the budget, with Greenspan on the economy, with Rumsfeld on Defense issues, with Coleman on aircraft noise. He signed bills, one on income tax reform; pushed the House to pass Revenue Sharing; and impounded $11 million in unused construction funds. He was interviewed by Tom Brokaw on the *Today Show* and held a press conference on the South Lawn of the White House. There he reported on Kissinger's progress in negotiating the problems of South Africa, and, in response to a question, answered that SALT prospects were improving but difficult problems were still to be resolved.

Ford formally opened his election campaign on September 15, 1976, in the city he had treasured since his college years: Ann Arbor, Michigan. To an overflow crowd in the University of Michigan's Crisler Arena, Ford presented a brief account of his performance in office—"restored trust in the White House . . . turned the economy around . . . peace and the capability and will to keep it." Dismissing "some mystic vision of the future," he again identified his down-to-earth goals for Americans' future: jobs, government economic policies that create jobs, homeownership for all willing to work and save, accessible and affordable health care, quality education for everyone, prevention of crime, and expansion of recreation facilities. One new initiative suggested by Ford was doubling the National Park System over the next ten years. Most important of all, he told the crowd, "We are at peace. No Americans are in combat anywhere on the earth and none are being drafted and I will keep it that way."

It was a good opening speech, comprehensive and realistic, absent of oratory, reflecting the stout and practical man Ford was. "It was what I wanted to say, where I wanted to say it, and I thought I had done well," he said later.

Preparing for the first televised debate, scheduled for September 23, 1976, in Philadelphia, Ford studied his briefing book on Carter's record, reviewed his own position on hundreds of issues, and practiced. With unemployment still high and the economy unstable, Ford calculated that this first debate, on economic and domestic policy, would be his toughest. "I thought if there was one area where Carter should do well, it would be here," Ford said. He had studied his opponent. "I disliked him in some respects. I detected a very egotistical person, and I don't like people with that characteristic," he said. "On the other hand, I was impressed by his articulate capability. He had a good mind. He was a pretty good showman, but just not the kind of person I would warm up to."

To coach Ford, Cheney and his staff set up a lectern, rigged spotlights, turned on cameras and subjected Ford to rigorous questioning. At the end of every session he studied videotapes of his performance and invited comment and criticism. On the eve of this vital face-to-face encounter with Carter, Ford was confident but realistic. "I hope to break even," he said.

On the night of the first debate, the cameras focused on Carter and Ford in Philadelphia's Walnut Street Theater, and Moderator Edwin Newman set the ground rules. Tension was high. Neither Ford nor Carter appeared to be at ease. Their responses seemed to have been memorized; both lacked spontaneity. Ford was the more specific, Carter the more conceptual. But neither Ford nor Carter enlightened the audience—estimated at some 100 million people. For the most part it was political attack, response, and counterattack, reruns of what each had been saying on his travels. Neither stumbled. Ford recounted what he had accomplished in two years; Carter promised to make the Federal government more economical and efficient. Ford came across as well-informed and competent; Carter as knowledgeable and persuasive. Both had stood in awkward silence, looking perplexed, during a twenty-seven-minute technical breakdown in broadcast audio.

The on-scene press scored it a draw, but the TV audience gave the edge to Ford. In fact, surveys after the debate indicated that Philadelphia had changed the political equation. Gallup, before that first debate, had Carter ahead by eighteen points; afterwards, Gallup reported that Carter's lead dropped to eight points.

After Philadelphia, Ford boarded Air Force One for a campaign trip through Louisiana, Mississippi, Alabama, and Florida. Reception was respectful but measured. Back at work in the Oval Office, he signed bills for land and water conservation, military construction, and veterans' benefits, vetoed appropriations for Labor and HEW, and reported on progress with his Administration's efforts to resolve the Cyprus conflict. Teeter came in to see President Ford with good news: Ford, so impossibly behind before the first debate, continued to gain.

Ford's post-Philadelphia optimism was brief. October brought bad news about the economy. Back in January Greenspan had advised, "If you submit an expansive budget everything will look good during the campaign. But if you win, you'll regret it because you will have inflation back, high interest rates, and other bad economic developments. If, on the other hand, you submit the more realistic budget you will probably have a hiatus in October that will be harmful politically. However, if you win the election, you will have a hell of a good economy for the next four years."

Given the choices, Ford had made a conscious decision to propose the budget that would over time improve the economy. "The other option would have meant spending by the Treasury, a bigger deficit, and reigniting inflation," Ford said. "That wouldn't have been the best thing for the country, and I just decided I would not do it. I thought I would rather gamble that we would win the election even though there would be a pause, and then have a healthy economy to start out the new term."

As it turned out, Ford said, "Greenspan was right. The news was bad in October. Unemployment went up, not much, but the perception was bad. That made the whole economic picture questionable."

Worse was to come. A disgruntled union official, Jesse Calhoon, head of the Marine Engineers Beneficial Association, told the press that his union had made cash payments to Ford's Congressional campaigns that he had never reported. Ford knew that the charges were false; his campaign and personal financial records had been examined and cleared by some 400 FBI agents and 6 IRS accountants before he was confirmed as Vice President, so he dismissed the charges at first. But newspapers made the union's accusations a potentially damaging campaign issue. The *New York Times* headlined its story: "Possible Covert Union Gifts to Ford from '64 to '74 Called Target of Inquiry by Watergate Prosecutor." For Ford, it was a dilemma. He wanted, urgently needed, an immediate resolution, but he would not intervene directly with Charles Ruff, a part-time Special Prosecutor, who was not expediting the investigation.

Determined to defend himself, Ford invited reporters into the Oval Office. He told them that all campaign contributions during his twenty-five years in the House had been properly reported, and that none had been diverted to personal use—as the FBI and IRS had confirmed. Ford reaffirmed the independence of the Special Prosecutor, and acknowledged that charges, once made, must be investigated—without interference. He told the press that he had instructed his staff, "Under no circumstances should they make contacts with either the Special Prosecutor or the Department of Justice." But he made a point of suggesting that the investigation be concluded quickly and quoted a legal aphorism: "Justice delayed is justice denied."

At the end of the press conference a reporter said: "Mr. President, you look more worried than I've seen you in a long time."

"I am more concerned about my personal reputation," Ford said, trying to mask his concern. In private he admitted: "I *was* worried. I had seen too many candidates defeated by false, last minute charges." The election was only thirty-two days away.

That afternoon, Cheney came in with still more bad news. Earl Butz, Ford's good friend and Secretary of Agriculture, had made a crudely offensive joke about black voters, and the degrading comment was about to be published in *New Times* magazine. In Cheney's account of Butz talking to fellow passengers on an airplane about the election, Butz had disdained the importance of the black vote with a vulgar characterization. One passenger who heard Butz's racist remark was the tattle John Dean, former Nixon counsel and Watergate conspirator. Dean gave the story to the press.

Ford, long aware that Butz was an irrepressible jokester, saw at once that this time Butz had gone too far. "Bring Earl in tomorrow morning," Ford told Cheney.

Before he saw Butz the next day, Ford decided that he would not ask for his immediate resignation. "He had been loyal to me, and I had built up a reputation for being loyal in reciprocation," Ford said. "I decided to see what Earl's own reaction was."

Ford rarely rebuked any subordinate; when he had to remonstrate at all, he never raised his voice. With his words deliberate and his voice even, Ford said: "Earl, the language and attitude attributed to you is not acceptable in my Administration. Such comments are offensive to me, and to the American people."

"I am sorry, Mr. President," Butz said. He admitted that the story was true and promised: "I will make a public apology."

The meeting lasted only minutes, and Ford called in Cheney. "Dick, now I don't want you to pressure Earl. As he sees the story develop he'll use his own good judgment, and I think his judgment will be that he will come in and say that he ought to step aside." Two days later Butz did come back to see Ford. "Mr. President," he said, "I goofed. I should have known better. I did not intend this to be a racial slur, but it's causing you an awful lot of trouble. So I'm going to submit my resignation." As Butz left the Oval Office, Ford saw tears in Butz's eyes.

The sequence of vexing events distracted Ford from preparing for the second debate with Carter—this one to be held in San Francisco with a focus on national security. "Foreign policy and national defense were my forte," Ford said, "so I expected to do well." Carter, despite his lack of experience or record in foreign policy, opened by boldly attacked Ford's record. In his first round, Carter said: ". . . . As far as foreign policy goes, Mr. Kissinger has been the president of this country." It was a cheap shot, touching a sensitive nerve with Ford, but he decided to ignore it. Instead, he pointed to successes, in Portugal, in Africa, and noted that Prime Minister Rabin of Israel had declared that the United States "is at a peak in its influence and power in the Middle East."

After more campaign slash-and-defense, Max Frankel of the *New York Times* suggested that the Helsinki Agreements accepted Soviet "domination in Eastern Europe." Ford defended Helsinki, and said: "There is no Soviet domination of Eastern Europe, and there never will be under a Ford Administration."

Frankel, former Moscow bureau chief for the *New York Times,* followed up: "Did I understand you to say, sir, that the Russians are not using Eastern Europe as their own sphere of influence and occupying most of the countries there and making sure with their troops that it's a Communist zone . . . ?"

"I don't believe, Mr. Frankel, that the Yugoslavians consider themselves dominated by the Soviet Union," Ford said. "I don't believe that the Romanians consider themselves dominated by the Soviet Union. I don't believe that the Poles consider themselves dominated by the Soviet Union. Each of these countries is independent, autonomous; it has its own territorial integrity."

Ford had made a mistake—a mistake of enormous consequence. Carter saw it at once and responded with sarcasm: "I would like to see Mr. Ford convince the Polish Americans and the Czech Americans and the Hungarian Americans in this country that those countries don't live under the domination and supervision of the Soviet Union behind the Iron Curtain."

Scowcroft, watching on television in a room offstage with Spencer, turned ashen. "We have a problem," he said aloud, knowing that as many as four Soviet divisions occupied Poland. But Ford, continuing to debate and concentrating on parrying Carter's charges of weakened defense and misguided foreign policy, did not realize that he had erred in flatly denying that the USSR dominated Poland and other countries in Eastern Europe. When the debate ended, he stopped by a rally in the St. Francis Hotel, then returned to a friend's guest house in San Francisco where he was staying. Believing he had performed well, Ford went to sleep.

Downtown, in the Holiday Inn, reporters were writing their leads: *Ford blunders in the debate on foreign policy, frees Poland.* Cheney, Spencer, Baker, Scowcroft, and Nessen, all mingling with the press, were trying to explain. Scowcroft put it best: "I think what the President was trying to say is that we do not recognize Soviet domination of Europe and that he took his trip to Eastern Europe—to Poland, to Romania, to Yugoslavia—to demonstrate, to symbolize their independence . . ." But neither Scowcroft nor anyone else could stop the hemorrhaging in the media; Ford's mistake would dominate the news that night and all the next day.

On the morning after the debate, Cheney went in first to suggest to Ford that he had misspoken and should issue a statement of clarification. Ford turned him down flat. "I know what I said and I have no reason to correct it," Ford said. Next was Spencer; another strong rebuff. Next was Scowcroft; the third angry rebuff. "Poor Dick Cheney. Poor Stu. Poor Brent," Ford said later. "I thought I was right in what I said. I was furious with anybody who even inferred I was wrong. My best friends. My best advisers. They had clarifications or whatever they called them. I argued with them. I was mad, really mad. I felt that the way the press had distorted what I said made me absolutely furious. And every one of the worst stubborn attributes I have came to life."

Teeter, watching at home in Ann Arbor, foresaw the consequences. In the next days, tracking polls confirmed his fears. "Ford went in to that debate even with Carter, and slowly gaining," Teeter said. "We were

stopped cold. Cold." He telephoned Cheney to suggest Ford acknowledge his mistake and issue a correction. "We're working on it," Cheney
said.

For two days Ford campaigned in California—in San Francisco,
down the coast to Los Angeles, Beverly Hills, the San Fernando Valley,
and Glendale, trying to regain the momentum of the week before. On
October 8, two days after the debate, Ford corrected himself: "Perhaps
I could have been more precise in what I said concerning Soviet domination of Poland," he told reporters in Glendale. "I recognize that in
Poland there are Soviet divisions. [But] I do not believe that the Polish
people over the long run . . . will ever condone domination by any foreign force."

"That was too damned late to have any impact," Ford said. "Delaying was the worst mistake I ever made politically. I don't know why I
was so stubborn. I don't know why I was so stupid in this case."

Indeed it was too late; the damage had been done. Ford's blunder
on Poland reminded the press, and the public, of the tales of Ford's
clumsiness—false ones initiated by Lyndon Johnson, but others real,
such as falling down the rain-swept airplane steps in Austria, and still
others in caricature, with Chevy Chase tripping himself on *Saturday
Night Live*.

After the clarification of his mistake in California, Ford flew east to
Oklahoma, made two stops in Texas, five in New York, and three in
New Jersey. Going on the attack, Ford singled out Carter's proposals
and record: "He wants to cut $15 billion out of your Army, your Navy,
your Air Force and Marine Corps . . . In the four years he was governor
of Georgia, state employees went up 25 percent, the cost of government
went up over 50 percent." In Washington, Ford predicted, Carter would
create "new government programs that would cost between $100 bil-
lion and $200 billion a year."

Diligently Ford also cited his two-year record—gains in employment, economic recovery, peace in the world. Crowds were good. People
listened with respect. But on the podium the candidate still lacked the
magnetic appeal and verve that comes naturally to the best political
performers.

One day in the Oval Office, Ford was discussing with Cheney and
Spencer how they could best generate excitement, invigorate the closing

weeks of the campaign. Ford mentioned that he had always admired President Truman's successful whistle-stop train campaign in 1948.

"Why don't I have a whistle stop campaign like Truman?" Ford asked.

"I don't think that's a good idea, Mr. President," Spencer said.

"Why not?" Ford asked.

"Because, Mr. President, you're no fuckin' good as a campaigner," Spencer said.

Ford, taken aback, frowned, then laughed. "I guess you're right, Stu."

But campaign Ford did. With seventeen days to go until Election Day, Ford took off again. His first stop was Iowa. Then the railroad whistle stop he wanted, truncated to the heartland of Illinois, closing out in Missouri, then back to Washington for Oval Office business and a press conference before briefings for the third and last debate of the 1976 campaign, in Williamsburg, Virginia, on October 22. For this event, reporters' questions were rambling and vague; the answers predictable and evasive. Neither Ford nor Carter committed a major error; neither revealed a new idea or initiative that might excite voters. Press and polls called this final debate a draw.

Determined to win, Ford put aside his resentment of the Reagan challenge and instructed his campaign staff to ask Reagan to campaign in California, Texas, Louisiana, and Mississippi. It was too late. Mike Deaver, Reagan's scheduler, informed Cheney that Reagan had a full calendar of commitments for other Republican candidates. No time was left. "Reagan did campaign for Ford," Meese said, "and he would have campaigned more. The governor felt it was because of the Ford staff that they didn't use him as much as they might have."

With less than two weeks to go before the election, Ford's campaign chiefs came up with their best plan yet to present Ford on television. Concerned that his speeches and the televised excerpts from his speeches rarely moved an audience, they searched for alternatives. Someone—Ford said it was Deardourff who first mentioned it to him—suggested a conversational Q&A, with Ford talking on camera, impromptu and live; not with a newsman but with a person who would represent and reflect the questions in the mind of the typical American voter.

The proposal was for Ford to go to the eight most populous states, schedule a full day of public appearances in each, and close with a half-hour of impromptu dialogue on live television with an engaging interlocutor. "Several names were suggested," Ford said, "including Joe Garagiola. I immediately thought Joe would be ideal. As a sports enthusiast I had followed his career, and I always liked him. He played hard, and when he got into the media, I liked his down-to-earth way of communicating. And I got to know him better when I went to the All-Star game in 1976. He had grown up on the streets of St. Louis and had developed sincere convictions about people and the country and our ideals. He was rugged looking, had a little fringe of hair around his ears, had a good strong physique, and a great sense of humor."

The plan succeeded. The Ford-Garagiola interviews did in fact show Ford at his best. Garagiola somehow seemed to symbolize and represent grassroots America; asking when the unemployed would have a job again, why an arms agreement with Russia was so important, whether the government would have enough money to pay Social Security in the future. Ford answered with facts, drawing on his experience in governing, in the conversational style that came naturally to him. Teeter's polls began to move Ford's way again.

After flying some 15,000 miles and speaking in seventeen states in the final weeks of his campaign, on election eve Ford landed back in Grand Rapids, the city that framed his life. This was the city of sterling American values that Ford never really left; the city that never left him. Exhausted, hoarse from a hundred unremarkable but impassioned appeals for support, he suppressed his emotions to convey his gratitude for the unprecedented throngs and fervent welcome the city granted to its favorite son. "It is hard to express one's deep sentiments about a community and an area that has been so good to [Betty and me]," he told the crowd, many of them old friends. "The wonderful experience of representing the Fifth Congressional District will be something that I will never forget."

At 7:15 a.m., Ford showed up at his polling place in a junior high school, cast his vote, and headed for the Kent County International Airport for a special occasion: the unveiling of a wall-size mural celebrating Ford's life and career. Seeing the mural for the first time was, Ford said, "the most emotional moment of the whole campaign. It was a picture of This Is Your Life. It really made you just get goose bumps all over."

Portrayed in heroic size figures by Paul Collins, a Grand Rapids artist, were Ford's mother and stepfather, the teenaged Ford as an Eagle Scout, as high school football star, and as Navy officer. There was his wedding with Betty, his service as Congressman, his taking the oath of office as President. Looking at the faces of his mother and stepfather, he wondered how they would have felt could they have been there. Struggling to keep his composure, Ford paid them tribute: "I owe everything to them and to their training, love, leadership. And what has ever been done by me in any way whatsoever, it's because of Jerry Ford Senior and Dorothy Ford."

Flying back to Washington, Ford basked in a glow of Election Day confidence. The final Gallup Poll put him ahead 47 percent to 46 percent. "I was unbelievably exhilarated," Ford said. "It tended to justify all the things we had done over the twenty-seven months. It made me feel good about the American public's reaction and to prove that if you kept your cool and did your job, we have a good chance to win."

Teeter's comparable surveys showed the race too close to call, but Ford's optimism was undiminished. From the Oval Office he telephoned Dole: "We have the momentum now, and I just know we're going to win." Through the afternoon he brought in, one by one, Morton, Baker, Teeter, Marsh, and Cheney. His voice so hoarse from marathon speechmaking that he could barely speak, he nevertheless conveyed his confidence and gratitude to each for their contributions to the campaign. "I thought every member of the team had performed well," he said, "and I wanted to show my appreciation for their dedication and hard work."

Expecting to win, Ford had an ambitious agenda for his full term. "We would unquestionably resolve a Salt II agreement with the Soviet Union before the expiration date of Salt I on October 3, 1977," Ford said. "We would move quickly to get action going from the momentum we had in the Middle East, working with Israel, Egypt, Jordan, and Syria to get a series of bilateral agreements that we would then take to a full-scale Geneva conference for a comprehensive settlement. We would continue the momentum we had in southern Africa to settle the Rhodesian and Namibia questions and other regional issues."

"On domestic policy, we would continue our restraint on the growth of Federal spending, give tax relief to middle income people and to the business community to stimulate the capital investment that produces jobs. By restraining spending, and with an expanding economy, we would have a balanced budget by Fiscal '80."

"On defense, for the Air Force increases for the B-1, MX, and Cruise Missile programs, and for the Navy a five-year ship building program. For The Army, a buildup in the mobilization reserve and a five percent increase over inflation for the M60 tank and other equipment. On energy, we would push our '75 proposals through Congress, with emphasis on incentives for domestic production, push for nuclear, clean coal, solar, geothermal. We would become more vigorous in deregulating the trucking industry and the airline industry, and direct independent commissions to simplify their procedures and regulations. On welfare, we would eliminate the hodge-podge that is costly, ineffective, abused, and replace it with aspects of the family assistance program."

Ford was certain that as an elected President he could work more effectively with Congress. "They would know I was going to be there four years," he said. "I would have more clout. I would have a mandate from the people so my status with the public would have been stronger, and consequently my influence with the Congress would be stronger."

Confident Ford was as he gathered family and friends to watch the election returns in the evening in the residence. All were there—Betty, Mike and Gail, Jack, Steve, and Susan—along with his new sidekick Garagiola, and the Garagiola family. There also were his guests: Bob and Elizabeth Dole; Senator Jacob Javits; Cheney; Teeter; Clara Powell, the Fords' former housekeeper in Virginia; Ford's brother Tom; Pete Secchia and Leon Parma, Ford's longtime close friends; Steve's classmate Kevin Kennedy; Steve's friend and campaign companion Greg Willard; and other friends of the Ford children. All found places around six television sets in the family sitting room, the private sitting room, and the wide corridor leading to the Queen's Bedroom and the Lincoln Bedroom.

The first returns on television surprised and alarmed the happy gathering. Carter took a long lead by sweeping the South and the border states of Kentucky, West Virginia, and Maryland, giving him more than 100 electoral votes. Teeter reported an unusually heavy Democratic turnout, particularly in precincts where blacks were concentrated. With two predictably Democratic states—Massachusetts and Rhode Island, plus the District of Columbia—the networks gave Carter an additional 21 electoral votes.

"The early returns were conclusive for Carter until about 11 o'clock," Ford remembered. "By that time ten or eleven states had gone for Carter. I looked pretty lonesome up there." Garagiola said to Ford: "It's all right, Prez. We've given up a couple of runs, but the ball game is only in the top of the fourth."

Around midnight Ford's chances looked up. He had won his first state, Indiana, and four New England states: Maine, Vermont, New Hampshire, and Connecticut. The networks called New Jersey for Ford, giving him another boost. Then, to his surprise and delight he won Virginia's electoral votes, which pundits predicted would go to Carter. With Virginia, Ford could count on 61 electoral votes, and he was gaining.

He was even more encouraged as returns from the Midwest began to flow in. He won handily in Michigan, Illinois, and Iowa. As the polls closed in the Mountain and Pacific time zones, Ford's electoral votes mounted. He swept seventeen states west of the Mississippi River—winning the plains, the Rocky Mountain states, Alaska, and two coastal prizes, Oregon and Washington. "By 1 o'clock, we could see that if we carried California, and if we carried Ohio and Hawaii, we were going to make it," Ford said.

Texas, passing its lead back and forth, was also a possibility. At 1:30 a.m., Ford telephoned John Connally. "We're going to win," Connally told Ford. "Before the night is out, you'll have Texas." Connally was wrong; twenty minutes later, NBC reported that Carter had won Texas. "That hurt," Ford told Garagiola. "That *really* hurt."

Teeter had advised Ford, at the campaign's beginning, that he must carry six of the eight most populous states. He had carried New Jersey, Illinois, and Michigan, but lost Pennsylvania and Texas. "It's still a helluva ball game," Ford told his guests. New York was still a question. At Javits's suggestion, Ford asked Teeter and Cheney to confer with them in the family dining room. Javits reported that it looked as though New York City, heavily Democratic, would wipe out Ford's upstate lead and deliver the state to Carter.

With New York in his column, Carter continued to maintain his early lead—by a wide margin in the popular vote; narrowly in electoral votes. Missouri, a state that Ford felt sure he would win, went to Carter. Ford was dismayed that he and the incumbent governor, Kit Bond, had both lost. Minnesota, predictably, fell to Carter. By 2:30 a.m., the networks were calculating that Carter had a total of 230 electoral votes, only 40 short of election.

California came through for Ford, bringing him a huge gain in spirit as well as electoral votes. "It was still close enough that there was a real potential for us," he said. "Wisconsin was a possibility. We really thought Wisconsin would be a Ford state. With California, if we carried Ohio and Hawaii, we were going to make it. Electorally. We were always going to be a million or a million and a half behind in the popular vote. But that didn't bother me. It happened two other times, as I recall, when a President won the electoral votes but not the popular vote."

By 2:40 a.m., Teeter advised Ford that four states were still undecided—Ohio, Hawaii, Mississippi, and Wisconsin. Ohio reported that Ford had a narrow lead of 2,000 votes. With the backing, organization, and enthusiasm of Governor James Rhodes, Ford was counting on his neighbor state. He knew that no Republican had ever won the Presidency without carrying Ohio. In Hawaii, Ford had led in the early voting, but with later returns he had fallen behind. Mississippi, slow in counting, remained a question mark.

At 3:00 a.m., Cheney and Teeter came in with new information, and President Ford gathered his guests in the west living room. Faces were grim. "No," Ford said, "this isn't a concession speech. I think Bob Teeter has some interesting information for us."

Teeter reported that Hawaii was close and still counting. "Chances in Wisconsin look good, even though the networks have given the state to Carter," Teeter said. "Ohio is still close, and it may be morning before we know about Ohio."

With the race in doubt, at 3:20 a.m., Ford said good night to his guests. "I went to bed knowing the odds were against me," Ford said. "We had to win Ohio and we had to win Hawaii. We were close enough in both to give us hope, but the possibility of gaining enough votes was no better than 2 to 1 against us. I was dead tired. I knew I had to get up in the morning and be happy if we were the winner, and be a responsible person and concede if we were not. There wasn't a darned thing I could do."

It had been a long day. Ford had been confident of victory in the closing weeks of campaigning and all through the day when the polls were open. Then, during the early evening he had been dismayed by Carter's state-by-state successes. By midnight, Ford was further disheartened at losing states he expected to win. Sometime after midnight he began to feel the Presidency slipping from his hands. Ever the optimist, he still believed he could win; ever the realist, he steeled himself to losing. "I reconciled myself to the fact that we had done our best," he said. "We had run a good campaign. I felt that in the national interest it was important for me and my family to portray ourselves as good losers. I was not going to appear dejected or a bad loser. I was going to face the change in circumstances straightforwardly."

Mrs. Ford, the children, and a few guests remained. Minutes after Ford retired, Mississippi delivered its 7 electoral votes to Carter, giving him a total of 273 electoral votes—three more than the necessary 270. At 3:30 a.m., John Chancellor announced on NBC that Jimmy Carter would be the 39th President of the United States.

As the Ford family and friends listened, "No one said a word," Willard said. "There were no tears, no sighs of disappointment, just several minutes of complete silence as the NBC correspondents chattered."

"Do we dare wake him?" Betty Ford asked her children. "No," they replied in unison. "Let him sleep."

Moments later, Carter appeared on television. Betty Ford smiled at the television screen, chuckled, and, with the wisdom born of experience, said: "Governor, you have no idea what you're in for here."

Not wanting the night to end, for an hour, she and the children regaled each other with funny campaign stories. "At 4:30 a.m., we decided to call it a night," Willard said. "I said to Mrs. Ford, 'I'm so sorry. I really thought we were going to pull it out.' She came over, took both of my hands quite firmly and said, 'Now listen. We're going to leave here in January with no regrets and many wonderful memories. And remember, when we leave, we'll have our heads up with lots of pride.'"

Ford woke at 8:30 the next morning. "I called Cheney right away, and he said: 'Mr. President, we lost. Although the final tabulation in Ohio is so close you could win that state. But no other state will give us the additional four votes.'"

At 9:00 a.m., Kennerly went to the family quarters to see if Ford was up. "He was, sitting alone in his bathrobe and slippers in the dining room, reading the paper and watching a small television set," Kennerly wrote in his memoir, *Shooter.* "'I guess we've had it,' I said glumly."

"'Looks that way,' he replied in a whisper, smiling at me."

"'It was great while it lasted,' I said."

"'I wouldn't have traded a minute of it,' he stated."

The final count, with Ford narrowly losing Ohio and Hawaii, was:

Carter: 24 states, 40,831,881 popular votes, 297 electoral votes.
Ford: 26 states, 39,148,634 popular votes, 240 electoral votes.

It was the closest electoral margin in sixty years, when Woodrow Wilson defeated Charles Evans Hughes.

Walking over to the Oval Office, Ford met with Marsh, Baker, Spencer, and Teeter. Marsh reported there had been enough irregularities in Ohio and Wisconsin to warrant challenges. Spencer and Teeter were ready with plans for recounts. Ford listened to the four and thought it over. "No," he said. "The election is over. We lost. I will not be a party to any recount or lawsuit in any state."

At 11:04 a.m., Ford telephoned Carter to congratulate him on his victory. Ford's voice was still too hoarse to read Carter his concession statement. He put Cheney on the telephone to read it to Carter. Betty Ford read it to the press.

With the election decided, Ford began the process to bring in the new government. To head the transition, and to manage the complex and plenary responsibility of handing over the Federal Executive Department from the leader of one political party to the leader of the opposing party, Ford chose Marsh, of whom he had once said: "Jack handles the most demanding mission with dispatch, diplomacy, and sound judgment." The transition from Ford to Carter was, by every standard, as Ford directed and Marsh executed, a commendable example of bipartisan cooperation in the public interest.

The second day after the election, not by chance, both Jerry and Betty Ford remembered that, for two years, it had been their plan to get out of politics at the end of 1976. "Betty and I never looked back," Ford said. "We said to each other, 'We've got new opportunities. So we better start planning, honestly, judiciously, responsibly.' Almost overnight we started looking down the road for things we had been deprived of during twenty-eight-and-a-half years of politics. We both saw the beginning of a new life."

Fourteen years later, in President Ford's post-Presidential office in Rancho Mirage, California, I asked him at the end of one of our many discussions, "What was the greatest disappointment in your life?"

Without hesitating he said, "Well, in my junior year at Michigan I didn't get to play as much football as I had hoped. We had Chuck Bernard, an all-American center, so I sat on the bench most of the time.

I played enough to win my letter, but not as much as I wanted to. My senior year, I was the starter at center, but we lost most of our games."

"But Mr. President," I said, "what about losing the election?"

He laughed. "Oh, yes. Well, that too." After a few moments of silence, he began to look back on his defeat in 1976. Yes, he was disappointed, yet full of pride in his record as President, in having campaigned on that record, and in coming so close. "I was sad, for myself and the family," he said. "They had all worked so hard. Mike in New England. Jack even debated Reagan at a Republican convention in Colorado. Steve and a buddy rented a mobile home and campaigned all over the western mountain states. Susan worked very hard and effectively. And Betty— she was the real star, our greatest asset. Of all the family she took the loss the hardest because she knew it meant so much to me."

"Having said all that, did I think it was a disaster that we lost? No. I was crestfallen. I never liked to lose. I thought we should have won on the merits. I was convinced that we deserved to have a chance to continue the policies and changes we had begun. Naturally I thought the best man with the best policies had lost. I still do. But I've competed enough in life, whether it's athletics or politics or law to know that sometimes you win; sometimes you lose. I never felt that when you lose you should crawl in your shell and tear yourself apart mentally and physically. Life is looking forward, not living in the past. I always looked down the road. There's another ball game. Let's get going."

Reflecting on why he lost, Ford offered a pro's analysis. "When it's that close, any one of ten or twelve factors could have been the cause," he said. "That adverse economic news in October was the most crucial factor. If it had not occurred in the statistical sense in September and October, I think I would have won the election. Unemployment was going up, just a point or two, but it was a change from the direction it had been for nine months. So the perception was negative. That was a bad break in timing. By the middle of November it was altogether different—unemployment was down, interest rates down, the economy headed up. If we could have just switched those November–December figures to September–October, we would have had a different result."

Ruefully, Ford acknowledged that he had hurt his chances with his San Francisco misstatement on Poland. "The truth is I won that debate," he said. "But when the press started to interpret my comments on Poland, they turned the public around. The pundits sat around afterward and emphasized twenty seconds out of an hour and a half. So I was mad, about as mad as I ever get. What I said was one hundred percent right. What happened twelve years later proved it."

Ford recalled, before he pardoned Nixon, telling his counsel and close friend Phil Buchen that it might cost him the Presidency. "No question the pardon had an impact on the election," he said. "But if I hadn't pardoned Nixon, we would have had a Nixon problem for two and a half years. The pardon got rid of Nixon, but it antagonized a number of people, so you had a balance of adversity there. There were people who were just unforgiving. There were people who thought Washington, because of Watergate and Vietnam, just stunk. And I was a victim of that attitude."[1]

In Ford's political assessment, the election was more his loss than Carter's victory. "It wasn't anything particular that Carter did. He had some phony campaign promises. We should have beaten him. But he handled the religion vote very shrewdly, and the South came through for him. If Ronald Reagan had campaigned for us in Texas and Mississippi, we might have carried those two states."

"After the Reagan challenge for the nomination, the party was not as unified as I hoped it would be. The tension and conflicts generated by the primaries and the serious conflicts at Kansas City left scars. There was severe disappointment among the dedicated Reagan people, and they were traditionally the best party workers. The troops who were disappointed just didn't get out and do as much as they might have done. We never captured in my behalf the zeal that some of the Reagan people at the grassroots had for him. Hard as we tried, we could not overcome that problem."

"Could the campaign have been better managed?" I asked.

"Oh, yes," Ford said. "We neglected the convention states in competing for the nomination, for example. We did improve as we went along, and we ran a good campaign—far better than our critics. I learned a long time ago: A losing campaign is always badly run; the campaign that wins is always well executed."

Ford found some election results inexplicable. "It's an enigma to me that we lost Delaware," he said. "Republicans won the governorship, the Senate race, and the single state Representative—three statewide

---

1. One Teeter poll indicated that 7 percent of Republicans decided to vote against Ford because he pardoned Nixon.

races, and I lost. How that happened in Delaware is beyond my comprehension." Ford was sure he knew why he lost Missouri: his Secretary of Transportation had recommended that a new St. Louis airport be located across the Mississippi River in Illinois, and his Secretary of Defense had closed a Missouri air base. "Right on substance," Ford said, "bad for the campaign."

His most painful surprise was losing Ohio. "Hell, we carried Cleveland and Cincinnati," Ford said. "To lose Ohio by 11,000 or so votes out of four million, to lose Ohio after carrying Michigan, Indiana, and Illinois. I know why—the Southern tier of Ohio is dyed-in-the-wool Bible belt, and Carter carried the Bible belt. Imagine, we lost Hawaii by only 7,400 votes out of about 290,000 votes.

"I honestly believe if the campaign had gone two more weeks we would have won. We had the momentum and the economic picture would have been better."

For a long moment, Ford paused, then with a wistful shake of his head, he said: "You know, Jim, it wouldn't have taken a lot for us to win."

CHAPTER 25

Epilogue

There was a time when Washington governed reasonably well; when the two political parties competed but cooperated; when those elected to direct the affairs of the United States recognized the national interest and placed first priority on acting to fulfill it. Among their accomplishments were the GI Bill, the Marshall Plan, the Interstate Highway System, NASA, and the laws that guarantee civil rights and voting rights to all U.S. citizens.

In times of national need, we relied on a long train of the meritorious— Arthur Vandenberg, Sam Rayburn, Everett Dirksen, Richard Russell, John Stennis, Lyndon Johnson, Hubert Humphrey, Wilbur Mills, John Byrnes, George Mahon, Jacob Javits, Mark Hatfield, Abraham Ribicoff, Howard Baker, Daniel Patrick Moynihan, Fritz Hollings, Warren Rudman, among others.

There is no finer example of the tradition of public men acting positively and instinctively in the public interest than the act that made Gerald R. Ford President of the United States. Two Democratic statesmen—Speaker Carl Albert and Senate Majority Leader Mike Mansfield—recognized in October of 1973 that a crisis without precedent required a man of integrity, character, temperament, and experience who would restore legitimacy to the Presidency. That man was the leader of the opposing party in the House of Representatives. Albert and Mansfield imposed their choice on the beleaguered Nixon. Not surprisingly, Jerry Ford's Congressional colleagues, those who knew him best, confirmed his merit and his trustworthiness by a landslide of a bipartisan endorsement.

Ford took over as President on August 9, 1974, as a result of events and circumstances that the United States had not before, or since, experienced. Three critical problems confronted him. He inherited a nation betrayed by Richard Nixon; deceived by a President who had corrupted the highest office in the land by covering up a crime of his own hand. In Watergate, Nixon—by defying Congress and the courts—had provoked the most dangerous Constitutional crisis since the Civil War. Second, Ford inherited a house divided over the Vietnam War. Half of the United States was rebelling in anger against a long, and to many, a senseless conflict in distant Asia that had cost more than 50,000 American lives and billions of dollars—a war that seemed to be lost. The other half of Americans regarded their opponents as defeatists, sunshine patriots; they resolved to win the war at whatever cost. Third, Ford inherited an economy mired in the worst recession since the Great Depression of the 1930s—inflation was rising; industry was closing its doors; millions were losing their jobs.

America was not at its best. For more than a decade violence had replaced reason. The assassinations of President John F. Kennedy, Robert Kennedy, and Martin Luther King Jr. had stained national honor. A young generation rebelled against authority; many regarded their government as the enemy. Race riots plagued the South. Illegal drugs addled the well-to-do as well as the poor. Mobs invaded public spaces; one gathered outside the White House gates yelling that President Nixon be sent to prison. Rumors swept Washington that Nixon would circle the White House with tanks to forestall a coup. Doubt and fear enveloped the nation's capital. Rage, malevolence, turbulence—this was Nixon's legacy to the nation and his successor.

Jerry Ford was President for only 2 years, 5 months, and 11 days—895 days in all—but in that time he changed America. His first priority was to calm the capital and the country, to restore legitimacy to the Presidency, to heal a wounded nation. This he accomplished. Primarily he did so by being the man he was—honest and trustworthy, the very opposite of his predecessor. With openness and confidence, with a firm and steady hand, Ford restored to the Oval Office the integrity all Americans expect of their President—a quality that had for too long been missing. With Ford, everyone—in the United States, and abroad—could believe the word of the President again. In a profound sense, Ford redeemed the nation's anguished soul. This intangible—returning America's trust in the Presidency, and faith in the future—was Ford's greatest single accomplishment.

Ford is most often remembered for his pardon of Nixon. No decision he made provoked such opposition or invoked such condemnation as his bold but Constitutional action to block the prosecution of Nixon. At the time, Nixon seemed to be the least deserving of compassion of all the Watergate criminals. The public, still enraged over Watergate, demanded punishment—not forgiveness. Consequently, Ford's pardon of Nixon was denounced in Federal courtrooms, on the floor of Congress, in the pages of newspapers, and on Main Street America.

Ford expected the decision would cost him in popular esteem: he was correct. In a day his Gallup Poll dropped sharply. Ford also calculated that it might well doom his chances for election, but he believed that pardoning Nixon was best for the country. Almost alone, Ford foresaw the consequences of a Nixon trial—that the protracted public spectacle of a former President in the dock would not only dominate the news and preoccupy the public; it would also distract Washington from the resolution of more pressing economic and international crises. It took years, but informed public opinion eventually supported Ford on the pardon. Whether viewed at the time or in the hindsight of history, Ford's decision to pardon Nixon was a singular example of political courage.

Not once during the rest of his life did Ford doubt that the pardon had been the right decision, at the right time, in the best interests of the country. Over the years, many of his initial critics turned about and agreed with him. Senator Ted Kennedy, for one, excoriated Ford for the pardon when it was granted; twenty-seven years later, Senator Kennedy presented to Ford the Kennedy Profile in Courage Award for acting on principle rather than popularity. No honor so pleased Ford in his post Presidency as the Kennedys' affirmation of his most contentious action.

At the time, and thereafter, the pardon overshadowed Ford's accomplishments as President. To his great credit, he ended the Vietnam War, which three Presidents before him had mismanaged. It was a humiliating ending to the war, but Congress, having cut off money for Vietnam, gave Ford no choice. The withdrawal he managed well, pulling out the last U.S. forces, saving American lives, and rescuing thousands of Vietnamese who had supported the American effort.

Ford also brought the country through the most pervasive economic crisis in forty years. He led America out of hard times and onto the road to prosperity. No President in modern times had a better understanding of economics. Relying on himself and good advisers, Ford blocked Congress' impulse to have the Federal government spend the way to recovery. Staunchly conservative in economic philosophy, Ford believed that the United States would thrive if private enterprise was freed from excessive government regulation and interference; that citizens would benefit from lower taxes and greater freedom to spend their own money. Ford's approach worked. By the end of his Presidency the increase in the cost of living had been cut from 12 to 5 percent, and 4 million new jobs had been created. Ford took pride in pointing out that when he left office, 88 million American were employed in useful, productive jobs—more than at any other time in U.S. history.

Ford's chief accomplishments as President appear, in retrospect, to have been almost routine, methodically achieved by steadiness and common sense. His decisions were careful; they lacked the drama that Presidents often stage to attract popular attention. He governed with so little bombast and boasting that history has made him the least celebrated of recent presidents. Edmund Morris, erudite presidential biographer, once observed: "Gerald Ford was our most underrated modern President." So matter-of-fact were Ford's accomplishments carried out that most have been discounted, if remembered at all. As the sage Jack Marsh said, "The Ford Administration is the lost chord of the American Presidency."

Every President learns the job on the job. At managing the office, Ford learned faster than most Presidents and better than many. Initially disorganized and inept, he recognized his need and recruited a qualified manager, Donald Rumsfeld, to coach him on how to be an executive. Within months, Ford became the confident new President, on his own; a strong executive relying on his experience and his encyclopedic knowledge of Federal spending and programs to advance his own modest goals and deep convictions. No expansionist, he believed that the Federal government was already too big and too expensive, with too many employees. To set an example, he cut his White House staff and urged Congress to cut Congressional staff. Unlike some conservative Presidents, Ford did not merely talk conservative doctrine—he governed as a conservative.

Outnumbered by free-spending Democrats in the House and Senate, Ford had no choice but to rely heavily on the Presidential power of the veto. He used the veto with considerable skill against waste, duplication, and costly new programs. To Ford, vetoing an act of Congress was never a negative action; the authority was there in the Constitution to give a President the prerogative to send a bad bill back to Congress for improvement. It worked. Of his sixty-six vetoes, only twelve were overridden. By rejecting flawed legislation and proposing improvements, Ford prevailed on Congress to pass better laws. By blocking dubious Congressional expenditures with his vetoes, Ford saved taxpayers uncounted billions of dollars.

Ford never articulated a soaring vision for the country, but foresight he had. More than once he anticipated the looming critical challenges to the nation, and proposed action. Convinced that the United States was endangered economically and strategically by growing dependence on foreign oil, in 1975 he sent Congress a comprehensive plan to conserve supplies and increase domestic production. Congress balked, fearing that the price of a gallon of gasoline at the pump—then in double digits—would rise by a nickel or so. Consequently, nearly four decades later, the United States remains an economy, a military, and a society dependent on foreign suppliers.

Ford foresaw that the Helsinki Agreements could be the wedge that opened Soviet society to freedom and independence, and signed those agreements despite vociferous opposition from Republicans and Democrats. As it turned out, he was right; ideals and enlightenment brought down the Iron Curtain. Ford warned that U.S. armed forces were overextended by well-intended commitments around the globe, and so it happened. He pointed out, during New York City's 1975 financial crisis, that "if we go on spending more than we have, providing more benefits and more services than we can pay for, then a day of reckoning will come to Washington and the whole country." Some forty years later, that day of reckoning is at hand. This was Ford, looking ahead. He paid little attention to the headline of the day; he took the long view.

Ford's crucial failure in office was his inability to win a full term. Four years rarely gives a President enough time to make major differences. As President Wilson said in 1913, one term is too short for "a great work of reform." And reform was badly needed after Nixon; yet Ford had only two and a half years in office.

In a capital enamored with show horses, Ford was a workhorse, comparable to a Clydesdale or a Percheron, big, muscular, intelligent, good-natured, willing to work. He was best at his desk in the Oval Office, managing the myriad problems and responsibilities of the Federal government. Management was far more to Ford's liking than the other essential of the Presidency—showmanship, performing on the White House stage and traveling to win favor with the public. In dealing with domestic and international problems, Ford was confident and stout, but the calm demeanor and steady judgment he displayed so impressively in the Oval Office did not show on the podium. An orator he manifestly was not. On television, his genial, likable personality simply did not convey. And television is the way and means to election. As much as any other factor, Ford's inability to master television cut short his time in office. Ford was a far better President than *candidate for* President.

I mentioned that to Ford during one of my interviews with him. His immediate response: "No doubt about that."

Ford's most critical national-security failure was his inability to negotiate a Salt II Treaty with the USSR. "If the Joint Chiefs had been more cooperative and helped us get the SALT agreement I proposed, it would have been better than the one finally agreed to," he said. "Negotiating with General Brown and Paul Nitze was more difficult than negotiating with Brezhnev." Without Pentagon support, Ford recognized that the Senate would reject any treaty with the USSR.

Ford could have done a better job of explaining and justifying the pardon of Nixon. In his rush to announce his action before it leaked to the press—which, in his judgment, would have caused such a hue and cry that the public might have risen to block it—he delivered a poorly crafted and poorly timed television address that failed to set forth a convincing premise for his action. Ford had a better case than his brief or his oral argument before the court of public opinion. Compounding the thin logic of the rationale he presented for his decision was the resignation of his press secretary in protest to the pardon; this provoked the press to make a hero of his spokesman, and Ford's action unconscionable. To make his plight worse, Ford misread popular opinion. He was the least vindictive of men; he believed Nixon had suffered enough by being forced out of the Presidency, and presumed that most Americans would agree. In truth, at that point the majority of Americans wanted vengeance.

To Ford, one political mistake he regretted was giving in to conservative Republicans' demands that he dump Rockefeller at the beginning of his 1976 campaign. "That was the most cowardly decision of my political life," Ford said publicly to a New York State political audience after he left office. Had Ford kept to his original plan to run with Rockefeller in 1976, the team probably would have carried New York State and thus been elected. On the other hand, had he not removed Rockefeller, Ford might well have lost the nomination to Reagan.

As a matter of principle, if Ford did not intend to keep Rockefeller on the 1976 ticket, he should not have nominated him at the outset. Once he made his choice, got him confirmed as his Vice President, and consistently commended his value as his stalwart vice chief, Ford should have stuck with Rockefeller. Dumping his Vice President was a shabby political maneuver, quite out of character with Ford's lifelong commitment to loyalty and justice. It was a rare example of Ford putting politics ahead of the public interest.

Perfect Ford's Administration was not, yet one accomplishment will grace U.S. history. He healed the nation after the deep wounds of Vietnam and Watergate; he led Americans to feel good about their country again. No other public man of his time could have succeeded in restoring the nation's exuberant spirit as effectively as Ford.

After he left the White House, Ford enjoyed private life in the resort communities of Rancho Mirage, California, and Beaver Creek, Colorado, for almost twenty-nine years. This was longer by a year than he spent in public office. For him and for Betty Ford, it was the good life—enjoying the prestige and gratitude of the country but no longer bound by the schedule and rigors of public duty. "Theirs was a lifelong love affair," their son Jack Ford once said, and that love affair deepened in their new circumstances. Free of imposed commitments, they enjoyed the company of old and new friends, continued the good works that had always appealed to them, and most of all, enjoyed each other's company. They paced their lives and mellowed in California's benign, sun-filled Coachella Valley, and Colorado's lofty crags and peaks. Then, two years after he left office, Ford and his four children faced a serious family crisis.

In California, as in Washington, Betty Ford continued to relieve pain from a pinched nerve with prescription drugs and alcohol. Over time, in Rancho Mirage, her dependence increased and her family became more and more concerned. In the spring of 1978 her four children intervened, led by Susan and her husband. Collectively, they confronted their mother with the problem, and persuaded her to enter the U.S. Navy's

Alcohol and Drug Rehabilitation hospital in Long Beach, California, for help. It was a painfully wrenching and embarrassing situation for her; indeed, for the entire Ford family.

Nevertheless, with her uncommon courage, Betty Ford admitted her addiction and entered the Long Beach center to rid herself of her dependence. With her usual candor and openness, she made her decision public. For her husband, Betty's months-long trial of the will and spirit was no easy passage.

"When Mom went through her alcoholism it was a defining moment for Dad and for their marriage," Steven Ford observed later. "I believe he felt that life's journey was not valuable unless he could reach the end with his partner."

After she had recovered, Betty Ford decided there was a pressing need for a facility where others could benefit from her experience and cure. With her husband's encouragement, and the encouragement and financial support of their friend and neighbor, Leonard Firestone, she founded the Betty Ford Center in Rancho Mirage, a nonprofit hospital for the treatment of those addicted to alcohol and drugs. Opened in 1982, the center is a complex of buildings on twenty acres on the Eisenhower Medical Center campus. At the time of her death, on July 9, 2011, the Betty Ford Center had helped more than 90,000 women and men recover from addiction. Some were well-known—Elizabeth Taylor, Johnny Cash, Liza Minnelli, Mickey Mantle—but most were from Middle America. "I wanted this to be a place for the Chicago taxi driver as well as the celebrity," Betty Ford once said.

For her accomplishment, her husband paid her a heartfelt tribute. In 1992 at the dedication of a new building on the tenth anniversary of the founding of the center, Ford said: "When the final tally is taken, her contributions to our country will be bigger than mine."

During the first of Ford's out-of-office years, he pondered running again for President in 1980. Carter, in his judgment, was mishandling national security, the economy, and the Federal budget. Ford was sure that he, and only he, could defeat Carter in a rematch. Ronald Reagan, Ford told the *New York Times'* Adam Clymer, would lose to Carter. "Every place I go and everything I hear, there is a growing, growing sentiment that Governor Reagan cannot win the election," he said to Clymer in a March 1, 1980, interview. "We don't want, cannot afford to have a replay of 1964." Reagan, Ford continued, "is perceived as a most conservative Republican. A very conservative Republican can't win in a national election."

Clearly, Ford wanted his old job back; the *New York Times*' interview was the first time he said so publicly. But he had organized no campaign. Life was good in California, and Ford had dreaded the ordeal of raising millions in campaign contributions and competing in the primaries. Talking to Clymer, Ford envisioned the slim possibility that the convention would deadlock—that neither Reagan, nor Bush, nor Baker, nor Connally could muster a majority of delegates. Then, Ford hoped, the delegates would turn to him as the candidate who could defeat Carter.

It was a vain hope. The Republican Party had changed. Thwarted in 1976, four years later conservatives ruled the party, and they were determined to nominate and elect Ronald Reagan. This year, 1980, was to be their year. With conviction, zeal, and organization, conservatives were systematically assembling the delegates Reagan needed to win the nomination.

Two weeks after Ford told the *New York Times* that he was available to be drafted, he counted up Reagan's victories in the primaries and convention states and calculated that Reagan had the delegates to be nominated on the first ballot. To clear the political air, Ford called in the press and announced he would not be a candidate. His entry, he said, "would divide the party," and party unity was imperative if Republicans were to defeat Carter. "I will support the nominee of my party with all the energy I have," Ford promised.

Except for that campaigning, Ford assumed that his political career was over. But one final opportunity would come Ford's way.

On June 5, 1980, Reagan, with his nomination assured, flew to Palm Springs to explore the possibility that Ford consider running as his Vice President. The idea of this "dream ticket" had been suggested to Reagan by Senator Paul Laxalt—Reagan's most experienced political practitioner—and by other Reagan advisers. Reagan liked the proposal, and initiated the meeting. For an hour and a half, Reagan and Ford talked in Ford's Rancho Mirage office, gradually patching up some of their past political differences. At the proper moment in their conversation, Reagan asked Ford to consider joining him on the ticket. He told Ford it would unite the party, that Ford would be a unique campaign asset, and that the country would benefit from his experience and knowledge of the Federal government if the "dream ticket" should be elected. Ford was flattered and said so. But he considered the offer a courtesy, and told Reagan that he would not be interested.

Six weeks later, on July 14, the first day of the Republican National Convention in Detroit, Reagan sent a message to Ford. As it was Ford's sixty-seventh birthday, he and his wife Nancy would like to come by, see him and Betty, and wish him a happy birthday. When they arrived at the Fords' suite, Reagan handed Ford a gift that was both apt and symbolic: a Native American peace pipe. To Ford, it was an unexpected token of goodwill and conveyed an unmistakable message. Forgiving by nature, he was more than ready to put aside their rivalry and their past conflicts in the interests of the party and the country. At this informal family get-together, Reagan again raised the possibility of Ford joining him on the ticket.

The idea was unprecedented but politically logical. Looking ahead, Reagan assumed his opponent, President Carter, would be tough to beat. Carter had the prestige and perquisites of the office. He had defeated Senator Ted Kennedy's challenge. He had the Democratic Party. He had the born-again vote. He had won the South in 1976 and could well win there again. Consequently, Reagan believed he needed to seize every possible political advantage if he were to defeat Carter. Plotting electoral strategy, Reagan's campaign managers contemplated that he would win the west, and that Ford could help take eastern states where he had won in 1976. The combination made sense: the two most popular leaders of the party joining their complementary strengths on the "dream ticket."

Up to that point, Ford had dismissed any notion of returning to Washington. But he had always been fired up by an unexpected challenge, and when the Reagan-Ford foursome broke up that July day, he agreed to consider Reagan's proposal.

Since Reagan had come to him, Ford assumed he could negotiate certain conditions on personnel and White House structure that would benefit Reagan and the governing process. For foreign policy and national defense, Ford would propose that Reagan bring Kissinger back as Secretary of State and Greenspan as chief adviser on economic and fiscal policy. On process, he had a plan. In his eight months as Nixon's Vice President, Ford had been dismayed at having no role in decision making. Perhaps, he thought, this might be the time to change that. His idea was to position the Vice President as the last signoff point on major programs and decisions prior to the President's consideration; in effect, as Vice President he would become the de facto chief of staff. To Ford, his plan had a corporate parallel: Reagan would be the chief executive officer and Ford the chief operating officer.

With these conditions in mind, Ford appointed Marsh, Kissinger, Greenspan, and Executive Assistant Bob Barrett to discuss possibilities with William Casey, Reagan's campaign manager, and Edwin Meese, Reagan's counsel. Their first meeting was friendly and exploratory. Their second meeting focused on Ford's terms, which went well beyond what Reagan's negotiators expected. They listened, but raised substantive questions about how the novel partnership would work.

Later, when Marsh briefed Ford on reactions by Casey and Meese, Ford concluded that his conditions were not likely to be met. "I got the impression that he was both comfortable and relieved with that decision," Marsh said.

As it happened, Meese, briefing Reagan after their second negotiating session, also advised that the proposed division of White House of authority was neither wise nor practical, and should not be accepted. Reagan agreed, but suggested they hold a third session and try once more to resolve differences. Up to that point, Reagan had deliberately put off considering any other vice presidential choice until Ford made his decision. Talking with Meese, Reagan agreed that it was time to consider alternatives, and that the best would be George H. W. Bush. He had performed well in his campaign, and ranked high in Reagan's private poll.

On the third night of the convention, Ford accepted an invitation to appear on CBS with Walter Cronkite. The central question: Would he accept the nomination for Vice President? Ford's response: It depends. Ford then proceeded to overplay his hand—in full view of convention delegates and the CBS national audience. He said that he would not be "a figurehead Vice President" but would "go there with the belief that I will play a meaningful role across the board in the basic and crucial and the important decisions that have to be made in a four-year period." That, Cronkite remarked, sounded like a "co-Presidency."

Reagan, in his suite watching Cronkite's talk with Ford, was shocked by the word "co-Presidency." Ford, he felt, had gone too far. "As I watched the interview," Reagan wrote, "it really hit me that we had some major problems with the idea. *Wait a minute,* I remember thinking, *this is really two Presidents he's talking about.*" As soon as Ford ended his conversation with Cronkite, Reagan telephoned Ford with a firm message: his offer of the Vice Presidency must be without conditions, and he needed an immediate decision.

By that time Ford had made his own decision. After the CBS interview, he told Barrett: "Bob, I'm just not going to do it. It wouldn't be fair to Betty." His mind made up, Ford went to Reagan's suite. "Look, this isn't going to work," Ford told Reagan. He defended his position: as a former President, he considered it appropriate for him to have more than the ordinary Vice Presidential responsibilities. However, Ford pointed out, his experience with Rockefeller had convinced him that a President should not, and cannot, delegate responsibilities assigned him by the Constitution. Therefore, Ford said, it would be best if Reagan made another choice for Vice President. The two parted with Ford's pledge to do everything he could to elect Reagan. Later, Reagan said, "He was a real gentleman."

Minutes after Ford left the suite, Reagan telephoned George H. W. Bush and asked: "Can you commit to fully endorse and support all my policies and the Republican platform?" Bush responded yes. With that commitment from Bush, Reagan asked him to be his candidate for Vice President. "George jumped at it without a moment's hesitation," Reagan said.

Declining a second term as Vice President marked a sort of continental divide in Ford's life. From that point on, he never again considered holding public office. But for him, retirement was out of the question; indeed, Ford became as busy as ever, devoting all his experience and physical stamina to new ventures. He had already been working on plans to preserve the history of his Presidency and his years in Congress. Both of his hometowns—Grand Rapids and Ann Arbor—wanted to preserve the papers and artifacts of Michigan's only President, so Ford split his choices. In Grand Rapids, he decided to build a museum to exhibit the mementoes of his life and political career. In Ann Arbor, on the University of Michigan campus, he would build a Presidential Library to preserve his official documents, and serve as a prime source for scholars and historians. The two projects would cost about $15 million. Ford approved the plans and set out to raise the money, traveling the country to solicit contributions from old friends and new. He succeeded. Both the museum and the library opened in 1981.

To ensure financial security for Betty, their four children, and himself, Ford decided to accept lucrative offers to join corporate boards. Beginning in 1981, he became a director of American Express, Citigroup, NASDAQ, Nova Pharmaceutical, Aerospace, Primerica, Pullman-Peabody, Santa Fe International, Shearson Lehman Brothers, Tesoro Petroleum, Texas Commerce Bancshares, Travelers Group, and Twentieth Century Fox, among others. Ford said he believed he was the first former President to join a corporate board. With some companies, he earned an additional fee as a consultant. "I thought, Why not make available my experience to good business people? I was criticized by some who thought it improper for a former President, but I met my commitments. I earned every cent I was paid."

In the corporate world, Ford worked just as hard as he had in public life. "We never had a better outside director," said James D. Robinson, then CEO of American Express. "President Ford not only attended every meeting, but he always came well prepared. He studied his briefing papers beforehand. He asked good questions. He made sound observations. After meetings, I would sometimes talk with him in private to discuss ego problems with high corporate officers. He always had good advice."

From his fees from board meetings, and speeches arranged by Hollywood mogul Norman Brokaw, Ford was soon traveling twenty or so days a month, and earning an annual income of seven figures. He and Betty built new homes for themselves—their expansive dream house in Rancho Mirage, California, and a 10,000-square-foot vacation house in Beaver Creek, Colorado. There, close to a ski slope and golf course he favored, he and Betty Ford provided rooms for their four children and spouses, a top floor dormitory for their grandchildren, and a swimming pool for exercise. There, with their growing family, they spent four months every summer, and holidays in the winter.

Ford enjoyed corporate life and its benefits, yet he never lost his deep interest in politics and public affairs. He continued to campaign for his party's candidates for the House and Senate, incumbent and prospective alike. At times he gave his Presidential successors advice—but only when asked. He became friends with former President Jimmy Carter, and together they sponsored independent enterprises in the public interest. In 1988, for example, the two former Presidents chaired American Agenda—a bipartisan initiative by experienced government officials to define and rank the major problems the new President, George H. W.

Bush, would face. On his own, Ford initiated an *amicus curiae* brief to the Supreme Court that influenced the court's 5-4 decision to continue affirmative action at the University of Michigan.

Ford's devotion to his alma mater deepened through the years. He was always proud of its reach and influence, and visited often, especially during football season. He took particular delight in delivering extemporaneous pep talks to the Michigan football team. On November 11, 2004, when Ford was 91 years old, he met the team on a spirited occasion. After greeting Ford as he arrived on the practice field, Coach Lloyd Carr lined everyone up for a group photograph. Then, Ford, Carr, and the full squad trooped into Schembechler Hall and Ford took the microphone. "I am your number-one fan," he began. "I watch every game I can. I also get the sports pages and read about the way you play." Then, in the words of the coach he had once been, he critiqued the team's performance game by game, wins and losses, and recognized those who played best. "Where is Braylon Edwards, who catches all the passes? Stand up, Braylon, let us recognize you . . . Where is the little guy runs through the line so well? Stand up, Mike Hart." Winding up his football talk Ford said: "Now football is great. But you came here also to learn. So go to class. Study. Do your best. What you take away from the classroom at Michigan can be more valuable than football in the years ahead."

In 1999, the trustees of the University of Michigan renamed their then eighty-five-year-old graduate school of government the Gerald R. Ford School of Public Policy, and soon expanded the school to include undergraduate as well as graduate students. To house its broad areas of training and scholarship, the university found a place on its campus to expand, and through the generosity primarily of Joan and Sanford Weill, built a 5-story, 85,000-square-foot brick building for some 350 students, undergraduates and graduate students alike. The Gerald R. Ford School of Public Policy is one of the top policy schools in the country—known for education, research, and policy engagement grounded in the social sciences. Alumni serve in government, work for domestic and international nonprofit organizations, consult and lead in the private sector, and more.

Summers, in Colorado, Ford hosted, with the American Enterprise Institute, the World Forum, a three-day gathering of government and business leaders to assess the state of the world, and to evaluate critical international issues such as national deficits, monetary issues, and free trade. The sessions, held in informal settings and off the record, brought together such notables as Margaret Thatcher, Helmut Schmidt, Valéry Giscard d'Estaing, and James Callaghan, along with Henry Kissinger, Alan Greenspan, Brent Scowcroft, leaders of the House and Senate, and fifty chief executive officers of corporations from nine countries. Initiated and organized by Ford, the Colorado meetings were designed to keep himself and former heads of allied governments up-to-date on events and problems confronting their successors in high office.

At home in Rancho Mirage, Ford kept regular office hours. Beginning his day with a swim, he spent the morning reading newspapers, poring over every page of the *Los Angeles Times*, the *New York Times*, the *Wall Street Journal, Time, Newsweek,* and finishing up with the *Grand Rapids Press.* "The local paper is where you find out whether what Washington has done actually works," he often said. The rest of the day he devoted to answering his mail, drafting his speeches, talking on the phone to old political friends, and reading. He was one of the handful of people in the country who actually read, and understood, the Federal budget. From time to time a political reporter would stop by to get his views. With his favorites, he spoke without reserve. "As long as he was busy, he was happy," Chief of Staff Penny Circle said.

In his late eighties, Ford began to slow the pace of his life. After both knees were replaced, his doctors told him he must give up skiing, but that he could still play golf. He did, and regularly hosted charity tournaments for professionals and celebrity amateurs. As the years advanced, his energy flagged. More and more he spent time with Betty and their children. Mike, Jack, Steve, Susan, all visited often. Ford was proud that all were succeeding in their chosen professions, and counted each the best of friends.

He never lost his passion for golf and the outdoors. In his last years, he would ride a cart along the course with one of his sons, play a few holes, and test his favorite clubs. Steven Ford remembered: "If he hit a long straight drive he would go home and crow like a rooster to his girlfriend."

The summer of 2006 was their last in Colorado. Doctors warned him that the 8,000-foot altitude would be hard on his heart, which was progressively weakening. But he and Betty overruled the medical advice. "They wanted one last summer together in Colorado, and decided to go despite the doctors," Steve said. "He loved looking at the mountains, the beautiful scenery, being outdoors." In Colorado, Ford's medical condition worsened, and doctors insisted he go back to sea level for his heart. In Rancho Mirage, Ford was confined in part to a walker and a wheelchair. As his eyes dimmed, one of his children would read the newspapers to him. Ford was well aware that his life was coming to an end, and he often said to Steve, "Take care of your Mom when I'm gone."

Just before Christmas, in 2006, Ford's heart weakened more, and he was confined to bed, and slept most of the time. On Christmas Day, Betty and the children gathered and knew the end was near. On the day after Christmas, the great heart that sustained him for ninety-three years had ceased.

[EDITOR'S NOTE: The manuscript ended here at the time of the author's death on September 15, 2011, at the age of 93. The following text is constructed from the author's detailed notes and his outline for the book's final pages.]

Presidential funerals are staged by a subordinate office of the U.S. Army, with as much or as little ceremony as the subject decides. President Ford directed that his be appropriate to the office, but with the relative modesty he had shown in life. Ford wanted his to focus on the highlights of his Washington experience and public life.

As he directed, his body was to be flown from California to Washington, carried by hearse through Virginia, past the house in Alexandria where they had lived, and past the World War II monument on the National Mall. As he had served in the Navy during World War II, Ford wanted the procession to stop briefly at that monument to recognize his service in the war. In Virginia and in Washington, hundreds of thousands of Americans stood by the roads, holding hands over hearts, saluting, weeping, and somberly honoring the President who had brought the nation through such difficult times.

He was taken to Capitol Hill, and carried up the steps by eight soldiers representing the Armed Forces, and into the Capitol through the House of Representatives, where more than sixty years earlier he had first taken the oath of office to begin his service; then to the Capitol Rotunda, where, for three days, thousands came to pay their respects as he lay in state.

On December 30, 2006, a short service was held. Of all the tributes, none was more poetic than Vice President Cheney, who said in part, "We were proud to call him our leader, grateful to know him as a man . . . Few have ever risen so high with so little guile or calculation . . .

"He was modest and manful; there was confidence and courage in his bearing. In judgment, he was sober and serious, unafraid of decisions, calm and steady by nature, always the still point in the turning wheel. He assumed power without assuming airs; he knew how to treat people. He answered courtesy with courtesy; he answered discourtesy with courtesy.

"This President's hardest decision was also among his first. And in September of 1974, Gerald Ford was almost alone in understanding that there can be no healing without pardon. The consensus holds that this decision cost him an election. That is very likely so. The criticism was fierce. But President Ford had larger concerns at heart. And it is far from the worst fate that a man should be remembered for his capacity to forgive.

"It was this man, Gerald R. Ford, who led our republic safely through a crisis that could have turned to catastrophe. We will never know what further unravelings, what greater malevolence might have come in that time of furies turned loose and hearts turned cold. But we do know this: America was spared the worst. And this was the doing of an American President. For all the grief that never came, for all the wounds that were never inflicted, the people of the United States will forever stand in debt to the good man and faithful servant we mourn tonight."

President Ford's body was taken out through the Senate, where he had presided over proceedings as Vice President, and then to Andrews Air Force Base. The plane that bore him home to Michigan dipped low over the Michigan stadium where he had played football, then on to Grand Rapids. All the city turned out to pay final respects.

The hearse took his body to downtown Grand Rapids to the tomb that had been built at his direction. Betty Ford said, "I will walk this last time with him," and his body was interred.

Epitaph
The late Thomas P. "Tip" O'Neill, former Democratic Speaker of the House, was Ford's political opponent, but also one of his closest friends. He spoke these words, now etched below Ford's bronze statue in the U.S. Capitol rotunda:

"God has been good to America, especially during difficult times. At the time of the Civil War, he gave us Abraham Lincoln. And at the time of Watergate, he gave us Gerald Ford—the right man at the right time who was able to put our Nation back together again."

In one of my final discussions with President Ford, I asked what he would like said of him as the epitaph of his life. He said, "One who strongly believed in all the good things about America. I love this country. I'm hopeful that for most of my life, I did something to make it even better."

Afterword

This book is in essence the one the author first set out to write in the early 1990s to chronicle the White House years of Gerald R. Ford. But President Ford's compelling early life story distracted the author—my father—on that first attempt; the more he learned about the self-made Michigan man who rose to Congress and the presidency, the more he was convinced that he should tell *that* story first. *Time and Chance: Gerald Ford's Appointment with History* was published 19 years ago, but the author never forgot his commitment to the initial task, or "Ford II" as he referred to it, and the White House years.

Following publication of *Time and Chance*, the author took part in the 1996 Character Above All lecture series on presidential history and recounted how President Ford restored stability and integrity to the Oval Office. Character was the essence of Gerald Ford's life, and of the author's life as well, so it's not surprising they had mingled destinies; honesty, good work, directness marked their lives and careers.

After leaving office, the President was generous with his time in discussions, interviews, and correspondence with the author. No subject was off limits, mutual respect was assured, and both men had the chance to reflect on the past and capture details and turning points in history. For that and for the privilege of serving the country in the White House, the author was always grateful.

In the introduction to his first book, *Politics U.S.A.*, published in 1960, the author seemed to predict his own move from journalism to government service some nine years later. He wrote of meeting Connecticut Governor Abraham Ribicoff and Nelson Rockefeller in 1958. Rockefeller was considering a run for New York governor and sketched the methods he would use to get things done if nominated and elected. The author, at that time an editor at *Newsweek* magazine, "listened with fascination" to Rockefeller and to Ribicoff, who explained like a military strategist how he had defeated bureaucrats and cut government spending.

"Political techniques have long interested me," the author wrote. He could not find a "how-to" book on winning and holding public office, so he determined to publish one. "I believe this book will truly inform people—those who want to go into politics, those who are in it now, and those who, as good citizens, simply want to find out more about it. I also hope that this book will contribute in some way to the public's understanding of how the democratic system works. What I set out to do was as difficult as it is simple: to tell the story the way it really is." Decades later, that same approach would serve him well in writing about Gerald Ford.

At the end of a long and fascinating tenure on the Capitol Hill staff of Senator Howard Baker Jr., in 1984 the author was reflective in a note to an old friend:

> My clear and singular first choice for a profession is politics . . . I enjoy the sense of being in public life, the demands of governing, the defining of choices, the study of human nature and motivation . . . I enlisted in politics as an idealist; I remain an idealist. The Greeks considered politics the ultimate responsibility of a citizen and the most noble of professions. So do I . . . I try not to take myself or my political associates all that seriously; but I do take the system very seriously. I believe profoundly that any one person can make a difference. On occasion, I believe I have made a difference. Moreover, politics is great fun. Journalism was good fun; this is better.

In the interim between *Time and Chance* and this book, my father wrote *Apostle Paul: A Novel of the Man Who Brought Christianity to the Western World*. He had always wondered how difficult it would be to write fiction. "Well," he said with a weary smile after it was done, "I sure found out." Then, in 2006 he turned his full attention back to "Ford II."

He passed away in late 2011, several pages shy of completing this manuscript. A new book by a writer recently deceased can perplex the publishing world, with no telegenic principal to press it on the talk show circuit. But supporters and advocates for President Ford and the author conspired for success.

Allen Moore worked in the Ford White House with my father, and Allen's careful review readied this manuscript for the professionals at University of Michigan Press. At the Press it found the right home. With patience and encouragement, editor Tom Dwyer made the project his own, and enlisted a colleague, Christina Milton, whose edits and suggestions made it a better book.

Through the years, the author depended on steady men and women in Michigan. William McNitt, archivist at the Gerald R. Ford Presidential Library, answered countless queries and ensured the author had his facts in order. Audiovisual archivists Kenneth Hafeli and Nancy Mirshah produced the author's photo "wish list" from Library archives.

At the Gerald R. Ford Presidential Foundation, Marty Allen and Joseph Calvaruso were long-time connections whose keen interest in the story helped move it forward. University of Michigan Alumni Robert P. "Bob" Strauss, a Public Policy professor at Carnegie Mellon University, was a firm advocate for the book's success. Peter Matson, the author's agent, kept it on track from his New York office, along with Emilie Jackson, his able assistant.

In the author's notes are the names of two men whose memory he kept close: "Vice President Nelson Rockefeller and Arthur Quern—The one knew and advocated what needed to be done. The other quietly got it done." The author never forgot that it was Governor Rockefeller of New York who drafted him in 1969, from *Newsweek* to the governor's staff, and opened a new career in politics and public service.

The author would have thanked by name each of the many men and women who generously gave their time, recollections, insights, and guidance to this book. Any attempt to list them here would leave out many whom he meant to include, but know that he was indebted to them all.

Finally, as he did in all his previous books, my father would surely have closed his own remarks with love and respect for his wife, Cherie Dawson Cannon, for the constancy of support and happiness in 60 years of marriage.

Scott Cannon
January 2013

Index